RIGHT ROMANCE

Cultural Inquiries in English Literature, 1400–1700
Rebecca Totaro, General Editor

ADVISORY BOARD

Joe Campana
Rice University

Hillary Ecklund
Loyola University, New Orleans

Katherine Eggert
University of Colorado, Boulder

Wendy Beth Hyman
Oberlin College & Conservatory

Julia Reinhardt Lupton
University of California, Irvine

Vin Nardizzi
The University of British Columbia

Gail Kern Paster
Folger Shakespeare Library

Garrett Sullivan
Penn State University

Tiffany Werth
University of California, Davis

Jessica Wolfe
University of North Carolina, Chapel Hill

Books in the Cultural Inquiries in English Literature, 1400–1700, series acknowledge the complex relationships that link disciplines in the pre-modern period and account for the lived experience represented in literary and cultural texts of the time. Scholars in this series reconnect fields often now considered distinct, including cuisine, ecology, cartography, the occult, meteorology, physiology, drama, popular print, and poetry.

RIGHT ROMANCE

*Heroic Subjectivity and Elect Community
in Seventeenth-Century England*

Emily Griffiths Jones

THE PENNSYLVANIA STATE UNIVERSITY PRESS
UNIVERSITY PARK, PENNSYLVANIA

Library of Congress Cataloging-in-Publication Data

Names: Jones, Emily Griffiths, 1983– author.
Title: Right romance : heroic subjectivity and elect community in seventeenth-century England / Emily Griffiths Jones.
Description: University Park, Pennsylvania : The Pennsylvania State University Press, 2019. | Series: Cultural inquiries in English literature, 1400–1700. | Includes bibliographical references and index.
Summary: "A study of romance, religion, and politics in seventeenth-century England, presenting a recontextualized understanding of romance as a multi-generic narrative structure or strategy rather than a prose genre"—Provided by publisher.
Identifiers: LCCN 2019028364 | ISBN 9780271084923 (cloth)
Subjects: LCSH: Romances, English—History and criticism. | English literature—Early modern, 1500–1700—History and criticism. | Romanticism—England—History—17th century. | Religion and literature—England—History—17th century. | Heroes in literature.
Classification: LCC PR438.R65 2019
LC record available at https://lccn.loc.gov/2019028364

An earlier version of a portion of chapter 2 was published as "Historical Romance and *Fin Amour* in Margaret Cavendish's *Life of William Cavendish*," special issue, ed. James Fitzmaurice and Sandro Jung, *English Studies* 92, no. 7 (2011): 756–70.

A portion of chapter 3 was published, in an earlier form, in "Milton's Counter-Revision of Romantic Structure in Paradise Regained," *Huntington Library Quarterly* 76, no. 1 (2013): 59–81, https://doi.org/10.1525/hlq.2013.76.1.59.

An earlier version of chapter 4 was published as "'My Victorious Triumphs Are All Thine': Romance and Elect Community in Lucy Hutchinson's Order and Disorder," *Studies in Philology* 112, no. 1 (2015): 162–93.

Copyright © 2019 Emily Griffiths Jones
All rights reserved

Published by The Pennsylvania State University Press,
University Park, PA 16802–1003

The Pennsylvania State University Press is a member of the Association of University Presses.

It is the policy of The Pennsylvania State University Press to use acid-free paper. Publications on uncoated stock satisfy the minimum requirements of American National Standard for Information Sciences—Permanence of Paper for Printed Library Material, ANSI Z39.48–1992.

for Tina
"the name of whose friendship carried me
above my own worth, and I fear hath left
me to play the ill poet in my own part"

and Patrick
who "would make a true history of a
more handsome management of love
than the best romances describe"

CONTENTS

Acknowledgments | ix

Introduction: Getting Romance Right | 1

1 Protestant Re-visions of Romance: Philip Sidney's *New Arcadia* and Edmund Spenser's *The Faerie Queene* | 29

2 "Heroical" Histories: Writing Lives into National Romance, 1648–1670 | 73

3 The Fall and the Pinnacle: Milton's Righting of Romance in *Paradise Lost* and *Paradise Regained* | 111

4 "My Victorious Triumphs Are All Thine": The Politics of Love and Elect Community in Lucy Hutchinson's *Order and Disorder* | 155

5 "In the Next World": John Bunyan, Aphra Behn, and the Imitation of Romance | 187

Conclusion | 227

Notes | 233
Bibliography | 253
Index | 265

ACKNOWLEDGMENTS

This project owes its existence to a marvelous reading community. I am deeply grateful, first, for the wisdom and support of Erin Murphy, a splendid adviser who has become a wonderful friend. Her rigorous questioning, sensitivity to nuance, and commitment to justice in her teaching and writing will continue to inspire me throughout my career. Chris Martin's superior insight into Sidney and Spenser has been invaluable, and his direction of my attention long ago to Greville's understudied *Life of Sidney* lent this book a structural and emotional coherence it would have otherwise lacked. I thank Amy Appleford, Bill Carroll, Jim Siemon, and James Winn for their brilliant instruction and guidance. I am especially indebted to James and to the Boston University Center for the Humanities for making essential travel and archival research possible in this project's early stages. At the Folger Shakespeare Library, my seminar leaders in Early Modern English Paleography and Researching the Archive have contributed their tremendous knowledge and advice: many thanks to Heather Wolfe, Peter Lake, and Nigel Smith, and to the colleagues and friends in both seminars who offered their feedback and support, around the seminar table and at the pub. Many of these chapters began as conference papers, which grew to maturity with help from the warm and insightful participants in the International Margaret Cavendish Society Conference, the Conference on John Milton, the Renaissance Society of America, the Shakespeare Association of America, and the International John Bunyan Society Conference. Special thanks to John Rogers for his generous and careful attention to my work on *Paradise Regained*, to an anonymous reader at *Studies in Philology* for valuable suggestions on my reading of Lucy Hutchinson, and to Diana Henderson and Marina Leslie for giving me the opportunity to speak on Aphra Behn at the Harvard seminar on Women and Culture in the Early Modern World. I am also deeply grateful to Diana, Pete Donaldson, Shankar Raman, and

Arthur Bahr for their unfailing kindness and mentorship as my colleagues at MIT. At the University of South Florida, I thank my new colleagues for their welcome, friendship, and support, especially Kristin Allukian, Cassie Childs, Jessica Cook, Nicole Discenza, Hunt Hawkins, Ylce Irizarry, Meredith Johnson, Nate Johnson, Steve Jones, Mark Leahy, Gary Lemons, John Lennon, Susan Mooney, Laura Runge, Elaine Smith, Lisa Starks, and Jacob Tootalian. The excellent graduate students in my Early Modern Romance seminar gave me the excitement, and the Humanities Institute provided the crucial funds, that I needed to finish this work. Rebecca Totaro encouraged me to send her the manuscript for this book long before that manuscript existed; her early enthusiasm and confidence were invaluable. I extend my gratitude to Kendra Boileau and Alex Vose, and to two anonymous readers for Penn State University Press, who kindly offered tremendous encouragement and learned advice.

When I first began work on this project, I was writing about personal loss and political trauma without having experienced either. By the time I finished it, I knew how both of these things could feel, and I hope that familiarity has made me that much more sensitive to the real lives and feelings of the men and women in this book, however many centuries ago they lived. Through everything, I owe much of my enduring enthusiasm for romance to a beloved fellowship of people whose formidable intelligence, exemplary virtue, and heroic spirits daily renew my hope concerning the genre of history. I thank Abby Ingham Lull, Sara Marie Massee, Kim Thompson Stiffler, Aimee Rose Formo, Maggie Beyer, and Kimmi Kresica for the gifts of their fandom and friendship. This project has become one of many efforts to "keep company . . . even after death" with Tina Blevins, our stellar Sidney, another "Architechtonical Master" without whom I, too, must "play the ill poet in my own part." Tragedy sits on one side, romance on the other: last and first, I thank Patrick Jones, the partner of my story, whose friendship, love, and gallantry are "more than the best romances describe."

This book occasionally uses manuscript transcription notation when quoting from unpublished texts. This notation preserves the original author's marks, including underlines and strikethroughs. It also commonly makes use of italics to indicate that the transcriber has inserted letters which the original author did not supply: for example, "ye" becomes "the," and "Sr" becomes "Sir."

Introduction

Getting Romance Right

In 1640, before the armed conflicts of the English Civil War began, royalist political philosopher Thomas Hobbes warned in his *Elements of Law* against the reading of romances, claiming that the pastime led to foolish delusion and vain pride: "The fiction (which also is imagination) of actions done by ourselves, which never were done, is glorying; but because it begetteth no appetite nor endeavour to any further attempt, it is merely vain and unprofitable; as when a man imagineth himself to do the actions whereof he readeth in some romant.... And this is called VAIN GLORY: and is exemplified in the fable by the fly sitting on the axletree, and saying to himself, What a dust do I raise!"[1] Reading romance, Hobbes proposes, produces ridiculous fancies in the "pusillanimous" person, whose subjective identification with the genre's heroes is so intense that he imagines himself to be greater than he is. In the most extreme cases, the result is "spiritual pride or madness": "The gallant madness of Don Quixote," Hobbes writes, is "an expression of such height of vain glory as reading of romants may produce" and may be compared to "the example of one that preached in Cheapside from a cart there, instead of a pulpit, that he himself was Christ."[2] The most ridiculous victim of a romance-reading imagination, for Hobbes, is the religious radical who believes himself to be the protagonist of a heroic story written not by man, but by God.

In 1651, when Hobbes published his better-known *Leviathan*, such people were no longer so easy to laugh at. The Puritan-dominated New Model Army, with Oliver Cromwell at its head, had successfully backed the forces of Parliament against those of King Charles I; Charles had been beheaded by a victorious parliamentary faction that owed its allegiance to God rather than the king; and the zealous and ambitious Cromwell was poised to become Lord Protector of England. In *Leviathan*, Hobbes's discussion of romance and imagination resembles that of the *Elements*, but romance has been unbound from the constraint that it "begetteth no appetite nor endeavour": "So when a man compoundeth the image of his own person with the image of the actions of another man, as when a man imagines himself a Hercules or an Alexander (which happeneth often to them that are much taken with reading of romances), it is . . . but a fiction of the mind."[3] Victoria Kahn offers a keen summation of the genre's progressive threat to Hobbesian political order in the years of civil war between the *Elements* and *Leviathan*:

> The danger here is not simply that the reader of romance will imagine himself a lover and knight errant . . . but that the reader of romance will imagine himself a Hercules or Alexander, that is, a military hero of epic proportions. . . . Romance vainglory is not simply unprofitable but dangerous, as it is when the parties to the civil war begin to imagine that their honor demands that they engage in violent conflict. Thus the errant activity of the imagination . . . is not simply associated with moral and epistemological error. . . . It is also associated with political error—with what Hobbes called "sedition and contempt."[4]

Hobbes's mid-century fear of romance was a reaction both to the fresh memory of the war and to a long English tradition of religiously inflected chivalric narratives that offered readers a heroic subject position with which to identify and a sense that their endeavors had the support of divine providence. His premise—that romance subjectivity is intrinsically unruly, encouraging personal pride but also subversive factionalism and resistance to authority—is foundational to this book. As we will see, subjects who imagined themselves as romance lovers or knights-errant might prove just as politically dangerous as those who thought of themselves as military heroes, since all these romance subjects share an assumption that one has been chosen for a life of heroic exceptionalism, predestined to prevail under extraordinary conditions and against extraordinary odds. In the decades that witnessed the fall of Charles I, the collapse of Cromwell's commonwealth, Charles II's restoration to the throne, and eventually the expulsion of the Stuart dynasty, English men and women of diverse ideological communities often expressed mistrust and contempt for romance as a vehicle for their opponents' vainglory—but at the same time, they found solace, along with grounds for resistance, in the romance mode's structural promise that suffering and disappointment would give way to the triumph of a story's true champions.

WHOSE ROMANCE?

> I shall not today attempt further to define the kinds of material I understand to be embraced within that shorthand description; and perhaps I could never succeed in intelligibly doing so. But I know it when I see it.
> —SUPREME COURT JUSTICE POTTER STEWART, *Jacobellis v. Ohio*, 1964

Before proceeding, I want to set forth a reasonably stable meaning for "romance" throughout this project, both because it can be tempting to apply to it Justice Potter Stewart's now famous, highly subjective test for the presence of pornography,[5] and because I use the term somewhat differently from most recent scholars. Indeed, many scholars who discuss romance do not attempt a precise definition of it, perhaps under the supposition that we all already know what we are talking about. Helen Cooper, seeking that definition, captures the consensus that romance encompasses a very large set of recognizable tropes or themes, including (but not limited to) "exotic settings, distant in time or place, or both; subject-matter concerning love or chivalry, or both; . . . high-ranking characters . . . ; quests; magic and the supernatural"; and "a concern with ideals" of heroic behavior.[6] Before the rise of the internet "meme," medievalists were using the word—denoting sameness or repetition—to describe romance's recurring elements: shipwrecks, ladies adrift at sea, abandoned children, unknown knights, rash promises, and many, many more. Cooper has proposed a definition based on the disqualifying *absence*, rather than the qualifying presence, of such tropes: "With romance, *any* of the features that might be taken as definitive for the genre may be absent in any particular case without damaging that sense of family resemblance, though the dissimilarity increases . . . in proportion as the various elements are missing."[7]

This kind of delineation, though, avoids fully explaining what it also allows for: the potential for extreme disparity between various works that are all commonly recognized as romances or as derived from a romance tradition. Many of the texts we consider in this book have remarkably few features in common. For example, Edmund Spenser's *The Faerie Queene* and Margaret Cavendish's *Assaulted and Pursued Chastity* both address love and desire, include episodes of battle, and share the trope of female virtue under threat. However, one romance is in verse and the other in prose; one is extremely long and the other quite short; one thrives on magic while the other eschews it; one avoids the plot device of shipwreck that the other employs repeatedly; and one champions heroic idealism, the other heroic pragmatism. If romance is an assemblage of tiles that form a recognizable mosaic, Spenser's and Cavendish's narratives would seem to produce two images that look practically nothing alike—and most of the other texts before us may seem similarly dissimilar. Importantly, a number of the texts I want to consider are not often identified or studied as romances at all, typically because they exhibit more obvious signs of falling into some other form, mode, or genre—including pastoral, epic, panegyric, biography, historiography, even political pamphlet.

So we require some further approach to romance that helps explain both why we usually *do* know it when we see it—even when one romance is superficially unlike another—and why it sometimes manages to slip unseen into other categories. Barbara Fuchs has recently proposed that we understand romance not as a genre or a mode but as a *strategy* for both outlining and complicating a quest narrative; romance as strategy is characterized by "hybridization and malleability," by its ability to reshape itself into syntheses with diverse forms of writing.[8] My work here continues to pursue Fuchs's effort "to deconstruct the many oppositions set up by literary history, such as romance versus epic or romance versus novel," and in this pursuit I am indebted to a synthesis of critical approaches new and old.[9] Before the structuralist movement fell into disfavor for its ahistorical method, Northrop

Frye also defined romance very broadly in terms of its whole rather than its parts. Frye identifies romance as our "secular scripture": if the Bible is "the epic of the creator, with God as its hero," then romance is "the epic of the creature, man's vision of his own life as a quest." This narrative entails a cycle of "descent" and "return" that fluctuates between two worlds: "a world associated with happiness, security, and peace," and "a world of exciting adventures, but adventures which involve separation, loneliness, humiliation, pain, and the threat of more pain." For Frye, the structure is recognizable for its positive teleology: "Most romances . . . begin with a departure" from the world of fulfillment into the lower world of desire—for love, for family, for power, for safety—"and end happily, with a return" to the realm that seemed lost. At the same time, Frye suggests, the world of desire, suffering, and adventure is critical to our imagination, since in the desired telos of the ideal world, "there is nothing to write about." Milton, who managed to write several books of *Paradise Lost* about life in Eden and in Heaven, might disagree with this last point, but Frye's structuralist model of a secular quest that echoes the scriptural narrative of fall and redemption—and that tends to be creatively fixated not just on the redemption but also on the fallenness, loss, and longing—will be vital to my more historically grounded study. Hobbes's seventeenth-century authoritarian politics, after all, were threatened not by the lovers, warriors, or miraculous events of romance fiction, but by a literary vision of real life that made people imagine themselves as heroes and history as the landscape of their romance. This strategy that transforms lived experience into coherent narrative and thrives in the temporal space between loss and recovery, tragedy and triumph, lies at the core of all the sixteenth- and seventeenth-century texts we will consider here, including those not normally studied as romance. Finally, Frye has suggested that "an identity between individual and social quests has always been latent in romance," a genre that feeds both "the need to experience as part of a community and the need to experience as a withdrawn individual."[10] This book is strongly concerned with the relationship between individual romance heroism and the construction of ideologically charged romance community—for if Hobbes was unsettled by one quixotic Christ in a cart, an armed fellowship of godly knights posed a more substantial problem.

Despite its importance, Frye's "secular scripture" is not the structuralist phrase most often cited in more recent treatments of the genre; that distinction must go to Patricia Parker's "inescapable romance."[11] Parker, too, understands romance to be a narrative mode that simultaneously seeks and defers the telos of its quest, but as her term indicates, the emphasis of her study is on the deferral—on romance's fundamental resistance to teleology, despite its heroes' orientation toward a goal. This sense of romance as an inherently meandering, even aimless form has become commonplace and has often been reproduced; recently, Dani Cavallaro defined romance as a "centerless text" that demands "a denial of conclusive solutions."[12] Unsurprisingly, then, romance is often contrasted with epic. David Quint has famously distinguished the two genres according to both structure and historical politics: "To the victors belongs epic, with its linear teleology; to the losers belongs romance, with its random or circular wandering. Put another way, the victors experience history as a coherent, end-directed story told by their own power; the losers experience a contingency that they are powerless to shape to their own ends."[13] This diametric opposition between romance and epic is relatively new in literary criticism—for Frye, romance was synonymous with "the epic of the creature"; for Hobbes, reading romances endowed men with delusions of epic grandeur; and for Philip Sidney in his *Defence of Poesie*, romances and epics are lumped together as "heroicall Poem[s]"[14]—and I believe that Quint's romance/epic binary, however often it has been rearticulated, is frequently unhelpful to an understanding of romance's role in the ideological politics of the seventeenth century (or any other period). This study does not position romance as the opposite of epic or any other genre. As Fuchs has demonstrated, we can find it infusing itself into various forms, often including its "ostensible opposites," because as a hybridizing strategy romance is inherently adaptive rather than antagonistic.[15] Contrary to Quint's model, both victors and losers may experience the history of their community as driven by human agency or by contingency or by divine providence, or by some combination of these, as we will see. Victors might see chance even in their victory; losers might strive to glimpse a providentially "coherent, end-directed story," even in their defeat.[16] Moreover, as Quint recognizes, victors may not remain victorious and losers may not remain cast down for long, which was certainly the case in seventeenth-century England. Romance, with its productive tension between teleological triumph and medial defeat or deferral, is uniquely suited for both victors and losers to locate themselves at different points on its narrative arc, and while both success and failure could certainly shape *how* political subjects and communities read and wrote romance in the seventeenth century, these vicissitudes did not initiate or terminate their engagement with it.

Cooper, who stands out among recent critics for identifying "the happy ending" (rather than endlessness) as "the characteristic most . . . definitive" of romance, draws our attention to Monika Fludernik's term "duplicitous teleology"—that is, "the gap between 'the characters' plotting on the level of the fictional world and that narrative's overall counter-plotting."[17] As Cooper puts it in the context of romance, "The reader will always know more than the protagonists (that they will survive their adventures, marry their beloved, win back their kingdom), but that knowledge is a shared assumption between author and audience that bypasses the characters themselves."[18] Seventeenth-century English men and women drawn to a narrative vision of their individual and communal stories as quests could position themselves at once as the characters, readers, and sometimes authors of the romance of history: while in the midst of profound political disappointment and personal doubt as characters ignorant of the future, they could presume an audience's knowledge of the full structure that promised to deliver them from their trials, and they could look to God as Author, their own authorial agency, or both to bring that deliverance about in the near or remote future. Frye has suggested that identifying romance as the genre of history allows one to interpret and represent "the maze without a plan and the maze not without a plan" as "two aspects of the same thing."[19] Because the strategy of romance insists on—and offers narrative meaning to—both success and failure, both the presence and absence of fulfillment, and both randomness and order, it belongs equally to history's victors and to its losers. Indeed, it allows its subjects to be both of these at once.

Beyond disturbing the assumption that romance is a genre primarily for losers, I also want to dismantle the critical commonplace that Civil War–era romance was a genre primarily for royalists. Certainly some royalists produced works of prose fiction, both long and short, especially during and after their exile under Cromwell's regime; however, historicist efforts to contextualize such works have led to a general impression that royalist romance was the only romance in town in the mid-seventeenth century. Anthony Welch's description of the genre as a literary realm to which defeated royalists fled for "privacy and stasis, a protective cocoon of rest from . . . political action," is normative (although Welch challenges this reading and points out that a turn to romance did not "set the royalists apart" entirely from republican writers).²⁰ A combination of Parker's anti-progressive structure, Quint's idea of romance as antithetical to the political engagement of the victors' epic, and a restriction of the mode to prose love stories risks mistaking one facet of seventeenth-century romance for the whole. Also common is a critical focus on romance as a genre for women (especially royalist women), and as a mid-century trend adopted into England from seventeenth-century continental (especially French) texts. When Nigel Smith rightly notes that "where romances were read, they could become the dominant way in which an individual understood him or herself," he is speaking specifically about recent continental models of the genre, focused on domesticity and psychology, which did indeed become popular among royalist women readers.²¹ Because seventeenth-century women certainly did produce and consume romance, important scholarship about women as writers and readers (by Mary Beth Rose, Helen Hackett, and Michelle Dowd and Julie Eckerle, among others) may contribute to a necessary understanding of women's engagement with the genre while indirectly downplaying romance's importance across and between genders during the period.²² Similarly, while it is worthwhile to recognize that seventeenth-century English romance was informed by continental styles, we lose a full sense of its nationalistic power when we disregard the genre's native tradition and that tradition's appeal to multiple ideological communities. As Fuchs, Cooper, and Jennifer Goodman have pointed out, English romance presents one of many challenges to conventional periodization, since this cherished medieval mode remained popular "well into the seventeenth century."²³

Historicist scholars who have challenged certain common assumptions about romance typically leave other assumptions intact. Erica Veevers, Ann Baynes Coiro, and Karen Britland have examined how earlier Stuart romance, instead of salving war wounds, celebrated monarchic power and thrived in court drama, poetry, and painting (as in Rubens's portrait of Charles I as Saint George rescuing Queen Henrietta Maria from the dragon); however, their focus remains restricted to royalist culture.²⁴ Annabel Patterson, Paul Salzman, Victoria Kahn, Amelia Zurcher, and Lois Potter have shown that mid-century romance, far from fleeing politics, could be intently political, often concerned not just with defeat but with resistance, recovery, and the maintenance of power; like me, Kahn and Zurcher read romance by both men and women, and Zurcher centers native romance by beginning with Sidney's *Arcadia*.²⁵ Lori Humphrey Newcomb and Nandini Das also consider the vitality of Renaissance romance as a long-standing English tradition and examine its sociopolitical appeal across lines of gender as well as class.[26] Again, though, all these treatments remain primarily focused on prose fiction, royalist writing, or both. Smith has proposed that we rethink the genre's royalist associations, arguing (as I do) that "romance was seen to be a political form by members of both sides of the political conflict" and drawing our attention to elements of romance in the republican James Harrington's *Oceana*; still, most of the romance that Smith considers is royalist, virtually all of it is long prose fiction, and he tacitly regards romance as a discrete genre separate from epic and other modes.[27]

In this book, I consider politically engaged romance that can be derived from a native English tradition in the writing of men and women on both sides of the Civil War. In calling for a "genuinely *historical*" treatment of romance in opposition to Frye's structuralist analysis, Fredric Jameson has argued that romance emerges in times of conflict between distinct socioeconomic paradigms, in which each viewpoint reads itself "in a magical, rather than a purely ethical, sense" as good and the opposition as evil; "romance as a form thus expresses a transitional moment" within a "society torn between past and future in such a way that the alternatives are grasped as hostile but somehow unrelated worlds."[28] I believe that romance's popularity and power amid the conflicts of the seventeenth century may be traceable to a fundamental disjunction between royalist and Puritan/republican ideologies in the way that Jameson suggests, but importantly, he understands romance as fundamentally *conservative*—"a cultural expression of a dominant class" that "has only too clearly the function of . . . providing a powerful internal deterrent against deviancy or subversion."[29] I want to argue that, much as we have overassociated romance with royalism, we have often overlooked its potential *radicalism* and resistance to power; after all, anti-royalist "deviancy and subversion" were exactly what Hobbes was afraid of. Medievalist Geraldine Heng has also proposed an important refinement to the Jamesonian idea of romance as evidence of a major historical rupture between two irreconcilable sides: for Heng, what makes romance is "the articulation of fantasy and history . . . as varieties of cultural work" in response to "communal trauma."[30] Tiffany Werth applies this theory to the Elizabethan period in her reading of early modern English romance as a negotiation of the turmoil of the Reformation; I extend it further into the conflicts of the seventeenth century.[31] Republicans and royalists shared the traumas of the

Civil War, even if they did not experience them in the same ways or at the same times, and for both sides, "romance be[came] a particularly effective tool for intermingling history and collective fantasy."[32] I mean for this book—with primary emphasis on Puritan and republican writers, whose often-intense investment in radical romance has received far less critical attention—to trace various paths between seventeenth-century communities' shared traumas and their co-created visions of history as romance.

ADAPTIVE ROMANCE

One reason that Puritan and republican romance has gone underrecognized and understudied, I believe, is that we have become accustomed to looking for the romance mode chiefly *in romances*—fanciful fictions (usually in prose) dedicated to love and war. Such texts were popular among mid-seventeenth-century royalists, and their opponents largely avoided them in part because of their association with royalism. In order to recognize romance in the work of godly republicans like John Milton and Lucy Hutchinson (or, for that matter, in royalist propaganda pamphlets or panegyric verse), we must bear in mind its structural premise—that life and history may be expressed as teleological heroic quests—and so be prepared to find that premise, and romance's many recurring tropes, strategically adapting themselves to other genres. Seventeenth-century English readers were used to finding romance outside of romances: as we will see, Milton complained of romance in Charles I's confessional *Eikon Basilike*, Hutchinson may have objected to romance in Milton's epic *Paradise Lost*, Margaret Cavendish derided romance in republican historiography like Hutchinson's, and Samuel Pepys scoffed that Cavendish lived her entire life like a romance.

It will be immediately clear from these examples that seventeenth-century readers habitually, even reflexively, condemned romance when and where they found it; Hobbes was hardly alone.[33] Most studies of romance note how roundly the genre was mocked and denounced in the early modern period, and much scholarship has proven that widespread critiques of romance went hand in hand with its widespread popularity, sometimes showing that even writers who disavowed romance tacitly employed it. My work takes largely for granted the fact that those who voiced their disapproval of romance often ended up reading and writing it anyway; I hope to go beyond simply locating romance in places where it is not "supposed" to be, in order to show what specifically it is doing there, what strategy it is adopting, why its authors embraced it against their own protestations, and the complex web of ideological functions it performs.

I propose that where we find explicit references to romance's tropes and memes, we also find often-implicit appeals to romance's structure—that is, to the narrative vision of individual subjectivity or communal history as a quest—and evidence of romance's function as "collective fantasy" within a traumatic historical moment. *Eikon Basilike*'s use of a captive princess's prayer from Sidney's *New Arcadia* offended Milton in large part because it insinuated that the king, too, was a godly romance hero enduring the abuses of the wicked; Milton's own references in *Areopagitica* to the "warfaring Christian" or the quest of Isis for Osiris are meant to reinforce his premise that history entails a long, often painfully deferred quest for divine truth. One fine example of a non-romance text that employs a romance trope in a gesture toward the larger form or strategy is John Donne's audacious sonnet "Show me dear Christ thy spouse":

> Show me dear Christ thy spouse, so bright and clear.
> What, is it she, which on the other shore
> Goes richly painted? or which robbed and tore
> Laments and mourns in Germany and here? . . .
> Dwells she with us, or like adventuring knights
> First travail we to seek and then make love?
> Betray kind husband thy spouse to our sights,
> And let mine amorous soul court thy mild dove,
> Who is most true, and pleasing to thee, then
> When she is embraced and open to most men.[34]

Donne's poem, a plea for enlightenment about the identity of God's Church in reaction to the political and personal trauma of the Reformation, compares Christians in search of this truth to knights-errant on an adulterous (yet holy) quest for "knowledge" of the Bride of Christ. God becomes the author of the romance of history, and believers become characters within it; the speaker prays that his ignorance and love-longing will be relieved by the still-obscured divine telos of his "travail." This appeal to an orthodox narrative is also doctrinally brash and ideologically subversive. The speaker's notion that his role as a Christian knight might license him (and a whole community of his fellows) to have spiritual sex with Christ's spouse, and his suggestion that the identity of the Church was still a romance riddle and might not be Anglican, make credible Hobbes's later anxiety that romance led people to imagine grandiose identities and actions for themselves, thus turning them recalcitrant to temporal authority.

Donne's startling leap from "embrac[ing]" a religion to pursuing free love, or having group sex, also evokes what Melissa Sanchez calls "queer" about ideological appropriations of eroticism in the Renaissance: "Love almost invariably inspires desires and fantasies that resist normalizing, rational structures . . . regardless of the gender of the persons involved."[35] Given that erotic love is one of romance's major constituents, my study of romance as an often-subversive strategy of political fantasy will make several queer "tangents," to use Carla Freccero and Carolyn Dinshaw's term, touching from time to time (most centrally in chapter 5) on the "heterogenous and indeterminate" affective bonds of romance communities.[36] I follow these writers and other queer scholarship on the early modern period in reading queerness not only through gender but through "attention to desire, fantasy, language, and . . . non-identitarian sexualities . . . uncovering a range of early modern variations on a . . . theme."[37] Finally, in light of the recent debate within queer studies on "unhistoricism" and the question of reading with a teleological view of history, it may bear noting up front that most of the writers I consider whose romance communities feature elements of queer eroticism—from Philip Sidney to Lucy Hutchinson to John Bunyan—are *adamantly* invested in a teleological reading of history.[38] Their reformist visions of history as romance depend on a narrative end in which worldly structures of oppressive power are defeated, within time and finally for all time; Hutchinson and Bunyan also represent reproductive futurism as a necessary (but importantly, not sufficient) means to this end. These early modern writers place queer eroticism and community in the service of a sacred telos; their subversive politics often employ discourses of futurism and teleology for the sake of resistance to authoritarian normativity in their present historical moment. Even Donne, noted previously, is a good example of what I mean: the sonnet's fantasy of transgressive sex is linked to the express purpose of bringing about the triumph of God's undefined, "indeterminate" True Church on earth and at the end of history. As romance adapts itself to a plenitude of genres, ideologies, and subjectivities, sometimes including queer ones, we may also need to adapt our understanding of queerness to appreciate its place in early modern romance.

Donne's turn to romance mode is explicit, even jarring, deliberately intended to produce a certain effect. However, subtler or less calculated uses of romance may help us better appreciate how easily accessible it was to, and how deeply embedded within, seventeenth-century England's cultural imagination. In the rest of this section, two manuscripts will exemplify romance's easy adaptability to other forms of writing, and its application to concerns individual and communal, private and public: Bishop Arthur Lake's series of sermons, *Christ's Conflict with and Conquest of the Tempter*; and a collection of letters from Mary Hatton to her fiancé, Randolph Helsby.

Lake's six sermons, preached at Worcester during Lent of 1613, were compiled into a neat manuscript in 1661, that they might be "first presented to Publik view"; however, they apparently never went to press.[39] The sermons explicate Matthew 4:1–12, Christ's temptation in the wilderness, and emphasize Jesus's exemplarity rather than his exceptionality. They employ the extended metaphor of chivalric combat, reaching back to the medieval English tradition of representing Christ as a knight or hero of romance, and so suggesting that tradition's enduring familiarity in the early and mid-seventeenth century. Readers of Milton's *Paradise Regained* often wonder why Milton chose the temptation in the wilderness, rather than the Passion, for his "sequel" to *Paradise Lost*; Lake understands the temptation and the crucifixion as linked battles of comparable importance, although only Christ's conquest in the first can be imitated by his followers. The devil will "[play] *the* Lion" in the cosmic conflict soon enough, "when the time will occasion us to consider Christs passion"; but for the time being, the foe appears "as a Serpent," both the dragon of romance and the wily antagonist of Eden (5).

Lake never evinces discomfort with his comparison of Christ to a secular martial hero in his title and throughout; his analysis relies early and often on his congregation's attunement to a romance of combat. Proposing in the first sermon that Christ is driven into the wilderness by the Holy Spirit not physically, but by "a kind of morall violence," Lake turns to other heroic examples to clarify his meaning: "A morall violence I call that, when ... the will [is] so resolute, that ... without dreading those dangers which will stop ordinarie courages, men adventure upon high attempts: we may call them Heroicall motions. Such as were *the* Acts of Moses, Ioshua, the Judges, the worthies of K. David in the old Testament (to say nothing of Alexander, Cyrus & others in prophane histories)" (12). Christ, like Cyrus (also a favorite exemplar of heroic virtue for Sidney in the *Defence of Poesie*), is drawn into battle with his adversary by the "Heroicall motions" that bolster his resolution. As his sermons progress, Lake tends to prefer the chivalric imagery of "prophane histories"—the term, for him, is remarkably free of moral baggage—over connections to the Old Testament. He warns his audience not to confuse true "Heroicall motions" with the kind of "desperate humours" that might provoke them into vainglorious mock tourneys with Satan: "The Lesson that wee must learn is, that wee may not be like unto *the* swaggerers, who stick not in [their] vanitie . . . to defie *the* devil & be bold to enter the lists with him: but manie of them have to theire cost proved how hardie they were" (12). Lake notes that the devil himself is urged forward by his own sense of martial vanity: "As in warfare, souldiers choose to set upon the markablest enemies, & thinke it the greatest honour to give such a one an overthrow: So is the devils malice speciallie bent against the eminentest servants of God" (5). Both combatants, then, understand themselves to be engaged in a romance of "courage," "adventure," and "honour," although only one is led by the "morall violence" of extraordinary providence. Crucially, Lake preemptively distinguishes between misguided Hobbesian romance and romance of some other, higher kind: the first may be the genre of vainglorious soldiers or of the devil, but the second—though it may look much like its antithesis—is justified because inspired by an authorial God.

Both Christ and Satan likewise possess their respective "weapons" of attack and strategies for defense—images Lake employs in his exhortations to his congregation to take Christ as an example for their own "Heroicall" spirituality. Because all of God's people have access to the same spiritual weaponry as their chief, "the difference between Adam & Christ, was not in *the* weapons whereby the devil was to be encountred, but in the use of the weapons. The second Adam had them & did use them, & made *the* devill feele *the* force of them" (19). While one of the devil's weapons is his manipulation of biblical text, Christ's godly employment of scripture is his spiritual armor, a metaphor that is itself scriptural in origin and available to all believers: "It must bee to us as armour not hangd up but putt on; seing Tentations will day and night sett on us, Texts of scripture must bee alwaies readie to repell them from us. . . . Wee see, that *the* Tempter gives no rest to Christ, but goeth on trying, Whether he be armed at all points. St Paul

... teacheth that wee have ... a spirituall armour to cover us from top to toe. And *that* wee have need to have it all on, God is pleased to shew us in *the* example of Christ" (18). As the community of Christian soldiers must learn, through Christ's chivalric conduct, the right uses of the weapons and armor at their disposal, so must they become familiar with the "politik" strategies of Satan's perverse romance: "For whereas in warre the field may bee forsaken ... politikly, as when an Armie maketh shew to flie, but with a purpose to draw *the* enemie into the more danger.... Even so doth the Tempter" (46). Lake warns that our spiritual combat is not merely an episode, but never ends while we live:

> Trulie is it said, The life of man is a warfare. During this life wee must ever stand upon our guard.... The greatest Captaines that profane histories doe mention, have never received greater blows than when, overjoyfull of a victorie, they have been fearelesse, & not expected the return of the enemie....
>
> But a greater Captaine than any is our Saviour Christ, even *the* Captain of *the* Lords armies: who standing out in our persons, representeth the Conditions of our state.... The Tempter doth watch us, how he may have opportunitie to assaile us: wee must never thinke *that* hee is *the* least time at one with us, Though wee doe not feele him setting on us. (20–21)

Both "the greatest Captaines that profane histories doe mention" and "*the* Captain of *the* Lords armies" stand as examples to the congregation, one negative and the other positive. For Lake, the entire life of each believer is always already a romance of combat—one that is indeed, in some sense, inescapable. The Lord's army is destined for a final conquest, but on the other face of this communal eschatological victory are a nearly infinite number of solitary battles with the serpent.

In the last sermon, Lake invites his audience to consider chivalric romance not just as a useful analogy, but as a real presence in the temptation episode and an essential element of Christian narrative. He urges reflection on the fact that the divine orchestration of chivalric narrative is itself necessary for the instruction of the godly: "Christ could have putt [the devil] off at the first approach: but hee would not. Hee stood out for us, & hee would be an Example unto us: an example, with what shield we should quench all *the* fierie darts of the devill, & *with* what sword we should putt him to flight: Christ would be a patterne unto us in both" (46–47). Humans are compelled to live within an ongoing narrative of conflict and conquest, but the Son of God freely chooses romance rather than instantaneous success, fitting his conduct to the genre of the fallen community he has come to deliver.

While Lake's sermons envision a Christian romance whose superficial resemblance to vainglorious fiction is distinguished by "Heroicall motions" of divine origin, the letters of Mary Hatton offer a reading of private life as romance,[40] as well as a preoccupation with the proper relationship between "Heroicall motions" and political action. The letters that we have from Hatton to Randolph Helsby mainly span their engagement between 1653 and 1655 (although a final letter in the collection, dated 1668, reveals a brief glimpse of an apparently happy marriage, along with a young son named Jack and a houseful of naughty servants). Crucially for our purposes, the pair's vibrant letters indicate that they also exchanged reading material, including romances. Evidently, they enjoyed both sixteenth-century classics (Helsby loans Hatton a "booke of mr Spen*es*ers") and contemporary texts. On one occasion, Helsby seems to have asked Hatton about her recent reading of a prose romance that the letters do not identify. She is less impressed by this particular romance than by Spenser's poetry, and offers Helsby her review:

> I do not methinks approve of stories of romaunce all so alike that they seem as if I had read *the* same one hundred times. Besides that how vain it was (for him which writt it) to make *the* yong gentle woman run awaie with a sweet hearte (her young*er* of manie years) when all were agreed upon *the* matche save only his more sober unckle. Tis all as olde as Helsby towre but this. . . . If you have not read itt I would advise you sadly if by my commendations you would waste a candell over itt. I had rather do some thing of more use than he that writ it by turning my wheel without a stop till some other had read throu itt in my stead. But it hath little bits in it that shewe he could not with carefullness & practise be without much commendation.[41]

At first glance, her report may look like a straightforward dismissal of the genre, like a critique of today's romance novels: they rely on absurd plot devices and are so packed with clichés that someone who has read one may as well have read them all. Hatton also gestures to her feminine domestic virtues by suggesting that she would rather be spinning than reading, and that her housework is "of more use" than either the composition or the consumption of such a romance.

However, if we were to take only this message from her letter, we would be ignoring much of what her negative review implies. Far from calling romances bad, Hatton is complaining that *this* one is a bad romance—and she seems to have read enough of them to distinguish the ones she enjoys from the ones that are "all so alike" that they resemble "one hundred" others she has seen already. In criticizing the lovers' gratuitous elopement, she suggests that this silly plot point is the work of an amateur, who nevertheless might "with carefullness & practise" come to produce something better later in his career, since he shows "little bits" of creative promise elsewhere. In essence, Hatton seems to regard herself not as a dabbler in romances, but as a connoisseur of them. In offering to tell the right kind of romance from the unworthy kind, she is not unlike Lake, different though their standards of judgment may be. Hatton concludes her review with another dual indication of her contempt for vain romance and her love for a truer version: "I do scorne & disdaine these trifling pass times & nought else can I learne from manie of them. There is so much more prettyness in your poetrie that I shall keep itt with all the rest."[42] The best love language, then, comes from Helsby directly to her. This, too, she critiques, with both playfulness and passion: "But why do you tell me that hath so small a portion that I am so very rich? There your similiter stoppeth. But when we are married you can then say in very truth that I shal be rich beyond all earthly riches with that affection you will give to me."[43] Better than reading an amorous romance, Hatton finds, is living in one—and her writing elsewhere reveals her inclination to think and speak about her relationship with Helsby in the effusive, ardent style of the love stories they both enjoy.

The conceptual vocabulary of romance helps Hatton express herself in times of trouble and fear, as well as on happy or amorous occasions. From a historical standpoint, by far the most noteworthy element of the Hatton/Helsby correspondence is its hint that Helsby, while a bachelor in London, may have been on the periphery of some subversive action against Cromwell. The plot must have died in its cradle (as Mary Hatton was anxious it should). Hatton, having heard something of it, reveals her feelings upon receiving his latest: "How greatly your letters reioyced me none can tell save one shipwrackd & draifting hither & thither halfe dead in the waving seas which at last suddenly eyeth the succours that seemed awhile agoe utterlie beyond the vision of even hope." Having communicated her intense relief through the stock romance devices of shipwreck and miraculous rescue, she hopes for similar providential protection for Helsby in his dangerous position, but frets over a distinction similar to the one Lake draws between the "Heroicall motions" of providence and the "desperate humours" that make men "bold to enter the lists" with the devil, "to theire costs." Hatton confesses her fear "to think how matters might ensue . . . to your ill fortune. Yet godd knoweth the unfearing trust I have in him for your well fare now & hereafter. . . . But liken unto any other things [hope and trust] may att tymes faill us when the cloudynesses of life blinde the eyes to the ever watchfull Saviour." Both she and Helsby are caught up in the "cloudyness" of a tempest that prevents them from knowing which heroic impulses are divine and which are vain, and which may likewise temporarily obstruct their faith in providential oversight. In the absence of this conviction, she desperately (and cryptically) advises him to "bear watchefully the changes till time ripens the fruits that you talke of," and not "to followe those who be placed lesse advantageously than the verie fewe others that can note discretely from their overseeing place the tymes & oportunities for fortunate action."[44]

Caught up in the seas and storms of life, Helsby lacks the clear perspective of history as narrative that "verie fewe" possess, which alone can reveal the best occasion for agency and determine whether one's "Heroicall motions" are valid or vainglorious. Such dangerous circumstances, she adds, may favor the few who are granted this vision—like, possibly, Cromwell himself—but are disastrous for others and may be unstable for all alike:

> It was not matteres of this favour that created <u>Olliver</u> (& others to be read of) but some suche matter did holpen the uncrowneing of the poore king.[45] Tis true tis out of the verie mudd & mire of the tyme that a bolde man of partes & some place, tho he may not pick his way, maye fly upwards to fortune, by his clear vision of the wayes that lead unto her (straightly or crookedly). But he who would over throwe him when there must wait upon patience to know if such an Olivers power can hold all he hath gotten. Of

all I have ever read this I conceive to be the greatest of trialls Conquerers can be putt to.⁴⁶

All that Hatton has "ever read," whether histories or romances of conquest, has made her wary of occasions that depend on the favor of "fortune," and she urges Helsby to wait with "patience" until both time and providence can illuminate the darkness of the age and determine whether his heroic impulse is destined for a successful end. Given that the idea remained confined to their private correspondence, Hatton seems vindicated in her fear that the national narrative was not on the side of her fiancé's drive toward public heroism. Her letters anticipate other texts throughout this book in their concern with the distinction (both light and serious) between vain versus right romance, with the disturbing difficulty of knowing whether one has correctly intuited one's role in the narrative of history, and with the tension between friends' and partners' subjective readings of life as genre.

RIGHT ROMANCE

Between Donne's, Lake's, and Hatton's writing, we have observed romance's adaptive facility: these texts feature romance beyond royalist prose fiction and outside of romances entirely. Taken together, they also illustrate several other factors crucial to this project. First, they show us that seventeenth-century English men and women who are attuned to romance are engaging not just with continental works, but also with England's medieval chivalric tradition and with sixteenth-century writers like Spenser. Second, they remind us that romance, while read by women, was not primarily a women's genre; it was also a genre of masculine fellowship (as in Donne's sonnet),⁴⁷ of communal Christianity (as in Lake's sermons), and of communication between men and women (as in Hatton's letters)—relations that might highlight divergent perspectives on how to read life as romance. These examples reveal romance not just as a mode of isolation or withdrawal, but also as a strategy for forging bonds between individuals and within groups, a genre for expressing and creating fellowship, as when Lake's Christ retreats alone into the wilderness in order to lead and strengthen his community of followers. Next, they offer further evidence of Hobbes's concern over the potency of romance subjectivity: subjects who identify with the heroes of romance perceive their power to resist not just Satan, but also church teaching or state leadership. Finally, they are each concerned in their own way with making, and sometimes worrying over, distinctions between right romance and wrong romance: if the first kind is inspired and justified by God, by true love, or by a clear vision of fortune's course, the second kind might be the vanity of the world, the flesh, and the devil; a silly waste of time; or a delusion that tempts would-be heroes toward danger and tragedy. How might those who believed in both wrong romance and right romance decide which was which, and what circumstances tested their belief in the usefulness of that distinction?

To explore these matters further, and to present a more complete picture of romance and communal ideology in seventeenth-century England, this book traces two interwoven threads. First, I examine the relationship between the individual romance subjectivity that Hobbes denounced as vainglorious and the formation of romance community based on a *shared* sense of heroic identity, which was even more threatening to established authority. Expanding on ideas proposed by scholars such as Sacvan Bercovitch, who finds romance at the root of Puritan subjectivity, mythmaking, and conquest in America,[48] and Michael McKeon, who links romance to nonconformist religious "enthusiasm" or (according to seventeenth-century critics like Hobbes) "claims to spirituality which reflect the pride of human sufficiency by being inadequately tied to rational . . . evidences,"[49] I argue that the heroic subjectivity offered by romance often correlated with the widespread Protestant belief in divine election.

Today, we are likely to associate the concept of election most strongly with the Calvinist doctrine of double predestination—the belief that God, at the beginning of time, marked out each human soul for either salvation or damnation. It bears noting right away, then, that many of the writers in this book do not seem to have believed in double predestination, and while all would have been exposed to Calvin's theology, most either had a complex relationship with it or plainly did not subscribe to it. The religious landscape of sixteenth- and seventeenth-century England was extraordinarily diverse, and many believers defy classification, as scholarship increasingly has shown. Of the writers I consider here who express some form of belief in divine election that they associate with the subjectivity of romance, perhaps only Lucy Hutchinson can with confidence be identified as an orthodox, hard-line Calvinist. Among the others, Philip Sidney belonged to a syncretistic, anti-dogmatic society of reformers; Edmund Spenser seems to have held moderate or ambiguously Calvinist beliefs; John Milton's faith was famously idiosyncratic; and John Bunyan is typically identified as a "nonconformist" or "dissenter" from the Anglican state church. When we consider the writers in these pages who pushed against an association between romance and divine election, the picture is equally diverse: Fulke Greville espoused Calvinist ideas but was deeply uncomfortable with romance as a model for life and history; Margaret Cavendish's religion—if indeed she had one—was also highly idiosyncratic and perhaps deistic; John Dryden was a High Church Anglican who became a Catholic; and Aphra Behn's ambiguous references to her own Catholic upbringing are difficult to verify. Throughout this book, I refer variously to the pro-election, pro-romance contingent as "Protestant" (the broadest applicable label), "reformist" (to indicate the bent of their religiopolitical activism), "republican" (with the exception of Sidney and Spenser), and "godly" or "Puritan." While this last label is as sticky and contentious as any other, I frequently choose to use it for two reasons. First, it is the name by which a theologically disparate group of people increasingly came to be known on the basis of their shared commitments to certain religious and political reforms. Second, and more important for this project, Jason Gleckman has argued that while "Puritans" diverged in many theological specifics, they were consistently firm on the controversial point of "assurance"—the "[intense belief] in the possibility of attaining a state whereby one was absolutely certain of one's election."[50] This deeply subjective certainty was one major aspect of the "vain glory" that Hobbes (among others) found both ridiculous and dangerous, and it is a feature that I believe we can discern in the various mental worlds of Sidney, Spenser, Hutchinson, Milton, and Bunyan. The idea of election may have meant something different for each of these writers, but I argue that for all of them it means a sacred status of which one may potentially receive assured signs—and that all of them associated this calling, and this assurance, with romance heroism.

Seventeenth-century subjects (especially, though not only, Puritans) who read themselves as the heroes of romance regularly attributed authorship of that romance to God; as characters predestined for trials and triumph within a divine narrative, they were essentially equivalent to the community of the elect. Their belief in their sacred heroism, as well as in their Christian salvation, finds its source in a private assured conviction of their election by God—an impression that can never be "tied to rational . . . evidences" and therefore cannot be proven false.[51] Both election and romance could draw individual believers together into a community united by its members' shared faith in their exceptionalism—a community that also, by its very nature, excluded the unregenerate who did not share its collective subjectivity. Like the private experience of conversion, which could then be shared and validated by others' similar experiences so that it also became a public and communal identity, romance could function as a powerful shibboleth, drawing its adherents together while excluding and resisting those who did not participate in the "right" kind of romance.[52]

Patterson and Potter have shown that romance-as-strategy could function as a code accessible only to members of the royalist community,[53] and Kahn and Welch have argued that royalists formed affective fellowships based on their prose romances of sentiment and sympathy.[54] Following them as well as Julie Crawford, who has shown how "the production of literature helped to create and sustain exclusive societies" among late sixteenth-century and early seventeenth-century reformers, I argue that Puritans and republicans formed exclusive romance communities of their own, based on both affective piety and a shared sense of elect exceptionalism.[55] Because royalists were not the only romance subjects, the Civil War and its aftermath meant an ongoing ideological battle over whose romance was the right romance: both sides mocked and condemned their enemies' manipulation of the genre while simultaneously appropriating and reclaiming it in order to represent their own champions, and their community, as the true heroes of national and sacred history. Peter Lake has shown in his work with Michael Questier how Puritans and their various rivals engaged in competition for control over major English cultural narratives, with one central field of contention being the appeal to individual conscience: a crucial value for Puritans, recusant Catholics, and others, one that by its very nature was profoundly subjective and might justify all manner of subversive politics.[56] My work here is comparable, centralizing romance as a key seventeenth-century cultural battleground, not least because of its deeply personal, malleable, and dangerous evocation of heroic subjectivity. I also examine, especially in later chapters, how this competition became increasingly self-conscious and sometimes self-critical: both republicans and royalists recognized that their rivalry over romance and its inherently nonrational subjectivity needed to be acknowledged and wrestled with, and began to suggest that individual heroism and communal identification might depend on romance's mediation between assurance and uncertainty. Finally, I address how postwar writers might turn to romance not merely to represent elect community, but to reconsider and reconstruct it, thinking critically about whether the genre might breach and repair the very divides in subjectivity and identity that it had been so instrumental in maintaining, and about where the limits of romance for constructing civic and religious narratives might lie.

In the second thread of this project, I explore how seventeenth-century writers who were drawn to romance contended with recurring problems of how to interpret and represent history as genre. As the structure of the form suggests, romance's length and its "duplicitous teleology" were well suited to the vagaries of an always-unfolding national history. But because of these vicissitudes, while romance subjectivity might be powerful, liberating, and inspiring, it also demanded experiences of failure, suffering, and ignorance, in which the genre of history or life might look much more like tragedy. To mitigate this burden, writers conceiving romances of elect community frequently imagined their characters—and by extension themselves—being granted some prophetic perspective on the complete teleological narrative of history. As we will see, such visions are often limited, fleeting, and unevenly bestowed on individual subjects. Like Mary Hatton, who could not foresee a happy end to Randolph Helsby's "Heroicall motions" through "the utter darkness & uncertaneties of the tymes," certain subjects and writers of romance were apt to express skepticism about, or feel excluded from, the confident narrative visions of others.[57] (We will find that this interpersonal friction is sometimes, though not always, gendered, as it is in the case of Hatton and Helsby.) I argue, then, that due to romance's long form and the problem of multiple ideological stances and subjectivities, we encounter many seventeenth-century struggles with the generic tension between providential romance and the tragedies of personal or national history. Finally, I propose that as writers reconsidered the formation and restrictions of elect community, they also strove to rethink strategic divides in romance, interrogating new ways of approaching mixed genre, narrative perspective, and heroic identity.

Beginning in 1588, the year that Fulke Greville began work on the publication of his late friend Philip Sidney's *New Arcadia*, and ending one hundred years later in 1688, the year that Aphra Behn published *Oroonoko* and the "Glorious Revolution" deposed the Stuart dynasty, this book reads across the divide between centuries in order to enable a new understanding of romance, heroic subjectivity, and elect community during the English Civil War, the Restoration, and its aftermath. In chapter 1, "Protestant Re-visions of Romance: Philip Sidney's *New Arcadia* and Edmund Spenser's *The Faerie Queene*," I consider the two key works that grappled with romance's civic potential and its limits for a newly Protestant state, and that profoundly influenced seventeenth-century approaches to the genre. Against critical claims that Sidney and Spenser judged romance too worldly to function in harmony with their godly patriotism, I argue that they each developed distinctive postures that acknowledged romance's challenges while affirming its Protestant resonances. Sidney's Pyrocles, asked to justify his erotic passion, counters that "they only know it which inwardly feel it," setting up a correspondence between the turn to romance and godly assurance: both rely on nonrational subjectivity to exclude the uninitiated from a community of believers.[58] By forming affective bonds through their mutual affinity for romance, Sidney's zealous lovers resist the tyranny of the unregenerate. Spenser, in turn, contends with romance's errant structure by portraying its tortuous temporality as a yoke to which an elect people must submit as they navigate the hard course of providential history, although his protagonists may be granted prophetic narrative perspective, in various forms, to help them bear this burden. Sidney's and Spenser's two models of romance—as a strategy by which communities construct, understand, and empower themselves, and as a temporal structure that endeavors to mediate between triumph and tragedy—would endure with widespread and multivalent applications amid the ideological conflicts of the next century.

Chapter 2 ("'Heroical' Histories: Writing Lives into National Romance, 1648–1670") examines how Sidney and Spenser's twin hermeneutics permeate four works of romance-inflected historiography composed by royalists and republicans during and after the Civil War, as both sides sought to mark their community and leaders as the true heroes of the national narrative. Two texts highlight Sidney and Spenser's complex mid-century reception: First, the 1648 pamphlet *The Faerie Leveller* extols Charles I as the living antitype of Spenser's Knight of Justice, casting Spenser as a prophet who forecasted an unlikely defeat for Cromwell and reclaiming him from his Puritan devotees by insisting that readers loyal to the king hold the real key to his allegory. Next, the 1652 first printing of Greville's *Life of the Renowned Sir Philip Sidney* wrestles with the relationship between Sidney's romance heroism and his tragic death, while allowing its diverse Interregnum audience to read him as either a chivalrous royalist or a godly proto-republican visionary. A second pair of works—the royalist Margaret Cavendish's and the parliamentarian

Lucy Hutchinson's memoirs of their war-hero husbands—diverge politically yet share a generic and gendered tension between the men's confident vision of history as romance and their wives' relative uncertainty. All four texts reveal ideological competition over the right uses of romance for representing individual and communal history as story, alongside a pervasive sense that that very strategy is fraught with problems of variable subjectivity and historical perspective.

Each remaining chapter pairs a republican writer with one or more royalist ones in order to illuminate these ongoing struggles over romance. In chapter 3 ("The Fall and the Pinnacle: Milton's Righting of Romance in *Paradise Lost* and *Paradise Regained*"), I explore both parties' efforts to contend with the problem of romance subjectivity and the experiences of contingency and defeat, reading Milton's post-Restoration biblical poetics against post-Regicide romances by Margaret Cavendish and Percy Herbert. Much as Kahn has proposed, Cavendish and Herbert offer their fellow royalists a rationalist way around Hobbes's distaste for romance, creating skeptical characters who accept and exploit the strategy's flexible subject positions and its indeterminacy between providence and fortune. Milton, however, assigns this relativism to Satan, pitting his anti-teleological skepticism against the protagonists' embattled faith and reaffirming a godly subjectivity unique to the community of the elect. Contrary to the common argument that Milton came to reject romance as too royalist, I show that he develops his own sense of Puritan right romance that embraces the gap between conviction and uncertainty and the distance between the promise of narrative fulfillment and the present imperceptibility of that end.

In the last two chapters, I consider late seventeenth-century writers' attempts to rethink romance in relationship to election, community, gender, and generic form. Chapter 4 ("'My Victorious Triumphs Are All Thine': The Politics of Love and Elect Community in Lucy Hutchinson's *Order and Disorder*") reads Hutchinson's Genesis epic against John Dryden's panegyric to the restored Charles II, "Astraea Redux." I argue that Dryden's poem, reconceiving romance as reparative rather than exclusionary, depicts the Restoration as the universalist telos to the turbulent national story: God blesses and elects all English people equally in their mystical marriage to Charles II, an ecstatic union that subsumes distinctions of gender and ideology by reinscribing all subjects as feminine in fallibility, as masculine by marriage, and as royalist. Hutchinson resists this triumphalist narrative, insisting in her turn to biblical romance that both teleological plot and redemptive eroticism are gifts reserved for the Puritan elect, and suggesting—somewhat differently than in her *Memoirs* of her husband—that male and female believers experience the burdens and the hopes of romance temporality equally, including prophetic glimpses of the still-remote "full Restoration."

The final chapter ("'In the Next World': John Bunyan, Aphra Behn, and the Imitation of Romance") considers part 2 of John Bunyan's *The Pilgrim's Progress* and Aphra Behn's *Oroonoko*, texts known for resistance to generic categorization. I aim to show how this complexity relates to both authors' self-conscious interrogation of romance and elect community, as they return at the dawn of the eighteenth century to questions much like those that challenged Spenser and Sidney a hundred years before: Can romance function as a meaningful model for history? What are its civic and religious applications and limitations? Behn affirms the genre's capacity to unite the diverse community of Oroonoko and his friends. Rather than being empowered or providentially protected, however, their group is destroyed by external foes and, more important, by internal weakness: the protagonists are too enamored of imitating the fictions of romance to protect one another from real violence. Behn enacts romance's recession in her transatlantic tragedy; her prophetic narrative vision as a royalist woman reveals not the New Jerusalem but the New World—a spatial and temporal zone she finds hostile to the ideas that allowed romance to flourish across ideological boundaries in seventeenth-century England. Bunyan, on the other hand, deliberately draws romance to the fore of his text, orchestrating productive conflicts between romance norms and nonconformist Christian allegory. Part 2 of *The Pilgrim's Progress* ultimately proposes that romance's value lies in its ability to imitate or stand for (rather than embody) sacred narrative form, to imagine new modes of godly eroticism and heroic agency, and to empower a nontraditional family of dissenters as they journey together not only to Paradise, but also into England's this-worldly future.

Cooper has suggested that romance's theme of socially stabilizing faithful love and its providential teleology grant the mode "the potential to lie at the heart of a Protestant national literature," and yet that "outside the *Faerie Queene* it does not often do so," perhaps because of a "cultural shift, from an assumption that literature exists to express an age or a nation's ideology to an assumption that it speaks with an individual voice at odds with the institutional requirements of Church and state."[59] This book tells a different story—one of how seventeenth-century writers *did* follow Spenser, Sidney, and their medieval predecessors in embedding romance at the core of their (mostly) Protestant nationalist mythmaking and individual subjectivity, sometimes for that very purpose of resisting and subverting "institutional" structures. What lies at the heart is often hidden, and we will sometimes need to search in nonobvious places. The quest to glimpse and understand romance is itself part of the point of concealing it: only what Bunyan calls "*the Godly mind*" (and what other writers describe in other terms) will be drawn to the right kind of romance, will recognize and read it in the right ways, and will claim a rightful place in its exclusive elect community.[60]

CHAPTER 1

Protestant Re-visions of Romance
Philip Sidney's New Arcadia *and Edmund Spenser's* The Faerie Queene

Before we can fully appreciate seventeenth-century writers' ideological appropriations of romance, we must consider the most influential English narratives from the end of the previous century that served as foundations for countless texts that followed them. Although we are examining them proleptically, Sir Philip Sidney's *New Arcadia* and Edmund Spenser's *The Faerie Queene* were both composed with one eye toward England's Protestant present and the other toward its troubled recent past. Near the sixteenth century's close, and in the wake of England's turmoil under the Tudor dynasty, Sidney and Spenser were keenly aware of romance's medieval Catholic history, and they were eager to reconsider the cherished mode's religious and civic potential for their newly Protestant state. What, they asked themselves and their readers, might romance come to mean for the community of God's church as it encountered trials and triumphs in the world? What kind of literary arena could it provide for contending with questions of England's faith, its monarchy, its history, and its destiny?

The aim of this chapter is not to present a complete picture of Sidney and Spenser's complex reformations of romance—a task already undertaken with skill by Tiffany Werth—nor to detail the full inheritance that Sidney and Spenser's engagement with romance's Protestant nationalist potential left to seventeenth-century Britons.[1] Rather, it is to explore four specific elements of their re-visions of the mode—two from each writer—that proved especially fruitful to the Civil War and Restoration writers featured in this book. Sidney's *New Arcadia* bequeathed to English romance two traits that would eventually inspire Thomas Hobbes's warnings about its subversive potential: first, an interiorized and powerfully malleable heroic subjectivity, derived from the hero's zealous faith in his or her vocation and protection by providence; and second, romance's related ability to function as an ideological litmus test, uniting an exceptional community of self-identified heroes and empowering them to exclude and resist those they see as hostile to their shared narrative. Spenser's *Faerie Queene* established two key points of tension in his patriotic Protestant romance-epic that prepared seventeenth-century writers to engage constructively with romance's structural challenges: first, a tension in genre, produced by providential romance's interplay with the tragic burdens of personal and national history; and second, a tension in subjectivity, produced by separate subjects' receipt of different, and not equally revelatory or comforting, prophetic visions of romance's long and errant form. Sidney and Spenser's twin legacies—of romance subjectivity and exclusive community, and of romance's productive problems of genre and narrative insight—would flourish with widespread applications and innovations amid the conflicts of the century to come.

ROMANCE SUBJECTIVITY AND COMMUNITY IN PHILIP SIDNEY'S *NEW ARCADIA*

At the age of thirty-one, Philip Sidney died of wounds inflicted at Zutphen in the Netherlands, where he fought a losing battle against Spain in the name of a unified Protestant Europe. Stories about his conduct on his deathbed immediately became the stuff of legend. The young poet-knight had composed a final song and had it performed as he lay dying; he had urged his grieving friends to philosophize with him about the comforts of eternal life; most famously, he had given his water to a dying foot soldier, assuring him, "Thy necessity is yet greater than mine."[2] By dying young, with gallantry, and in service to his faith and his queen, Sidney catapulted his reputation from an aristocratic writer of romance fiction to an exemplary hero of the romance of English history—the story of the Protestant state's triumph over adversity, which, like Sidney's own *Arcadia*, remained unfinished.

In the decades that followed, English readers of disparate ideologies would shore up Sidney's reputation as the ideal soldier, scholar, subject, poet, lover, and Christian, all in one.³ Much contemporary Sidney criticism has been a reaction against this legend, an effort to unearth the historical Philip Sidney beneath layers of literary hyperbole. In his seminal study on Sidney and his religion, Andrew Weiner proposed to correct "the romantic image of the courtier-lover-poet that was for so long an obstacle to the understanding of his works" by revealing the "real" Sidney, a serious-minded scholar whose Protestant zeal jarred with Elizabeth I's more moderate stance.⁴ Blair Worden continued the project in his expansive allegorical reading of Sidney's *Arcadia* as an earnest, religiously reformist critique of Elizabethan policy.⁵ The struggle toward an accurate representation of Sidney's politically engaged Protestant identity, as distinct from "romantic" mythmaking, has been undertaken by many scholars and has always been bound up with the question of how to read his work. He has been described as a Calvinist (most notably by Weiner), a Puritan (by Alan Sinfield),⁶ a "forward Protestant" (by Worden), and even perhaps a crypto-Catholic (by Katherine Duncan-Jones).⁷ But Sidney's idiosyncratic expressions of faith—entangled as they often are in his own literary criticism, his poetry, and his prose romance—for a long time frustrated attempts to affix a label.⁸ Indeed, as the many descriptions indicate, early modern religious identity was not easily demarcated; English Protestantisms were and would remain widely variable. Robert Stillman has recently cut through this Gordian knot by arguing persuasively that Sidney belonged to a small and underrecognized multinational community of "Philippists": admirers of Luther's colleague Philip Melanchthon.⁹

The Philippists did not call themselves by this name, or by any for that matter; the French reformer Hubert Languet, who had been Melanchthon's student and who became Sidney's mentor in turn, was fond of referring to people who shared their convictions and their purposes as *les notres*—"our own." Termed "Philippists" by fellow Protestants of divergent beliefs, they were humanists uncomfortable with theological hairsplitting and open to compromise: optimistic about free will and moderate on the efficacy of good works, Melanchthon and his followers rejected the doctrine of double predestination because it made God appear a tyrant, and as political activists they opposed themselves to earthly tyranny in all its forms. Stillman has argued for an understanding of Sidney's faith and his writing as syncretistic and "inclusive," welcoming to a doctrinally diverse readership (including freethinking Catholics) for the sake of unity against ignorance and oppression, especially of the Popish and Spanish varieties.[10] I want to show here that Sidney's *New Arcadia* demonstrates both the winning inclusivity and the alluring *exclusivity* of his religiopolitics. To choose loving fellowship over rivalry and to join the fight against tyranny is to gain membership in the community of *les notres*, to become "one of us"—and so to cease being "one of them," the masses of unenlightened barbarians, fools, and slaves.

Readings of Sidney's work that have assigned him a dogmatic creed like Calvinism have typically coincided with arguments that his literary career is didactic in a strange, ironic way. If Sidney believed in the total depravity of the will and passions, then the *Defence of Poesie* must be interpreted as a self-contradictory indictment of secular poetics, and *Arcadia* must be a mock-heroic romance about what not to do, as Weiner, Sinfield, Worden, and others have contended in various ways.[11] Weiner speaks for many when he says of the *Old Arcadia* that "Sidney did not intend [his protagonists] to be exemplars of heroism" and that the characters' amorous exploits distract them from political ethics and spiritual virtue.[12] Such claims are easier to make about the shorter, finished *Old Arcadia*, in which the princely heroes end up guilty of unchastity and attempted rape.[13] However, Sidney's revised, incomplete *New Arcadia*—which his friend Fulke Greville upheld as more representative of Sidney's values and in which the princes are somewhat better behaved—has received similar treatment. Worden argues that the *New Arcadia*'s erotic escapades still point to the moral that godly stoicism must rule over a statesman's desires; Victor Skretkowicz claims that Sidney uses his audience's familiarity with Heliodoran Greek romance "to demonstrate how all sense of political and social responsibility can be eroded by passion";[14] while Clare Kinney, Mary Ellen Lamb, and Alex Davis interpret the revision's extensive metadiscourse about its own genre as evidence that Sidney really meant to indict romance as self-indulgent.[15] The *New Arcadia*—widely read and well loved in the late sixteenth and seventeenth centuries—is indeed the text that best illustrates Sidney's conscious, careful Protestant engagement with romance.[16] However, I propose that when we read it in light of Sidney's Philippism, rather than with recourse to a theology of total depravity or a political philosophy at odds with passion and pleasure, we find that the *New Arcadia* functions not as a self-consuming artifact created to perform its own moral critique,[17] but as a sincere—if also playful—"heroicall Poem," like those celebrated in the *Defence*, which asserts Sidney's conviction of erotic romance's real value in constructing a syncretistic reformist community.[18]

One critic in Sidney's lifetime who might have needed to be convinced of the value of romance was his own Philippist mentor. Hubert Languet's hopes for his protégé's activism were high, perhaps oppressively so.[19] Stillman notes that in their correspondence, Languet habitually imagines Sidney as "an actor in a drama scripted by God," a hero with a "providentially appointed" destiny to thwart the "tragedies" always being authored by the tyrannical forces of Catholic Europe. Yet he also seems to have been chronically anxious about the degradation of this young warrior into "another, very different Philip Sidney—a Sidney too easily seduced by pleasure, luxury, ease and what his mentor refers to most often as idleness."[20] These twin visions of Sidney—the divinely ordained tyrant fighter and the lazy hedonist seduced away from his quest—look remarkably like the dual natures of Pyrocles and Musidorus, who divert from their shared career of righteous tyrannomachy to pursue love in Arcadia. Critics have tended to assume, like Languet, that this digression discredits or even degrades the princes. Musidorus thinks so too, at first, when he discovers Pyrocles dressed as a woman to get closer to Philoclea, and before he himself falls in love with Pamela. But I argue that Sidney sees the potential for nobility, even sanctity, in both civic and erotic pursuits. In Melissa Sanchez's view, this element might set the *New Arcadia* apart from its antecedents: "Numerous Greek and medieval romances depict passion in obsessive and excruciating terms. . . . But early modern erotic literature is unique in that it sees human desire, in all of its glorious perversity, as the source of political order, not its enemy."[21] Helen Cooper, meanwhile, argues that in medieval romance, "the desirability of desire, male and female, *was* widely acknowledged as a part of God's design for the universe" and as a political good—yet suggests that eroticism in the *Arcadias* was essentially too bizarre for Sidney himself to have been advocating this.[22] In what follows, I hope to show that love's strangeness in the *New Arcadia* is concomitant with its ecstatic Christian resonances. Moreover (in a reading I share with Sanchez), when tyranny reemerges to shatter the lovers' retreat, their love and their assurance of its rightness grant them new ways of fighting. Sidney's literary answer to his mentor's anxieties over a tragic turn to history is not drama or epic, but romance—a site for negotiating intergenerational conflict, as Nandini Das has suggested, and a mode that predicts the hero's final victory over evil and in which his public service may be entwined with his private passions.[23] The *New Arcadia* acknowledges the pitfalls of worldly love—its silliness, its selfishness, its inextricability from lust—yet still commits it to the service of a divine providence fully engaged in worldly politics. With his characteristic lighthearted seriousness, Sidney makes erotic romance first an instrument of individual heroic faith, and then a communal weapon against the tragedy of tyranny.

"They Only Know It Which Inwardly Feel It": The Subjectivity of Romance

Melanchthon and his followers understood the salvation of the Christian soul as a narrative formula unfolding in time. In creation, God embeds seeds of truth in every human mind, which the Philippists termed *notitiae* (notices or notions). The believer, often by degrees, becomes increasingly awakened to them, and by following these signposts arrives at a powerful faith, understood both as "the self's unreserved commitment to God" and as "the certainty of the self's knowledge about its relationship to God."[24] This relationship entails extraordinary love, but also extraordinary responsibility, as Languet fretfully insisted to Sidney: responsibility to identify the story of God's church triumphant as one's own story, and to undertake the heroic task of making that triumph real in the temporal world. After all, the victory of the reformed Church was also a narrative in progress, a communal story woven from the stories of each individual member. Sidney's *New Arcadia* differs from the *Old* partly in its multiplicity of interlaced narratives: there are many accounts of love conducted either nobly or ignobly, many parallel obstacles and losses, many recognitions and reunions. At the same time, Sidney insists that service to love is an intensely subjective experience, a patterned, recurring process that is nevertheless intimately and singularly felt by each individual. The degrees through which Pyrocles, Musidorus, Pamela, and Philoclea each fall in love and submit to Love as a divine force are recounted for us in detail: each of the four protagonists first becomes receptive to love as an idea after witnessing its workings in others, then undergoes a profound inner revelation of its power through irresistible desire for a particular person, and finally ecstatically embraces it as a godlike authority that evokes the believer's extraordinary devotion. This process can be mapped onto the Philippist narrative of salvation that progresses from signs to "certainty," and although Melanchthon's followers rejected predestination (all people were gifted with *notitiae* and could choose whether to heed them), Sidney's stages of love might also be recognized by readers of other creeds. After all, a long theological tradition compared Christian devotion to erotic love, as often illustrated through the Song of Songs, and Plato's "ladder" from earthly to heavenly love (a favorite topic of Sidney's) had been repopularized for both Protestant and Catholic readers by Castiglione's *Courtier*. Readers versed in Calvinist theology might see in Sidney's process a secular echo of the *ordo salutis*: according to this alternative narrative formula, God's elect children would receive an outward call to faith that preceded a life-altering inner calling, an assured conviction that one was chosen by God for his church and owed this special status not to one's own worthiness but to God's irresistible grace. The fact that doctrinally diverse readers might see shadows of familiar salvation stories in Sidney's romance is a testament to Sidney's religious syncretism, but also to the allure of membership in a sacred narrative, whether of a predestinate elect or a more ecumenical elite.

Pyrocles, Sidney's most "fiery" hero and the first to find himself overwhelmed with desire to devote himself to Love, is moved by many external signs of love's power prior to his internal experience of its full force. Before arriving in Arcadia, he is loved by the real Zelmane, who disguises herself as a boy and dies in his service, and whose name and appearance he later adopts to woo Philoclea. Pyrocles confesses to Philoclea that "something there was" in the dying Zelmane's devotion, "which, when I saw a picture of yours, brought again her figure into my remembrance, and made my heart as apt to receive the wound, as the power of your beauty with unresistable force to pierce."[25] When Pyrocles hears the "true" romance of Argalus and Parthenia and witnesses their joyful reunion, he is so affected by it that "a change [is] grown" in him: he slips into a contemplative melancholy, mysterious to his friends, as he feels his own inclination toward love (48). Sidney's fellow Philippists, among them the French Huguenot philosopher Philippe Duplessis-Mornay, held that God endows all his creation with an inclination to love their fellow creatures; Sidney eroticizes this divinely orchestrated tendency.[26] Calvinist readers, meanwhile, would be familiar with the idea that authentic conversion must be preceded by receptiveness to the testimony of scripture and of the faithful. Finally, Pyrocles explains to Musidorus that upon seeing Philoclea's image, "once my heart was made tender ... it received quickly a cruel impression of that wonderful passion which to be defined is impossible, because no words reach to the strange nature of it. They only know it which inwardly feel it; it is called love" (78). This moment, lexically recognizable to doctrinally diverse readers as the "mollifying of the heart" of the convert, marks a permanent change in Pyrocles as he yields himself entirely to the power that has claimed him, now able to "inwardly feel" the sign of his vocation to a new kind of heroism.[27]

However, this emotional triumph raises intellectual problems. When Pyrocles tells Musidorus of the profound inward alteration he has undergone, he has changed outwardly as well and is now dressed as the Amazon Zelmane, the better to win Philoclea without arousing her parents' suspicion. Musidorus responds skeptically to Pyrocles's erotic evangelism, disturbed by his friend's feminization and his concomitant interest in sexual, rather than soldierly, conquest. Anticipating later critics who argue that Sidney's *New Arcadia* condemns the ungodliness and passivity of romance, Musidorus berates Pyrocles for abandoning his manly virtue in pursuit of lust and demands a teleological justification: "The beginning being so excellent, I would gladly know the end" (75). For Sidney's community, this is exactly the right question: Melanchthon has been described as a "relentlessly teleological" thinker, and Philippist intellectuals took care to extend their philosophical premises through to their ultimate purposes (a prime example is the *Defence*'s assertion that the end of a poet's fantasy must be the real cultivation of virtue).[28] But Pyrocles has an answer. Without denying his desire for Philoclea, Pyrocles insists that his stated "end" of "enjoying" her refers beyond sexual consummation to Neoplatonic delight in spiritual beauty and virtue, "the end to which it is directed; which end ends not" (75). But this ardent yet cryptic assertion of his passion's moral teleology fails to convince Musidorus, and Pyrocles turns instead to a declaration of love's inexpressible transformative power, forced to acknowledge that "they only know it which inwardly feel it" (78).[29] Yet this admission works to his advantage: his erotic conversion has endowed him with a subjective certainty that cannot, and need not, be justified to others who do not yet possess it themselves. The subjectivity of his newfound love of Love proves—to him, if not to anyone else—that rather than falling from grace, he has only just now attained it. This appeal stymies counterargument despite, and because of, its illogic; Pyrocles's claim to a *notitia* or an inward calling that justifies his radical devotion is unfalsifiable.

Pyrocles's "end" assurance marks the beginning of Musidorus's own conversion narrative. His reluctant consent to help Pyrocles/Zelmane woo Philoclea results in his first sight of her sister Pamela, and he is "presently stricken" with his own profound interior change, seemingly awakened to the *notitia* of the human inclination to love in the image of their creator: "Can any man resist his creation? Certainly, by love we are made, and to love we are made" (108, 106). When Zelmane teases him for his change of heart, he acknowledges his conversion in explicitly religious terms. "'I recant, I recant!' cried Musidorus; and withal falling down prostrate," he utters a prayer for forgiveness that might be addressed to an inexorable God as well as to the "spirit of love": "Have compassion of me, and let thy glory be as great in pardoning them that be submitted to thee, as in conquering those that were rebellious" (106). Moreover, he suddenly finds himself possessed with the exact same faith that he derided in Pyrocles: "'O heaven and earth!' said Musidorus. 'To what a pass are our minds brought, that from the right line of virtue are wried to these crooked shifts! But O love, it is thou that doost it. . . . Thou disguisest our bodies and disfigurest our minds; but indeed thou hast reason, for though the ways be foul, the journey's end is most fair and honourable'" (109). Musidorus, having now "inwardly [felt]" the transfiguring force of Love, joins Pyrocles as a devotee of its mysteries and so shares his certainty that Love imposes a teleological narrative on the faithful lover's "journey," no matter how "crooked" it may appear along the way. As a member of Love's chosen fellowship, he becomes convinced that he can now perceive the "end" he once mocked. His subjective assurance of his calling, and of the end-directed heroic romance plot associated with it, constantly protects and renews itself.

In Philoclea, the last of the lovers to undergo conversion, Sidney treats the fear and the ecstasy of submission to divinity most earnestly. While the other protagonists attempt to describe their new vocations to others with limited success, Philoclea's is the only process we observe from the heroine's private perspective, and her transformation is terrible and wonderful. She, too, is attracted at first by witnessing the signs of love at work outside of her, in the form of Zelmane's gazes and sighs, which Philoclea innocently imitates "till at the last, poor soul, ere she were aware, she accepted . . . not only the sign, but the passion signified" (145). Upon realizing that she is, as she believes, in love with another woman, Philoclea falls into a conviction of her own depravity common in conversion stories, much like the near despair described by both Luther and Calvin (though observable in pre-Reformation Catholic writers such as Margery Kempe) and prominent in personal declarations of faith, from Anne Lok's 1560 *Meditation of a Penitent Sinner* to John Bunyan's 1666 *Grace Abounding to the Chief of Sinners*. Though Philoclea prays for aid from the "great hidden deities which have their working in the ebbing and flowing of our estates," she presumes herself forsaken by them: "No, no, you cannot help me! Sin must be the mother, and shame the daughter of my affection" (149). But the Philippist Sidney represents the faithful soul's self-horror at her depravity not as a direct path toward salvation (as Calvin did), but as an obstacle that she must see beyond in order to willingly assent to her new vocation and begin participating in the divine narrative that will transform her and, through her, the world. The oracle has already directed Philoclea's "estate" to the surprising love that she admits she feels, and at last her hope and faith in Love's superior providence conquer her despair and doubt: "Alas then, O love, why doost thou in thy beautiful sampler set such a work for my desire to take out, which is as much impossible? And yet, alas, why do I thus condemn my fortune before I hear what she can say for herself? What do I, silly wench, know what love hath prepared for me? . . . Away, then, all vain examinations of why and how. Thou lovest me, excellent Zelmane, and I love thee. . . . I am wholly given over unto thee" (174–75). Readers know that Philoclea's faith is warranted, and that "love hath prepared" a plot twist that will vindicate her desire, since the lesbian amazon turns out to have been Pyrocles, destined to marry Philoclea all along. But from Philoclea's perspective, not knowing the end of her romance, this declaration represents an extraordinary commitment to Love's service. Her great uncertainty about why she has been chosen and what her calling means is outstripped by a greater certainty that she belongs to Love and to Zelmane, and that her life must now be dedicated to this story.

Cooper would presumably trace Philoclea's extraordinary subjectivity to the heroines of medieval romance, where "a sense of women as 'subjects' . . . with a self-conscious awareness of their own place in the scheme of things, first begins to develop. This self-awareness is linked to the awakening of their sexuality; and women's sexuality is centrally regarded as positive, to the point where it is one of the key factors that enables a restoration of social and providential order. Such an emphasis functions as a strong generic marker—this is what romance is *about*."³⁰ Remarkably, though, Cooper does not see this sacred and pro-social sex positivity in Sidney's work, instead finding that his "gender confusions" are meant to be "disturbing" to early modern readers, "not least because they do not have . . . traditional value behind them and do not acquire any inherent value of their own."³¹ I argue that the romance of the *New Arcadia* is, quite emphatically, "about" the sacred and political value of sexual and even queer love, in agreement with Sanchez and with Julie Crawford, who sees in Philoclea a sympathetic openness to queer desire. Crawford argues that Philoclea's "sapphic" moment is meant to appeal directly to the subjectivity of Sidney's women readers (including his sister Mary and their mutual female friends), whom he trusts uniquely "to identify with [polyvalent] desire and its complications."³² Crawford rejects "the argument that Sidney was embarrassed about" his playful, transgressive erotic writing; far from it, she contends, he counted on a sensitive interpretive community to enjoy his romance's playfulness and understand its seriousness simultaneously.³³ There may be something inherently queer, in Sanchez's sense of encouraging "desires and fantasies that resist normalizing, rational structures," in this ideal community and its way of reading.³⁴ Crawford and Mary Ellen Lamb have suggested that Sidney's romance urges *all* its readers to "read like women";³⁵ it seeks an audience receptive to a thrilling liberty of feelings, meanings, and affective relationships, not only for private pleasure, but also for the sake of passionate public resistance to authoritarian structures of power—a subject we will revisit shortly.

The nature of Sidney's writing, not just in the *New Arcadia* but also in the *Defence of Poesie* or *Astrophil and Stella*, is to court scandal and silliness while demanding to be taken as heartfelt and serious. Writing of the *Defence*, Stillman beautifully articulates Sidney's characteristic earnest playfulness or playful earnestness, along with the risks that result from rejecting it: "The playfulness of his text is irrepressible, constant, and nowhere more visible or more serious than in his purposeful toying with the boundary lines between the secular and the sacred"; Sidney "cultivates a teasing, deliberately coy mode of discourse that *relates* while refusing to *equate*."³⁶ If we assume that Philoclea's queer erotic and spiritual ecstasy cannot be compatible with sincere and devout faith, then un-Sidneian "heavy-handed irony" forces us wrongly to conclude that his work performs "parodic deconstruction of its own arguments," with Sidney's ardent Protestantism crowding out and condemning the ardent humanism and eroticism of his text—when, in reality, "Sidney's piety is sufficiently cosmopolitan to be unembarrassed" by analogies between queer desire and divine love.[37] If Sidney is not ashamed to suggest (as he does in the *Defence*) that a godly poet might channel his heroic energies into erotic verse, there is no reason to think that when Pyrocles and Philoclea embrace Love as new converts called to serve by resisting the normal and the rational, they are really being impious and unheroic.

At the same time that Sidney revels in the seriocomic parallels between erotic romance and Christian vocation, however, he plays up the controversies inherent in the comparison. He himself sees both the emotional necessity of "knowing" that one is "chosen"—his protagonists' certainty is central to their identity and actions as devotees of Love—and the practical and moral hazards of the same idea. However sure individuals may feel of their heroic subjectivity within a divinely plotted narrative, this assurance is inward and self-affirming; it cannot be proven to others unless others choose to accept it as an echo of what they have come to believe about themselves, and so it must always be insular. Sidney highlights the fact that a character's role in the *New Arcadia* is difficult to evaluate without some form of "external" knowledge, and such knowledge is not always easy to come by. We know that Philoclea is right to give herself to Zelmane because we know what the oracle has promised, but Philoclea's parents are both also crazed with love for Zelmane and make themselves ridiculous in pursuing her, just as Pyrocles arguably makes himself ridiculous by becoming Zelmane to pursue Philoclea—how, then, do we know that Philoclea and Pyrocles are the heroes of a romance while Basilius and Gynecia are the butts of a farce? As readers, we can consider the oracle's prophecy, but Basilius also knows what the oracle has said, while Philoclea does not; he turns out not to understand it, and she turns out not to need it. We can also rely on Sidney's authorial authority: he has structured the romance to make the young lovers the primary protagonists, and our cultural familiarity with the genre tells us to accept their actions and expect their happiness. Yet the *New Arcadia*'s characters have no knowledge of Sidney as author and must put their faith in the providence of "hidden deities" and in their own feelings; in this, they are in the same unsteady boat as Sidney's readers, who must eventually put down their books and return to judgments and actions in the real world. Moreover, among the revisions to the *New Arcadia* are its many peripheral narratives and figures, which are far less predictable. Who would imagine, after reading the short and sweet romance of Argalus and Parthenia in the early chapters of book 1, that these faithful lovers would reappear in book 3, only to die tragically for each other at the hands of Amphialus? And Amphialus himself—whose name suggests ambivalence and ambiguity—may pose the greatest problem. Like Pyrocles, he adores Philoclea; like both princes, he holds high chivalric ideals but fails to be consistent in upholding them. When the *New Arcadia* breaks off, Amphialus has just attempted suicide out of remorse for persecuting the princesses and lies on the point of death, but Queen Helen has arrived with a vow to try to heal her beloved. In Anna Weamys's 1651 continuation of the romance, she succeeds and they marry, but Sidney never completes the redemption of the fallen knight that he leads us to believe might be possible.[38]

The legitimacy of a hero's romance subjectivity cannot be judged until the narrative has reached its all-important end. We know how the *New Arcadia* ends, thanks to the oracle—or do we? When the romance breaks off, we may assume that the lovers will triumph and enjoy each other at last, but we do not know *how* this happy ending can arrive out of ongoing suffering and war, and we do not know what other tragedies might haunt them along the way. The text constantly questions whether the flawed heroes' convictions are correct and their actions virtuous, insofar as they are aligned with providential design—which in turn raises the theological question, intimately familiar to Sidney and his contemporaries, of whether individuals possess the positive agency to contribute meaningfully to what providence has already ordained. As a Philippist, Sidney leans toward a model in which the human will ("infected," as Sidney calls it in the *Defence*, but not totally depraved) cooperates with providence in a rather messy, paradoxical way.[39] Translated into the secular narrative of the *New Arcadia*, a person can deliberately embark on a life of romance, as Pyrocles and Musidorus do after being raised on tales of heroism: "They determined . . . to see more of the world, and to employ those gifts esteemed rare in them, to the good of mankind; and therefore would themselves . . . go privately to seek exercises of their virtue, thinking it not so worthy to be brought to heroical effects by fortune or necessity (like Ulysses and Aeneas) as by one's own choice and working" (179). And yet it may be that the princes' choice of romance is the product of their having already been chosen by it, since at their birth the heavens showed "tokens of the coming forth of an heroical virtue. . . . Only love was threatened and promised to [them] . . . as both the tempest and haven of their best years" (163). Sidney provides no conclusive answer about the relationship between romance subjectivity and divine authority. But one thing is certain, as we will see: for the fellowship of romance's faithful subjects, the extraordinary love that may be a tempest and a threat serves also as a haven and a promise.

Les Notres *and* Les Autres: *Romance Community, Exclusion, and Resistance*

Romance subjectivity, like religious assurance, is for Sidney a powerful (if problematic) way of knowing oneself. It also proves a powerful and problematic way of building community. In stubbornly setting himself apart from the still-unregenerate Musidorus, Pyrocles also imagines a soon-to-be-realized plural network of select converts, "they only" who "inwardly feel" as he does. The Protestant resonance of Sidney's erotic narrative bolsters individual resolution and fosters a resolute community *between* individuals who share a recognition of the outward form and inward effects of romance. This community strengthens its sense of identity and heroic purpose as it grows, and it thrives on telling tales of amorous romance, which inspire and delight each of its members by reiterating their own ecstatic experiences of being chosen and mastered by Love. Stillman's reading of a "cosmopolitan" Sidney emphasizes his "magical inclusivity"—his ability to foster humanist agreement between readers of diverse national and confessional identities and to urge them to unite against their common enemies: ignorance, tyranny, and the papist politicians that weaponize both.[40] Without discounting Sidney's open-mindedness and ecumenical appeal, we must keep in mind that his brand of inclusivity necessarily functions on a concomitant principle of *exclusivity*. To accept his invitation into a new order of enlightenment, liberty, and reformed religion means immediately setting oneself apart from, and if necessary in opposition to, others who remain unregenerate—not (yet?) true servants of God, still (always?) slaves to tyrants and to themselves. This principle is manifest in the term Languet favors for the Philippists and their allies: *les notres*, which implicitly bars all others who are not "one of us." However welcoming the fellowship may be, one must belong either to *les notres* or to *les autres*—the others.

The spiritual and intellectual community formed by Languet, Mornay, and other friends and family (including, as Crawford has emphasized, many freethinking women) was an enduring force in Sidney's life and writing.[41]

And in his romance, the subjectivity Pyrocles articulates to explain his *singular* devotion and actions ("They only know it which inwardly feel it") gestures toward a *they*—a community of fellows with the capacity to join him in serving Love. Pyrocles's singular faith soon gives rise to this very community, as Musidorus, Philoclea, Pamela, and other peripheral characters devote themselves to Love and to one another. The communal telling of heroic love stories is an essential element of the *New Arcadia*'s fellowship: Pamela listens with increasing attraction to Musidorus's true tales of the princes' chivalric deeds; Philoclea rejoices in the narrative teleology of Pyrocles's past "perils, for, since I have you here out of them, even the remembrance of them is pleasant" (233-34); and Musidorus feels increasingly bound first to Strephon and Claius, and then to Argalus and Parthenia, after hearing the stories of their love. Pyrocles's metric—to feel is to know, to know is to understand, to understand is to be one of us—allows the *New Arcadia*'s chosen heroes to recognize one another and to reject others who neither feel nor understand. Their community is indeed inclusive, in a sense: it can admit common shepherds like Strephon and Claius, united in "love-fellowship" through their mutual love of Urania (5); it thrives on the steadfastness of its female members more than on the emotional and egocentric heroism of its men; and, as we have seen, its sense of Love as a deity can adapt itself to multiple religious perspectives in Sidney's real world. However, that community is also rigorously exclusive. In a distinction that may offer a rebuke to both the scolding Languet and the "gerontocracy" of Elizabeth's regime, it is limited to the young, who must defend themselves from the jaded skepticism of oldsters like Kalander (who scoffs at the idea of Neoplatonic shepherds devoted to heavenly beauty), as well as from the domineering lusts of the princesses' parents. More important, there are certain people the community bars absolutely as enemies to its nature. These foes match Melanchthon's: the ignorant masses—best represented by the vulgar shepherd family of Dametas, Miso, and Mopsa—and tyrants whose god is their own enslaving will, of whom Cecropia is chief.

While Musidorus recounts his own personal romance to win over Pamela, Mopsa snores her way through it, too dull to appreciate either its high style or its hidden purpose. Her ignorance is also central to the funniest of the *New Arcadia*'s embedded romance narratives. Pamela, Philoclea, and Pyrocles/Zelmane are spending their day in chivalric storytelling when they are interrupted by Mopsa's clumsy fairy tale about a princess and her enchanted lover:

> "In time past," said she, "there was a king (the mightiest man in all his country), that had by his wife the fairest daughter that ever did eat pap.... So, one day, as his daughter was sitting in her window playing upon a harp, as sweet as any rose, and combing her head with a comb all of precious stones, there came in a knight into the court upon a goodly horse—one, hair of gold; and the other, of silver. And so, the knight, casting up his eyes to the window, did fall into such love with her that he grew not worth the bread he eat; till ... with daily diligence and grisly groans he wan her affection, so that they agreed to run away together. And so, in May, when all true hearts rejoice, they stale out of the castle, without staying so much as for their breakfast. Now, forsooth, as they went together, often all to-kissing one another, the knight told her he was brought up among the water-nymphs, who had so bewitched him that if he were ever asked his name he must presently vanish away: and therefore charged her upon his blessing that she never ask him what he was.... And so, a great while she kept his commandment; till once, passing through a cruel wilderness, as dark as pitch, her mouth so watered that she could not choose but ask him the question. And then he, making the greivousest complaints ... vanished quite away; and she lay down, casting forth as pitiful cries as any shritch-owl. But having lain so, wet by the rain and burned by the sun, five days and five nights, she gat up and went over many a high hill and many a deep river, till she came to an aunt's house of hers, and came and cried to her for help. And she, for pity, gave her a nut, and bad her never open her nut till she was come to the extremist misery that ever tongue could speake of. And so, she went, and she went ... till she came to a second aunt. And she gave her another nut." (214)

Here Philoclea interrupts (presumably dismayed by the appearance of the second aunt with her second nut), Zelmane requests that the princesses resume the aristocratic (and intratextually true) romance of Plangus and Erona, and the *New Arcadia* returns to its usual high style.

Superficially, Mopsa's story is ridiculous in the same way as Chaucer's *Tale of Sir Thopas*, which is also mercifully interrupted: it is crammed so full of romance clichés—nonpareiled beauties, unknown knights, lovesick pleas, weird taboos, rash promises, meandering quests—that it ceases to be simply conventional and becomes parody. Yet as Clare Kinney has observed, Sidney's *New Arcadia* shares almost all the same features: Pyrocles and Musidorus indulge in hyperbolic celebrations of their ladies' beauty, conceal their identities, and wander through any number of loosely correlated adventures before arriving in Arcadia and relating the stories of these very exploits to the princesses.[42] Making a distinction based on truth value proves largely unhelpful: Mopsa's story may be a fantasy, but the protagonists' "true" stories take part in that fantasy's traditions and tropes, and Sidney acknowledges that his own text is the product of fancy as well. How, then, should we distinguish between Mopsa's bad romance and the heroic community's narratives, or even the romance of the *New Arcadia* itself?

We should not, according to Kinney's reader-response critique: we are meant first to laugh at Mopsa's digression, but then to realize that the whole "morally and aesthetically self-subverting" text shares the same perverse idolatry of Love and the same interminable structure.[43] Alex Davis agrees: "When Sidney writes the *Arcadia*, he behaves exactly like Mopsa.... The effect is playful, but also ambivalent—even rather scathingly self-disgusted."[44] Werth has objected to reading Sidney's romance as self-critique, noting one element in Mopsa's tale that is conspicuously absent from the rest of the *New Arcadia*: magic. She argues that Mopsa's mistakes allow Sidney to imagine a new Protestant romance distinct from an unreformed version of the genre, suggesting that because Sidney and many of his Elizabethan readers would have associated the "fabulous devices" in Mopsa's romance with popish mystification, Sidney can use her clumsy effort to distinguish romance's "seductive qualities" from its godly potential.[45]

Werth offers an important corrective to the perspective that Sidney wrote romance only to undermine it. However, another aspect of Mopsa's tale may be even more central to Sidney's project. While her story is bursting at the seams with recognizable tropes, it lacks what Sidney's heroes regard as romance's most important features: an inspiration toward virtue and the promise of an ending.[46] Patricia Parker has famously defined romance as "inescapable" and dedicated to the allure of errancy, but as we have seen, the *New Arcadia*'s protagonists become deeply invested in a "fair and honourable" end to their own story, zealously convinced of its providential teleology.[47] As Philoclea explains when she asks Pyrocles to tell her of his past dangers, errant perils and adventures lend delight to providential romance's narrative pattern—but only when the errancy is linked to a secure end. Mopsa, on the other hand, is so delighted by the cosmetics of the genre—the pretty lovers, their fineries and food, their amorous dalliances, their emotional excesses—that she loses sight of its teleology, content to roam indefinitely across the romance landscape from aunt to aunt and nut to nut. Sidney highlights this endlessness by having Mopsa sprinkle her story with one "and so" after another: she has no eye toward an ending, since her pleasure in (non)narrative rests solely in the next "next." Magic and meandering, for her, have displaced providence and purpose; no matter how many hills and rivers her princess traverses, Mopsa will never be granted membership in the heroes' community of romance lovers because her ignorant, unreformed story is going nowhere.

Notably, the *New Arcadia*'s contrast between Mopsa and the young royals corresponds to Fredric Jameson's argument that romance is fundamentally conservative and classist; crucially, though, Sidney and his heroes will turn their elite romance to radical ends. Again in a manner consistent with Jameson, the text urges us to judge the protagonists as good by the power that their subjectivity grants them over evil—but for Jameson, "evil" is whatever threatens structures of authority with "absolute difference," while for Sidney, evil chiefly *is* absolutist authoritarian power that oppresses difference.[48] The Philippists saw the twin obstacles to God's people's reformation of Europe as ignorance, which might sometimes be enlightened, and tyranny, which must either be corrected or destroyed. The lovers' sense of right romance becomes a guide that ultimately does much more than exclude vulgarians like Mopsa; it grants their community the insubstantial yet indestructible authority to resist an ungodly tyrant who resembles the foes of Sidney's England and his reformist movement. In the *New Arcadia*'s most substantive addition, the community of lovers is tormented by Cecropia, who aims to marry her son Amphialus to one of the princesses and so secure Arcadia for herself. Cecropia's ties to a host of despised Catholic symbols and monarchs have been enumerated by a number of scholars.[49] But given the cultural links between Catholicism and romance that Werth suggests forced Sidney to be cautious with the genre, it is especially remarkable that Sidney characterizes Cecropia's evil through her *rejection* of romance. The

Cecropia episode positions tyranny on one side and romance on the other, as Sidney's protagonists together confront her scorn and hatred for the most important elements of the genre. With the *New Arcadia*'s revised emphasis on "the political virtues of love," romance becomes both a sign and a means of godly resistance.[50]

Cecropia repeatedly insists that love is nothing more than a mask for lust, that all self-proclaimed followers of Love are liars or fools, and that their devotion is a delusional excuse for inaction and impotence. This, of course, is the platform on which some critics have tried to place Sidney himself—and yet Sidney uses Cecropia to show that contempt for romance is evidence not of piety or statesmanship, but of self-love and abuse of power. The oppressor sneers at the idea of a divine Love, privileges masculine action over feminine affect, and renounces belief in any inherent structure to the narrative she inhabits. In resistance to her tyranny, the protagonists increasingly assume the virtues of stoicism, patience, and faith in providence, but critically, they do so without ever turning away from their enthusiasm for romance. Cecropia's villainy illustrates, perhaps much more clearly than the flawed virtue of the heroes, Sidney's commitment to a reformed romance for a reformed religion. There may well be something threateningly nonrational in the lovers' dedication to Love and in their conviction that they have been chosen to advance a romance narrative, but Sidney here represents their subversive subjectivity as a threat chiefly to the enemies of God and his community of reform and liberation.

The enmity between cynical tyranny and faith in romance is first played out between Cecropia and her son Amphialus, whose zeal for Love is tested and found wanting. Cecropia makes war on Basilius and kidnaps his daughters, along with Pyrocles/Zelmane, for the sake of the noble but conflicted Amphialus, who is the next heir to the throne of Arcadia after the princesses and is sick with unrequited love for Philoclea. But immediately after seizing his beloved for him, Cecropia begins a campaign to quash her son's impulses toward romance, mocking his love as an emasculating weakness and an obstacle to his political and sexual ambitions. When Amphialus laments that his honor and courtesy forbid him from keeping Philoclea prisoner, his mother scoffs at his "pretty, intricate follies" and advises him that Love will only prove "the instrument of [his] subjection" (319–20). Cecropia understands just enough about the values of romance to know that they demand the "subjection" of the lover to Love and to the beloved, antithetical to the self-love and self-aggrandizement of the tyrant. Amphialus knows this, too, and tries to protest that "lust may well be a tyrant, but true love, where it is indeed, it is a servant. . . . Did ever man's eye look thorough love upon the majesty of virtue shining through beauty, but that he became—as it well became him—a captive? And is it the style of a captive to write, 'Our will and pleasure'?" (401–2). But Cecropia only denies that any such thing as "true love" exists: all Amphialus really wants is sex, so he should simply "show [him]self a man," rape Philoclea, and get back to business (403). Her belief that a romance hero must be an emasculated man too weak for politics—which some scholars have attributed to Sidney himself—is presented here by Sidney not as sound reformed doctrine, but as a heresy directed toward oppression, the faithless creed of Protestant England's Machiavellian foes. Amphialus, allowing this anti-romance advice to corrupt his better judgment and purer *notitiae*, becomes a victim of his mother's tyranny and a tyrant to Philoclea in turn.

Cecropia's lack of credence in Love is twinned with her disbelief in God. In urging Pamela to discard her chastity, she attempts to persuade her that belief in divinity is the response of "foolish folks" to random phenomena beyond their comprehension (359). Sidney models Cecropia's philosophy on Lucretius's *De Rerum Natura*, with its emphasis on contingency over divine purpose: "All things follow but the course of their own nature—saving only man, who, while by the pregnancy of his imagination he strives to things supernatural, meanwhile he loseth his own natural felicity" (359).[51] The same proto-Hobbesian "imagination" that has urged Amphialus to woo with chivalry has driven Pamela into an excess of piety (which, unbeknownst to Cecropia, is also linked to her love for Musidorus). Cecropia cites Pamela's difference from "vulgar" people like Mopsa as evidence of her worthiness to be a law unto herself, since the only truly enlightened are those who break from the ignorant masses by rejecting a spiritual shape or end to human events: "But in you, niece, whose excellency is such as it need not to be held up by the staff of vulgar opinions, I would not you should love virtue servilely, for fear of I know not what . . . for else, to think that those powers—if there be any such—above are moved either by the eloquence of our prayers or in a chafe by the folly of our actions caries as much reason as if flies should think that men take great care which of them hums sweetest, and which of them flies nimblest" (358–59). As the Philippist epitome of the Counter-Reformation tyrant, Cecropia weaponizes the ignorant by turning them against Basilius, while also sneering at their servile credulity for believing in the religious instruments of their subjection.

In resistance to Cecropia's anti-romance atheism, Sidney's princesses find an opportunity to attain the height of their heroism, which (as Sanchez has also argued) begins to take on an increasingly Christian cast while remaining rooted in faithfulness to Love.⁵² Pamela, aflame with "virtuous anger," rails against Cecropia's disavowal of the providential teleology that grants the lovers their sense of heroic purpose and community: "I will not here call all your senses to witness, which can hear nor see nothing . . . of the unspeakableness of [God's] wisdom. *Each thing being directed to an end, and an end of preservation* . . . then must nothing, no, not the estate of flies (which you with so unsavoury scorn did jest at) be unknown unto him" (361–62; emphasis mine). Pyrocles, Musidorus, and Philoclea have all previously emphasized their faith in Love's all-important "end" in some heavenly purpose; the sensible stoic Pamela here reveals for the first time that she, too, feels a powerful sense of membership in a sacred teleological narrative that Cecropia eschews. She threatens her aunt that one day, the shape of the story will be made all too clear to her: "The time will come when thou shalt know that power by feeling it . . . and shalt only perceive him to have been a creator in thy destruction!" (363). Sidney's narrator, who rarely surfaces to insert his own moral judgments, steps in to agree: "But Cecropia, like a bat which, though it have eyes to discern that there is a sun, yet hath so evil eyes that it cannot delight in the sun, found a truth but could not love it" and "went away, repining but not repenting" (363). The Calvinist belief in innate reprobation need not be distinguished here from the Philippist belief that one can willingly cooperate with one's salvation or damnation; Cecropia illustrates both. Her refusal to be moved by Pamela's testimony also echoes Sidney's discussion of "the abominable tyrant Alexander Pheraus" in the *Defence*, whose corrupt nature recoils from poetry: "He that was not ashamed to make matters for tragedies, yet could not resist the sweet violence of a tragedy. And if it wrought no further good in him, it was that he in despite of himself withdrew himself from harkening to that which might mollify his hardened heart."⁵³

Tragedy was the genre that Sidney's Philippist community associated with tyranny; one member, Scottish playwright George Buchanan, made his name writing tragedies depicting the hubris and the fall of tyrants, as did Sidney's friend Greville. Sidney maintains this association but prefers romance as an alternative literary mode of resistance. While Mopsa's anti-romance reads as parody, Cecropia's anti-romance has a genre of its own: rather than perceiving herself as a heroine within a romance ordained by a divine power, she imagines that she stands outside of a tragedy orchestrated by herself, despising any dependency on an external narrative or creator. "Though many times fortune failed me, yet did I never fail myself," she boasts to Amphialus, and sets about authoring her own story in defiance of fortune (319). Cecropia conducts her captives' "tragedy" with a flair for dramatic spectacle, withdrawing "the curtains ... from before the windows of Zelmane and of Philoclea" to present them with the staged illusion of Pamela's execution, later to feign Philoclea's beheading also (424–25). But these illusions are all the substance of the tragedy that Cecropia can author. She proves incapable of altering the providential plot of the protagonists' romance, which stays its course despite her disruptions and disbelief, and when she meets her own demise by falling "ere she were aware" from her castle wall, her spectacular drama turns out to have been out of her control (440).

A number of readers have observed that Cecropia's tyranny lends Sidney's princesses a resemblance to the heroines of Protestant martyrology, combatting temptation and oppression with their reliance on the freedom and integrity of the individual conscience.[54] "Thou mayest well rack this silly body, but me thou canst never overthrow," vows Pamela, while Philoclea refuses to yield to those who would treat her as a "slave," declaring "liberty" to be "more dear than life itself" (422, 322). As Musidorus and Pyrocles liberated nations from tyrants during their chivalric adventures, Pamela and Philoclea take a stand for liberty amid their own trials, epitomizing Crawford's argument for "the political nature of female constancy," which is "best understood not as passive or patient suffering, but rather as an active achievement of the will, and thus as a statement of power."[55] All the while, they never feel called to turn away from romance. On the contrary, "to all [their trials], virtue and love resisted, strengthened one by the other when each found itself over-vehemently assaulted" (419). Sanchez notes the irony of Cecropia's belief that love "is the instrument of subjection," when "true love in fact sustains the princesses' resistance" (320).[56] Philoclea's refusal to sully herself with slavery to Amphialus is coterminous with her refusal to be untrue to Pyrocles (to whom she first dedicated herself in a heady assertion of queer liberation when she still knew him as Zelmane), while Pamela's unconquerable mind "softened in her, when with open wings [her thoughts] flew to Musidorus. . . . Then would she fortify her resolution . . . taking the counsel of virtue, and comfort of love" (422). In Sanchez's words, Pamela becomes "a central contestant in the civil war that surrounds her, rather than its passive object," and it is "her passion for Musidorus," not her stoicism, "that assures her victory."⁵⁷ Her flight to the subjective freedom of imaginative communion with her beloved demolishes Worden's claim that "lovers . . . are subjected to a dependency incompatible with true liberty, the liberty within."⁵⁸ Contrary to readings of *Arcadia* as self-critical anti-romance, in which love compels free minds to enslave themselves and surrender their virtue, love in the Cecropia episode is the comrade of virtue and liberty, the core of the heroes' refusal to surrender their heroic subjectivity or pervert its end.

Daniel Lochman has argued that the *New Arcadia*, which begins with the "triangulated love-fellowship" among Strephon, Claius, and Urania, "works toward a quadratic fellowship among the royals" that "suggests an affection extended laterally in impassioned acts of justice."⁵⁹ In Sidney's revision from the legalistic *Old Arcadia* to the *New*, the lovers' resistance to Cecropia by cleaving to their faith in providential romance and in each other imagines a mode of justice driven not by laws, but by love, passion, and empathy—by a Philippist "certainty of the self's knowledge about its relationship to God" and God in others. In another Sidneian parallel between the sacred and the secular, when Philoclea reveals to Pyrocles that she has not really been executed, his rush of renewed faith in the mysterious unfolding of a providential narrative is indistinguishable from his ecstasy in discovering that his beloved, like Christ, is not dead but alive. "Death was not strong enough to divide thy love from me," Philoclea joyfully affirms (438). Although the *New Arcadia* breaks off unfinished, we may see Sidney's romance weaving straight, queer, secular, and sacred bonds together into the fabric of a community that the weapons of tyranny cannot rend asunder.

Of course, the problem of the unfinishedness lingers. Cecropia's death does not exorcise the specter of tragedy from the romance; her fall is followed by her son's attempt at suicide, and the lovers remain threatened by her allies, their ends left unresolved. Despite Pamela's prediction of Cecropia's ultimate providential doom, the captives vacillate between perceiving that their love "comes between [them] and death" and assuming that they will not escape alive (451). Duncan-Jones has described the "account of the long and unproductive siege of Cecropia's fortress, culminating in the bungled suicide of Amphialus," as a "dark ... vision of stagnation and defeat," speculating that Sidney may have believed his own career was "in the final act of a tragedy."[60] Yet Sidney's writing and his Philippist Protestantism give us every reason to doubt that he would change his mind about the genre of Christian history, or of his book. In both contexts, providence offers repeated assurances of a final victory and a long-delayed wedding celebration for the heroes. Still, the time remaining until that consummation is never clear; many knights devoted to romance—Argalus, Parthenia, the real Zelmane, Sidney—will die in its service; and the forces of tyranny (like the forces of virtue) outlast individual defeats. Julianne Werlin has said that "for Sidney, narrative [can] model providence's opacity as well as its lucidity," and the opacity of providence is why romance narrative, and the community that coheres around it, are vital.[61] For as long as "the end to which it is directed, which end ends not," remains clouded, the individual and communal subjectivity of romance provides the tools for living faithfully under oppression and for resisting it (75). Strephon and Claius's resolution in the *New Arcadia*'s opening pages holds as true for its closing ones: the fellowship's power rests in its calling to "love with joy in the midst of all woes" (4).

TWO NARRATIVE PERSPECTIVES AND THE WEIGHT OF ROMANCE IN EDMUND SPENSER'S *THE FAERIE QUEENE*

In response to Languet's fretting, Cecropia's sneering, and critics' deconstructions, Sidney and his growing community of heroes maintain that romance is not a detriment to the spirit or a distraction from sacred duty. Instead, it instills the convictions that strengthen the spirit and cements the connections that enable sacred duty's performance. Among Spenser scholars, we find more widespread agreement that *The Faerie Queene* represents Spenser's good-faith effort at a Protestant reformation of romance, rather than an ironic critique of it.[62] Also widespread, though, is the conclusion that this effort was doomed to failure. Such arguments tend to cite the ineradicability of evil in the poem, or Spenser's inability to draw the errant paths of his characters (and of his entire massive text) to a final conclusion; *The Faerie Queene* shares the *New Arcadia*'s challenging unfinishedness. Harry Berger detects "a faint echo of hopelessness" in the impossibility of redemption for characters who persist in sin and ignorance;[63] John King suggests that Redcrosse's yielding to Duessa's seduction connotes "the moral failure of [erotic] romance" as a genre;[64] Andrew King terms *The Faerie Queene* a "[movement] away from romance," in that the genre and Spenser's Protestant eschatology continually foil each other;[65] and David Mikics argues that Spenser's plot gets "out of hand in a way that adulterates and frustrates moral point," and that romance, with its "easier delights," "looks inadequate to the providential didactic meaning that Spenser attaches to it."[66] This last concept—that romance is easy, or delightful, and therefore evades attempts to reform it— runs through decades of major Spenserian scholarship. Parker, in *Inescapable Romance*, introduces the idea that Faerie Land is characterized by the pleasures of errancy and adventure, at the same time that Spenser's knights often experience "the sorrow of wandering."[67] This important nuance of sadness, though, is less prevalent in Clare Kinney's recent claim that Spenser is "acutely aware that structural errancy and a persistent delight in wandering by the way—the deferral of ending that Patricia Parker has argued defines the mode—can beguile the poem as well as its questers, trapping both in 'Errours endlesse traine.'"[68] Since Parker, many critics have extended the idea that romance is inescapable to the idea that it is always escaping, much like the irredeemable villains Archimago and Duessa. Does the delight inherent in the adventures of *The Faerie Queene* undermine its effort to reform romance, or its heroes' striving toward godly knighthood?

I want to argue here that it does not—but *not* because Spenser makes his reformed romance readily compatible with pleasure and "love with joy," the way Sidney does. Spenser concurs with Sidney that romance is not a delightful distraction from duty, but for the poet and his protagonists; this is chiefly because romance often proves not a delight but an obligation. Spenser tells Raleigh that it ought to delight its readers, and heroes like the Redcrosse Knight may initially be eager for its pleasures and rewards; as the romance progresses, however, the mode that its audience continues to enjoy transforms for the figures within it. Rather than a thrilling distraction from their sacred calling, romance becomes the painful means by which they enact that calling. The persistent sense of melancholy in books 1 and 3 of *The Faerie Queene* stems not from Spenser's failure to reform romance, but rather from his success, as the uneasy accord between human and divine narrative generates a burden that the protagonists must consciously assume.[69] Spenser's Protestant reformation of the genre would offer seventeenth-century writers a model not of irresistible ravishment by the "[easy] delights" of romance, but of willing submission to its hardships. I am also particularly concerned with another legacy that Spenser left his successors, two distinct archetypes of exceptional perspective on communal narrative, which many later writers would feel compelled either to reiterate or to reconsider. While the Redcrosse Knight is brought to a mountaintop and shown a transcendent vision of his final destination, the elect city of New Jerusalem, the lady knight Britomart is never shown the assurances she craves of a happy ending to her story and must accept the incomplete narrative of her progeny that she is told by the prophet Merlin. And indeed, her personal story does not end so very happily: we hear that her chivalric prowess and erotic fulfillment will lead to early widowhood and the many sorrows of her descendants. Romance subjectivity, according to Spenser, might mean either visionary conviction or confusion and constraint.

The sections that follow consider the third and first books of *The Faerie Queene* in reverse order—the better to reflect, first, Britomart's position near the beginning of her heroic narrative when she hears Merlin's prophecy versus Redcrosse's position near the end of his when he receives his sight of the New Jerusalem; and second, my proposition that her narrative vision is one of uncertain mediality rather than assured finality. Both knights, though, come to share Spenser's Protestant nationalist sense of the weight of romance. Importantly, while this burden is common to the Knights of Maidenhead and to allies of their fellowship, part of the weight of Spenser's romance is the experience of seeming to bear it mostly alone. Sidney conceived of romance subjectivity differently—in the *New Arcadia*, the specter of tragedy is often eclipsed by the protagonists' ardent, even ecstatic conviction, in the face of uncertainty and adversity, of their membership in a chosen fellowship of love—but for the heroes of *The Faerie Queene*, the subjective experience of romance is frequently not one of validation within a like-minded community, but of confusion and isolation within the sparsely populated landscape of Faerie Land. Undoubtedly that community exists—Britomart travels for a while with Redcrosse, they both travel with Guyon, they all encounter Arthur, and they exchange aid against an ideological "other," the Catholic-conflated Saracens—but these partnerships are temporary respites. To Spenser, a Protestant reformation of romance required special attention to the mode's tension between narrative certainty and doubt or suspense, between the threads of community and the loneliness of the heroic subject.[70] This difference between the great romancers of the Elizabethan age may seem odd in light of the probability that Spenser's personal theology owed more than Sidney's to Calvinism and to its doctrine of election: Spenser could, and occasionally does, refer to the communion of God's elect saints as the joint protagonists of a massive nationalistic Christian narrative.[71] Nevertheless, in *The Faerie Queene*, to be chosen for romance means often to be alone and in doubt, delivered and sustained in crucial moments by the real presence of an elect fellowship before returning to the isolation of the quest. For Britomart, the community of romance is spread across centuries of history in the form of her British progeny, known to her only through prophecy and separated by lifetimes from their foremother and from each other. For Redcrosse, it ultimately takes the form of the communion of saints who await him in the New Jerusalem—the final destination where his romance duty both directs and forbids him to go.

Britomart at the Root of Romance: The "Hard Beginne" of Elect Heroism

Book 3 of *The Faerie Queene* begins the story of Britomart, the female Knight of Chastity, and her quest to find her future husband, Artegall, the Knight of Justice. The psychosomatic intensity of Britomart's desire for Artegall is a hallmark of cross-period romance, as Cooper has shown: the "theme of the actively desiring and faithful woman . . . defines a work as romance almost as decisively as does a happy ending. . . . The presence of such a woman at the centre indeed promises the happy ending. . . . Furthermore, as the romances make clear, the happiness is not just a personal matter. The strong and loving heroine is typically an heiress, even the founder of a family or a dynasty."[72] Cooper refers to Britomart as the early modern epitome of this theme—yet I wish to show here that Britomart's role in Spenser's romance crucially depends on her active, faithful pursuit of what she knows will be a personally *unhappy* ending, in which her dynastic line is of ambivalent value.

Britomart's physically excruciating longing for Artegall is symptomatic of the pain that participation in the romance mode will cause her both before and after their union. After seeing his image in a magic mirror, she suddenly feels herself "Sad, solemne, sowre, and full of fancies fraile / . . . yet wist she nether how, nor why"; she describes her anguish as an "vlcer" that "groweth daily more and more."[73] Spenser's treatment of erotic and martial romance through Britomart recalls Sidney's in some respects. First, his attention to her private thoughts and subjective experiences is reminiscent of Sidney's lovers' interior monologues, and as in the *New Arcadia*, the potential godliness of true love is shown *not* by its capacity to be controlled by the lover's disciplined reason, nor even by prayer, but by the irrepressible zeal of its devotion. Spenser's narrator reminds us that "loue, that is in gentle brest begonne, / No ydle charmes so lightly may remoue," and that Britomart retains "no powre / Nor guidaunce of her selfe," since she and her desire are now vehicles for divine will (3.2.51, 49). Next, as Sidney's Pyrocles avows, love must find an "end" in "enjoying," "which end ends not." Britomart sets out in quest of her future husband and learns from Merlin that she and Artegall are destined to produce "Most famous fruites of matrimoniall bowre": a line of the chosen heroes of Britain, which stretches beyond the horizon of the future (3.3.3). Further, she proves that for Spenser, too, "both men and women are called to Christian militancy."[74] Finally, according to Kimberly Coles's beautiful queer reading of book 3, Spenser, like Sidney, "imagines love as the vehicle for reform" and sees this love as nonnormative.[75] Coles reads Scudamour/Amoret's erotic fusion into each other at the end of *The Faerie Queene*'s 1590 first edition as an allegory for the communal body of the church, which is sustained not by the "production of progeny" but by "the denial of material categories of subjectivity, like gender, that define and divide us."[76]

However, the similarities between Spenser's erotic romance and Sidney's also run up against limits. While Sidney's heroes find pleasure and solidarity in their love of Love and of one another, Britomart's quest for Artegall begins and ends in solitary sorrow.[77] Further, Coles's reading rests on two points: first, the 1590 ending of the poem that Spenser had to excise for the romance to continue, and second, an argument for Amoret as the "hero" of book 3, even though Britomart is the "champion."[78] Book 3 remains concerned with the struggles of Britomart as its central protagonist, and Spenser's queer image of the hermaphrodite is a transcendent *potential* conclusion for *The Faerie Queene* that must ultimately be displaced and deferred. I want to argue not against Coles's reading, but alongside of it, that Britomart's female heroism is defined both by its transgressive desire, militancy, and errancy *and* by Britomart's willingness to submit to a painfully mundane future in which she hangs up her sword and becomes a wife and mother, only to suffer the death of her beloved husband and the often tragic fates of their offspring. Moreover, as Coles observes, the story Britomart must take upon herself as an idealized figure of Elizabeth is not even sufficient: "The founding of the Protestant Church can only be imagined by looking beyond the body of Elizabeth, beyond the production of progeny, and beyond the present time."[79]

The romance of *The Faerie Queene* must indeed transcend Britomart—and part of her heroic calling is that she, knowing that, must serve out her ancillary role in it anyway.

At the outset of book 3, the tradition of erotic romance initially does seem rooted in reproduction: God has ordained Britomart's virtuous love and childbearing to sustain his historical narrative and to reveal the glory of its conclusion—particularly with regard to the newly Protestant English state as his elect nation. Spenser's narrator describes Merlin's prophecy to Britomart as the teleological story of "My glorious Soueraines goodly auncestrye" (3.3.4); and as the prophecy recounts Britain's historical past, it also gestures toward Elizabeth's reign and—more problematically—to the chosen state's eschatological future. With love's patriotic and providential purpose in mind, Merlin urges Britomart not to be dismayed by the "hard beginne" of erotic desire "that meetes [her] in the dore" and affirms that her passion for Artegall is indeed predestined and commended by God (3.3.21):

> It was not, Britomart, thy wandring eye,
> Glauncing vnwares in charmed looking glas,
> But the streight course of heuenly destiny,
> Led with eternall prouidence, that has
> Guyded thy glaunce, to bring his will to pas . . .
> Therefore submit thy wayes vnto his will,
> And doe by all dew meanes thy destiny fulfill. (3.3.24)

Merlin suggests that secular romance tropes (like magically imbued objects and love at first sight) are of value insofar as they are instruments of "eternall prouidence" working out its will. Britomart's "wandring" quest is made "streight" by "heuenly destiny," and so erotic romance is wedded to nationalistic epic (for now, in a conspicuously unqueer way). Under Spenser's reformation, Britomart's quest for her beloved is justified not by her own desire, but by God's: the romance heroine becomes an agent of sacred history and is called to yield to the fulfillment of her providential purpose.

The "hard beginne" of Britomart's love, Merlin tells her, ultimately forecasts both British and divine triumph:

> For so must all things excellent begin,
> And eke enrooted deepe must be that Tree,

> Whose big embodied braunches shall not lin,
> Till they to heuens hight forth stretched bee.
> For from thy wombe a famous Progenee
> Shall spring, out of the aunciant Troian blood,
> Which shall reuiue the sleeping memoree
> Of those same antique Peres, the heuens brood....
> Renowmed kings, and sacred Emperours,
> Thy fruitfull Ofspring, shall from thee descend...
> And their decayed kingdomes shall amend:
> The feeble Britons, broken with long warre,
> They shall vpreare, and mightily defend
> Against their forren foe, that commes from farre,
> Till vniversall peace compound all ciuill iarre. (3.3.22–23)

Merlin's prophecy positions Britomart "deepe" at the root of the "Tree" of her "Progenee"; like the tree's branches, Britomart's heroic destiny must be "embodied," narratively and physically "big" with the long line of champions that will proceed "from [her] wombe." Merlin promises temporal fame and historical victory to Britomart and her descendants—the "auncient Troian blood," born and beloved of the pagan gods, will "reuiue" to conquer Europe, rescue the downtrodden Britons, and institute a Pax Britannica—but his nationalist prophecy is also suggestive of eschatological history and irenic apocalypse. Britomart's progeny is "the heuens brood" in a Protestant sense as well as a pagan one; her maternal "Tree" of God's elect heroes will grow "to heuens hight," and their victories over "their forren foe" will one day "extend" God's elect nation "through all lands," resulting in "vniversall peace" and the end of history itself. The providential plan of sacred time is thus founded on Britomart's private erotic destiny and her reproductive body. The will of providence, however, is beginning to look suspiciously like English jingoism, and this patriotic glibness raises questions about what might happen if the human-led state should fail to submit to the guidance of God.

Indeed, Merlin's revelation of Britomart's providential role leads her nurse Glauce to question the role of human agency in her quest: "what needes her to toyle," she demands, "sith fates can make / Way for themselues, their purpose to pertake?" (3.3.25). The prophet's response attempts to effect a union between divine will and human action: "Indeede the fates are firme, / And may not shrinck, though all the world do shake: / Yet ought mens good endeuours them confirme, / And guyde the heauenly causes to their constant terme" (3.3.25). Providence must be infallible, but the righteous "ought" to act in order to "confirme" it; their direction of "heauenly causes" to their destined end is a sign that they have been chosen for that very task. The purpose of heroic adventure in Spenser's reformed romance, then, is not to *create* a new narrative, but to *represent* and *enact* one's alignment with a preordained narrative and with the God that authored it—more or less. Spenser does not always seem to hew to the most strictly deterministic forms of Protestant theology:[8c] Merlin later tells Britomart that her son will enjoy peace "if" he can achieve victory over his enemies, and the question of individual agency reopens, together with the potential for temporal failure (3.3.30). While Spenser never undermines the power of providence, the *necessity* of human action to the divine romance remains a paradox— one that will go on to bedevil seventeenth-century writers.

Likewise, Merlin's neatly summarized initial revelation of the future is only the simplest version of the whole story of Britomart's obligation and its outcome. As he elaborates on the progress of Elizabeth I's "goodly auncestrye," further complex implications of Britomart's duty emerge. The newly married heroine will journey from fairyland to Britain, her husband's "natiue soyle," to fight the "forreine Paynims" that have usurped the land (3.3.27), but both the chivalric and erotic components of her private romance have fixed limits:

> Long time ye both in armes shall beare great sway,
> Till thy wombes burden thee from them do call,
> And his last fate him from thee take away,
> Too rathe cut off by practise criminall
> Of secrete foes, that him shall make in mischiefe fall. (3.3.28)

Before Britomart has even begun her transgressive adventure, Merlin informs her that her martial heroism will be cut short by the all-too-ordinary pains of motherhood; before she has even met her beloved, she learns of his untimely and violent death. Merlin's prophecy strips Britomart of the option to dwell solely within the realm of erotic or chivalric romance. For the sake of her elect progeny and its destiny, Britomart must begin her quest already aware of its privately unhappy ending and of the constraints on her martial glory.

Her "wombes burden" begins to reveal the weight of romance. Notably, Spenser seems to regard Britomart's destined return to female norms as a godly requirement but also as a personal hardship that asks our sympathy. A role in the reformed romance demands sacrifice for providence and patriotism before it promises reward—even, and especially, for the narrative's chosen protagonists. After one knight's stories of love and combat have ended, the larger romance continues, now spurred forward not just by action, but by submission.

As Merlin's prophecy continues, it appears as a densely compressed romance in itself, with like action and submission required of all its heroes as the centuries pass. Britomart's descendants experience so many trials, triumphs, and defeats that their narrative progress often disappears beneath a veneer of historical contingency and even tragedy. Her grandson is destined to succeed his predecessors "In kingdome, but not in felicity," losing what his father gained to "froward fortune"; his own son will then "Auenge his fathers losse" and reclaim victory from their enemies, but only until *his* descendant falters, "and then the raine / Of Britons eke with him attonce shall dye" (3.3.31, 40). However, Merlin indicates that ill fortune is not a vicissitude of history, but yet another instrument of divine will: "For th'heauens haue decreed, to displace / The *Britons*, for their sinnes dew punishment, / And to the *Saxons* ouer-give their gouernment" (3.3.41). A future virtuous descendant must also submit his secular heroism to the sacred romance and refrain from going into battle to redeem his people, "by vision staide from his intent" (3.3.41). Like the scriptural Hebrews, the Britons are doomed to lose the rewards of their success because of their forgetfulness of its source.

Spenser's biblical typology and Merlin's visionary power together produce a moment of temporal and generic confusion, with the prophet grieving for the Britons' decline as though it has already occurred: "O who shal helpe me to lament, and mourne / The royall seed, the antique *Troian* blood, / Whose Empire lenger here, then euer any stood" (3.3.42). Hearing Merlin foretell "woe, and woe, and euerlasting woe" to her progeny, Britomart is confounded by her romance's apparent turn to tragedy (3.3.42):

> The Damzell was full deepe empassioned,
> Both for his griefe, and for her peoples sake,
> Whose future woes so plaine he fashioned,
> And sighing sore, at length him thus bespake;

> Ah but will heuens fury neuer slake,
> Nor vengeaunce huge relent it selfe at last?
> Will not long misery late mercy make,
> But shall their name for euer be defaste,
> And quite from off the earth their memory be raste? (3.3.43)

Merlin cuts their mutual mourning short and assures her that despite appearances, her narrative is not a tragedy and the elect nation of her descendants will rise again:

> Nay but the terme (said he) is limited,
> That in this thraldome Britons shall abide . . .
> For twise fowre hundreth yeares shalbe supplide,
> Ere they vnto their former rule restor'd shalbee . . .
> Yet during this their most obscuritee,
> Their beames shall oft breake forth, that men then faire may see. (3.3.44)

The Britons' fall proves to be a false ending, a mistaking of romance for tragedy through the fallibility of individual subjectivity. In further resemblance to the Israelites, the Britons await a predestined restoration, despite the long duration of their "thraldome." In the meantime the elect nation will continue to produce heroes who manifest the glory of God and his chosen people, projecting a more complete vision of history that pierces though "obscuritee." Finally, after eight hundred years, the "goodly auncestrye" of Elizabeth I is complete: "when the terme is full accomplishid," the Tudor family will arise like "a sparke of fire" from "where it lurked in exile" and "reclame" the throne of England (3.3.48). Merlin's vision of the Tudor dynasty, culminating in Elizabeth's glorious reign, again conjures the imagery of irenic apocalypse:

> Thenceforth eternall vnion shall be made
> Betweene the nations different afore,
> And sacred Peace shall louingly persuade
> The warlike minds, to learne her goodly lore,
> And ciuile armes to exercise no more:
> Then shall a royall Virgin raine, which shall
> Stretch her white rod ouer the *Belgicke* shore,

> And the great Castle smite so sore with all,
> That it shall make him shake, and shortly learn to fall. (3.3.49)

For a moment, this providential triumph appears to conclude Merlin's prophecy and the long, turbulent romance of Britomart and her descendants. The Tudors unite nations and establish concord, and Elizabeth allies with the Protestant Low Countries ("the *Belgicke* shore") and overcomes the menace of Catholic Spain ("the great Castle"). Spenser's own age, in which England has emerged as a newly Protestant and newly powerful nation, seems to be the natural telos of Britomart's narrative: all her sacrifices, and all the trials, victories, and defeats of her "royall seed," have led to this moment.

"But yet the end is not," pronounces Merlin suddenly, and these are his final words in the poem (3.3.50). Immediately upon indicating that more of the story remains to be told, he falls silent, "As ouercomen of the spirites powre, / Or other ghastly spectacle dismayd, / That secretly he saw, yet note discoure" (3.3.50). If he can indeed see more, Britomart's (and our) access to his vision has been cut off. One "ending" of her romance after another has proved to be an illusion, and the true end remains hidden. Of course, Spenser is not Merlin, and he cannot reveal England's future beyond Elizabeth's reign, but the weight of the prophet's silence imports more than ignorance. Despite the flourishing of the English nation and the Protestant religion after many centuries, history continues, and the divine romance is incomplete.[81] Elizabeth, just recently celebrated in Merlin's prophecy as "the hope of Protestantism," now finds herself in Britomart's position: she must enact, and submit to, her own role in the narrative, whatever that might be.[82] Glauce's query again applies: *must* she do anything in particular to advance the sacred story? But Elizabeth's failure to follow Britomart's example casts an ominous shadow over the unanswerable question: her refusal to relinquish her role as virgin warrior in favor of the motherhood that will sustain the chosen nation threatens to overlay romance with tragedy once more. Among others, Coles calls the prophecy a "critique of [Elizabeth's] family practices," and King notes that "at issue here is an imaginative reception of Elizabeth that sees her unfitness to sustain a romance-epic narrative of ongoing perfection. She truly is . . . a dead end for the quest."[83] The divine plot jars with the personal and political actions that Elizabeth has already taken, and Spenser and his readers must contend with the knowledge that, so soon after England's return to Protestantism, the path to providential triumph is once again as invisible as it is inevitable. Even now, at a triumphant peak in the action, the next steps for "heuens brood" are more obscure than ever. Here, then, is where readers have found incompatibility between romance and Protestant nationalism: King returns to Glauce's question about the needfulness of Britomart's heroic agency as an inquiry that "could be revised to assume the reader's perspective: why bother reading this work, since the generic signals at the most basic representative level tell us that it is a romance, shaped toward moral victory and sustaining throughout a sense of providence? However . . . that end never happens. Glauce's question . . . is simplistic because it fails to recognize how Spenser's work struggles to attain the values and meaning of romance—how *The Faerie Queene* is, at its deepest level, in the process of becoming romance, and equally in danger of failing to become that world."[84] This link between Glauce and the reader seems right, but I differ with King on the subject of why Glauce's question misses the point. It is impossible that God's providence could fail, whether in the realm of *The Faerie Queene* or in Spenser's Protestant worldview. Glauce's question is "simplistic" not because it does not recognize the "danger" of the failure of romance, but because it equates the inevitable with the straightforward and easy. Paradoxically, failure is impossible, and yet the very nature of Spenser's romance is that the attainment of the inevitable is *almost* prohibitively long, painful, and difficult—a heroic undertaking indeed.

Britomart embarks on her erotic quest having learned only that her personal story is at best one of mixed joy, sorrow, sacrifice, and consolation; that her descendants' destinies are equally variable; and that the ultimate end belongs to a providential authority that has set a hard limit to what she may know. She lies "enrooted deepe" beneath the "Tree" of her progeny's future and must be told about the "braunches" she cannot see, and the limbs that grow "to heuens hight" stretch beyond the reach even of prophetic human eyes. Merlin's vague and imperfect promise about the glorious "end" of Britomart's love affair does not suffuse her with ecstatic zeal, as it does for Sidney's heroes, but with a sense of resignation. Likening herself to a "feeble barke . . . tossed long" on a "Huge sea of sorrow," she prays for a break in the tempest, "The which may bring my ship, ere it be rent, / Vnto the gladsome port of her intent" (3.4.8, 10). In the midst of her "priuy griefe," she takes comfort not in anticipation of chivalric success or erotic fulfillment, but in the "intent" of her distant and dispersed community, finding

>   good reliefe,
> Through hope of those, which Merlin had her told
> Should of her name and nation be chiefe,
> And fetch their being from the sacred mould
> Of her immortall womb, to be in heauen enrold. (3.4.11)

Britomart assumes extraordinary freedom in stealing away from her father's castle and venturing into the romance landscape disguised as a man, but her story's "hard beginne" does not look much like a thrilling escape. Rather, she is told from the outset that she must bear, reproductively and psychologically, the genre's weight. Importantly, though, Crawford's argument on "the political nature of female constancy" applies to Britomart as it does to Sidney's heroines: her extremely "active" acceptance of the burden of romance is "a statement of power" that surpasses even the strength of the Virgin Queen.[85] As Coles acknowledges, "the narrative fixation of [book 3] is undeniably upon family generation," and while this is not the end of the story, Britomart's heroic duty is to commit her body, as a warrior and as a mother, to that middle portion.[86] The book's "radical" 1590 ending in "a new self 'that moves directly from time into eternity on the basis of its mutual devotion, rather than its production of progeny,'" offers a radiant queer image of chaste erotic communion that its "champion" must safeguard for others but not enjoy herself, and Spenser withdraws this image in his 1596 revision, so that readers who identify themselves with Britomart's elect nation must share with her the weight of romance.[87] To be one of God's chosen is to be assigned a hero's role in the divine story, but that role means actively submitting to an unutterably long narrative within time, perhaps unable even to glimpse eternity, let alone move directly there. The romance will not end with the defeat of an enemy, the consummation of a marriage, or the birth of an heir. These generic conventions may recur again and again, and they are always cause for celebration, "But yet the end is not."

Redcrosse on the Mountaintop: The Ends of Romance

Near the end of book 1, the Knight of Holiness is also granted a vision of the providential shape of his Protestant romance. His transcendent perspective, while more revelatory and more final than Britomart's tempered promise, likewise proves subject to the burdens of Spenser's reformation of the mode.

Guided to the summit of a mountain by Contemplation, the Redcrosse Knight learns his true identity, as all unknown heroes of romance eventually must. Unsurprisingly, he is of royal blood (and therefore, as convention dictates, naturally inclined toward the heroism he has already demonstrated):

> For well I wote, thou springst from ancient race
> Of Saxon kinges . . .
> From thence a Faery thee vnweeting reft. . . .
> Thence she thee brought into this Faery lond,
> And in an heaped furrow did thee hyde,
> Where thee a Ploughman all vnweeting fond . . .
> Whereof Georgos he thee gaue to name;
> Till prickt with courage, and thy forces pryde,
> To Fary court thou cam'st to seeke for fame,
> And proue thy puissaunt armes, as seemes thee best became. (1.10.65–66)

Moreover, he is "sprong out from English race": like Britomart's destined spouse Artegall, he belongs to the elect nation that, like him, has recently undergone purification to a state of holiness (1.10.60).[88] Stolen into Faerie Land, he is adopted by a ploughman (whom many scholars have linked to Langland's Piers Plowman, another recipient of sacred revelation through a mountaintop vision) and given a name—Georgos, after the earth in which he lay. Now risen to a higher state, the "man of earth" is destined to be exalted as "thine owne nations frend / And Patrone: thou Saint George shalt called bee, / *Saint George* of mery England, the signe of victoree" (1.10.52, 61). The story of Redcrosse's mysterious identity, like that of Britomart and Artegall's love, culminates in a sanctified nationalistic purpose.

This conventional revelation of personal and patriotic identity merges with a reformed, implicitly Calvinist revelation of Redcrosse's elect spiritual condition.[89] Contemplation shows him, still "far off" from where they stand, "A litle path, that was both steepe and long, / Which to a goodly Citty led his vew," and identifies it as the eternal dwelling place of God's elect (1.10.55):

> Faire knight (quoth he) Hierusalem that is,
> The new Hierusalem, that God has built
> For those to dwell in, that are chosen his,
> His chosen people purg'd from sinfull guilt . . .

> Now are they Saints all in that Citty sam,
> More deare vnto their God, then younglings to their dam. (1.10.57)

When Redcrosse admires the distant Jerusalem as the most beautiful city he has ever seen (surpassing Gloriana's city of Cleopolis, its worldly type, and by implication Elizabeth's kingdom), Contemplation promises him that he, too, is destined to dwell there after the accomplishment of his earthly adventures:[90]

> Then peaceably thy painefull pilgrimage
> To yonder same Hierusalem doe bend,
> Where is for thee ordaind a blessed end:
> For thou emongst those Saints, whom thou doest see,
> Shalt be a Saint. (1.10.61)

To Redcrosse's fear that he, "Vnworthy wretch... of so great grace," cannot deserve this final reward, Contemplation replies that human effort plays no part in the Calvinist romance of salvation, in which the trials of all the elect point to the same end, regardless of merit: "These that haue it attaynd, were in like cace / As wretched men, and liued in like paine" (1.10.62). Redcrosse, often estranged from faithful companions, learns at last of his membership in a community that knows and shares his story of sin, suffering, and redemption.

Yet these two great revelations are accompanied by others that reiterate the "paine" of the narrative instead of relieving it. Contemplation informs Redcrosse that his election to romance heroism is ultimately a calling that transcends such heroism and compels him to abandon it. Like Britomart, he must follow the patterns of romance only insofar as their purpose accords with God's, and as before, the divine romance outlasts the mortal one. Redcrosse's "seruice" to the Faerie Queen is "worthy," as is his aid of Una, yet even these acts have no merit in themselves, and the hero must be prepared to forsake them for the higher end that they represent (1.10.60):

> But when thou famous victory hast wonne...
> Thenceforth the suitt of earthly conquest shonne,
> And wash thy hands from guilt of bloody field:
> For blood can nought but sin, & wars but sorrows yield. (1.10.61)

When Contemplation condemns the worldliness of romance, Redcrosse experiences shock and dismay at the prospect of abandoning the fruits of his career: "But deeds of armes must I at last be faine, / And Ladies loue to leaue so dearely bought?" (1.10.62). Contemplation replies that romance's conventions are useless once the narrative has attained its ends—that is, its purpose and its true finality. In Jerusalem, the symbolism of the genre's martial and erotic tropes dissipates into the truths they signify, and the signs alone become meaningless: "What need of armes, where peace doth ay remaine, / (Said he) and bitter battailes all are fought? / As for loose loues they'are vaine, and vanish into nought" (1.10.62). The love of ladies and the love of glory are no more than types of the love of God and of his will, as well as potential distractions from it; they may first be redeemed, but are finally supplanted, by their antitype.

We might expect this commandment that Redcrosse give up his worldly heroism to be his final lesson, and even to constitute Spenser's supposed acknowledgment that his poem must "move away from romance."[91] But Redcrosse's sacrifice is neither his last nor his heaviest burden, and it is not Spenser's ultimate position on the challenging mode. Upon hearing this latest revelation, the young knight who was so eager for romance at the poem's beginning becomes just as zealous to set it aside. If the holiness of his adventures is indeed inferior to the holiness of their end, the Knight of Holiness is suddenly desperate to have his story over already, to dispense forever with the "deeds of armes" and "Ladies loue" that he had clung to only a few lines ago, and to be absorbed into the elect community of saints:

> O let me not (quoth he) then turne againe
> Backe to the world, whose ioyes so fruitlesse are;
> But let me heare for aie in peace remaine,
> Or streight way on that last long voiage fare,
> That nothing may my present hope empare. (1.10.63)

But Contemplation admonishes his latest display of overhasty virtue with an authority that also echoes Merlin's final pronouncement: "That may not be" (1.10.63). Like Britomart, who "needs . . . toile" even though the end result of that labor has been predestined, Redcrosse's obligation to his role in the divine romance does not end simply because the hero has received a vision of its ending: "ne maist thou yitt / Forgoe that royal maides bequeathed care . . . //

Till from her cursed foe thou haue her freely quitt" (1.10.63). As a sign of his election, Redcrosse has been granted not just a prophecy, but a personal sight of the entire narrative from a sacred height, where he can glimpse a perfect interpretation of the story and its telos. However, this extraordinary vision of the ends of romance takes place above and apart from the ongoing narrative below; and having seen it, Redcrosse must re-descend into his unfinished story. Despite his longing to dispense with romance and proceed on a "streight way," his "present hope" must again be "empare[d]" by doubt and the threat of tragic turns, and he must return to relative isolation while the promise of community again recedes into abstraction and invisibility.

Crucially for Spenser's reformation of romance, immediately after devaluing the worldly version of the mode as a veneer over its immutable, eternal telos, Contemplation revalues it as a form of submission to that same end.[92] Redcrosse's greatest burden is to return to romance after he has seen its end and has ceased to desire it, enacting conventional heroism for God's glory rather than his own. The Knight of Holiness has a duty to perform his mortal role—protecting Una, fighting the Dragon, restoring her usurped kingdom—because these actions symbolize his alignment with divine order and help bring it to pass. His allegorical defense of the True Church, combat with Satan, and restoration of Eden all clearly reflect Christ's progress, although Saint George of England is not Christ, but his elect imitator. Even Christ's heroism on earth mirrors his final triumph at the end of time without removing the need for it, and vice versa. Despite their hierarchical relationship, neither worldly romance nor its eschatological counterpart precludes the other. Spenser insists on the paradox that the same conventional plot that is "vaine" and "nought" for the united community of the elect in Jerusalem is essential for the dispersed community of the elect still on the path there.[93] Put another way, Redcrosse's mountaintop revelation lets him perceive that he is a character in an allegorical romance, ultimately authored by God, not Spenser. As such, he must reenter his narrative armed with an understanding of its shape and outcome, but he cannot yet cease to be a character or a symbol. Redcrosse pledges, with God's "grace," to "Abett that virgins cause disconsolate," but he exhibits a new sense of dissatisfaction with his knightly adventures, eager to "returne vnto this place, / To walke this way in Pilgrims poore estate" (1.10.64).

While Britomart is only told that she is chosen and must choose to believe it and to fight for her promised progeny, despite the tragedies she knows will befall them, Redcrosse has visual confirmation of his election and of the eschatological unreality of tragedy for God's elect. Nevertheless, the gap between the two heroes' perspectives quickly begins to shrink (though not to close) once Redcrosse re-descends into the lower landscape of romance. His new vision is barely sustainable in tandem with his everyday sight:

> adowne he looked to the grownd,
> To haue returnd, but dazed were his eyne,
> Through passing brightnes, which did quite confound
> His feeble sence, and too exceeding shyne.
> So darke are earthly thinges compard to things diuine.[94] (1.10.67)

Redcrosse must struggle to reacclimate himself to his earthly purpose, but when at last "himselfe he gan to fynd," he returns down the mountain "to Vna, who him ioyd to see, / And after litle rest, gan him desyre, / Of her aduenture mindfull for to bee" (1.10.68). Their romance renews, and book 1 of *The Faerie Queene* approaches its climax in Redcrosse's battle with the Dragon.

The last two cantos of book 1 reiterate Contemplation's and Merlin's warnings that temporal endings are illusions, for better and for worse. Redcrosse's combat with the Dragon appears to end twice in defeat before the knight triumphs on the third day. The restored king of Eden makes Redcrosse his heir and grants him Una's hand, "By dew desert of noble cheualree" (1.12.20). After all, love and a throne conventionally reward the hero after his trials, which Una's father assumes are finally past: "since now safe ye seised haue the shore, / And well arriued are, (high God be blest) / Let vs deuize of ease and euerlasting rest" (1.12.17). But Redcrosse has seen "euerlasting rest" and knows it is not to be found here. Even his worldly adventures are not yet over, as he still owes years of allegiance to Gloriana against her pagan enemies "by the faith, which I to armes haue plight," before he can return to marry Una (1.12.18). In his allegorical defeat of Satan and liberation of Truth, Redcrosse seems to have accomplished the highest ends imaginable for Protestant heroism, but he must repeat similar symbolic acts again and again. His "faith . . . to armes" and to virtuous ladies stands for his duty to God—until, finally, it does not, when the providential end of allegorical romance causes all mere symbols to "vanish into nought." In the meantime, its chosen heroes encounter the usual trials and the usual triumphs; Spenser's narrator informs us that Redcrosse's betrothal to Una is celebrated with "The vsuall ioyes at knitting of loues band" (1.12.40). But yet the end is not:

> Yet swimming in that sea of blisfull ioy,
> He nought forgot, how he whilome had sworne . . .
> Vnto his Faery Queene backe to retourne:
> The which he shortly did, and Vna left to mourne.[95] (1.12.41)

Mikics and others have seen this deferral of the marriage as evidence that "romance energy, as the pure willful movement of plot, escapes providential closure when Red Crosse . . . once again departs in search of chivalric excitement . . . yet again the victim of the short attention span encouraged by a hyperactive questing mentality."[96] But this interpretation emphasizes only the pleasure of adventure that Parker sees as endemic to *The Faerie Queene*, again at the expense of her acknowledgment of "the sorrow of wandering"—which, I argue, lies at the heart of Spenser's reformation of romance.[97] Redcrosse's departure from Eden and from Una is much more melancholy than "hyperactive"—we should feel here not energetic lightness but weight—and the quest drive comes not from Redcrosse's own will, but from the commandments of his monarch and his God. Far from "escap[ing] providential closure," his burden is that he *cannot* escape from providential narrative prematurely. Ultimately more like Britomart than unlike her, Redcrosse subordinates his desire to the advancement of his nation, and must subordinate both callings to divine will. All of Britomart's chivalry is devoted to the tree of her elect descendants, even though she will only ever see the nearest branches, and all of Redcrosse's is dedicated to the community in Eden and the communion of the New Jerusalem, from both of which he is exiled. "The Patron of true Holinesse" discovers that true holiness is neither conventional romance heroism nor the ascetic abdication of it (1.1.argument). Rather, the elect hero is called to an ongoing, often painful submission to the ends of romance: to the mode's real and allegorical providential purpose, and to its remote but ever-certain erasure.

The narrator of *The Faerie Queene* often addresses his audience as though he himself were another member of his elect community of heroes questing in relative isolation, speaking at one remove from their story but with the same guiding sense of the conventional tropes and narrative patterns of romance. He, too, is laden with a sense of duty to a community—to his Protestant readers, to his own Queen Gloriana, and to the God whose providential will for England he hopes to illustrate.[98] Notably, his rhetorical postures align him more with Britomart's medial perspective than with Redcrosse's final one: like her, he compares himself and his poem more than once to a "feeble bark" whose "wearie course" is beset by "stormie surges" as it struggles to avoid going "astray" (1.12.1, 6.12.1). At times, he expresses faith in the providential direction of his venture—even in the final completed book of his unfinished epic, the ship "Still winneth way, ne hath her compasse lost" (6.12.1)—but in the "vnperfite" final canto of *The Faerie Queene*'s fragmentary continuation, he grieves for the tragedies of the temporal world and for his own lack of Redcrosse's heavenly vision. His contemplation of mutability has made him "loath this state of life so tickle . . . // Whose flowring pride, so fading and so fickle, / Short Time shall soon cut down with his consuming sickle" (7.8.1). This is conventional imagery not for a romance of providence, but for the tragedy of fortune: struggling to produce his impossibly long poem, disappointed by his lack of favor with Elizabeth, and near the end of his life, Spenser (like Sidney, but more acutely) represents tragedy as always encroaching on the borders of romance. His reformist narrative, however, weighs this anxiety against a re-vision of romance not just as a mode that is threatened by tragedy, but—as Cooper anticipates—as a mode that involves and subsumes tragedy.[99] Negotiating between the experience of contingency and the faith that at the end of time "all shall rest eternally / With Him that is the God of Sabbaoth hight," *The Faerie Queene*'s last line prays for the vision granted to Redcrosse but withheld from the poet, who does not stand on a prophetic peak but struggles "enrooted" somewhere in the branches of history: "O that great Sabbaoth God, graunt me that Sabaoths sight" (7.8.2). As sixteenth-century Protestants striving toward a pious and patriotic reformation of the genre so beloved by medieval Catholic England, Spenser offers his readers a sense of romance's often isolating weight (a narrative burden eased to uneven extents by various insights into the narrative's long-form structure), while Sidney conceives of romance's insubstantial yet mighty individual and communal subjectivity. Together, both would stand as powerful models for seventeenth-century writers to adopt, and to adapt, when England's civil conflicts plunged the nation into another religious and political tempest.

CHAPTER 2

"Heroical" Histories

Writing Lives into National Romance, 1648–1670

We have seen how Sidney's *New Arcadia* envisions romance as the source of a heroic subjectivity that mimics a range of Protestant experiences of election or vocation. From there, romance becomes a test of faith that draws believers into an exclusive, potentially subversive community. In this chapter, we examine how this model of romance informs four works of heroic historiography composed by royalists and republicans during and after the English civil wars. Despite their ideological diversity, these works all share Sidney's fascination with romance's capacity to situate individuals and communities within a providential narrative, to empower them to exclude and resist the unregenerate or unenlightened, and to distinguish their understanding of right romance from outsiders' or opponents' perversions of the genre. During the tempestuous decades in which the balance of power, and control over the telling of England's story, shifted from royalists to republicans and back again, both sides mocked or condemned their enemies' manipulation of romance while openly or tacitly appropriating it in order to mark their community and its leaders as the true heroes of the national narrative. Romance emerged as a battleground between royalists and republicans in the years of the civil wars and beyond.

Through Spenser's *Faerie Queene*, we have seen that nationalistic romance offered its subjects not only confidence and power, but also a narrative frame that demanded, and lent meaning to, uncertainty and pain. The burden of the genre might be eased by a visionary perspective on the story's promised end, but not all narrative visions are equal: a hero like Redcrosse may be graced with a transcendent sight of the full arc of the plot they inhabit, but others like Britomart are exhorted to have faith in a telos to their story that they cannot see and may not enjoy. In the middle of the seventeenth century, due to romance's long form and the problem of conflicting subjectivities, we encounter many examples of writers struggling with the tension between providential romance and tragic or haphazard human history, often employing variations of Spenser's archetypes of disparate perspectives on the ends of romance. The historiographies in this chapter share a Spenserian awareness that romance is fraught with, and perhaps uniquely equipped to navigate, problems of uneven personal and historical perspective.

We begin with two texts that deal with the complex mid-century reception of Sidney and Spenser as writers and political icons. First, the 1648 pamphlet *The Faerie Leveller* extols Charles I as the antitype of Spenser's Knight of Justice, casting Spenser as a prophet who foresaw defeat for Cromwell and reclaiming him from his Puritan devotees by insisting that royalist readers alone hold the key to his allegory. Next, the 1652 first printing of Fulke Greville's *Life of the Renowned Sir Philip Sidney* wrestles with the discrepancy between Sidney's romance heroism and his tragic death, and between the author and his subject's views of history as genre, while allowing its diverse Interregnum audience to read Sidney as either an emblem of nostalgic royalism or a godly proto-republican visionary. A second pair, the royalist Margaret Cavendish's and the republican Lucy Hutchinson's biographies of their war-hero husbands, are ideological opposites but share a keen sense of generic and gendered tension between the men's confident identification with romance and their wives' struggle to define and reconcile their own narrative roles in England's story. John Hutchinson and William Cavendish define their heroism through both their wartime chivalry and their passionate love for God and the king; meanwhile, the women who write their lives must labor to ensure that their heroic subjectivity does not exclude their wives, as well as their enemies, from the glorious ends of their personal and national narratives.

SPENSER AS ROYALIST PROPHET: THE "PRINCE OF JUSTICE" AND HIS
FOLLOWERS IN SAMUEL SHEPPARD'S *THE FAERIE LEVELLER*

In July 1648, with the war going badly for the royalists, the royalist newsbook *Mercurius Elencticus* advertised an anonymous pamphlet: *The Faerie Leveller* purported to offer "a lively representation of our times" through an excerpt of book 5 of Spenser's *Faerie Queene*.[1] In this episode, Artegall, the Knight of Justice, and his squire, Talus, humiliate and defeat a giant who has seduced many disciples by pledging to "suppresse" the rule of tyrants: "And Lordings curbe that Commons over-aw: / And all the wealth of rich-men to the poore will draw."[2] The pamphleteer, identified by Marissa Nicosia as Samuel Sheppard, posits that Spenser's romance foresaw the "subverters of well-settled States . . . lately risen up and now raigneing amongst us": these Levellers "were discryed long agoe in Queene *Elizabeths* dayes, and then graphically described by the Prince of English Poets *Edmund Spenser*, whose verses then propheticall are now become historicall in our dayes" (3).[3] Adding that Spenser's *Faerie Queene* is "Allegoricall, and needes a little explanation," Sheppard offers his audience a "key of the work" that "[applies] all to these times": Artegall, "Prince of justice," is identified as Charles I, and "Talus his Executioner" as "The Kings forces" (4). The "Gyant Leveller" is "Col. Oliver Cromwell, L. G. of the Sts. Army." As Nicosia, John King, and Clark Hulse each point out, Sheppard disregards the fact that Cromwell was "no friend" to the most radical reformers who fought under him, equating Cromwell's policies with the Levellers' promotion of total "equallity" (6).[4]

As King notes, "Spenser's moralism and Protestant zeal made him a favorite of seventeenth-century Puritans," but his support for Elizabeth and his moderate social politics offered royalists an opportunity to claim him as their own.[5] *The Faerie Leveller* asserts their right to English epic romance by reidentifying Spenser not as a Puritan forerunner but as a royalist prophet. Charles I, too, is reimagined as the hero of England's historical romance: endowed with a distinctive set of royalist virtues, the Prince of Justice embodies the "compleat Gentleman," worthy of popular reverence and emulation (4). Sheppard seeks to undermine the Puritans' claim not just to Spenser, but to other instruments of ideology. Anagrams, typology, and biblical exegesis, the tools of radical preachers and prophets, assume royalist meaning in *The Faerie Leveller*; conscience and individual judgment, the subversive bywords of religious and political reformers, are repositioned to side with the king; and providential romance itself, which for Spenser and his Puritan admirers (like Milton) promised eschatological triumph for the godly, here foretells worldly victory over Cromwell for the embattled Charles. Notably, the short pamphlet disregards Spenser's sense of national romance's length and weight, predicting that the king's increasingly unlikely victory would come easily and soon.[6] Instead, Sheppard's approach owes much to Sidney's model of community and resistance through heroic subjectivity. Using *The Faerie Queene* as its romance text/test, the pamphlet mocks the self-proclaimed "godly," reconstitutes an enlightened community of royalist readers who exclusively possess the right "key" to Spenser's romance, and calls on those loyal to the heroic Charles to resist the rebels by hewing to their own interior conviction of providential favor.

The Faerie Leveller's title page immediately signals that its attitude to the Puritan opposition is simultaneously derisive and appropriative. A sardonic note indicates that the pamphlet was "Printed . . . in the yeare of their Saintships ungodly Revelling for a godly Levelling. 1648." This mockery of impious zealotry is accompanied by an anagram that endows wordplay with spiritual significance, as Puritan preachers and prophets liked to do: "Parliaments Army" is rearranged on the next line as "Paritie mar's al men."[7] While the pamphlet's first foray into providential wordplay appears witty and apt, a second anagram is conspicuously less felicitous: after identifying the "Gyant Leveller" as Cromwell, Sheppard notes the portent that "the Letters of [his] name fall into this Anagram. / Oliver Cromewell. Com' our vil' Leveller" (4). This attempt is stretched and strained to the point of absurdity: even with an extra "e" inserted into Cromwell's name, there are clearly not enough vowels to make up the sinister invocation that follows; "w," "v," and "u" must all be treated as interchangeable; and amid all the obvious clumsiness, an additional "l" sneaks in. "Com' our vil' Leveller" looks less like a genuine attempt at providential anagrammatics and more like an intentionally ridiculous imitation of "their Saintships'" predilection for silly verbal mysticism—a parody of their arrogant presumption of exclusive access to divine code.

Yet the pamphlet is more than simply parodic. Its repeated invocations of scripture mimic Puritan zeal, but they also reclaim scriptural exegesis for the royalist cause. Sheppard introduces biblical typology to *The Faerie Leveller* when he compares his scavenged text to a marvel from the book of Judges: "here is meat out of the Eater, sweet hony to be found in the carkasse of a slaine Lyon; do thou but with *Jonathan* taste of it, and thou shalt have thy sight cleared in some remarkable matters, which before thou didst not discerne" (3).⁸ Sheppard brings new life and fresh meaning to an old poem while promising literary and religious enlightenment to his readers.⁹ Cromwell's fate, too, is anticipated both typologically and poetically: "I dismisse him with . . . the Traytor *Judas*, Act I. 25. *who by transgression fell, that he might go to his owne place.* And his complices with *Thomas Sternehold*, version of the 10 v. of the 3. *Psalme.* / Destroy their false conspiracies, that they may come to naught: / Subvert them in their heapes of sinne, that have rebellion wrought" (4). Predictions of divine vengeance, Sheppard demonstrates, are not only the province of anti-royalist rebels; the community of those loyal to the king is entitled to its own biblical and poetic hermeneutics. Moreover, his display of exegetical ability helps mark him as an enlightened follower of the scripturally authoritative Prince of Justice, as we will see.

The Faerie Leveller moves from its appropriation of scripture and providential wordplay to its reinvention of *The Faerie Queene* itself—which, like the introductory anagrams, requires some manipulation of the source material in order to bolster its royalist exclusivity. Sheppard claims to have found his prophecy in Spenser's "first Booke," which "containes the Legend of Justice, the most universall vertue" (4). Of course, Justice is the subject of the *fifth* book, and Spenser never assigns it this special distinction. But the undoubtedly conscious fudging of the books' order, and the citation of justice as the "most universall" heroic attribute, lend the episode of Artegall and the Giant a prominence it lacks in the original poem. Sheppard also undertakes to reshape the king's romance identity: the young Charles I liked to imagine himself as Saint George, as in Rubens's portrait of his union with Henrietta Maria over the corpse of the slain dragon; but against the backdrop of 1648, Sheppard transforms him into a different knight, associated less with love and chivalry and more with order and diplomacy.¹⁰

The Faerie Leveller is perhaps more anxious to recast Charles as the hero of England's national romance than to vilify Cromwell or prophesy an unlikely outcome for the war. Again, Sheppard takes liberties with the original text in order to perfect the literary typology through which Artegall/Charles becomes the charismatic pillar of the "real" godly community. By summarizing the episode preceding the encounter with the Giant in book 5, canto 2—in which Artegall and Talus defeat the oppressive tax collector

Pollente and his daughter Munera, a figure for bribery—he leaves out its full text, extracting the story's heroic value while jettisoning the troubling specifics less suitable for Charles as Prince of Justice. Pollente and Munera are both listed in Sheppard's "key of the work": he now symbolizes the "prevalent over awing Faction in the two houses," while she represents the "intolerable Tax-raisers" who "must first be apprehended and brought to justice, ere [Cromwell's] army be quelled" (4).[11] Their episode is distilled into a short summary—"Arthegall the Champion of Justice, with the assistance of Talus his Groome betokening execution of Law, having overcome all illegall arbitrary oppressive power; under the person of Pollente, a barbarous Saracen, strengthened by his Daughter Munera importing bribes and taxes: He proceeds to suppress the Gyant Ring leader to the faction of Levellers" (4)—and into a quatrain, composed by Sheppard, placed to give the impression that the episode with the Giant begins a new canto: "Arthegall with his Groome Talus / having Pollente quel'd: / And drown'd his Daughter Munera, / they on their journey wel'd" (5).

This selective inclusion serves two ends. First, it allows for the tidy introduction of Artegall/Charles as an equitable peacemaker who subdues faction and oppression, even though the pamphlet's prophetic "key" is imperfect: in Spenser's text, Pollente is the tax raiser, while Munera stands for corruption and greed, evils less clearly restricted to Parliamentarian rule. Second, it imagines a trial for the Prince of Justice from which he emerges morally untarnished. Spenser's melancholy approach to romance often questions its heroes' successful embodiment of their virtues, as with Artegall in 5.2. The knight first shrinks from his mission out of "pitty" for the elegant Munera (5.2.25), but then permits Talus to exact a brutal and merciless punishment:

> Yet for no pitty would he change the course
> Of Iustice, which in Talus hand did lye;
> Who rudely hayld her forth without remorse,
> Still holding vp her suppliant hands on hye,
> And kneeling at his feete submissiuely.
> But he her suppliant hands, those hands of gold,
> And eke her feete, those feete of silver trye,
> Which sought vnrighteousnesse, and iustice sold,
> Chopt off, and nayld on high, that all might them behold. (5.2.26)

Talus then throws her, still "In vaine loud crying," from her wall, drowns her in the river below, and destroys her wealth rather than restoring it to the oppressed people (5.2.27). Spenser highlights Artegall's tendencies toward both misguided compassion and extreme retribution in the form of the implacable Talus, who regularly handles the ugliest elements of his master's vocation. Sheppard's vague summary thus permits Artegall/Charles to appear against the "Gyant Leveller" unsullied by the disturbing residue of his overthrow of institutionalized oppression.

As their encounter unfolds, Sheppard engineers a set of heroic attributes for the Prince of Justice that recommend him as a community leader preferable to the Giant. His Artegall must be sincerely devout, fair, and compassionate in order to expose and overcome his Cromwellian foe's false pretense to these virtues. Both Spenser's poem and Sheppard's pamphlet juxtapose the Giant's bad reading of scripture with Artegall's superior exegesis. While the Giant interprets Isaiah 40:4 to license his reformist rebellion—"Therefore will I throw downe those mountaines high, / And make them levell with the lowly plaine" (7)—Artegall offers a corrective reading of the same passage as a testimony to God's power as divine monarch:

> All in the power of their great maker lye:
> All Creatures must obey the voice of the most high. . . .
> The hills do not the lowly Dales disdaine.
> The Dales do not the lofty hills envy.
> He maketh Kings to sit in Soveraignty.
> He maketh Subjects to their power obey. (8)

This contrast between the Leveller's radical, self-serving exegesis and the hero's conservative correction recalls Sheppard's efforts to undermine the biblical rhetoric of the "Saints": Sheppard presents himself as a faithful imitator of the Prince, and the Puritans' usual tools transform to support royalist values. None may "shunne" God's "Soveraigne power," Artegall warns—least of all the Leveller who acknowledges no supremacy but his own and only pretends to godliness to demolish the order of a providence "Whose counsells depth thou canst not understand" (8). Artegall/Charles lays claim to truer devotion and a better grasp on scripture than the hypocrites who oppose him; the earthly Prince speaks best for the king of Heaven.

Finally, *The Faerie Leveller* reinterprets a rather weak moment for Spenser's Artegall to shape its readers' final impression of Charles's heroic persona. Once Talus has slain the Giant, the peasants rise up in anger against Artegall:

> He much was troubled, ne wist what to doe,
> For loath he was his noble hands t'embrew,
> In the base blood of such a Rascall crew. . . .
> Therefore he Talus to them sent t'enquire
> The cause of their array, and truce for to desire. (11)

In *The Faerie Queene*, this stanza again reveals Artegall's deficiencies: faced with exercising justice on weaker offenders, he is stymied, and as usual, he sends Talus to protect his reputation and handle the hard work. Sheppard, rather than eliding this problem as with the similarly uncomfortable Munera episode, allows its meaning to shift, transforming the Caroline Artegall into a different hero than Spenser's Knight of Justice. As a "Prince," not a knight, the Artegall of *The Faerie Leveller* need not deal with the demands of a warrior's code. His "troubled" mind suggests love for his misguided subjects, instead of anxiety over an unequal conflict; his concern with keeping his "noble hands" clean from "base blood" comes across as royal dignity instead of snobbery or diffidence; and his delegation of Talus to preserve order looks more like peaceful, pragmatic diplomacy than a shirking of duty. By the time the "Raskall Rout" has fled, another vexed occasion for Spenser's Artegall has become an ennobling one for Charles's Spenserian persona (11). The monarch as romance hero seems pious instead of sanctimonious, decorously proud rather than arrogant, and just and courageous yet equitable, merciful, and benevolent. The assistance of Talus, instead of calling his heroism into question, refines and shapes it: with necessary violence securely in the hands of the allegorical army, he is free to be well-spoken, courtly, and wisely paternal, not warlike, rash, or punitive.

Having both parodied and repossessed Puritan tactics, and having turned Artegall's heroism and fallibility alike to Charles's advantage, *The Faerie Leveller* employs its most potent strategy to unite readers behind the royalist cause and its champion: it turns Spenser's romance into an invitation to join an exclusive enlightened community. Sheppard claims in his preface that he has "revised" Spenser's prophetic poetry "for the undeceiving of simple people, too apt to be induced into an high conceipt and overweening opinion of such Deceivers, and too ready to be seduced by their specious pretences," and he explains Spenser's intent "to set forth a compleat Gentleman, accomplisht with all vertues adorning a truly noble Person" (3–4). King suggests that Sheppard attempts to influence common readers by "tak[ing] Spenser's purpose . . . as an argument in favor of royalty and the gentry."[12] However, Sheppard does more than reinforce a Jamesonian hierarchy: he offers his readers a chance to use romance to elevate themselves above "simple people." We read that the leveling Giant is "admired much of Fooles, Women, and Boyes" and that "the vulgar did about him flocke, / And cluster thick unto his leasings vaine: / (Like foolish Flies about a hony crocke) / In hope by him great benefit to gaine" (5, 6). Although the readers are initially treated as "simple," as they read on they are tacitly encouraged not to count themselves among these gullible, emasculated masses, and to follow the "sweet hony" of Spenser's prophetic wisdom in resistance to the Leveller's dishonest "crocke." They are urged to read as "Gentle[men]" or "noble Person[s]" who can distinguish and so imitate true heroic virtue, as Sheppard has already done. Modifying Sidney's vision of a heroic subjectivity that enables members of a community to discern between right romance and misappropriations of the genre, Sheppard implies that his audience's possession of the "key" to Spenser's text gives them an opportunity. Siding with the Prince of Justice can make even a poor subject more princely and raise his cultural status within an exclusive community of enlightened royalist readers.

By its end, *The Faerie Leveller* has offered its audience the subjectivity to judge between the Giants heroism and Artegall's. Artegall acknowledges that the truth may not be self-evident, and he champions discernment rather than blind obedience: "But in the minde the doome of right must be . . . // And judge whether with truth or falsehood they agree" (10). A preference for the Giant or Artegall, and a choice of sides in the war, must ultimately be a subjective matter.[13] As in the *New Arcadia*, this royalist appeal to Protestant ideas—the superior subjectivity of the godly and the supremacy of the individual conscience—is both powerful and dangerous. Sidney envisioned history as a romance of providence legible to the faithful, and Sheppard assumes that all "noble" minds will be drawn to the king's cause and to faith in its success. Yet such subjectivity remains troublesome, as Sidney had been aware: one may mistake one's calling and develop a perverted sense of heroism, and one may side just as easily with the Giant as with Artegall. Milton's *Eikonoklastes*, published the next year (after any possibility of royalist triumph had collapsed), shows what it means for every subject's mind to be his own and proves that Spenser's romance was exclusive to no faction: "If there were a man of iron, such as *Talus*, by our Poet *Spencer*, is fain'd to be," who could reform England "expeditiously, without those deceitfull formes and circumstances of Law.... I say God send it don, whether by one *Talus*, or by a thousand."[14] In the judgment of Milton and other reformist republicans, Talus and the Giant's mass of followers might join forces, with overwhelming results.

SIDNEY AS REPUBLICAN SAINT: READING FULKE GREVILLE'S *LIFE OF THE RENOWNED SIR PHILIP SIDNEY* IN 1652

While Sheppard offers a striking royalist appropriation of a sixteenth-century romance writer more often associated with Milton's Puritan poetics, Fulke Greville's *Life of the Renowned Sir Philip Sidney* reminds us that Sidney, whose romance style was imitated by many royalists, was at least as slippery as Spenser.[15] The subjectivity of romance proved as crucial to seventeenth-century curators of his heroic memory as it had been to the fictional heroes of his *New Arcadia*. The few who now read Greville's *Life of Sidney* remark on its generic complexity and singular approach to life writing.[16] Indeed, Greville wrote the *Life* not as a biography but as a dedication of a volume of plays to his dead friend; it is not a chronological memoir so much as an account of Sidney's knightly prowess and a treatise on his Protestant politics, which Greville shared. Greville claims that he wrote it as a personal exercise, "to keep company with [Sidney], even after death," and "to entertaine, and instruct [him] selfe," but he anticipates a wider audience, "esteem[ing] [Sidney's] actions, words, and conversation, the daintiest treasure my mind ... can at this day impart with our posteritie."[17] He never published the work, though, perhaps judging it unwise to wax nostalgic for Elizabeth I and her independent-minded courtier while employed by James I's divine right regime in the 1610s.

In 1652, the *Life of Sidney* was printed for the first time. Only three years earlier, England had executed Charles I and become a nominal republic dominated by Puritan leadership. The "posteritie" reading the *Life* were doing so under wildly different circumstances than Greville could have imagined, and this new audience likely viewed Greville's portrait of Sidney through their own visions of themselves. Peter Herman points out that although Greville celebrated Elizabeth and (especially) Sidney as opponents of absolute monarchy, the *Life*'s printer mainly published royalist writing, and proposes that by 1652, "a book idealizing a popular earlier monarch and one of her glittering courtiers would likely be interpreted as a defense of England's monarchy in general and the late Charles in particular. The implied contrast would not be with a monarch attempting to impose absolutism, but with a Parliament trying to rule without a king."[8] While this interpretation highlights how context and ideology had the power to "[alter] the reception of a text" and of a celebrated national figure, Herman's claim that "in 1652, the 'horizons' circumscribing this text had, in effect, moved 180 degrees" underestimates what he himself calls "the fluidity of reputation in the seventeenth century."[19] Readers across the political spectrum in 1652 could locate the evils of absolutism wherever they pleased and could embrace the gallant Sidney as a nostalgic emblem of romantic royalism/royalist romance *or* a prophetic figure of romantic republicanism/republican romance.[20]

In accepting Herman's reading of a royalist (mis)appropriation of Sidney, we should also consider how Sidney's sixteenth-century Philippism, religiously reformist and politically anti-absolutist, might just as easily be (mis-)recognized by Puritans decades later as their theology and their republicanism.[21] An anti-royalist public could gaze backward into history through the *Life* to imagine Sidney preparing the way for the godly state, sacrificing himself in the name of a victory over tyranny he would not survive to see.[22] While this subjectivity recasts Sidney as a hero of a new providential romance and a pillar of its living community—a community likelier than the less dogmatic Sidney, perhaps, to identify itself as God's "elect"—his death for the reformist cause complicates the *Life*'s genre. While *The Faerie Leveller* reimagined Spenser through a Sidneian approach to subjective romance without anticipating the tragedy that soon befell Charles I, the *Life of Sidney* required readers in 1652 to contend with a melancholy Spenserian view of the genre of history: Greville depicts his friend's romance heroism as beset by tragedy. Narrative subjectivity makes Sidney's outlook unlike Greville's, which is in turn separate from the perspectives of multiple mid-century communities.

Readers of any ideology looking for a hero needed little imagination to see Sidney as a real-life knight seemingly sprung from fictional romance. The Sidney of the *Life* resembles the idealized heroes of chivalry, embodying all manly virtues and pursuits.[23] Greville compares him to Hercules (41) and Aeneas (90), and remembers him as "a true modell of Worth; A man fit for ... what Action soever is greatest, and hardest amongst men: Withall, such a lover of Mankind, and Goodnesse, that whosoever had any reall parts, in him found comfort, participation, and protection to the uttermost of his power" (38). Crucially, Sidney's excellence is recognized best by those who share his "reall parts." As in the *New Arcadia*, romance heroism is not appreciable by all observers; it is a concept nurtured within a community of similar minds and mutual values, which offers "comfort, participation, and protection" to members of its shared narrative. Greville may have thought his testimony would appeal to a coterie of aristocratic readers, but in 1652 the audience that could approve Sidney's worth, and so locate themselves within a morally elite class or community, was much larger.

While Sidney's romance heroism lends him broad ideological appeal, the exact nature and telos of that heroism arguably have a more republican than royalist cast. Greville's praise of Sidney's knighthood stresses his magnetic power to draw an admiring community of excellence into coherence around him; he leads as first among equals. His skill in arms is evident chiefly through the emulation of his compatriots: "Souldiers honoured him, and were so honoured by him, as no man thought he marched under the true Banner of *Mars*, that had not obtained Sir *Philip Sidney*'s approbation" (39). His communitarian charisma extends beyond the battlefield: every "Artificer of extraordinary fame ... [made] himself known to this famous Spirit, and found him his true friend without hire; and the common *Rende-vous* of Worth in his time" (39). This role as the pillar of a fellowship formed by the gifted and honorable is more important than any of Sidney's individual accomplishments. Textually resurrected in 1652, Sidney could be celebrated afresh in the Interregnum as the hero of an ostensibly egalitarian community of worthies. Under his influence, everyone of "any reall parts" is moved to enrich his own virtues—a result, Greville claims, that Sidney actively sought. In praising Sidney's literary talent, Greville emphasizes his true purpose: "His end was not writing, even while he wrote ... but ... to make himself, and others, not in words or opinion, but in life, and action, good and great. In which Architechtonical art he was such a Master, with so commending, and yet equall waies amongst men, that whersoever he went, he was beloved, and obeyed: yea into what Action soever he came ... the whole managing of the business, not by usurpation, or violence, but (as it were) by right, and acknowledgment, falling into his hands, as into a naturall Center" (21).[24] The "Architechtonical Master" acts as a poet or "maker" not chiefly of words but of people.²⁵ Both his writing and his life work toward the "end" of romance as Sidney himself presents it in the *New Arcadia* and the *Defence of Poesie*: to inspire an audience to show their "reall parts" by making themselves "good and great" in the world beyond the story.²⁶ Crucially for republican readers of the *Life*, Sidney both inspires and surpasses his fellows based on merit. He becomes "first" among those he regards as "equall" to himself "not by usurpation" but "by right" of virtue and by "acknowledgment" of others.²⁷ Although he, like Greville, was dedicated to the monarchy he served, a 1652 audience could imagine Sidney as a founding father of utopian meritocracy.

At least as important for Puritan readers is the fact that Sidney's civic merit is excelled only by his reformist piety; his "true-heartednesse to the Reformed Religion" directs his politics and, all too often, obstructs his success in his own time (42). For Sidney, reform is essential for "Peace, Safetie, and Freedome," and "to temporize with the Enemies of our Faith" is "false-heartednesse to God and man" (42). While Sidney sees service to Protestantism as coterminous with service to England, his zeal often inspires resistance to state authority. Although Greville praises Sidney for "his chief ends being . . . the honour of his Maker, and service of his Prince, or Country," these three ideals are not always aligned in the *Life* (47). Republican readers would surely appreciate Greville's insinuation that service to the monarch and service to the country were distinct, and Puritan readers could hardly miss the theme that godliness, along with the sense of heroic subjectivity that it imparts to Sidney, dominates his other concerns whenever conflict emerges between them. For instance, Greville takes pleasure in recounting the knight's boldness before his queen in the name of Protestant egalitarianism.²⁸ After Sidney makes plans to duel with an insulting nobleman and Elizabeth urges him to defer to the earl's superior rank, he politely agrees not to pursue the quarrel, but first reminds her that "that place [of nobility] was never intended for privilege to wrong: witness her self, who how Soveraign soever she were by Throne, Birth, Education, and Nature; yet was she content to . . . govern all her rights by [her subjects'] laws" (80). The hero's contention that monarchs are not above the law would have been daring when Greville first wrote the *Life* under James I, but this had become a foundational tenet of the English republic in 1652. Sidney also feels called to act in riskier situations: fearing that a marriage between Elizabeth and the Catholic Anjou would result in "a precipitate absoluteness" of monarchy, he warns her that "he foresaw, and prophesied, that the very first breach of Gods ordinance, in matching herself with a Prince of a diverse faith, would infallibly carry with it some piece of the rending destiny, which Solomon, and those other Princes justly felt, for having ventured to weigh the immortall wisdom in even scales, with mortall conveniency" (63–64). If Sidney's claim to prophetic vision and his unwillingness to "biace Gods immortall truth to the fantasies of mortall Princes" made him a Protestant hero in Greville's lifetime, it could only intensify his glory under the Puritan republic (60).

While Sidney's claim to divinely granted foresight enhances his heroic leadership of a godly community, Greville's representation of him as a prophet makes the *Life* vulnerable to the same generic tensions that arise in *The Faerie Queene*'s moments of prophetic vision. After Sidney's death cuts short his often-frustrated efforts to establish a pan-European Protestant league to resist Catholic tyranny, Greville terms his friend "Sir Philip, our unbelieved Cassandra," at once celebrating and grieving Sidney as a visionary whose wisdom went unheeded during his lifetime (129). Greville conjures an image of Sidney overlooking sacred narrative much as Spenser's Merlin or Redcrosse do, "lift[ing] up his active spirit into an universall prospect of time.... The placing of his thoughts upon which high pinnacle, layd the present Map of the Christian world underneath him" (90–91).[29] From his mental "pinnacle," Sidney sees nations' roles within the romance of history: he witnesses "that creeping Monarchie of Rome" menacing Europe, and Spain "mixing the temporall, and spirituall sword, to their crafty conquering ends" (94, 97). Sidney perceives that these Catholic monarchs are "no anointed deputies of God, but rather lively Images of the dark Prince ... who ever ruines his ends with over-building," and is certain of their final fate: "the vengeance of God must necessarily" fall on tyranny (130). Unlike the hesitant Protestant rulers who lack his heroic spirit and vision, Sidney trusts that "though this justice of the Almighty be many times slow, & therefore neglected," the community of the godly is destined to triumph, while their enemies are always already doomed (131).

Greville weighs Sidney's faith in the providential romance of history and in his own heroic subjectivity against an awareness that progress is "slow"; like the visions of Merlin and Redcrosse, Sidney's "universall prospect of time" reveals the trajectory of history but cannot hasten that narrative's conclusion. Before the final victory of the godly, Sidney is destined to die at Zutphen, the "last scene of this Tragedy" as Greville sees it (159).[30] Sidney sacrifices himself for the future he foresees—a tragic end to pave the way for a romance ending. Puritans reading from the hindsight of 1652 might imagine that the end for which he fought was still at hand, or had even come to pass in the form of a militant godly republic (which had finally dispensed with a king who was, at best, a lukewarm leader of God's chosen nation or, at worst, a "lively Image of the dark Prince"). Greville, though, cannot see Sidney's vision or muster such confidence, and his text confronts audiences with the tension between Sidneian romance and Grevillian tragedy.

The *Life*, originally conceived not as a memoir but as a preface to a collection of political tragedies, ends with a fraught discussion of Greville and his friend's separate artistic visions and generic sensibilities.[31] While Sidney was famous for his romance, Greville had become known for his tragic drama. Noting that his works illustrate the corruption of power, Greville indicates a strong preference for the historical realism of tragedy over romance—revealing his skepticism of Sidney's vision of history as romance. He finds tragic history "fitter to hold the attention of the Reader, than . . . the strangeness . . . of witty Fictions; in which the affections, or imagination, may perchance find exercise, and entertainment, but the memory and judgement no enriching at all" (244). In this criticism of romance as emotionally engaging yet intellectually and morally vapid, Greville accords with many of his contemporaries, but not with Sidney, who championed heroic fiction in the *Defence of Poesie* and by writing *Arcadia*. Keenly aware that he and his friend traveled different generic paths, Greville follows his personal rejection of romance with a strange, difficult passage that offers earnest yet halting praise for *Arcadia* and its author:

> My Noble Friend had that dexterity . . . to make the Arcadian Antiques beautifie the Margents of his works; yet the honour which (I beare him record) he never affected, I leave unto him, with this addition, that his end in them was not vanishing pleasure alone, but morall Images, and Examples, (as directing threds) to guide every man through the confusing Labyrinth of his own desires, and life: So that howsoever I liked them not too well (even in that unperfected shape they were) to condescend that such delicate (though inferior) Pictures of himselfe, should be suppressed; yet I do wish that work may be the last in this kind, presuming no man that followes can ever reach, much lesse go beyond that excellent intended patterne of his. (244–45)

Greville vacillates between defending his own decision to write history as tragedy instead of romance and defending Sidney's decision to write romance instead of a more serious genre. He proposes that his friend was the far superior poet, claiming that his own "creeping Genius" was forced to be "more fixed upon the Images of Life, than the Images of Wit" (245)— but he adds that if Sidney was better able to imagine romance because his gifts were of a higher order than Greville's, he was unique in possessing such vision. Sidney may have had the "dexterity" to fill *Arcadia* with "morall Images" for a godly life, yet Greville hopes that no other writer will try to imitate his example and be doomed to failure. Greville's overwrought prose and parenthetical digressions suggest a dizzying ambivalence toward Sidney's agenda.[32] Consigned to "beautifie the Margents" of Sidney's career, *Arcadia* is literally marginalized. Greville holds that Sidney ought to be famous for his romance but that "he never affected" such renown. He half defends *Arcadia* by noting that its end is not *only* "vanishing pleasure" and finds it too excellent to "be suppressed" after his death, although it is unfinished and "inferior" to his true greatness. Finally, he concludes by "wish[ing] that work may be the last in this kind." Sidney alone was capable of writing godly romance and of living according to the example he portrayed. His tragic demise, Greville anticipates, marks the fall of England's last romance hero, the death of romance as a viable English genre, and possibly the permanent decline of the godly community.

The question of England's future looms throughout the *Life*: what will happen now, after Sidney's valiant death, to the chosen nation and the chivalric fellowship which, in life, he drew together and upheld? Early in the text, Greville extols Sidney as a beacon guiding England: "Did not his country . . . take knowledge of him as a Light, or leading Star[?]" (7). But this brightness fades as Greville laments England's loss of his friend's wisdom: "He would have found, or made a way through all the traverses, even of the most weak and irregular times. But it pleased God in this decrepit age of the world, not to restore the image of her ancient vigour in him, otherwise than as in a lightning before death" (43). Sidney is here a marvel of ages past rather than a model for the future, an ephemeral "lightning" instead of an enduring "Light." In his life, as in his fiction, he has offered a fleeting image of heroic virtue; but God has deprived the sinful world of his perfection, and Sidney's capacity to inspire greatness in others may have become diminished, not enhanced, by his death. This communal loss, Greville claims, is his own greatest grief: his stoicism and his faith forbid him "to complain of God for taking him . . . yet for the sincere affection I bear to my Prince, and Country, my prayer to God is, that this Worth, and Way may not fatally be buried with him" (43). The *Life* cannot seem to keep from suggesting, though, that the romance "Way" may indeed have died along with the man who epitomized it.

In the early seventeenth century, Greville read the romance of the dead as the tragedy of the living. While his nostalgic melancholia might have resonated with royalist readers in 1652, a Puritan republican audience would have had less reason to relate to his lament for Sidneian romance as decayed or impotent. Readers of the *Life* who identified with the community of the godly were free to rethink the genre of history once more, and to see Sidney not as the last remnant of a bygone age of chivalry but as the first knight of the new republic, a hero whose providential romance lived on and posthumously validated his prophetic vision from his mental pinnacle. As the *Life* concludes, Greville advises the reader of his tragedies to "look on that Stage wherein himself is an Actor, even the state he lives in, and for every part he may perchance find a Player, and for every Line . . . an instance of life, beyond the Authors intention" (246–47). The *Life*'s mid-century factions would have seen multiple ways to "find out some affinity, or resemblance" between their own age and Sidneian romance, and republican readers might have had an especially easy time of it (247). If Sidney's prophetic perspective could be seen to have borne fruit in Interregnum England, then perhaps his life could be reclaimed from past marvel to present model. The generic anxieties that dogged Greville might not have troubled 1652's republican readers, who could flatter themselves that they, Sidney's latter-day community, had continued or even perfected his heroic work. But those anxieties must have been keenly felt by those whose royal romance had taken a tragic turn, and they would return with a vengeance for republicans after 1660, when England's political narrative reversed course once again.

"NO OTHER WILL, BUT YOUR MAJESTIES PLEASURE": THE EROTIC
POLITICS OF MARGARET CAVENDISH'S *LIFE OF WILLIAM CAVENDISH*

When Samuel Pepys stayed up all night reading Margaret Cavendish's biography of her husband William, Duke of Newcastle, he was evidently scandalized by its adulation of its still-living subject. Cavendish published

The Life of the Thrice Noble, High and Puissant Prince William Cavendishe in 1667 to memorialize his "Sufferings, Losses, and ill-Fortunes" and boast of his "Loyal, Heroick and Prudent Actions" in service to the royal family.[33] Pepys found more fantasy than fact in the *Life* and in his impression of its author, calling her husband "an ass to suffer her to write what she writes of him" and famously pronouncing her "a mad, conceited, ridiculous woman" whose "whole story . . . is a romance, and all she does is romantic."[34]

Probably aware of her reputation as a lavish eccentric, Cavendish prefaces the *Life of William* with an explicit refusal to allow romance conventions to interfere with more reputable genres: she refers to the royalists' defeat as a "Tragedy" and calls her account of her husband's role in it a "true Heroical history" (c1v). Given that even in the seventeenth century "romance was very often construed as a vehicle of royalist ideology," Cavendish takes pains to associate romance's infiltration of historiography with Puritan republicanism.[35] Her family's opponents, she insists, are the party guilty of "telling Romansical Falshoods for Historical Truths" and writing "in a mystical and allegorical style . . . out of Policy to amuse and deceive the People" (c2r, d1r). She accuses Parliamentarian sympathizers of writing nominal histories that "contain nothing but Falshoods and Chimeraes" and of fictionalizing their commanders by "comparing some of them to Moses, and some others to all the great and most famous Heroes" (d1r).[36] Having tarnished the marriage of historiography and heroic entertainment as the manipulative tool of her enemies, Cavendish vows to shun the manner of writers whose emphasis on the "mystical Designs" of history render their accounts "but pleasant Romances" (b2v).[37] Despite all this, Pepys was not wrong to identify a "romantic" conceit in the *Life of William*. Indeed, Cavendish intends this very design: even as she rejects romance as an appropriate genre for life writing, her case for William's royalist heroism is firmly grounded in romance convention.[38]

In its plot alone, the *Life of William* can hardly help merging romance and history. After all, it traces the usurpation of a kingdom, the trials of a long exile, and the ultimate restoration of the rightful ruler—a prototypical romance pattern that William, in the *Life*, implicitly trusts will translate into historical reality.[39] But most important, the biography takes its dominant theme from a romance tradition dating back to the Middle Ages: *fin amour*, an extremity of erotic devotion characterized by the lover's limitless willingness to suffer for the sake of an often remote and indifferent beloved.[40] Although the *fin amour* tradition is of French origin, as are the later romances that Victoria Kahn and others have proposed as Cavendish's sources,⁴¹ by her own report Cavendish never managed to learn much French, and in any case the concept had quickly spread into England through texts like Thomas Malory's *Mort d'Arthur* and thrived throughout the sixteenth and seventeenth centuries, featuring prominently in romances such as Sidney's *New Arcadia* and Spenser's *Faerie Queene*.⁴² In the *New Arcadia*, we have seen how the private intensity of love can imbue a hero with a powerful subjective sense of exceptionalism and public purpose, and Cavendish employs *fin amour* to the same end in the *Life of William*. But perhaps surprisingly, the love plot of her "Heroical history" does not chiefly concern her relationship with her husband.⁴³ Instead of celebrating the romance of the Cavendishes' marriage, the *Life*'s focal figures in the *fin amour* tradition are her husband and King Charles II, with William in the role of the long-suffering lover and the king as the beloved "master"—as Cavendish often terms him.

Kahn has briefly remarked on this homoerotic dynamic in her discussion of the "romance of contract" in the *Life*, which portrays William as the king's "unrequited" lover; she and Melissa Sanchez argue persuasively that his unconditional devotion finds a "countermodel" in the contractual paradigm of love and governance that Cavendish envisions in her prose romances.⁴⁴ While Kahn's and Sanchez's readings are more concerned with these prose fictions and their departure from William's principle of passionate obedience, I propose that we look more closely at the romance within the *Life of William*. As we explore how Cavendish merges historiography with romance, we can see her simultaneously resisting and engaging productively with William's noncontractual model, and grappling with her complex relationship to romance as a royalist woman. We also find here another illustration of the potential queerness of the emotional bonds formed by romance subjectivity. Carolyn Dinshaw and Carla Freccero have stressed how "queer histories are made of affective relations" in which sex is "heterogenous and indeterminate," accommodating heterosexuality as well as "sex's irreducible interrelatedness with other cultural phenomena"—in this case, romance, royalism, and the monarch/subject relationship.⁴⁵ As Sanchez puts it, "Since love was thought to inspire political consent and service, attention to the 'queer'—peculiar and eccentric—nature of eros also accentuates the queer side of politics."⁴⁶ In the *Life*, Cavendish represents William's "political affects" as "counter to ideals of rational and 'normal' desire" in ways that frustrate his wife, but not because they compromise his heterosexuality—rather, because "regardless of ... gender" they constitute a model for royalist subjecthood that she finds both dangerous and useful.[47] Her incorporation of *fin amour* into her ostensibly anti-romance history helps her construct both a heroic subject position for her husband and a platform for her own anti-absolutist royalist identity.

Although the erotic/political spectrum of romance also offers Cavendish the model of egalitarian love between men (as in Greville's *Life of Sidney* and, again, *Arcadia*),[48] she finds special use for the model of romance devotion founded on unconditional humility rather than mutual duty. William's heroism depends not on a reciprocated relationship with King Charles, but on his renunciation of a reciprocal contract between monarch and subject. For Sanchez, Cavendish "stresses a perverse component of sovereignty" imagined through "compromised, even degrading, erotic unions" that constitute her critique of William's "misplaced fidelity and self-sacrifice."[49] I argue, though, that Cavendish represents her husband's love for Charles ambivalently and that his consensual humiliation is only half of the picture: as "master," the king holds infinite affective and material power over his servant, yet he also takes on the less dignified role of the fickle mistress, while William's abjection elevates him to the height of royalist integrity and moral potency.[50] By Cavendish's design, he has many rivals for the king's good graces but no equal in devotion. The *Life of William* is thus concerned not with an elect or elite community, but with exceptional individualism: it creates for William a singular romance in which even his wife does not share, and which she simultaneously resents and celebrates.

Cavendish's dedication of her work to King Charles II concludes with a pointed assertion: "I have heard him often say, He loves Your Royal Person so dearly, that He would most willingly, upon all occasions, sacrifice his Life and Posterity for Your Majesty" (n2r, n2v). The *Life* continually demonstrates her husband's singular royalist heroism through this boundless sacrifice for his master the king, whom he repeatedly professes to love more than his own wife and children, despite Charles's failure to respond in kind. William understands his role as a royalist subject through the lens of romance, and Cavendish authenticates her husband's heroism by stressing his unwavering fidelity to the mode's most extreme erotic ideals: where all other subjects fall short, his love remains perfectly unselfish. Yet at the same time, as several readers have observed, the dedication to the king and the entirety of the *Life* are a thinly veiled petition for long-overdue royal favor.[51] Even as William's character simultaneously marginalizes and strengthens himself by disclaiming any reward for his love, Margaret Cavendish never loses sight of her husband's practical contributions to the royalist cause and the harsh arithmetic of her family's losses as a consequence of his devotion. The result is a generically complicated text founded on the productive tension between the historiographic account-keeping of Margaret Cavendish as the *Life*'s narrator and the romance subjectivity of William as its hero.

James Fitzmaurice has suggested that William's commitment to suffer for the king without complaint demonstrates masculine stoicism that conceals his "private anger and bitterness," while Sanchez's focus on the Petrarchan tradition reads his "suffering, not joy, as evidence of true love."[52] Yet William's devotion consistently appears not as resignation or pain but as *happiness* to suffer: "I have heard him say out of a passionate Zeal and Loyalty, That he would willingly sacrifice himself, and all his Posterity, for the sake of his Majesty, and the Royal Race. Nor did he ever repine either at his losses or sufferings, but rejoyced rather that he was able to suffer for His King and Countrey" (I1r). William sees his suffering not as a necessary evil but as a joy and a privilege—an attitude compatible with the tropes of erotic romance, and with Sanchez's understanding of political eroticism as queer or "perverse" precisely *because* it often portrays pain as pleasurable. Cavendish imitates countless images of lovesickness in early modern romance and poetry in writing William's mercurial enjoyment of this dynamic, as when, afraid that Charles has been lost in battle, "[he] fell into so violent a Passion, that I verily believed it would have endanger'd his life; but when afterwards the happy news came of His Majesties safe arrival in France, never any Subject could rejoice more then my Lord did" (T1v).

William regards his bond with the king as singular, personal, and intimate, grounded largely in the fact that he helped educate him in the prince's youth. (His attachment may support Will Fisher's claim that early modern eroticism was defined by "a range of different distinctions," including "gender, age, and status" and, in Eve Sedgwick's words, "a certain relation of age or power," which could "change over time.")[53] Cavendish's contemporaries attest to this special tie: the Earl of Clarendon writes that the Duke of Newcastle's love for Charles I was surpassed only by his "more extraordinary devotion for . . . the prince."[54] The Cavendish family's political enemy Lucy Hutchinson, who was also their neighbor in Nottinghamshire, puts it differently in her *Memoirs* of her own husband: "no man was a greater prince in all [the north of England]" than William Cavendish, "till a foolish ambition of glorious slavery carried him to court, where he ran himself much into debt, to purchase neglects of the king . . . and scorns of the proud courtiers."[55] Of course, the "glorious slavery" that the republican Hutchinson disdains is perfectly consistent with the ideals of William's royalist *fin amour*. In order to prove his love through willing and joyful suffering, the lover in the *fin amour* tradition must necessarily serve a beloved who exacts such sacrifice from him indefinitely and without any guarantee of reward or reciprocity. As Sanchez puts it, "Since voluntary suffering is the most persuasive evidence of love . . . only a corresponding sacrifice on the part of the beloved distinguishes the relation between friends . . . from that between master and slave"—and an erotic master/mistress is just what William's romance requires.[56] Charles II, as Cavendish represents him, performs this role perfectly and has yet to requite his servant. Throughout most of the *Life*, he is conspicuous by his absence as William serves him from afar, and their primary interactions are indeed defined by the king's "neglects." Time and again, Charles takes William's fidelity for granted while keeping him at arm's length, permitting him to live in poverty in exile, failing to repair his ruined estate, and declining to admit him into the inner circle of his government or his graces.

Importantly for my argument, Margaret Cavendish chooses to emphasize their royalist compatriots' bewilderment over William's love. His extreme selflessness is incomprehensible, even undesirable, to observers standing outside the love relationship as William has defined it, but his subjective romance for one disregards anyone too self-interested to imitate his devotion. Showing the ideological malleability of English romance, Cavendish manages to merge Hobbes's anxiety over heroic exceptionalism with Sidney's delight in exclusive erotic experience, and without recourse to Sidney's emphasis on Protestant assurance and godly community. In fact, membership in a like-minded community would diminish William, as one story shows: "My Lord entertaining one time some Gentlemen with a merry Discourse, told them, that he would not keep them Company except they had done and sufferd as much for their King and Country as he had. They answer'd, That they had not a power answerable to my Lords. My Lord replied, They should do their endeavour according to their Abilities: No, said they, if we did, we should be like your Self, lose all, and get but little for our pains" (Aaa2r, Aaa2v) The "merry Discourse" turns suddenly serious when the gentlemen acknowledge their own instincts for self-preservation and the king's apparent indifference to William's suffering. In an ingenious maneuver typical of her style in the *Life*, Cavendish manages all at once to highlight Charles's coldness, William's reckless refusal to safeguard himself, and the extraordinary heroism that exalts him far above his practical fellows, whose anti-romance calculation prevents them from attaining, or even admiring, his courtly perfection.

We eventually find that William is well aware of the singularity of his devotion and of its mystifying effect on others, despite his indifference to their objections. After Charles's restoration produces no substantial honors for the Cavendishes, William finally resolves to retire to the country to make the best of the remnants of his estate. But first, he goes to the king to seek permission and to dispel any rumors about his motives: "Sir, said he to His Majesty, I am not ignorant, that many believe I am discontented; and 'tis probable they'l say, I retire through discontent: But I take God to witness, That I am in no kind or ways displeas'd; for I am so joyed at your Majesties happy Restauration, that I cannot be sad or troubled for any Concern to my own particular; but whatsoever Your Majesty is pleased to command me, were it to sacrifice my Life, I shall most obediently perform it; for I have no other Will, but Your Majesties Pleasure" (Aa1r). With this final vow, "he kisse[s] His Majesty's hand" and departs to Nottinghamshire, where his affairs lie in ruins (Aa1r). Anticipating that court gossips will presume his lack of royal favor has bred bitterness and ill will, William reiterates that his model of love demands the *abandonment* of will, or rather the total submission of one's will to the desires of one's beloved—an act that strengthens the lover to his own sublime satisfaction even as it diminishes him in the eyes of outsiders. Having already sacrificed his assets, he would happily give infinitely more to prove that his love has no limit, and that it is too "joyed" within its own sphere to regard the incredulity of others. The subjectivity that isolates him also insulates him. Even if the historical Duke of Newcastle was "profoundly disappointed to find himself excluded from the king's inner circle," as Anna Battigelli has claimed,[57] the literary William Cavendish, as authored by his wife, thrives on this exclusion because it enables *his* exclusion of all other subjects as lesser lovers, who cannot understand his devotion because they have never "inwardly [felt] it."[58]

Cavendish must partly endorse William's model of romance in order to authenticate his heroism, but as much as her narrative glorifies his singular preference for the king above his own wife, we can easily see how royalist *fin amour* might create problems within their marriage. Whenever Margaret appears in the *Life*—sometimes as an active participant, more often as an observer and counselor—her persona reiterates the preface's skeptical distaste for using romance to interpret one's role in history. Cavendish frequently seems to insert herself into the narrative for the express purpose of serving as a counterweight, even an antagonist, to William's romance sensibilities. Despite being a prototypical consumer (and producer) of romance as a royalist woman, and despite her personal reputation, she is far from embracing the genre as a political model without serious interrogation; in fact, constructing herself as the wife of a romance hero only makes her stance more complicated. According to Sanchez, the purpose of the *Life* is "to challenge the equation of love, virtue, and sacrifice that has so damaged her husband," and we must treat this motive seriously in order to appreciate the part it plays in Cavendish's writing of what is (as I argue) her more multivalent, even paradoxical, "form of activism."[59]

Very occasionally, Margaret's cool rationality overcomes her husband's most ardent romance impulses, as when Charles has gone missing at sea and she manages to dissuade William from sailing off aimlessly to go look for him. Far more often, though, Cavendish pits Margaret's skepticism against William's romance heroism only to have the generic conventions of romance prevail—or at least, only to depict Margaret being gently chided by her husband for neglecting his ideals of honor, patience, absolute loyalty, and faith in a romance telos to the royalists' history. After detailing their poverty in exile, Cavendish stresses his enduring confidence in a happy ending to the royalist story: "In this Condition (and how little soever the appearance was) my Lord was never without hopes of seeing yet . . . a happy issue of all his misfortunes and sufferings, especially of the Restauration of His most Gracious King and Master, to His Throne . . . whereof he always had assured Hopes" (U2r, U2v). William is not merely hopeful, but "assured" that "Restauration" will come to pass. In fact, the "little appearance" of any hope for success only makes him more so, since William is a reader of romance and assumes that the same final victory that is generically inevitable must first appear to be virtually impossible. His assuredness stands in marked contrast to his wife's freely admitted doubt: "Whensoever I expressed how little faith I had in it, he would gently reprove me, saying, I believ'd least, what I desir'd most; and could never be happy if I endeavour'd to exclude all hopes, and entertain'd nothing but doubts and fears" (U2v).

From our position of hindsight after the historical Restoration, William's extraordinary faith or foresight appears entirely vindicated, but as readers in the midst of the narrative, we can easily imagine ourselves feeling Margaret's misgivings. And so when his faith comes to fruition, Cavendish allows—even encourages—us to imagine that her husband's singular romance offered him a special vision of historical narrative that his more rational wife lacked. When Margaret asks, "What kind of Fate it was, that restored our Gracious King . . . to His Throne," William gently corrects her terminology by making room for divine providence: "It was a blessed kind of Fate" (Zz2v).[60] Of course, the providential ending to the royalist romance that William has anticipated proves limited, as he himself is granted little share in the king's glorious restoration. He does, however, enjoy a humbler moment of private restoration in the text: returning home after years in exile, he experiences tavern fare as a glorious feast, "and the noise of some scraping Fidlers, he thought the pleasantest harmony that ever he had heard" (Z1r). This sublimity is soon intruded upon by the arrival of the practical Margaret, who finds his London lodgings "not fit for a Person of his Rank and Quality, nor of the capacity to contain all his Family" (Z2v). But once more, her husband "gently reprove[s] [her] for [her] rashness and impatience" and stays in the city to await his master's arrival (Z2v).

We know that William is fulfilled, having always made his happiness conditional upon the king's; but Margaret continues to struggle with her role relative to his romance for one. At times, as Sanchez argues, she uses her awkward position as a platform for interrogating and "oppos[ing] absolutism."[61] Questioning William's perception of the monarch/subject relationship as a passionate but unidirectional bond between a master and a devoted servant, Margaret declares "that I had observed Great Princes were not like the Sun, which . . . nourish[es] and comfort[s] sublunary Creatures; but [Princes'] glory . . . proceeded rather from the Ceremony which they received from their subjects" (Aaa2r). She dismisses a common defense of monarchy itself: that it mirrors the created world and is therefore both natural and divinely ordained. But William, unmoved, cherishes the astronomical analogy that Margaret rejects. *Fin amour* makes him a happy "sublunary creature" comforted by his master's sun; all "glory" flows from one source and all duty from the other, to the satisfaction of both parties and the consternation of those observing from outside the closed royal solar system. Cavendish stages this debate over royalist political philosophy without revealing a clear winner. She leaves that judgment to her readers; and the royal reader to which the text is dedicated, at least, is presumably meant to find William's position worthy and admirable.

Finally, Margaret expresses outright scorn for *fin amour* after the Restoration because of its failure to guarantee gratification for the lover, and William simply responds with enduring resolution to make it the ongoing basis of his life and service to the king: "I have heard him say several times, That his love to his gracious Master King Charles the Second, was above the love he bore to his Wife, Children, and all his Posterity, nay to his own life: And when, since His Return into England, I answer'd him, That I observed His Gracious Master did not love him so well as he lov'd Him; he replied, That he cared not whether His Majesty lov'd him again or not; for he was resolved to love him" (Zz2r). Sanchez represents this moment as Cavendish's "political protest" against a "melodramatic" and dangerous political narrative that eroticizes abjection "even in the face of betrayal," which William has "too credulously accepted."[62] This is true, but this moment of open conflict between spouses also reads as a definitive climax in which Margaret's rational victory is succeeded, and perhaps superseded, by William's emotional triumph. He already knows that his love for the king renounces expectation and defies explanation. Since "they only know it, which inwardly feel it," as the *New Arcadia* puts it, love becomes an end and a good in itself. Its virtue is only heightened by William's acceptance of his master's indifference, and his commitment to it sets him apart from and above all of Charles's more pragmatic but less heroic subjects, including his own wife. As Fitzmaurice notes, her angry cynicism "only serves to make her depiction of her husband's amiability come more to the fore."[63] We should not, though, take this as a sign of Cavendish's (or her character's) marginalization: to use Julie Crawford's formulation, this is not a case of Margaret Cavendish trying to "find a voice" and failing, but of her bid for "economic survival and socioeconomic ambition," her proffering of "criticism and advice," and her deliberate "experimentation" with genre.[64] In Cavendish's brilliant and careful political maneuver, she can protest and his romance can still prevail.

Cavendish's juxtaposition of William and Margaret's views throughout the *Life* raises an inevitable question. Is her skepticism in her intranarrative role as the hero's wife meant as a genuine critique of William's romance and of absolute devotion to the monarchy, or does she intend to magnify William's heroism in the eyes of her readers (including Charles II) by emphasizing his loyalty to his love in the face of his wife's pragmatic, rationalist temptations? The answer to this either/or question, I think, can only be yes—both. William confirms his role as the ultimate hero of the royalist romance by staying steadfast to his preeminent relationship with the king, even when his devotion yields no clear advantage and jars with his secondary duties to his secondary beloved. At the same time, Cavendish uses William's stunningly disinterested heroism as a means to protest absolutism and to advocate for his worldly interests, since he will not do so himself. Because he has sought the least, he deserves the most, and Charles's failure to bestow favor commensurate with William's "Actions and Sufferings" leaves both the king and *fin amour* as a political model open to criticism. Cavendish manages to idealize her husband's romance principles without compromising her own rational ones, combining both sets of values in an effort to perfect the narrative arc of William's romance by moving the king to the requital her husband deserves. Realpolitik and romance, often seeming opposites throughout the *Life*, finally function in mutual service to each other.

We might be able to see the legacy of William's commitment to *fin amour* in Cavendish's romance fiction. Kahn has argued that the heroines of Cavendish's romances (one of whom appears in the next chapter) embody royalist subjecthood in their unification of erotic passion and political pragmatism,[65] but in the *Life of William*, the erotics are all William's and the pragmatics are all Margaret's. Only when her rationality and his queer devotion operate in concert can the *Life of William* function, in Cavendish's terms, as a "Heroical" history that speaks on their mutual behalf. Under Kahn's formulation, as a married couple they become a unified subject. Despite Cavendish's prefatory posturing on the incompatibility of romance with historiographic and political concerns, she ultimately seems to find that a contentious marriage of rational skepticism and romance vision offers her a position of strength for negotiating her relationship to her enemies, her husband, and her king.

"MORE . . . THAN THE BEST ROMANCES DESCRIBE": PURITAN HEROISM AND GENDERED GENRE IN LUCY HUTCHINSON'S *MEMOIRS OF THE LIFE OF COLONEL HUTCHINSON*

Lucy Hutchinson—who did, in fact, compare her husband to Moses—is surely the sort of Puritan writer Margaret Cavendish had in mind when she disdained "mystical" historiography with "Romansical" overtones. For Hutchinson, the backdrop of history is a translucent screen through which the godly can witness a shadow battle between cosmic forces of good and evil. The recent civil war, she explains in her *Memoirs of the Life of Colonel Hutchinson*, is just one episode in an ongoing "spirituall combate."[66] Proposing in the *Memoirs* to situate the war within this larger narrative before returning to John Hutchinson's life, Hutchinson approaches Britain's past century with a mixture of analytical historiography and vivid literary imagination. Mary, Queen of Scots, assumes the stock role of the "wicked Queene" of "bloody lustfull temper" who menaces her Protestant rival, much as Cecropia or Duessa (fictional echoes of Mary) do in Sidney's and Spenser's romances, while Elizabeth is protected "by the good providence of God" (39, 41). Mary's son James is guilty of more than bad policy: he also nurses a "secrett designe of revenge upon the godly" after his mother's death (43). Throughout this struggle between the "children of darknesse" and the "children of light" (44), God "most miraculously order[s] providences" for the "preservation" of his chosen people (49), and the conclusion of the romance of history is never in doubt: however many battles may appear "more successfull to the devill," the war will at last "happily be decided" when "the Prince of Peace come to conclude the controversie" (281).

The *Memoirs of the Life of Colonel Hutchinson*, together with Lucy Hutchinson's brief autobiographical fragment, makes a remarkable companion piece to Cavendish's *Life of William*. David Norbrook, in his excellent overview of the relationships between the Hutchinsons and the Cavendishes (neighbors in Nottinghamshire) and between the women's heroic biographies of their husbands, notes that "it is possible that [Hutchinson] wrote the *Memoirs* in the knowledge of the Duchess's work on her husband's life . . . and that this was a spur to making her work ideologically quite distinct from Cavendish's writing."[67] Such a distinction might entail rejecting the "romantic" conceit that Pepys perceived; however, Hutchinson's engagement with romance is much more like Cavendish's than not, and reading the romance of the *Memoirs* helps us better appreciate the common ground, the contested territory, and the hard boundaries between Cavendish and Hutchinson as politically active women writing heroic historiography.

Much like Cavendish, Hutchinson disavows romance as a frivolous, culturally tarnished genre, only to return to it repeatedly as the best vehicle for conveying her subject's singular heroism. As Susan Cook observes, "She allows for the reader's knowledge of several narrative modes and manners. For example, when talking of the hard-won Puritan success at Nottingham, she writes, 'If it were a romance, one should say . . . that the heroes did it out of excesse of gallantry . . . but we are relating wonders of Providence'" (114).⁶⁸ Cook suggests that although Hutchinson's style "seems to veer naturally toward" romance, "it seems to be in opposition" to her Puritan historiographical project.⁶⁹ N. H. Keeble has claimed that Hutchinson avoids romance in the *Memoirs* because she regards it as too feminine for a text concerned with "masculine discourse: war, politics, and patriarchal religion."⁷⁰ But as we will see, not only is romance a fundamental component of Hutchinson's historiography, she at times presents it (as does Cavendish) as a man's mode with which she has a challenging relationship. Romance and providential history, which Hutchinson presents in the Nottingham episode as opposites, are often aligned in the *Memoirs*, and as Devoney Looser and others have noted, romance proves indispensable for memorializing John Hutchinson as a republican hero, a Puritan saint, and—more important than in Cavendish's *Life*—a devoted spouse.⁷¹ The romance of the *Memoirs* is again chiefly one of love: like Sidney's heroes and Spenser's Britomart, John experiences his divine calling to romance in no small part through the providential direction of his erotic life. But whereas Cavendish downplays the eroticism of marriage to focus on William's love for the king, Hutchinson struggles with the interplay between her and John's mutual passion and his even more passionate devotion to God—and the wife of the *Memoirs*, too, ultimately takes second place in her husband's heart as John increasingly pursues his heroic destiny to serve his first love. Part of Hutchinson's labor is to carve out some sense of her own heroic subjectivity as a Puritan republican wife who does not always share her husband's narrative vision of the romance of history—a harder task than Cavendish's comparable endeavor in the more secular *Life*.⁷² Like Cavendish, she writes to interrogate the idea of a personal and political life lived as romance, and her husband's assurance of the value of this model evokes her own doubt;

but unlike Cavendish, she writes ultimately to endorse right romance as a model for heroism and a vision for history—one that her republican community and she herself must strive to follow, despite its difficulty.

Hutchinson's text actually opens with an expression of female romance subjectivity. Her autobiographical fragment frames the *Memoirs* by writing Lucy, as well as John, into the plot of English history as a godly heroine who has been chosen to enter the story at just the right time. "Att the time of my birth," Hutchinson writes, the eternal conflict between darkness and light was just "working up into that tempest wherein I have shar'd many perills ... and many more mercies, consolations and preservations" (281). Being born into a historical "tempest" is a "mercy" because it positions her at a crux within the divine narrative that gives her the potential both to witness the marvelous and to perform heroic action (282). Hutchinson's account of her birth further suggests her heroic potential: her mother dreams while pregnant that she catches a falling star, which she is told "signified she should have a daughter of some extraordinary eminency" (287). Hutchinson moves to diminish this startling claim by suggesting that the dream, "like such vaine prophecies, wrought as farre as it could its own accomplishment" in the form of her parents' special indulgence (287). Her introduction of herself as a potential heroine surrounded by the romance tropes of tempests and prophetic signs, in tandem with her disclaimer that such motifs are "vaine" and silly, characterizes her hybrid historiography.

Thrilling as Hutchinson's militant assertion of her own heroic agency is, like Spenser's Britomart she eventually becomes compelled to reconcile it to widowhood and tragedy, and the ambiguous promise of prophecy is challenged by the appearance of a more assured romance subjectivity.[73] Her account of her life breaks off while she is still a child, and the bulk of her life writing celebrates the heroism of her husband, grounded primarily in his assured narrative vision of history, not in a mother's "vaine" dream. John Hutchinson, too, is marked by marvels in infancy: "flung" from a runaway carriage, the baby is saved "by the good providence of God," which "reserv[es]" him for "a more glorious death" as a champion of the godly (21).[74] His life continues to be secured by providence in his adulthood, to the point that he comforts himself after the Restoration that "the Lord had not thus eminently preserv'd him for nothing, but that he was yett kept for some eminent service" for the "Good Old Cause" of republicanism (234). John matures into a man whose physical beauty (gorgeously detailed in a striking blazon) is enhanced by the indefinable allure that so many heroes of romance possess: his "countenance ... carried in it something of magnanimity and majesty mixt with sweetenesse, that ... bespoke love and awe in all that saw him" (3).[75] This special "something" aids him even on the plane of "spirituall combate": "So were all the children of darknesse convinc'd by his light that they were in awe more of his vertue than his authority" (206). As soon as John—like his wife, apparently a believer in both divine election and double predestination—attains assurance that God "ha[s] bene pleas'd to chuse him out of the corrupted masse of lost mankind," he resolves to enter public life, incensed at the injustices endured by his godly countrymen (35). Notably, Hutchinson separates her accounts of her husband's religious calling and his parliamentary debut with "a short digression from our particular actions" to her history of Protestant England (37), but this separation also creates an important link: John's private, subjective assurance of his election heralds his public activity and his commitment to stand with the "children of light" in the unfolding providential narrative in which he is now a chosen hero.[76] Like Sidney's princes or Spenser's knights, he has been called to challenge tyrants and to defend truth, and his election is of a piece with his heroic subjectivity.

At the core of his romance, though, we encounter not combat, but love. Concluding her account of the pair's courtship, Hutchinson tells us she has left much unsaid: "I shall passe by all the little amorous relations, which if I would take the paynes to relate, would make a true history of a more handsome management of love than the best romances describe; for these are to be forgotten as the vanities of youth, not worthy mention among the greater transactions of his life" (32). Her comment again blends Puritan sobriety with authorial coyness: of course erotic romance is a worldly vanity "not worthy" of the Colonel's "greater" heroism, and yet if we knew all that she could tell us, we would see that John Hutchinson is as perfect an erotic hero as a martial one. But Hutchinson is being disingenuous in her claim that she will "passe by" romance here: her story of the courtship has already lasted several pages by the time she makes her disclaimer, and it has indulged in plenty of romance conventions. It begins by mentioning the unfit lovers whom John has avoided: predestined for a bride who shares his spiritual nobility, he steers clear of the "fine snares" of "vaine weomen" hoping to "entangle" him (28). Hutchinson insists that John remains providentially ordained for the right kind of eroticism: "Wealth and beauty thus in vaine tempted him, for it was not yett his time of love; but it was not farre off" (26). Narrative suspense builds as we foresee an approaching destiny of which the hero remains ignorant; in this Puritan descendant of Sidney and Spenser's reformations of erotic romance, the elect hero's elect beloved will soon produce an interior effect in him that no other woman could.

Hutchinson's Puritan romance even reclaims magic, as John's travels take him to a house marked by a mysterious blessing or curse: according to local legend, it is a place "so fatall for love that never any young disengag'd person went thither who return'd againe free," but John only "laugh[s]" at this fantasy (27). As readers are likely to intuit and as Julie Eckerle has noted, "a combination of pride and scorn for love is the downfall of many a romance hero, and so it is" for John Hutchinson.[77] The magic begins to work when he discovers some books belonging to a lady called Lucy, who is currently not at home. Like some particularly precocious lovers (including Sidney's Pyrocles and Spenser's Britomart), John appears to fall in love *before* first sight, and Hutchinson unfolds his virtuous passion in a sequence that echoes Sidney's accounts of love's inexorable progress. "He began first to be sorrie she was gone before he had seene her . . . then he grew to love to heare mention of her"; when told of Lucy's supposedly unfeminine "reserv'd and studious" manner and her poetic talent, "it so much enflam'd Mr. Hutchinson's desire of seeing her that he began to wonder at himselfe that his heart, which had ever had such an indifferency for the most excellent of weomenkind, should have so strong impulses towards a stranger he never saw" (28–29). When he is given the false impression that Lucy has married another suitor, the critical moment of transformation by love is upon him: "Mr. Hutchinson immediately turn'd pale as ashes, and felt a fainting to seize his spiritts . . . the distemper of his mind had infected his body with a cold sweate and such a dispersion of spiritt that all the courage he could at present recollect was little enough to keepe him allive" (30). Despite his pride in his godly rationalism, John now "remember'd the story was told him when he came downe, and began to believe there was some magick in the place which enchanted men" (30).

But Hutchinson is careful to remind us that magic cannot be the first cause of the love story in the *Memoirs*. In a "light person" not granted John's elect heroism, she suggests, such "an extravagant perplexity of soule" over love would not be "admirable"; in him, though, it signifies the inward "effect of a miraculous power of providence, leading him to her that was destin'd to make his future joy" (30).[78] God's election legitimizes John's half-ironic realization that his life has become a romance; and when Lucy finally arrives, she partakes in this heroic subjectivity and takes her place with countless heroines of medieval romance, "surpriz'd with some unusuall liking in her soule" at first sight of John despite her parallel history of "indifferency" toward other men (31).[79] As the author of their romance, God has chosen them for himself and for each other. Only now does Hutchinson elide the rest of their courtship, barring her readers from the intimate details that surpass "the best romances" and adding "only this": "That never was there a passion more ardent and lesse idolatrous; he loved her better than his life, with unexpressable tendernesse and kindnesse, had a most high oblieging esteeme of her, yet still considerd honour, religion, and duty above her" (32).

This final qualification, which may seem a pious afterthought to Hutchinson's passionate and entertaining account, points to the heart of her testimony to John's Puritan heroism and introduces us to important tensions in the genre of the *Memoirs* and between husband and wife. Much as William Cavendish's idealized representation as a royalist hero stems from his absolute devotion to his master in lieu of his wife or his own interests, John Hutchinson emerges as the right hero for a godly republic because, for all his ardor for Lucy, "he lov[es] God above her" (10).[80] If he possesses such a sincere attachment to the "little amorous relations" of his marriage, which are already better "than the best romances," then his willingness to subordinate them to the greater romance of providential history becomes all the more heroic—much as Spenser's Redcrosse and Britomart embody Protestant heroism only once they learn first to surrender their human plots to the divine plot, and then to integrate them. Crucially, John is granted Redcrosse's narrative prospect that enables him to glimpse God's glorious end—the assured visionary gift that Britomart, Fulke Greville, Margaret Cavendish, and eventually Lucy Hutchinson perceive they lack. Also paralleling Greville's Sidney, who can see the "universall prospect" of the Christian world from a mental "pinnacle," John is "led up to see" a "soule-refreshing view" in his mind's eye of "the promis'd land . . . as made him forget on what side of the river he stood, while by faith he tooke possession of future glory, and resign'd himselfe in the assured hope of returning with the Lord and his greate Armie of Saints" (36). In hard times, John often tries to comfort his wife with this vision, while Lucy must rely on his mediated testimony and her dubious hope as she navigates between the triumphant romance of God's elect and her tragic personal loss.[81]

The tone of the *Memoirs* shifts once Hutchinson has concluded the romance of John's amorous adventures with his happy marriage to Lucy: the rest tells of the Colonel's devotion not to his wife, but to his nation and his God. The theme of the hero's "actions and sufferings" becomes a refrain in the *Memoirs* as in Cavendish's *Life*, and again, heroic action must be redefined to incorporate heroic sufferance once the subject's personal and political hopes are frustrated. Fortunately for John Hutchinson, like his royalist counterpart, he "ever [has] most vigor and chearefullnesse" when he has the most pain to endure (202). In a plot structure reminiscent of the *New Arcadia*, John's military heroism must yield to patience during his postwar imprisonment. Once the Restoration dashes the republicans' hopes he vows, with romance rhetoric resembling William Cavendish's, that having "made shipwrack of all things but a good conscience," "if the sacrifice of him might conduce to the publick peace . . . he should freely submit his life and fortunes to their dispose" (228). But as John grows increasingly committed to living a romance, even if that means giving his life for its end, Lucy increasingly sinks into Fulke Greville's impression that the hero's magnanimity must end in tragedy.

The Lucy of the *Memoirs* is forced into a position strikingly like Margaret's in the *Life of William*: as her husband's secondary love, she shares in many of his "actions and sufferings" for God and country, yet often finds herself standing, sometimes defiantly, between him and his heroic calling. Realizing that John is "ambitious of being a publick sacrifice," Lucy "herein only in her whole life, resolv[es] to disobey him": she forges an affidavit in his name to beg pardon for his role in the regicide (229).[82] The letter temporarily has the right effect on the judges, but an adverse one on John and on their marriage: "His wife, who thought she had never deserv'd so well of him . . . never displeas'd him more in her life, and had much adoe to perswade him to be contented with his deliverance. . . . But being by her convinc'd that God's eminent appearance seem'd to have singled him out for preservation, he with thankes acquiesced . . . and beg'd humbly of God to enlighten him" (234). The Colonel can never be "contented" to put his life or his wife before God, although insofar as Lucy can persuade him that her design accords with the divine narrative, he accepts it while remaining watchful for the proper providential occasion for his "eminent" action. And when he is taken back into custody, he (again like William Cavendish) admonishes his wife for doubting that their present misfortunes conceal a providential telos: "Mrs. Hutchinson was exceedingly sad, but he encourag'd and kindly chid her out of it . . . and told her if she had but patience to waite the event, she would see it all for the best" (249).

Confident in his private narrative vision that his own story and the story of England as a godly state are inextricably interlaced, John points Lucy to evidence both of his own elect status and of the predestined triumph of the elect nation. The combination of his high spirits and his low station are a sure sign of the glory to come, "for if he had flourisht while all the people of God were corrected, he should have fear'd he had not bene accounted among his children" (265). Again, John's assurance of his election is connected to his heroic subjectivity and his solidarity with the community of the godly; if his story lacked romance structure, complete with loss and sorrow, he would not know he was one of the chosen. He is equally sure that the romance of the "children of light," which necessitates their trials, must conclude with the triumph of their cause:

> He gave her reasons why she should hope and be assur'd that this cause would revive, because the interest of God was so much involv'd in it. . . . She told him she did not doubt but the cause would revive. "But," sayd she, "notwithstanding all your resolution, I know this will conquer the weaknesse of your constitution, and you will die in prison." He replied, "I thinke I shall not; but if I doe, my blood will be so innocent I shall advance the cause more by my death, hasting the vengeance of God upon my unjust enemies, than I could doe by all the actions of my life." (264)

Lucy has faith enough not to reject John's testimony that the Puritans' story will end well, but she doubts his conviction that the plot of his own life is so bound to it that even his death would spur its progress, for England's and his own heroic glory. Struggling to reconcile long-form communal romance to imminent personal tragedy, she is "a little" encouraged, but "her devining heart," which possesses its own generic foresight, is "not to be comforted" (249).

As the *Memoirs* and John Hutchinson's life approach their respective ends, the subjective and generic distance between husband and wife increases. While Lucy grows all the more miserable in her "horrible toyle" for John's material welfare, John grows all the more happy in his long-deferred fulfillment of his spiritual destiny, "never more pleasant and contented in his whole life" (264). His death in prison, foreseen by Lucy, concludes her tragedy while cementing his romance. While ill, he finds himself "incomparably well, and full of faith" as his "continuall study of the Scriptures did infinitely ravish his soule": his eroticized love of God detaches from the youthful sexual passion that prefigured it (270–71). His final thoughts of his absent wife convey wistful sympathy without descending to grief or disrupting his pristine contentment: "When some nam'd Mrs. Hutchinson, [he] sayd, 'Alas, how will she be surpriz'd!' He fetched a sigh, and within a little while departed, his countenance settling so amiably and cheerfully in death that he lookt after he was dead as he us'd to do when he was best pleas'd in life" (272).

Like Cavendish, Hutchinson is committed to the sincere glorification of her husband's romance heroism even as she simultaneously invites her readers' sympathy, and perhaps their anger, over her own story's tragic end. But while Cavendish declines to prioritize either William's romance or Margaret's rationality and makes political hay of the generic hodgepodge that results, Hutchinson suggests that her struggle to read and write John's life in a spirit of fidelity to his narrative vision is symptomatic of her own weakness in devotion, both to John and to God. And so Hutchinson the writer strives to perform and encourage an assuredness of providential romance that Lucy the character could not achieve, and her prefatory note invokes a faithful community that Lucy seems unable to perceive in the body of the text. Chastising herself for her tendency to become mired in the "amorous relations" that John could enjoy yet subordinate, and for her difficulty in following his example of putting God before all other loves, she bestows on her children and her community both the *Memoirs* and the task of remaining "united" in carrying on John Hutchinson's quest:

> Let not excesse of love and delight in the streame make us forgett the fountaine: he and all his excellencies came from God, and flow'd back into their owne spring. There lett us seeke them, thither lett us hasten after him.... Our conjunction, if wee had any with him, was undissoluble; if wee were knitt together by one spiritt into one body of Christ, wee are so still; if wee were mutually united in one love of God, good men, and goodnesse, wee are so still. What is it

then we waile in his remoove? The distance? Faithlesse fooles! 'tis sorrow only makes it. (3)

Rather than spend the rest of her life indulging in her tragic loss, Hutchinson presses herself and her audience to regard John's death—and the decline of his political cause—as the middle, not the end, of the communal history of "God, good men, and goodnesse." The genre of the text shifts again, from tragedy back to a form of romance higher than the narrative of their marriage. In order to accomplish this reascent, however, Hutchinson must perform a heroic labor akin to Britomart's in *The Faerie Queene*: she must fight (and write) for the cause, despite her personal loss of the love that is so central to her individual romance story, and she must accept another's vision of history in the absence of any revelation of her own personal "soule-refreshing view."

John Hutchinson has valiantly fulfilled his role in the romance of his temporal and spiritual family and has risen above it, and now serves as a guide to those who must continue to live and progress within it: "Wee may mourne . . . that wee want his guide and assistance in our way; and yett, if our teares did not putt our our eies, wee should see him, even in heaven, holding forth his flaming lamp of vertuous examples and precepts to light us through the darke world" (3). To fcllow the example of John's heroism is to further advance the narrative of the elect, as he anticipated before his death, while to "persue [the] sad remembrance" of it is to "ramble into an inextricable wildernesse"—an anti-teleological, pseudo-romance substitute for the romance of providence (63). Yet this exhortation contrasts sharply with the eerie wandering that Hutchinson imagines for Lucy at the very end of the *Memoirs*: "The spring after [his death] there came [to the prison] an apparition of a gentlewoman in mourning, in such a habitt as Mrs. Hutchinson us'd to weare there . . . and was often seene walking in the Colonell's chamber" (277). While still alive, Hutchinson suggests that Lucy has become a ghost who haunts her beloved husband's cell.[83] This final literary fancy blends the supernatural elements of romance with the perturbed spirits of tragedy while leaving the author-narrator of the *Memoirs* not quite unified with her character and not quite consistent on the matter of the genre of history. Perhaps more than anything else, she recalls Spenser's paradoxical position in the final pages of *The Faerie Queene*, striving to keep writing and insisting that the ship of his romance "Still winneth way" while evoking, with that very image, Britomart's "feeble barke" adrift on a "sea of sorrow," the "Sabaoths sight" in his prayers but not in his possession (6.12.1, 3.4.8, 7.8.2). Hutchinson's labor to reconcile the romance of the elect with the tragic experiences that befall them, and to represent a heroic subjectivity for male and female "children of light" with equal potential for faithful submission and assured vision, would prove to be an ongoing project in her epic *Order and Disorder*.

CHAPTER 3

The Fall and the Pinnacle

Milton's Righting of Romance in Paradise Lost *and* Paradise Regained

The fact that both Puritans and royalists could believe that Spenser's allegorical romance spoke for their community's cause and that Sidney was their ancestral champion—and the ease with which both Cavendish and Hutchinson could sneer at romance as their enemies' hobbyhorse before embracing it as a strategy for representing their husbands' heroism—confirm Sidney's sixteenth-century hope and Hobbes's seventeenth-century fear that romance was protean and subversive, all the more powerful for the conviction it enabled. Hobbes was not alone in his mid-century anxiety: although post-Regicide royalists and post-Restoration republicans continued their battle for romance as a genre that could accommodate and explain both heroic victories and crushing disappointments, this competition grew increasingly self-conscious. Both communities were aware that the generic conflict, and the easily manipulated subjectivity that occasioned it, needed to be faced and wrestled with. In Sir Percy Herbert's postwar royalist romance *The Princess Cloria*, the beleaguered king Euarchus articulates the problem of romance subjectivity run amok when he wonders "what assurances" he and his allies can possibly have of their own heroism "when every one pretends to be in the right, both in his belief and proceedings?"[1]

Many writers did not, however, assume along with Hobbes that the best answer was to reject romance. Instead, their works became less invested solely in individual and communal faith in providential favor—the sort of unfalsifiable certainty that disturbed Hobbes—and more concerned with how a narrative's protagonists might negotiate between belief and uncertainty, and between the hope of future success and the present realities of delay, contingency, and failure. The trials Cavendish and Hutchinson faced in navigating between their husbands' romance visions and their own doubts proved, in other mid-century texts, to be the very essence of romance. This chapter explores the ongoing, increasingly metageneric ideological struggle, with particular emphasis on John Milton's turning (back) to romance in his post-Restoration poems—for while royalists are well-known for their enduring engagement with the genre, Milton is broadly considered to have forsaken it in frustration as his career progressed.

"FREE AND GENTLE SPIRITS": MILTON'S IDEA OF ROMANCE AND ELECT COMMUNITY

The young Milton's love for romance is a matter of record. In his 1642 anti-episcopal pamphlet *An Apology for Smectymnuus*, he credits his moral education to his fanciful reading, recalling how his "younger feet wandered . . . among those lofty fables and romances, which recount in solemn cantos the deeds of knighthood."[2] His youthful tastes figure prominently in his masque *Comus* and throughout his later prose.[3] *Areopagitica* features the chivalric metaphor of "the true warfaring Christian" and his quest for Truth, and praises "our sage and serious Poet Spenser" as a master teacher.[4] The allegorical search for truth reappears in *Of Education*, and Spenserian and folk romance imagery features even in the *Doctrine and Discipline of Divorce*, where Milton again envisions history as a heroic narrative in which chosen protagonists defend Truth from "serpentine" error: at select times, God "calls together the prudent and religious counsels of men . . . to be the sole advocate[s] of a discountenanced truth: . . . a high enterprise and a hard, and such as every seventh son of a seventh son does not venture on."[5]

But as political tensions escalated, and as his enemies increasingly defined royalist heroism and history through the language and structure of romance, Milton's youthful enthusiasm for the genre quickly seemed to cool. In his 1650 *Eikonoklastes*, Milton denounces romance as an ungodly, insincere tool with which Charles I and his followers manipulate popular sentiment. Milton's polemic excoriates the royalists' propagandistic, and brilliantly successful, *Eikon Basilike* for attributing to Charles a seemingly heartfelt prayer that was in fact plagiarized from "no serious book, but the vain amatorious poem of Sir Philip Sidney's *Arcadia*—a book in that kind full of worth and wit, but among religious thoughts and duties not worthy to be named."[6] If he is filching prayers from romances, the king must be more slavishly devoted to the "sweet rhapsodies of heathenism and knight-errantry" than to his people's God.[7] Milton was clearly familiar enough with Sidney's *New Arcadia* to recognize a passage cribbed from it,[8] but if the royalists were now claiming Sidney for their own in a war of arms and ideas, he was compelled to disdain the book as witty enough (for a romance), but otherwise "not worthy." The religious zeal and romance rhetoric that often fit hand in glove in Milton's earlier writing appeared to become incompatible.

Eikonoklastes is often regarded as Milton's last word on romance. While a few Miltonists (most recently Colin Lahive) have suggested that he remained committed to the genre's godly potential,[9] more have judged that its royalist associations overshadowed his enthusiasm, and that his distaste for it spread into his later epics, *Paradise Lost* and *Paradise Regained*. George Williamson finds that Milton ultimately rejected romance as too Cavalier; Stanley Fish and Regina Schwartz both propose that Milton was ideologically motivated to abandon genre altogether, in favor of a poetics of divine temporality that resisted conventional narrative; and David Loewenstein and Luke Taylor suggest that crushing political disappointment left Milton jaded about optimistic genres after the Restoration.[10] Annabel Patterson and others make the crucial point that both positive and negative views of romance seem to coexist in Milton's late poetry, but nearly all conclude that Milton saw something about the genre as finally and fundamentally fallen: that its usurpation by the royalists led to "his sense that the romantic mode, cultural or political, was irretrievably spoiled."[11]

Scholars who argue for Milton's break with romance overwhelmingly cite its associations with royalist ideology as his primary reason for rejecting it.[12] However, historicist critics have often put too much stock in romance's being an obviously royalist genre, as Nigel Smith and Amelia Zurcher have pointed out,[13] and Lahive has shown that Milton "was not seen by early readers to be rejecting romance but using it in his imagined representation of the biblical narrative."[14] Finally, we must keep in mind that even the young

Milton had, unsurprisingly, his own idiosyncratic sense of what romance meant for him. Defending both his sexual morality and his reading habits in the *Apology for Smectymnuus*, Milton claims that tales of knighthood taught him "that every free and gentle spirit, without that oath, ought to be born a knight, nor needed to expect the gilt spur, or the laying of a sword upon his shoulder to stir him up . . . to secure and protect the weakness of any attempted chastity."[15] Milton identifies romance, while often predicated on love and desire, as the genre that teaches chastity and virtue—at least, to "free and gentle spirit[s]," an ambiguous class of people who are somehow born knights, never needing to be so appointed by any earthly king. Like Sidney, Milton indicates that those called to resist unrighteousness in the world are also those endowed with the ability to read romance right, and to identify with the subjectivity of its heroes.

"Free and gentle" are themselves words with a rich romance heritage and a significant range of meaning in medieval through Miltonic English. In Chaucer's day, "free" meant noble by birth and conduct—the practical freedom of landed gentry that supposedly correlated with courtesy and generosity.[16] When Milton refers to freedom of the spirit, his radical rhetoric of personal liberty is rooted in the fancied medieval freedom of the elite few to live life as romance. Following Sidney, Milton originates from a Jamesonian premise of romance as conservative, then revolutionizes it. We are more familiar today with "gentle" as a socioeconomic marker, though its slippage into an ethical sense is old: the fairy woman of the *Wife of Bath's Tale* admonishes the snobbish knight that "gentillesse" comes not from birth but from "vertuous lyvyng" and the imitation of Christ (1122). In the *Doctrine and Discipline of Divorce*, Milton returns to the notion of an innately gentle spirit when he conflates the ability to charitably interpret scripture with the capacity to feel "true" erotic love: someone who insists that Christ forbade divorce to couples who cannot love each other, he insists, did "never know or feel what it is to love truly. . . . There is none that can estimate the evil and the affliction of a naturall hatred in matrimony, unlesse he have a soul gentle anough and spacious anough to contemplate what is true love."[17] For Milton, as for Sidney's Pyrocles, the subjective knowledge of true love is a gift granted only to some, and with it comes the hero's privilege of pursuing love's commands and the knight's responsibility to be, like Spenser's Redcrosse, "sole advocate of a discountenanced truth." Others with "soul[s] gentle anough" will approve and join the quest, but Milton assumes that this radical romance community is small, "such as every seventh son of a seventh son does not venture" into.

Milton's expression that he wrote *Paradise Lost* for an audience "fit . . . though few" is famous (7.31), and it seems sensible to associate this readership with the "free and gentle" right readers and self-identified knights of the much older *Apology* and the "gentle" souls who are given to understand both scripture and true love. The "fit . . . though few" also appears to echo the Father's heterodox three-pronged theology of election in book 3:

> Some I have chosen of peculiar grace
> Elect above the rest; so is my will:
> The rest shall hear me call, and oft be warnd
> Thir sinful state. . . .
> And I will place within them as a guide
> My Umpire Conscience, whom if they will hear,
> Light after light well us'd they shall attain,
> And to the end persisting, safe arrive.
> This my long sufferance and my day of grace
> They who neglect and scorn, shall never taste;
> But hard be hard'nd, blind be blinded more,
> That they may stumble on, and deeper fall;
> And none but such from mercy I exclude. (3.183–202)

Scholars like Dennis Danielson, Stephen Fallon, and Debora Shuger have worked to unpack Milton's idiosyncratic understanding of election in these lines.[18] Most important for us are the first two: although God grants the possibility of salvation to all, and ensures the "safe arriv[al]" of all who heed the voice of "Conscience," he has also "chosen" for "Some" to be "Elect above the rest." If this group is not distinguished by their sole salvation, which is bestowed far more broadly, then what makes them special? God does not say, except that they are beneficiaries of "peculiar grace." Fallon proposes that Milton's idea of an extra-elect speaks to his pathological "need to be outstanding in as many ways as possible."[19] The diagnosis may be fair, but I suggest that Milton really only ever saw one way of being outstanding "from among the general run of souls," a way simultaneously spiritual, intellectual, moral, and literary.[20] To be "Elect above the rest" means to be a "free and gentle spirit" who feels, alike in reading romance or scripture, that he has been "borne a Knight"—of chastity, of love, of truth, of liberty—and must dedicate his life to his God-given subjective vocation. It means to identify with Virtue's "true Servants" in *Comus* who eschew "frail and feverish" common lives in favor of a quest for "that Golden Key / That opes the Palace of Eternity" (8–14).[21] It means membership in a community of the "fit ... though few" who possess the "peculiar grace" to read in the right way.

Milton shares with many of his predecessors and contemporaries the sense that romance belongs to a fellowship, perhaps divinely appointed to stand "above the rest," who feel more deeply, seek truth more purely, and see the narrative arcs of politics and history more clearly. I argue that his career sustains a commitment to romance for an elect community defined partly in opposition to those who would "kidnap" romance, to use Frye's term, for unfree ends.[22] Rather than trusting these polemics for Milton's final word on the genre, we might look to his greatest poetry instead. Romance as a Puritan literary mode is very much alive in *Paradise Lost*, and especially in *Paradise Regained*, despite aspects of these texts that appear anti-romantic. In fact, Milton may actually have found romance *more* useful to his ideology, not less, after 1660.

Milton's late poems contain both positive and negative gestures toward romance not because of his ambivalence, but because they embody a struggle between an ungodly, implicitly royalist perversion of the mode and a more sincerely romantic Puritan alternative. This struggle is concerned less with the early Caroline approaches to romance cited by Patterson than with the much more recent royalist romances and semi-historical romans à clef of the 1650s and 1660s. While these texts retained many of the genre's tropes, featuring the meandering adventures and hardships of exiled aristocrats, they made substantial revisions to structural premises such as providential plot. As Paul Salzman and Victoria Kahn have shown, although the restoration of Charles II seemed to align history with romance's common theme of royal dispossession and recovery, the king's supporters were disturbed enough by the upheaval of the Interregnum that their treatment of the genre was irrevocably altered, haunted by historical contingency and the instability of heroic subjectivity.[23] In this chapter, Herbert's *The Princess Cloria* and Margaret Cavendish's postwar prose romance *Assaulted and Pursued Chastity* will exemplify the royalist revisions that Milton counters with his own reassertions of Puritan romance. We will then turn to three of Milton's poetic perspectives on historical time, narrative, and genre, ordered by their chronology within Christian history: first *Paradise Lost*, followed by the early but fundamental *Nativity Ode*, and concluding with Milton's truly final word on romance, *Paradise Regained*.

WORLDS WITHIN ONESELF: ROYALIST ROMANCES OF PRAGMATIC PROVIDENCE

The unique structural characteristics of postwar royalist fiction have been well characterized by Salzman, whose analysis begins to reveal much about the most immediate romance backdrop to Milton's 1671 poem. Salzman argues that the royalist narratives reacting to the demise of Charles I and the eventual return of Charles II fundamentally revise several assumptions about the narrative structure and didactic goals of the genre. Postwar royalist romances thrive on ambiguity instead of absolutes, offering their readers "questions rather than answers" about the nature of providence and heroic virtue.[24] Their dispossessed and disillusioned characters wonder about the extent of God's role in human events and hence about their own responsibilities, unsure whether to interpret the tempest of history as a divinely structured plot or a series of contingencies dependent on the interaction of individual agency with uncontrollable fortune. As Smith, Kahn, and others have discussed, the writers of such romances were engaging directly not just with their ideological opponents, but with the anti-romance political philosophy of their fellow royalist Hobbes, who was particularly alarmed by the genre's chaotic potential to convince anyone of his or her special status as a hero ordained and justified by providential decree.[25] Instead of shunning romance altogether, some royalist writers set out to attempt a quasi-Hobbesian variant. In denying the certainty of providential authorship and of any divine source of heroic subjectivity, they continued to combat Puritan theology while confronting their own doubts; in acknowledging the remoteness or silence of a heavenly authority, they continued to resist republicanism by insisting on the need for a heroic earthly authority to provide for the common good by determining and imposing the most effective political and narrative order.

Herbert's *The Princess Cloria*, a coded roman à clef begun in exile during the 1650s and printed in England after the Restoration, epitomizes the royalist revision of romance in its self-conscious anxiety over heroic subjectivity and providential narrative structure.[26] As Salzman has noted,

Cloria's protagonists are not atheists, but they continually question "whether [divine] power [has] any consideration or regard to our actions" (361). Prince Arethusius (Herbert's figure for Charles II) finds himself so stymied by the machinations of religious zealots that he sometimes doubts religion's value and purpose: "Scarce can it be believed, there are any Gods in Heaven, or at the most that minde our actions upon earth" (463). Throughout the narrative, characters flirt with the conclusion that "either [the Gods'] Justice or [their] Power" must be lacking (555). Herbert does introduce other sympathetic figures who offer pious consolation to the heroes, such as the priest Hephestion, who advises that ignorant humans must "observe ... continually, both a perfect charity, and an entire patience" (320). These have the sound of Milton's favorite virtues, but unlike most of Milton's heroes, the inhabitants of *Cloria* fear that they may be practicing them in a vacuum, valuing patience for its own sake rather than as the expectation of the fulfillment of providential order. In the context of Hephestion's advice, "perfect charity" and "entire patience" are tools for survival in a world without assurances; they seem more like the armor of resignation than the weapons of faith.

Herbert's characters express unresolvable doubt and discomfort about how providence ought to be understood as a force operating within history. Locrinus conflates divine providence with an impersonal "predominate fate" that has used the "strange period" of civil war "for the punishing of wickedness" (539–40). While Arethusius might conceivably trust in providence to eventually reward righteousness rather than dispassionately punish evil, he instead grounds his hope that he may one day regain the throne in "the instability of things," or the vague vicissitudes of time, which "would of necessity at last bring him to his Rights" (445). Not God, but Arethusius's subjects, awash in cosmic uncertainty, will ultimately depend on a mortal monarch to restore (or impose) order, much as Hobbes's political philosophy prescribes. Salzman notes that Arethusius's ultimate return to power is made retroactively "inevitable" by the historical fact of Charles II's restoration and is then "gladly embraced by fiction"—that is, history happens to have conformed to romance's conventional shape—but Herbert's king's happy ending is not obviously the work of any providential power internal to his story.[27]

As an inhabitant of a formulaic genre that nevertheless acknowledges no providential formula, the romance hero Arethusius ironically arrives at a personal philosophy that embraces many of Hobbes's most anti-romance principles. He finally finds comfort in his stoical avowal that "man was a world within him self, being not to be deprived of an inward felicity by any power or tyranny, if he proved not the destroyer thereof by his own passions" (416). Much as Hephestion's "perfect charity" and "entire patience" resemble Miltonic virtues but prove different, Arethusius's "world within him self" might sound like Milton's "Paradise within" (12.587), but it is not. In *Cloria*'s universe, which might be ruled by a cold providence, "predominate fate," or atomistic chance—or some vague combination of these—Arethusius must weather the tempest of history through clear-eyed self-reliance, not through faith in the unseen. He turns inward not for divine guidance, but because his only certain reference is himself, and his own judgment leads him to a pragmatic philosophy in which one's outward actions may not match one's inner idea of heroism: in order to be an effective ruler, Arethusius resolves, "sometimes we must dissemble towards people. . . . I cannot deny it" (392). He comes to the Hobbesian conclusion that while his duty as king compels him to act for the good of his kingdom, he has no external "assurances" about the right course of action, and so the nature of that public good, and the substance of that action, must be his to determine as best he can. By acknowledging the instability of romance and the self-imposed nature of heroic subjectivity, he is free to take control of the navigation of his story while also benevolently controlling others.

Margaret Cavendish's style of romance, while less melancholy than Herbert's *Cloria* and less overtly historically coded, luxuriates in subjective inner worlds as sources of consolation and delight. The conclusion to her romance of science and invention, *The Blazing World*, celebrates the author's absolute monarchy over "the Worlds I have made" and urges readers to turn to their own "Minds, Fancies, or Imaginations" to "create Worlds of their own, and Govern themselves as they please."[28] Cavendish shares Herbert's principle of wariness about crediting a narrative plan to divine providence and places similar emphasis on politic pragmatism and self-reliance. As we have seen in her *Life of William*, Cavendish deeply mistrusts any human claim to know the mind of God, associating such assertions with her Puritan enemies.[29] In her *Philosophical Letters*, she derides those who claim to hold "the Key of Divine Providence": "I believe God did never give or lend it to any man; for surely, God, who is infinitely Wise, would never intrust so frail and foolish a Creature as Man, with it, as to let him know his secret Counsels, Acts, and Decrees. But setting aside Pride and Presumption, Sense and Reason may easily perceive, that Man ... is not made with such infinite Excellence, as to pierce into the least secrets of God; Wherefore I am in a maze when I hear of such men, which pretend to know so much."[30] Cavendish strips such dangerous presumption from her definition of providence in *The World's Olio* as the *human* ability "to observe the Effect of Things, and to compare the past with the present, as to guess, and so to provide for the Future."[31] In the *Life of William*, Cavendish disdains the Puritans' vision of history as a narrative authored by God's providence, in which heroism belongs exclusively to the godly; in her own romances, she releases herself from accountability to William's model of the genre and holds her most fanciful narratives to the standards of rational historiography and natural philosophy. Her fictions reformulate romance's reliance on providential plot: as in *The World's Olio*, providence signifies not God's design for human affairs, but characters' potential to provide for themselves, to reason and act in order to chart their own future, rather than attempting to strain for a glimpse of a sacred narrative vision that might explain their random circumstances. Rather than inhabiting a preexisting, predestined narrative, they create their own narratives out of apparent chaos.

In Cavendish's 1656 *Assaulted and Pursued Chastity*, both heroine and narrator regard human providence as their guiding principle. "Travellia" (the self-appellation she keeps longest) is abandoned by an unscrupulous guardian "to Chance, Time, and Fortune."[32] The lady set adrift on fortune's tide is a common trope in early modern, medieval, and classical romance, but her destiny is usually safely controlled by providential forces. Travellia, however, must provide for her own ends. While she and other characters occasionally refer to the gods, she presumes no knowledge of how they influence human life, apart from her belief that Heaven helps those who help themselves. Upon "considering" her "dangerous condition" at finding her virginity for sale in a brothel, Travellia reflects "that the Gods would not hear her, if she lasily called for help and watch'd for Miracles neglecting Naturall means," so she resolves to escape "and trust herself againe to chance; by reason there could not be more danger than where she was in" (Ff3r). While Travellia never rejects outright the potential for miracles, she determines that there is neither logic nor virtue in expecting one to save her now. Divine providence, in her experience, can only be mediated through pragmatic human providence, and so she turns to "Naturall means" and judges future contingencies less dangerous than the certainties of the present.

Yet, while she often acknowledges the roles of "Chance" and "Fortune" in aiding or frustrating mortal endeavors, Travellia leaves as little as possible to their random disposal. Most notably, she gets ahold of a gun by exploiting a servant's romance-reading imagination, concocting a parodic story about the prophecy of a "wise Wizard" to justify her request for it, then hides it in anticipation of future need and eventually uses it to shoot her would-be rapist (Ff3v). Although she deceives the "simple Wench" by pretending that the gun can perform a supernatural charm to protect her from evil, its purpose in Cavendish's rational narrative—as opposed to Travellia's opportunistically fanciful one—is comically naturalistic (Ff3v). Neither the gun nor her escape come to Travellia miraculously or by happenstance; she provides both for herself. And while she harbors a Hobbesian disdain for romance as full of "impossibilities . . . ridiculous to reason" (despite inhabiting one herself),[33] she is well aware of the genre's power to manipulate others' passions—a power she exploits to further her own rational romance (Ff4v).[34]

Like her fictional heroine, the authorial Cavendish's narrative vision for *Assaulted and Pursued Chastity* is founded not on providential "impossibilities," but on human nature and the relationship between probability and contingency. Her rational romance attributes unhappy events, such as defeat in battle, to Fortune: Travellia's father observes that "nothing [is] more subject to Chance than War, and that the valiantest and wisest Men might fall by Fortunes hand" (Ll3v). Cavendish even ensures that felicitous events that would go unremarked in many romances must not make hers "ridiculous to reason." When the Prince receives word that his first wife has died, leaving him free to marry Travellia, the message reaches him despite the fact that he has been abroad in disguise for many years; yet it arrives not by supernatural or even authorial intervention, but thanks to the pragmatic providence of his loyal subjects, who, "although they knew not where he was, yet they sent Letters into several Countryes, in hope some might light into his hands" (Mm1v). *Assaulted and Pursued Chastity* may follow a conventional romance trajectory through long trials to fulfilled desires, but Cavendish charts its narrative progress through the confluence of chance, human discernment, and statistical logic.

At the height of her narrative, Travellia becomes an evangelist on behalf of pragmatic providence. Shipwrecked and held captive by natives who plan to sacrifice her to their gods, she patiently studies her captors until the ideal opportunity, then astounds them with a sermon in their own language on how "[their] ignorance hath lead [them] wrong wayes" despite their well-meaning piety (Hh3v). She persuades the natives to forsake their superstitious zeal and become "a civilized people" (Hh4v) by explaining that while the gods certainly "governe all their Works," they do so in a surprising manner:

> The Gods made [Chance] by their providence when they made man, for man hath no more knowledge of the transitory things of the world than what chance gives them, who is an unjust distributer. ... None have perfect knowledge, for the Gods mix mans nature with such an aspiring ambition; that if they had a perfect knowledge ... of the first cause; and the effects produced there from, they would have warr'd with the Gods, and strove to usurp their authority, so busie and vain-glorious hath the Gods made the minds of men. Wherefore the Gods governe the world by ignorance. (Hh3v)

Throughout Cavendish's body of works, "providence" refers almost always to human prudence; here, Travellia employs the word just once in a metaphysical sense. This divine providence has a single design for creation: to order it by creating disorder. It protects human affairs not by bestowing prophetic visions on the chosen faithful or by guiding them toward a sacred end, but by frustrating such a teleology and any mortal claim to know it, since if man could truly perceive divine order, the result of that heady knowledge would be spiritual chaos, a Hobbesian war in Heaven. The function of divine providence, Travellia concludes, is to necessitate *human* providence. For despite Chance's regency in the material world, it cannot intrude into the realm of individual reason and subjectivity: "For the Soul is a kind of God in it self, to direct and guide those things that are inferior to it; to perceive and descry into those things that are far above it, to create by invention, to delight in contemplations" (Hh3v–Hh4r). While divine providence makes the world subject to contingency, human providence allows pragmatic self-reliance to withstand Chance. Travellia regards randomness as intrinsic to the universe and achieves a happy ending through her ability to "provide for the Future" by owning her own secular subjectivity, analyzing patterns of experience, and making the best of contingency.[35] Rather than pretending to a vision of predestined sacred narrative, she creates her own narrative out of apparent chaos. In Catherine Gallagher's terminology, much as Herbert's Arethusius is convinced by his trials of the need to act as *roi absolu*, Travellia steps up to perform as *moi absolu*, "a kind of God in [her] self."³⁶

Kahn has described postwar royalist romance as "a crisis of genre": after the execution of Charles I, and despite the eventual restoration of his son, the royalists required a "revised ... form" of romance in order to sustain it as a mode suitable for their traumatized community, one that could account for individual subjectivity and for the tragic vicissitudes of history while emphasizing the need for pragmatic personal rule over the self and others.³⁷ This "crisis" manifests itself through romances that retain their conventional narrative arc—from loss through wandering trials to eventual renewal—but take nothing else for granted. While Herbert laments the loss of naïve providential romance, and Cavendish is more cheerfully ironic in embracing new perspectives on subjectivity and narrative, both writers feel compelled to raise similar questions: Is the structure of plot—whether historical or fanciful—guided by providence, fate, random chance, human agency, or a combination of these? Can we reliably distinguish between these forces anyway? What constitutes heroic identity amid such structural and spiritual ambiguity? Herbert's and Cavendish's responses are likewise similar: creation is barred from knowledge of divine providence, if such a thing exists; pragmatic and secular self-reliance is essential, since the "world within" is an individual's only constant reference amid external turmoil; and because events occur apparently at random, a successful figure of authority must act to impose political order, while a successful search for narrative order requires self-possession of one's own persona and plot. Patience is often rewarded in these romances, but it is not the Miltonic version of the virtue: for Herbert and Cavendish, it signifies either resignation or calculated compromise, a waiting for a better chance, not for the providential "fullness of time." The result, in Kahn's words, is "an ironic self-consciousness about literary convention and genre," a tongue-in-cheek "detachment from the conventions of romance" that coexists with the royalist reliance on romance's political usefulness as a narrative of tribulation and restoration.³⁸

PARADISE LOST: TWO FALLS INTO TWO ROMANCES

Given *The Princess Cloria* and *Assaulted and Pursued Chastity* as models of the latest variations on seventeenth-century romance, Milton's knotty approach to the genre in his late poetry becomes easier to untangle. The new royalist paradigm of the pragmatic, individualistic hero struggling to contend with the winds of fortune—treated with seriousness and sincerity by writers like Herbert and Cavendish—appears in Milton's work as something far more sinister. George Williamson has claimed that *Paradise Lost*'s romance elements belong "to the forces of evil. If the 'true warfaring Christian' had once been a 'Knight in Arms,' he had defected to the other side" by the time Milton wrote his epic.[39] As Williamson, Patterson, and others have noted, Milton clearly associates Satan and his confederates with many of the trappings of romance. They are compared to "Faerie Elves" (1.781) or "Aerie Knights" who "Prick forth" across the landscape of a weirdly Spenserian Hell (2.536); their martial ranks resemble

> what resounds
> In Fable or Romance of Uthers Son
> Begirt with British and Armoric Knights;
> And all who since, Baptiz'd or Infidel
> Jousted in Aspramont or Montalban,
> Damasco, or Marocco, or Trebisond
> Or whom Biserta sent from Afric shore
> When Charlemain with all his peerage fell
> By Fontarabbia. (1.579–87)

Satan casts himself as a romance hero, claiming to believe in his own version of the fortunate fall, by which his "wandring quest" undertaken "with lonely steps" may one day appear "More glorious" (2.828–30, 16). The chivalric narratives the young Milton loved appear to have been corrupted, co-opted by God's enemies. Patterson argues as much—yet she also points out the puzzle that "much of what Milton condemned" about romance, "he also managed to retain in one way or another" elsewhere in *Paradise Lost*.[40] Kinney observes a similar seeming contradiction: "[Satan's] fallen romance is never entirely transcended. . . . One might even suggest that Adam and Eve's 'wandering steps and slow' at the conclusion of Book 12 will carry them out of Christian epic and into this most errant of genres."[41] I propose that what the poem presents us with, between Satan's wandering steps and Adam's, are two parallel falls into romance, and two parallel visions of romance's structure. In light of Herbert's and Cavendish's texts, the relationship in *Paradise Lost* between bad romance and right—indeed godly—romance appears less contradictory and mysterious: Satan falls into the royalist romance of the exiled subject of fortune, while Adam and Eve fall into the providential romance of God's elect community.

Lahive, too, has called for closer attention to *Paradise Lost*'s double romance, the "pure" form of the genre set against the "tinsel trappings" that Milton rejects at 9.3.[42] Crucially, though, Satanic and godly romance are differentiated by more than aesthetics. Williamson proposes that Milton grew to reject narratives of war and chivalry in favor of those "Of Patience and Heroic Martyrdom" (9.32),[43] and it is true that Satan is associated with the spectacular trappings of romance such as knight-errantry and tournaments—but these outward signs are not wholly absent from the poem's positive turns to the genre. Moreover, as postwar royalist romances show, Milton was hardly alone in coming to prefer a heroic ethic of patient endurance over one of martial prowess. The ugly reality of civil war had soured royalists and republicans alike on the glories of chivalry, and the most famous "Heroic Martyr" of the age was surely Charles I himself. Milton does not straightforwardly condemn romance in *Paradise Lost*, nor does he merely oppose a gaudy romance of war to a sober narrative of obedience to God. Instead, he actively resists the *revisionist* royalist romance of patience and self-integrity by assigning its unique characteristics to the fallen angels and by combating it with a providential romance that extols corrective Puritan forms of the same traits. Where royalist writers deal with the universal accessibility of heroic subjectivity by decoupling it from divine favor, Milton insists more strongly than ever on the authenticity of an exceptional subjectivity for those "Elect above the rest." Where they make room for tragedy, contingency, and doubt by displacing providence, he proposes that these apparent threats to romance reassert the value of a providential understanding of the genre.

Once we have identified the distinctive features of postwar royalist romance—deliberate murkiness about predestined narrative, valorization of individualism and strength of will, and a thematic blend of fatalism and pragmatism—the prevalence of these features in *Paradise Lost*'s infernal romance is uncanny. The poem's first two books in particular, set in Hell and focused on Satan, pursue the thematic concerns of writers like Cavendish and Herbert, suggesting that regardless of what texts in particular Milton knew, he remained as familiar as he had been in his pamphleteering days with popular royalist strategies of manipulating history as story. Book 2, for instance, opens with Satan calling his followers to a council on how they may be restored to their "just inheritance of old," and "by what best way, / Whether of open Warr or covert guile" (2.38, 41). The debate that follows resembles conversations in *Cloria* and other royalist romans à clef about the proper actions for the deposed prince and his community of followers: should the exiles fight, wait, plot, or do all these things at the times they deem best?[44] While the unsubtle and belligerent Moloch, like a demonic variation on Herbert's passionately martial figure for James II, urges open war with the foe who has driven them from their "just inheritance," Belial advises pragmatic patience: "To suffer, as to doe, / Our strength is equal," he claims, suggesting that "since fate inevitable / Subdues us," the fallen angels should delay action until they discover "what chance, what change" might be "Worth waiting" (2.197–200, 222–23). Mammon agrees, stressing the royalist virtues of policy and self-reliance: he favors "peaceful Counsels" and proposes that they "might rise / By pollicy, and long process of time" (2.279, 296–97). Instead of relying on "force impossible," they ought to embrace the liberty and "inward felicity" that *Cloria*'s Arethusius recommends, which comes only from accepting the self-sufficiency of one's subjectivity: "Let us . . . // rather seek / Our own good from our selves" (2.249–53). Finally, Beelzebub, "Majestic though in ruin" and radiating the "Princely counsel" and "public care" of a royal exile like Herbert's hero (2.303–5), voices Satan's plan to tempt humanity into the same false beliefs that the devils share: once they have fallen from their own "inheritance" into Hell's perverse narrative, they, too, "shall curse / Thir frail Originals, and faded bliss" (2.374–75). Having thus determined their plan of action, the devils disperse, comforting and entertaining themselves by recasting recent events within the mold of royalist historical romance: they compose tales of "Thir own Heroic deeds and hapless fall / By doom of Battel; and complain that Fate / Free Vertue should enthrall to Force or Chance" (2.549–51).

Milton here parodies another trend that should now be familiar. The devils are notoriously vague whenever they ponder the origins of their story or contemplate its future course: is their narrative shaped by divine will, impersonal fate, contingency, or personal agency? Beelzebub questions whether God's "high Supremacy" is "upheld by strength, or Chance, or Fate" (1.132–33); Mammon imagines that "him to unthrone we then / May hope, when everlasting Fate shall yeild / To fickle Chance" (2.231–33); and

Satan proposes that heroic resolution "Will once more lift us up, in spight of Fate," speculating that "perhaps . . . / with neighbouring Arms / And opportune excursion we may chance / Re-enter Heav'n" (2.393–97). All three lack clarity about which of these forces orders events and how they stand in relation to one another. Can chance overcome fate? Can action subdue fortune? Satan even equates "chance" with "Arms / And opportune excursion," which seem to belong to the deliberative sphere of skill and careful planning. Like the royalists' heroes, they avoid settling on a cosmology that could definitively structure or frustrate their narrative and are skeptical that God's design might supersede fate, contingency, or strategy. Satan resolves, "If then his Providence / Out of our evil seek to bring forth good, / Our labour must be to pervert that end, . . . // Which oft times may succeed": with fortune's favor, politic consideration and timely action might prove more influential than a mysterious, ambiguous God (1.162–66).

The fallen angels' doubt that divine providence controls history leads them to seek other means of explaining their story's past and determining its future. Much as Arethusius finds solace in his belief that ' man was a world within him self, being not to be deprived of an inward felicity by any power or tyranny," and as Travellia lives by the maxim that "the Soul is a kind of God in it self," the community of devils console themselves by deriving their heroic subjectivity not from conviction of God's favor, but from the secular supremacy of the individual will. "[T]he mind and spirit remains / Invincible," pronounces Beelzebub (1.139–40), anticipating Satan's more famous declaration: "The mind is its own place, and in it self / Can make a Heav'n of Hell, a Hell of Heav'n. / What matter where, if I be still the same[?]" (1.254–56). Milton's refiguration of the exiled prince justifies his rule by boasting "A mind not to be chang'd by Place or Time" (1.253). Such dauntless constancy also allows him to claim that he and his followers have won a moral victory: "What though the field be lost? / All is not lost; th' unconquerable Will . . . // And courage never to submit or yield: / And what is else not to be overcome?" (1.105–9). The passive self-reliance characteristic of Herbert's Arethusius soon leads Satan into an active self-reliance typical of Cavendish's heroes as well: "Let us not slip th' occasion" to regain the upper hand, he urges, since all occasions within his narrative are potentially equal and must be analyzed as logistical rather than providential opportunities (1.178). Indeed, Satan places the same emphasis on Hobbesian pragmatic providence that Cavendish and Travellia do: looking back on his defeat, he considers that "through experience of this great event/ ... in foresight much advanc't, / We may with more successful hope resolve" to make war against Heaven (1.118–21). His narrative vision comes only from personal experience; in Cavendish's words, by "observ[ing] the Effect of Things," and "compar[ing] the past with the present," he aims "to provide for the Future" that he and his community desire.

Imitating the heroes of postwar royalist romance, Satan attempts to create his own order out of what looks to him like a disorderly universe by turning to a "world within him self" for guidance. But within a Miltonic narrative cosmology, such profoundly secular and self-reflexive heroic subjectivity is doomed. Milton ensures that instead of finding a "Paradise within" himself, Satan instead discovers, "Which way I flie is Hell; my self am Hell" (4.75). His world within is a world insulated from both divine guidance and providential hope. Amid all of Satan's pretensions to romance, we must not forget that he does not even believe in the narrative he takes such pains to construct. His claims to romance heroism are gestures calculated to shore up his rule and motivate his subjects; he feels no internal conviction of their truth. When he urges his followers to exercise their own capacity for rational providence to regain their lost inheritance, he is "Vaunting aloud, but wrackt with deep despair" (1.126). In this despair, he clings all the more closely to his relativistic, revisionist "world within," but forsakes a major structural pillar of romance, unable to imagine a happy ending to his own story: "So farwell Hope ... / all Good to me is lost" (4.108–9). Satan's illusory romance collapses into infinite tragedy.

Maureen Quilligan has said of Satan and his followers that "in effect, their story is over" before it begins: "Having already fallen ... they are no longer free to choose the one thing that would give their story a plot—a developing climactic chronology. All they can do is repeat their mistakes."[45] In adopting the royalist romance of restoration as the official narrative model for their cause, the fallen angels abandon the teleological romance of the godly for tragic parody: as they "[reason] high / Of Providence, Foreknowledge, Will and Fate, / Fixt Fate, free will, foreknowledg absolute," they "[find] no end, in wandring mazes lost" (2.558–61). Wandering movement, of course, is endemic to romance's structure and to its characters' paths, as Milton reminds us in the closing lines of *Paradise Lost*. But the devils' wandering—unlike that of Adam and Eve when they descend into the romance landscape beyond Eden—is doomed to have "no end," no telos.

The errancies of God's community of chosen heroes will finally lead them to reunion with the divine, but those who embark on a quest divorced from Providence are "lost" in a maze without an exit. Absent any sincere effort at mediation between an errant middle and a teleological end, this endless romance is not really romance at all: the devils, using the royalist model, are doing it wrong. Milton's narrator concludes that their version, with its "Vain wisdom" and "false Philosophie," may possess the "pleasing sorcerie" to "charm / Pain for a while or anguish, and excite / Fallacious hope, or arm th' obdured brest / With stubborn patience as with triple steel," but it lacks any power to produce a perfectible story of loss and restoration (2.565–69).

Time and again, Milton's fallen angels demonstrate postwar royalist perspectives on the absence or inaccessibility of inherent narrative order and the need to create a substitute. They also display what Milton (like many Puritans) saw as a royalist affinity for ostentatiously packaging their own history in romance frivolity (the sort of behavior that he also mocked and denounced in *Eikonoklastes*). Romance as parody dominates books 1 and 2 of *Paradise Lost*—and yet, as a number of readers have perceived, the poem's overall attitude toward it is not obviously or simply parodic. Considered comprehensively, romance as a strategy emerges as one of Milton's many "things indifferent," neither godly nor ungodly in itself, but only insofar as it is handled and interpreted. The first two books of *Paradise Lost* explore the dire implications of a romance devoid of providential structure; the last two, on the other hand, "assert Eternal Providence" as the author of the arc of time (1.25). Adam and Eve's fall into romance comes with new terms for a right understanding of it, including a rejection of both fatalism and the power of conventional heroism; an emphasis on the insufficiency of the individual mind to interpret or control the plot of history; an insistence on the authenticity of a special narrative perspective for those whom God has chosen for such a vision; and a reaffirmation of romance structure that, by providential design, is simultaneously errant and teleological.

Book 11 opens with Adam and Eve "in lowliest plight" but declared newly "Regenerat" (11.1, 5). As the first sinful and repentant members of God's elect community, they have fallen into a romance that is Puritan and providential, whereas Satan's was royalist and secular. God pronounces the entirety of their plot as individual believers, declined from "Happiness / And Immortalitie" to "Death . . . / after Life / Tri'd in sharp tribulation" but ultimately "up with Heav'n and Earth renewd" (11.66). The larger romance of the entire community throughout history remains for Adam to learn from the archangel Michael during the final two books. Michael comes to Adam in a fitting shape, one that suggests that Satan and his secular model must not be allowed to monopolize romance aesthetics: he appears in "A militarie Vest" like those "worn by Kings and Heroes old," armed with his "Sword, / Satans dire dread" (11.241–48), entering Adam and Eve's new romance world in his knightly form as the hero of heaven's army and the vanquisher of "the dragon" Satan.[46] Milton may further intend for him to evoke the image of Saint George, England's dragonslayer, who is of course also Spenser's Redcrosse Knight, another godly hero who receives a sacred vision of time and genre on the peak of a mountain. (Milton also represents, and genders, a version of Spenser's other archetype of prophetic reception here: while Adam "to foresight [wakes]" on high, Eve "sleep[s] below," assured in dreams that "the Promis'd Seed," her progeny, "shall all restore" [11.368, 12.623].) In the vision Michael will reveal to Adam, several other types of the final battle against the Satanic serpent will take place, and Adam (now in Redcrosse's position) will learn with difficulty to reject wrong perspectives on romance in favor of the providential model reserved for the regenerate, avoiding the royalist-inflected errors into which the devils fell.

Like Contemplation leading Redcrosse, Adam's literary progenitor and historical progeny, Michael and Adam "both ascend / In the Visions of God" to the hill

> Of Paradise the highest, from whose top
> The Hemisphere of Earth in cleerest Ken
> Stretcht out to amplest reach of prospect lay.
> Not higher that Hill nor wider looking round,
> Whereon for different cause the Tempter set
> Our second Adam in the Wilderness,
> To shew him all Earths Kingdomes and thir Glory. (11.376–84)

Regina Schwartz has noted that Milton here typologically anticipates the yet-unwritten *Paradise Regained* and suggests the challenge that Adam faces in his mountaintop vision: "The analogy is not to a place of definitive revelation, but to a place of temptation, and the temptation that Adam faces in the final books is to view the prospect of what lay before him and want to possess it." Schwartz argues that Adam's desire "to *possess* that entire story, to 'know' his future rather than to determine it... is, in Stanley Fish's phrase, the 'temptation of plot.'"[47] But for Fish and Schwartz, to succumb to the temptation of plot is to misread divine nonnarrative, independent of worldly time, as human narrative. What Adam and later Jesus, as I will argue, must really learn to do on their respective visionary hills is accept sacred time *as* a still-unfolding narrative, and as one that they, called to trust in God's authorial providence, have limited power to "determine." Unlike Satan and the heroes of postwar royalist romance, who strive to determine their own destinies in the absence of providential certainty, the protagonists of Milton's Puritan romance demonstrate the superior authenticity of their heroic subjectivity by living in willing accordance within the plot predestined by God.[48] The urge to leap to the end of the romance while bypassing the tortuous experience of the middle—to possess the full story at once while elevated to a God's-eye view without enduring the limited human perspective of embeddedness within narrative—is the temptation of *non*-plot. Satan will fall to this temptation, and press Jesus to do the same, in *Paradise Regained*; in *The Faerie Queene*, as we have seen, Redcrosse begs for permanent residency on the visionary peak and for a premature exit from his romance, which his guide forbids. On the mountain with Michael, Adam, too, keeps imposing his understanding of history over the providential plot, and prematurely presumes a conclusion to the story that winds and stretches on, often to his dismay. As he must learn from his own guide, the long and burdensome middle of the romance must precede the sure but distant conclusion, historical time must precede apocalyptic timelessness, and only divine story can point the way to the story's end.

Much as the fallen Eve contemplates suicide, and as Satan's concealed reaction to his own fall is an ouroboros of despair, Adam is first tempted away from narrative temporality upon witnessing death: "O miserable Mankind, to what fall / Degraded, to what wretched state reserv'd! / Better end heer unborn" (11.500–502). Like Herbert's exiles, he questions whether a providential hand can oversee such "inhuman pains"; only after Michael reinterprets death as the result of human faithlessness does Adam "yeild it just" (11.511). As his vision of history continues, Adam faces both the temptations of *wrong* romance and the temptation of *non*-romance again and again, and must learn to renounce both before his redescent into the "lower World," where individual and communal narrative unfolds within time (11.283).

Adam is first confronted with the tropes of "Soft" and "amorous" romance as he views the courtship and marriage of his progeny with "A Beavie of fair Women" (11.582–84). This vision "Of love and youth not lost" holds strong allure for the man who had recently defended his own erotic passion for his wife: "Much better seems this Vision, and more hope / Of peaceful dayes portends . . . / Here Nature seems fulfill'd in all her ends" (11.599–602). Adam makes two mistakes here: his attraction to the courtly romance of "these fair Atheists," and his assumption that wooing and marriage can in themselves signify the "ends" of nature and of his descendants' story (11.625).[49] Yet once Michael corrects him, he reacts too vehemently and, like many readers since, interprets this errant mode as feminine, inextricably associated with womanish wiles.[50] Scolded by his guide once more, he is next presented with another, more typically masculine, romance spectacle: a "cruel Tournament" of war between "Giants of . . . bould emprise" (11.652, 642). Michael is quick to denounce this chivalric variant, too, in which destruction and conquest are "Valour and Heroic Vertu call'd," though Adam already finds war less appealing than the love story (11.690). The last alternative corrupt narrative that he must resist is the one that appeals most to the war-weary royalists and the fallen angels, which valorizes pragmatic policy over both love and war. Neither the "Council" of the "grave" nor the "luxurie" of the peaceful can produce a happy ending, much to Adam's sorrow (11.661–2, 715):

> I had hope
> When violence was ceas't, and Warr on Earth,
> All would have then gon well, peace would have crownd
> With length of happy dayes the race of men;
> But I was farr deceav'd; for now I see
> Peace to corrupt no less than Warr to waste. (11.779–84)

Godless peace, Michael explains, is godless war's twin—both are "great exploits, but of true vertu void," each leading endlessly into the other (11.790). Neither love, nor war, nor politic and indulgent peace can underpin a teleological narrative with the power to redeem fallen humanity.

Faced with all this failure, Adam goes back to lamenting creation's new narrative temporality and regrets his view of its plot. The end of the romance of history, he now assumes, must really be tragedy: "those few escap't" on

Noah's ark, he grieves, "Famin and anguish will at last consume / Wandring that watrie Desert" (11.777–79). He has forgotten both the providential structure of the godly community's story and the providential source of his vision of it:

> O Visions ill foreseen! better had I
> Liv'd ignorant of future! . . .
>   Let no man seek
> Henceforth to be foretold what shall befall
> Him or his Children, evil he may be sure. (11.763–72)

David Loewenstein, reading Milton's work through the hermeneutic of drama, sees Adam's vision on the summit as evidence that Milton could not shake the sense that a fallen, tragic mode pervades historical narrative, despite holding out simultaneous hope for history as "divine comedy."[51] Romance, known onstage as tragicomedy, helps us navigate this generic divide. We have seen other writers struggle with tragedy as the close companion of romance, and the life and second coming of Christ guaranteed for Milton that the structure of romance existed internal to time as well as externally as time's telos. In believing that history will always and can only end tragically, Adam again speaks too soon. While the visions of book 11 teach him to reject bad romance in all its guises, they also lead him into another, maybe more deadly, temptation: to despair of the genre's promise altogether, as Satan secretly does. Michael's continued narrative in book 12 serves to reeducate Adam to recognize *right* romance as the true genre of history and to embrace it despite its structural challenges. Crucially, the final book of *Paradise Lost* returns to the most recognizable romance tropes that the poem has previously associated with Satan's army—the wandering quest and heroic combat—and reclaims them for the providential romance of a Puritan community. It also warns against the devils' and the royalists' greatest story-making error as Milton perceives it: failure to entrust the shape of events to God's often occluded design.

Unable to view the romance of providence, unlike its secular substitutes, with his deficient "mortal sight," Adam relies on Michael to narrate the rest of history (12.9). The archangel unfolds his story through one type after another of Jesus's wandering in the wilderness and his battles with Satan. First, Abraham escapes the tyranny of Nimrod and leads his people—"one peculiar Nation" selected "From all the rest"—into "a land unknown" (12.111–12, 134). Later, Moses and Aaron liberate the community of God's chosen from slavery and "return / With glory and spoile back to thir promis'd Land" through "the wide Wilderness" (12.171–72, 224). Along the way, they engage in allegorical chivalric combat with the Pharaoh, taming "The River-dragon" with "ten wounds," and in real warfare with other nations: "the rest / Were long to tell," demurs Michael in the conventional romance glossing of minor adventures, "how many Battels fought, / How many Kings destroyd, and Kingdoms won" (12.190–91, 260–62). Joshua, Moses's successor, is the next hero to foreshadow the eponymous Jesus, "His Name and Office bearing, who shall quell / The adversarie Serpent, and bring back / Through the worlds wilderness long wanderd man / Safe to eternal Paradise of rest" (12.311–14). All these figures, Michael assures Adam, prepare the way for "the true / Anointed King *Messiah*," the hero of the right royal romance, "born / Barr'd of his right" but destined at last to "ascend / The Throne hereditarie" of his father (12.358–60, 369–70).

Yet the very romance tropes that enlighten Adam about the elect community's providential plot become a source of further confusion to him: he tends to overliteralize Michael's metaphors and to revert to his old habits of rashly assuming knowledge of the story's shape and end. In his joy at the introduction of the Messiah, he does both:

> O Prophet of glad tidings, finisher
> Of utmost hope! now clear I understand
> What oft my steddiest thoughts have searcht in vain . . .
> Needs must the Serpent now his capital bruise
> Expect with mortal pain: say where and when
> Thir fight, what stroke shall bruise the Victors heel. (12.375–85)

Although the last hero has indeed entered the story, Adam's haste to declare it "finish[ed]," and to proclaim that "now . . . [he] understand[s]" what he had missed before, misses the mark. He has been disposed both to mourn and to celebrate prematurely since the start of his vision, and he had responded with similar exultation to Michael's account of Abraham's success (12.270–77). Michael must again correct him: "Dream not of thir fight, / As of a Duel, or the local wounds / Of head or heel" (12.386–88). Clearly, the imagery of the divine romance has inspired Adam, but he remains at risk of understanding the genre strictly through the secular tropes that have ensnared the devils. His graver mistake is to presume that *now* he understands, that the great battle must surely occur *now*: he is still poised to use his heroic subjectivity to justify seizing his own occasions, to strive toward the end of his personal narrative rather than live fully immersed within his community's providential plot. And just as the fight between the Satan and the Son will not resemble a human duel, its temporality resists easy placement within human history.

As Schwartz has discussed, the Son's destined combat with the devil appears both endlessly repeated and indefinitely forestalled as Michael draws his narrative to a close. Satan's defeat first seems accomplished at Jesus's birth, but the bruising of the serpent's head must be performed again through his perfect obedience to God (12.393–97), again during his sacrifice on the cross (12.427–33), and once more at his harrowing of Hell and reascension into Heaven (12.451–57). Yet even then, the divine romance remains unfinished: Michael explains that after the "deliverer's" victory, "the few / His faithful" will resume their roles as the narrative's elect community of earthly heroes, armed "With spiritual Armour" in resistance to "The enemies of truth" (12.479–91). Their spiritual chivalry will last as long as time itself, until the Son returns "to dissolve" his enemy—a verb that itself vaporizes the weight of the previous warlike imagery—and to establish "Ages of endless date" (12.546–49). The end of time marks the final end of the romance; until then, both history and genre stretch on toward an indistinct vanishing point. Schwartz argues that Michael's lesson in deferral indicates that sacred time is fundamentally nonnarrative and resistant to teleology—that "Adam cannot get there, Adam cannot see there, because there is no 'there' there"—but Michael is quite clear that a "there" that is not *here* is not the same as a "there" that will never be anywhere.[52] Adam must learn not that the romance and its end are unattainable or unreal, but that they do not belong to him to possess or identify. The hardest challenge he faces on the visionary summit is to distinguish the ways in which reading history as a romance can enlighten him from the ways in which it can only make wandering in darkness bearable.[53]

By the time Adam descends from the mountain of metanarrative back to the lower world of lived narrative—and back to Eve, consoled by her dreams of the hero that will spring from the tree of her descendants—his perspective on the structure of history is neither transcendently clear nor existentially murky. Unlike the protagonists of royalist or Satanic romance, he feels compelled neither to control his story nor to despair of its meaning. We might recognize the "mystical" zeal of Cavendish's stereotypical Puritan in Adam's vow "ever to observe / [God's] providence, and on him sole depend, / Mercifull over all his works, with good / Still overcoming evil," but we no longer see any pretense to *possess* the "key" of that providence (12.563–66). Like his prayer for forgiveness, his full view of the romance of time has brought him "Strength added from above, new hope to spring / Out of despair, joy, but with fear yet linkt" (11.138–39). As Adam and Eve take their "wandring steps" out of paradise and into the world of Michael's errant narrative, they share "one Faith unanimous though sad, / With cause for evils past, yet much more cheer'd / With meditation on the happie end" (12.648, 603–5). For both Milton and his royalist opponents, the romance of an individual life or of a community's history offers not a straight path to knowledge, but a wandering course through which the heroes can perceive the limits of knowledge and yet keep moving. But in Miltonic romance, only the promise of providential structure, and the chastened legitimacy of heroic subjectivity granted by God, can justify that movement and lend it direction.

"ON THE MORNING OF CHRIST'S NATIVITY": THE PERSISTENCE OF HISTORY

Milton's 1629 poem celebrating the birth of Jesus, "On the Morning of Christ's Nativity," offers an important link between the fall of man and the regaining of paradise as moments within Christian history. Composed half a lifetime before Milton wrote his epics on the Nativity's prequel and sequel, the lyric illuminates the coherence of his career's commitment to a poetics of sacred temporality and sacred genre. While Milton honed his approach to narrative in his later poetry and incorporated heightened politics into his postwar treatment of romance, he was also returning in *Paradise Lost* and *Paradise Regained* to ideas that had dominated his earliest work.

The young Milton's *Nativity Ode* opens with a jubilance that anticipates Adam's naïve delight at the prospect of collapsing vast stretches of narrative into *now*:

> This is the month, and this the happy morn
> Wherein the Son of Heav'n's eternal King,

> Of wedded Maid, and Virgin Mother born,
> Our great redemption from above did bring;
> For so the holy sages once did sing,
> That he our deadly forfeit should release,
> And with his Father work us a perpetual peace. (1–7)

Verbs in past and conditional future tenses are circumscribed by the "now" and "forever" implied in the stanza's first and last lines; the poem's narrator dips us into historical time and then draws us upward out of it with the ecstatic promise that we are about to be granted our own vision of an event that transcends history. His enthusiasm flourishes throughout the *Nativity Ode*'s first half, permeating the world of the poem like the music of the angelic chorus:

> Nature that heard such sound
> Beneath the hollow round
> Of Cynthia's seat, the Airy region thrilling,
> Now was almost won
> To think her part was don,
> And that her raign had here its last fulfilling. (101–6)

The narrator's supposition of what Nature "almost" thinks again resembles Adam's untimely conclusion upon witnessing his progeny's amorous romance: "Here Nature seems fulfill'd in all her ends" (11.602). As David Quint has argued, the *Nativity Ode* is a conscious exercise in this kind of narrative prematurity.[54] The eager poet's fantasies of temporal perfection reach beyond Adam's: he imagines that, hearing the music of the spheres that heralds Christ's birth, "Time will run back, and fetch the age of gold" (135). Rather than merely stopping, time (as in the opening stanza) will effectively implode into infinity, drawn into a singularity that is both cosmogonic and apocalyptic "Yea Truth, and Justice then / Will down return to men," and "Hell it self will pass away," while "Heav'n as at some festivall, / Will open wide the Gates of her high Palace Hall" (139–41, 147–48). Quint has observed that Milton's speaker enjoys a flirtation with universalism here as he imagines a defunct Hell and a communally inclusive Heaven.[55] Like either Redcrosse or Adam on their summits, the speaker is poised to grasp and possess the entirety of the story at once, to wind up the thread of history so that its entirety is visible, with the end result that time and plot, and perhaps even the exceptional subjectivity of the elect, no longer carry useful meaning.

We already know what Contemplation or Michael would say, and a guiding voice likewise enters the *Nativity Ode* to temper the poet's antinarrative zeal: "But wisest Fate says no, / This must not yet be so" (149–50).[56] As Adam must keep accepting the deferral of the final battle with the serpent, the speaker is forced to admit that the birth of Christ spells neither the fulfillment of nature nor the end of the Christian plot: "The Babe lies yet in smiling infancy, / That on the bitter cross / Must redeem our loss, / So both himself and us to glorify" (151–54). Time, history, and their sorrows persist. Having established that the poem remains set definitively inside of historical time, Milton offers a brief but sudden glimpse of the ongoing story's antagonist, characterizing him with an image that is medieval or Spenserian as well as biblical:

> from this happy day
> Th' old Dragon under ground
> In straiter limits bound,
> Not half so far casts his usurped sway,
> And wroth to see his Kingdom fail,
> Swindges the scaly Horrour of his foulded tail. (167–72)

Satan here appears as the Dragon of both Revelation and England's foundational romance, destined for eventual combat with the Christian narrative's chivalric hero(es). The Dragon's role in the *Nativity Ode* is small, but startling and complex: technically, the stanza he dominates reports that the birth of Christ has struck a decisive blow that constrains his power, but the monster's abrupt appearance serves as an alarming warning that the final battle has yet to take place. The Dragon may be "bound," but he remains a menacing creature, lurking "under ground" in all his rage and "scaly Horrour." Like the peasants in book 1 of *The Faerie Queene* who run to see the spectacle of the defeated Satanic dragon, but dread "Some lingring life within his hollow brest," we are encouraged to celebrate the enemy's predestined doom as though it were already accomplished, and yet to fear his persistent power (1.12.10). Milton evokes a similar sense of temporal ambivalence in the stanza's opening lines: "And then at last our bliss / Full and perfect is, / But now begins" (165–67). In these few words, we are reminded that the romance of history concludes in "bliss," but that we can only have faith in this finality from our imperfect vantage point somewhere in the melancholy middle of a very long story—and yet that the present moment promises and anticipates the joy of the ending.

This limited perspective may sound similar to the ambivalent and mediated consolation offered to Spenser's Britomart or to *Paradise Lost*'s Eve, and Milton's figure for the heroic acceptance of it is again an expectant mother. The last stanza of the poem presents a powerful corrective to the temporal acrobatics of the first, as time, motion, and creation rest in momentary contemplation and communion with Mary:

> But see the Virgin blest,
> Hath laid her Babe to rest.
> Time is our tedious Song should here have ending:
> Heav'n's youngest teemed Star,
> Hath fixed her polished Car,
> Her sleeping Lord with Handmaid Lamp attending:
> And all about the Courtly Stable,
> Bright-harnest Angels sit in order serviceable. (237–44)

While Balachandra Rajan has seen in this final stanza a moment of "crystalline joy," other readers have been less optimistic.[57] J. Martin Evans finds Milton's conclusion emblematic of a sad "poetry of absence" that characterizes the *Nativity Ode*: the scene of "rest" in the stable holds us "trapped in the long-drawn-out 'moment' of transition preceding the millennium," able dimly "to apprehend the paradisal state of perfection," but excluded from dwelling within it.[58] Evans opposes his interpretation to Rajan's; however, these two positions need not be mutually exclusive. The poem does press us to acknowledge the absence of paradise, justice, harmony, and vision external to history; but it also points us to an understanding of this absence as *present absence*—not eternal, though keenly felt for now—and to a perception of a form of divine presence within the absence. Much as Adam descends from his mountaintop vision in neither joy nor sorrow but "peace of thought" (12.558), the small community in the stable at the end of the *Nativity Ode* "does achieve a measure of readiness and composure."[59] The stillness of the tableau vivant in the poem's last stanza mediates between celebration and melancholy, between the absence of an apocalyptic Messiah and the presence of the newborn baby, an emblem not of action and conclusion but of potential and beginning. As the figures in and around the stable all fall silent to wait on the infant Jesus "in order serviceable," we are left with an image of patience as pristine presentness, of contentment with providential narrative as it is imperfectly understood, with "sitting" inside a moment inside of history.[60] Mary, the poet, the star, and the angels share this "crystalline" moment with one another and with the reader—but on this occasion of his birth, the Son of God is the focus of their experience rather than a participant in it. More than forty years later, Milton's last poem returns to the themes of his early ode, but *Paradise Regained* allows us to witness the adult Jesus's own human contentions with the problems and promises of subjectivity, time, and genre.

PARADISE REGAINED: A NEW "CHANCE AT TRUE ROMANCE"

Published four decades after *Comus*, *Paradise Regained* stands as Milton's only other work that does not merely allude to or contain elements of romance, but arguably *is* structurally a romance from beginning to end. The poem opens with one of the genre's archetypal premises: an unknown hero raised in obscurity suddenly discovers that he is the son of a king and heir to a usurped kingdom, and must then face the personal and practical implications of his identity. The Jesus of book 1 is "the Son of *Joseph* deem'd ... as then obscure, / Unmarkt, unknown" (1.23–25). Having grown to "youths full flowr" (1.67), he learns the truth of his birth from his mother:

> thou art no Son of mortal man;
> Though men esteem thee low of Parentage,
> Thy Father is the Eternal King, who rules
> All Heaven and Earth, Angels and Sons of men,
> A messenger from God fore-told ...
> Thou shouldst be great and sit on David's Throne,
> And of thy Kingdom there should be no end. (1.234–41)

Over the course of Milton's brief epic,[61] Jesus withdraws from society to wander through an isolated landscape, encounters and defeats his mortal enemy, and returns to the world confident in his heroic identity and in the providential teleology of his life's story. Milton's use of romance's conventions and its structure is deliberate and sincere, as I will argue, but *Paradise Regained*'s relationship to the genre is certainly more complicated than it appears in this cursory sketch of the plot. Jesus's story may be a romance in itself, but the hero must resist a Satanic presentation of romance that seems equally conventional in its chivalric content and its narrative about heroic action in pursuit of a lost paternal inheritance. Given the generically charged nature of the opponents' combat, what is Milton's final attitude toward romance in *Paradise Regained*?

This question was once the subject of extensive critical conversation. Nearly fifty years ago, Barbara Lewalski described "Jesus' adventure and conquest over Satan in the Wilderness" as "the true, fully achieved Romance Quest" in which the hero "antitypes the romance knights" and "achieves, as Adam did not and as fallen man cannot, the highest romance purposes."[62] Her reading of Miltons poem as a bold experiment with genre that "exalt[s] [the romance ethos] to the order of perfection" accords with Northrop Frye's description of *Paradise Regained* as "a parody of a dragon-killing romance, or, more accurately," as "the reality of which the dragon-killing romance is a parody."[63] Stanley Fish visited the poem once in 1971 and again in 1983. His earlier essay on the Son's "Inaction and Silence" hesitates to break from Lewalski and Frye's pro-romance reading: while he argues that the audience faces a "literary temptation" in its expectation of an active hero, he concludes that heroic action finally becomes "purified" by complete submission to God and so is "now not only allowed, but enjoined."[64] However, Fish's return to the poem in 1983 implies that reading it as a romance is impossible after all. This later essay—Schwartz's source for the idea of "temptation of plot"—redefines the core trial for both Jesus and the reader as a temptation not just to heroic action, but to narrative itself. Fish contends that Satan makes a "continual effort . . . to persuade the Son of God that the Son himself is a character in a plot, in a narrative where every change of scene brings new opportunities and new risks," and that "what defeats Satan finally is the Son's inability or unwillingness . . . to recognize the fact that there is a plot at all."[65] Even the final temptation on the pinnacle is not the "climax" of a "plot," Fish concludes: "There is no final moment in *Paradise Regained*. In this last scene, which ends nothing, the Son does no more or less than he does before and will have to do again." Jesus's active inaction is not a definitive triumph but an ongoing process: the poem's events (or nonevents) are removed "from the story line of a plot into a timeless realm where they are eternally occurring."[66] Rather than perfecting romance, Fish decides, the Son both refuses the heroism that characterizes the genre and erases the temporality that enables its structure. Finally, Annabel Patterson's 1983 essay on *Paradise Regained*, "Milton's Last Chance at True Romance," concludes that this last chance ultimately fails to redeem the genre. "The poem appears to be constructed on rigorously antiromantic lines," she argues, as it avoids a clear sense of a beginning, a middle, and an end, and portrays the genre's tropes and trappings as Satanic temptations to be rejected in favor of an ambiguous "new Christian narrative whose rules are yet to be revealed."[67] Within the same publication in the same year, Patterson and Fish each determined that Milton was politically and religiously motivated to exclude *Paradise Regained* from traditional categories of genre and narrative temporality; their consensus marked the poem's "last chance at true romance" in Milton studies, and twenty years of critical conversation on *Paradise Regained*'s relationship to romance came to an end.

I hope to show here that the matter has not been settled, and that a historical consideration of post-Restoration contexts can strengthen Lewalski and Frye's structuralist instincts about the poem's genre. *Paradise Regained* does not abandon outworn romance in order to escape its temptations; like *Paradise Lost*, it counters the *new* royalist romance by assigning its innovative characteristics to Satan and by combating it with a Puritan alternative. Satan's temptation in *Paradise Regained* is indeed literary, but Jesus's resistance and his triumph are no less so: while Satan's self-conscious assumptions and uncertainties about heroic narrative bear all the hallmarks of the royalist genre in crisis and seem more anxious than ever, Jesus becomes progressively more assured that providential romance is the genre of human history, and that his heroic subjectivity is authentically sacred, self-sufficient proof against his enemies. One of the forces that the hero of Milton's "dragon-killing romance" must overcome is a usurping rival form of the genre itself.[68]

Paradise Regained opens as Jesus "One day forth walk'd alone, the Spirit leading" into the wilderness, armed only with his tentative new knowledge of his identity and purpose and "Musing and much revolving in his brest, / How best the mighty work he might begin / Of Saviour to mankind" (1.185–89). Having withdrawn from the world into the indeterminate landscape of romance, he soon encounters another of the genre's well-known figures: "an aged man in Rural weeds" who offers the wandering hero his assistance

(1.314).⁶⁹ Scholars have long noted this seemingly innocuous old hermit's resemblance to Spenser's crafty villain Archimago; unlike Spenser's Redcrosse Knight (another unknown, untried hero traversing the wilderness on an errand of holiness), Jesus easily recognizes his foe, and his romantic and metaromantic battle with Satan begins. Satan's anxiety over the dethroned heir's uncertain future and his plan for regaining his father's kingdom again parallels concerns in postwar royalist romance, and at *Paradise Lost*'s infernal council, about which active or passive postures the exile should adopt. The ensuing temptations are accordingly varied, as Satan alternately urges Jesus to rely on martial force, on pragmatic patience, and on his wits. This new heroic narrative offers many possible paths to triumph, as long as its protagonist, like Cavendish's Travellia, acts to provide for his own ends and does anything other than stand around waiting for divine aid (as one might in passé romances that are "ridiculous to reason").

The order of Satan's temptations corresponds to the order in which Adam must learn to reject false heroics in *Paradise Lost*: first love, then war, then shallow peace. As Salzman has remarked, eroticism plays a relatively minor role in postwar royalist romance, and Satan wastes little time in confirming that Jesus is immune to the sensual charms of women modeled on the ladies of archaic Arthurian texts, "Fairer then feign'd of old, or fabl'd since / Of Fairy Damsels met in Forest wide / By Knights of *Logres*, or of *Lyones*, / *Lancelot* or *Pelleas*, or *Pellenore*" (2.358–61).⁷⁰ Instead, he turns to allures of romance that feature more prominently in postwar heroic texts: the temptations of combat and of politics. He begins by warning Jesus that his "years are ripe, and over-ripe" for the martial display by which the untried hero of chivalric romance conventionally proves his mettle (3.31), and for which Arethusius's younger brother in *Cloria* particularly yearns. Such is Jesus's "skill," Satan suggests, that were he "sought to deeds / That might require th' array of war . . . all the world / Could not sustain [his] Prowess":

> These God-like Vertues wherefore dost thou hide?
> Affecting private life, or more obscure
> In savage Wilderness, wherefore deprive
> All Earth her wonder at thy acts, thy self
> The fame and glory, glory the reward
> That sole excites to high attempts the flame
> Of most erected Spirits[?] (3.16–30)

Jesus responds by scorning the conventional quest for reputation as "false glory, attributed / To things not glorious, men not worthy of fame," in language reminiscent of Michael's to Adam (3.69–70). Moreover, he rejects martial action as a means of demonstrating heroic virtue:

> They err who count it glorious to subdue
> By Conquest far and wide, to over-run
> Large Countries, and in field great Battels win,
> Great Cities by assault: what do these Worthies,
> But rob and spoil, burn, slaughter, and enslave
> Peaceable Nations[?] (3.71–76)

Conquest and victory in battle, the chivalric hero's badges of honor, are denounced as excuses for wanton destruction and as the cornerstones of tyranny: the conquering champion's only motive and reward, Jesus argues, is to become the unlawful king of an unconsenting people.

After linking martial chivalry to the corruption of monarchy, Jesus counters that any earthly glory must be gained "By deeds of peace, by wisdom eminent, / By patience, temperance" (3.91–92). Yet as Adam learns in *Paradise Lost*, peace is not without its own perils. In *Cloria*, an inclination toward peaceful prudence rather than glorious violence distinguishes Arethusius from his rash brother; but as we have seen, Arethusius's cautiousness works in tandem with his authoritarian political ambition. Lewalski has pointed out that Milton suspects the entire premise of heroic ambition in his later work: in *Paradise Lost*, Eve "assumes the faulty heroism of a knight-errant looking for adventures to prove her unaided virtue" when the trials of romance will "come unsought" (9.366), while Jesus, who functions in *Paradise Regained* not only as second Adam but also as second Eve, instead accepts the trials that God has ordained, crucially seeking not his own glory, "but his / Who sent me" (3.106–7).[71] Heroic patience, for Milton, can never be politic in Arethusius's sense—though it is certainly *political* in allowing Jesus to resist his adversary.[72] Jesus is waiting not for the right time to exercise his own pragmatic providence, as Arethusius and Travellia do, but for divine providence "To exercise him" (1.156).

Having failed to move Jesus to action by encouraging him to go out in search of unknown adventure to prove his worth, Satan turns to a more specific quest—one that constitutes the plot of countless royal romances, including *Cloria* and the real life of Charles II. As the unrecognized heir to a kingdom, he insists, Jesus must surely answer the clear call of narrative destiny:

> Of glory as thou wilt, said he, so deem,
> Worth or not worth the seeking, let it pass:
> But to a Kingdom thou art born, ordain'd
> To sit upon thy Father David's Throne;
> By Mothers side thy Father, though thy right
> Be now in powerful hands that will not part
> Easily from possession won with arms . . .
>   and think'st thou to regain
> Thy right by sitting still or thus retiring? (3.150–56, 163–64)

Now knowing Jesus's hatred of monarchical oppression, Satan reminds him that his father's throne has been usurped by the Romans, who have ruled the realm as tyrants. If Jesus is truly the long-lost heir of David, then the obvious task before him is to reclaim his royal right, end the usurpers' tyranny, and establish a reign of virtue: "Raign then; what canst thou better do the while?" (3.180). According to Satan, Jesus is bound by all the obligations of royal romance: he has a "monster" (as Satan terms Tiberius) to "expel," an ancestral right to reclaim, a people to liberate, a prophecy to fulfill (4.100). Alongside these old traditions, Satan incorporates the revised royalist theme of politic calculation, proposing to his adversary that "Zeal and Duty are not slow; / But on Occasions forelock watchful wait. / They themselves rather are occasion best" (3.172–74). In other words, the dispossessed hero remains passive and patient only in anticipation of the right opportunity, which his own "Zeal and Duty" can help bring about. Indeed, these virtues "are occasion" in "themselves"; the right time for action in royalist romance is dictated not by providence, but by the hero's internal political barometer. Jesus refuses to adopt this revisionary rhetoric, insisting that "All things are best fulfil'd in their due time," which "The Father in his purpose hath decreed, / He in whose hand all times and seasons roul" (3.182, 186–87). Providential temporality, not royal birthright, political contingency, or secular subjectivity, determines the proper "occasions" for the hero's struggles and his eventual victory.[73]

In a final effort to motivate Jesus to yield to the pressures of his artificial narrative, Satan shows him the battling armies of Parthia and Scythia, which Milton's narrator links to the chivalric Roland cycle in a lengthy metaphor reminiscent of *Paradise Lost* 1.579–87:

> Such forces met not, nor so wide a camp,
> When Agrican with all his Northern powers
> Besieg'd Albracca, as Romances tell;
> The City of Gallaphrone, from thence to win
> The fairest of her Sex Angelica
> His daughter, sought by many Prowest Knights,
> Both Paynim, and the Peers of Charlemane.
> Such and so numerous was thir Chivalrie;
> At sight whereof the Fiend yet more presum'd,
> And to our Saviour thus his words renew'd. (3.337–46)

Satan claims that he has shown Jesus this spectacle to inspire him along his course: he will never regain his "foretold" kingdom "unless [he] / Endeavour[s], as [his] Father *David* did" (3.351–53). He attempts to attach Jesus to earthly hereditary succession by offering him his royal ancestor as a model of political virtue—as Herbert's Euarchus functions for Arethusius, and the historical Charles I for his son and his subjects—and also to persuade him that a providential plan for his heroic story is indeterminate at best, and perhaps nonexistent. Fate and prophecy may interact with chance and individual agency in some nebulous way, but no outcome can be guaranteed: "prediction still / In all things, and all men, supposes means, / Without means us'd, what it predicts revokes" (3.354–56). This reliance on pragmatic providence again parallels Cavendish's conviction that the gods are most helpful to those who help themselves. Satan's case accords with the postwar royalist stance that romance is founded on the uneasy collaboration of uncertain fortune and opportunistic heroism. Within this model, the hero may either "wait" or "Endeavour" to reclaim his right; both options require politic judgment and self-generated authority, since faith in providence alone answers no questions and ensures no victory.

Earlier in the poem, Jesus had privately acknowledged that he once found the royal romance of usurpation and restoration compelling.[74] Before his discovery of his identity from Mary and the exercising of his heroic subjectivity in the wilderness, the young hero (like the boy reader of the *Apology for Smectymnuus*) fantasized about himself as a knight of truth and justice, aspiring to something close to the zealous martial chivalry that Satan now proffers:

> victorious deeds
> Flam'd in my heart, heroic acts, one while
> To rescue Israel from the Roman yoke,
> Then to subdue and quell o're all the earth
> Brute violence and proud Tyrannick pow'r,
> Till truth were freed, and equity restor'd. (1.215–20)

However, as he comes to understand his surprising identity and the nature of his quest, his perspective on romance matures, and he exposes Satan's heroic narrative as a perverse veneer parodying and obscuring the true divine plot. In Jesus's rereading, it is Satan, not Tiberius and the Romans, who has "usurp't" the earthly kingdom and must be overcome, and who "first made" all "monster[s]" in need of expulsion (4.127–29, 183). As for the enslaved Israelites, their suffering under Roman rule is their own divinely ordained trial and a fit punishment for their idolatry, and their deliverance will come without any need for good fortune, politic "occasion," or monarchic might, since God "at length, time to himself best known. . . . May bring them back repentant and sincere' in accordance with his divine "providence" (3.433–35, 440). The time for action belongs to God to determine. In response to Satan's insistence that he fill an authoritative void by acting as *roi absolu* of his people and as *moi absolu* of his narrative, Jesus rebuffs these false absolutes as the desperate skeptic's substitutes for the one true absolute, which will prevail no matter how long it may remain concealed by political disaster or disappointment.

Finally, Jesus rejects Satan's assumption that his mission to reclaim his kingdom is that of the worldly royal hero and must therefore be accomplished by worldly royalist means:

> Know therefore when my season comes to sit
> On David's Throne, it shall be like a tree
> Spreading and over-shadowing all the Earth,
> Or as a stone that shall to pieces dash
> All Monarchies besides throughout the world,
> And of my Kingdom there shall be no end:

>   Means there shall be to this, but what the means,
>   Is not for thee to know, nor me to tell. (4.146–53)

Jesus's declaration that his romance is explicitly anti-royalist, the death knell for "All Monarchies besides," settles the matter of his narrative's ideology while refusing to answer any questions about its progress or its telos. Yet even as he dismisses martial chivalry and worldly ambition as elements of his narrative, he stresses that narrative's temporal reality and the conventionality of its inevitable end. As in book 12 of *Paradise Lost*, the Christian champion's victory is indefinitely forestalled yet absolutely assured: contrary to Fish's case that Jesus must resist the temptation of teleological plot, he reiterates that his "season" will come, that his story's glorious ending is guaranteed, and that this ending does, in fact, involve the forceful conquest of enemies and the recovery of a kingdom.[75] Satan has been right about the most basic tropes of his romance of kingship, but entirely wrong about their packaging and about the "means" that govern their progress. That progress is certain, but Satan—despite his insistence on fixed rules for heroic success—is too committed to his own revision of romance to believe in narrative certainty, and therefore cannot conceive of the middle of the story that ensures the transcendent end.

Jesus's declaration that the true story of his recovery of his father's throne is "not for [Satan] to know, nor [him] to tell" recalls the Lady's rebuff of Comus—"Fain would I somthing say, yet to what end? / Thou hast nor Eare, nor Soul to apprehend / The sublime notion" (783–85). It should also remind us of other examples in this book of the exclusionary power of divinely inspired heroic subjectivity and the stunted ability of the unregenerate to produce or comprehend right romance. Satan's temptations that Jesus replace God's romance with an inferior revision may be deceitful, but they also correspond to Satan's own willfully faulty understanding of the genre. Being "compos'd of lies / From the beginning" (1.407–8), Satan tells himself the same lies about the nature of romance narrative (as in *Paradise Lost*). His suggestion that Jesus's success hinges on the collaboration of politic action and fortune mirrors his speech to his followers, where he proposes that they take urgent measures to "learn" Jesus's identity in order to assess their "danger" that stands "on the utmost edge / Of hazard" (1.91–95). Satan's gambling terminology again suggests his Cavendishesque belief that chance and agency together govern affairs; accordingly, he imagines that he may yet "subvert"

God's plan for his Son if he acts swiftly (1.124). Even so, his stance on the nature of fate vacillates throughout this poem, too, continuing to present conflicting views on the muddled powers of personal agency, impersonal fortune, random contingency, and providence. Both Jesus and Milton's narrator are unequivocal that God's providence is the driving force behind the narrative of history: Jesus reproves ancient philosophers, and by implication Herbert's forlorn characters, for "accus[ing] [God] under usual names, / Fortune and Fate, as one regardless quite / Of mortal things" (4.316–18), while the narrator reminds us that Satan, "unweeting" and "contrary" to his own perceived purpose, "fulfill'd / The purpos'd Counsel pre-ordain'd and fixt / Of the most High" (1 126–28). However, Satan can neither admit such certainty nor fully shake it. Despite his suggestion to himself and his crew that they can act to influence their fate, elsewhere he admits once more that he despairs of altering God's judgment: "all hope is lost / Of my reception into grace; what worse? / For where no hope is left, is left no fear" (3.204–6). Like Arethusius, Satan finds it easier to conceive of divinity as the inexorable punisher of wickedness than as the assured ally of virtue. His hopeless courage serves only to inspire further fruitless action and, with it, further delusional hope; the circularity of Satan's belief and behavior locks him into an anti-teleological pattern entirely opposed to the shape of heroic romance, despite his apparent affinity for recent royalist treatments of the genre. Ironically, while Satan does indeed attempt to convince Jesus that he is a character in a certain kind of chivalric story, as Fish suggests, Jesus's heroic subjectivity has already made him aware that he *is* a character in the ultimate plot, while Satan is finally defeated by his *own* "inability or unwillingness . . . to recognize" that that plot exists.[76] Having rejected a real developing narrative for himself, Satan cannot conceive that his adversary could possess one without relying on the illusion of "hazard" to direct its progress.

Satan's inability or refusal to grasp the full sense of an ending to God's or his own story throws his most seemingly candid speech in the poem into sharp relief. When Jesus demands to know the reason for his solicitousness—"Know'st thou not that my rising is thy fall, / And my promotion will be thy destruction?" (3.201–2)—Satan replies that he has grown weary of waiting to learn the nature of his doom, since it is already certain:

> If there be worse, the expectation more
> Of worse torments me then the feeling can.

> I would be at the worst; worst is my Port,
> My harbour and my ultimate repose,
> The end I would attain, my final good. (3.207–11)

Claiming to be eager for the conclusion of the divine narrative, he irrationally justifies his attempts to provoke Jesus into alleviating his uncertainty by alleging that he already knows how the story ends. Jesus declines to sympathize with Satan's suffering and cuts through the knot of his illogical claim to simultaneous suspense and despair:

> My time I told thee (and that time for thee
> Were better farthest off) is not yet come;
> When that comes think not thou to find me slack
> On my part aught endeavouring, or to need
> Thy politic maxims, or that cumbersome
> Luggage of war there shewn me, argument
> Of human weakness rather then of strength. (3.396–402)

Beyond banishing "politic maxims" and the "Luggage of war" as signs of the "weakness" of secular romance, Jesus speaks only of his narrative's certain progress toward its actively heroic climax, and gestures parenthetically toward his enemy's willful ignorance. Satan is granted no insight into the divine plot because he refuses to believe that any such insight is possible or that any such plot exists. And he cannot in fact conceive of the story's end; if he could, he would have no desire to hasten it. Satan pleads for relief from the romance reader's illusory suspense; Jesus ominously informs him that if he understood the author's providential plot, he would be in no suspense at all.

The effect of Jesus's words is often to frustrate not only his adversary, but the audience, too. The heroic subjectivity of Milton's protagonist is so intensely private, exclusive, and defiant that it has been excluding and repelling readers for centuries. As a result, *Paradise Regained* has developed a reputation for being a difficult, narratively unconventional poem of indeterminacy, negation, inaction, and silence. Fish, Patterson, and Schwartz all broadly agree that Satan's goal is to press Jesus into making certain statements about his divinity and taking actions that confirm it, and that Jesus resists him by refusing to provide answers that would violate the ambiguity of the sacred (or, for that matter, give the reader any satisfying information).

This argument is sensible from a very specific angle, but we must be careful about how we understand Satanic "certainty" as opposed to divine "ambiguity." Satan, committed to a royalist romance discourse, actually harps on ambiguity and uncertainty as absolute facts before grasping at their opposites. Just as it is he who experiences the real difficulty in thinking of himself as a hero within a teleological plot, it is he who keeps insisting on narrative ambiguity and the inauthenticity of divinely bestowed heroic subjectivity, as in his warning that prophecy does not entail predestination (3.354–56), his willful claim that the title "Son of God . . . bears no single sence" (4.517), and his final grand tirade before setting Jesus on the pinnacle of the temple:

> if I read aught in Heaven,
> Or Heav'n write aught of Fate, by what the Stars . . .
> In their conjunction met, give me to spell,
> Sorrows, and labours, opposition, hate
> Attends thee, scorns, reproaches, injuries,
> Violence and stripes, and lastly cruel death.
> A Kingdom they portend thee, but what Kingdom,
> Real or Allegoric I discern not,
> Nor when, eternal sure, as without end,
> Without beginning; for no date prefixt
> Directs me in the Starry Rubric set. (4.382–93)

With this last gasp of malicious frustration, Satan articulates all the confusions of his revised romance at once: Is he reading the text of Heaven or of fate?[77] Can a hero's suffering really be a meaningful precondition of his triumph? Is Jesus's kingship 'real,' or only a convenient metaphor? Finally, his confusion leads him to proclaim that, because *he* cannot discern its structure, the narrative itself must be inherently unstructured and meaningless: there are no ends, no beginnings, no coherent middles. He is obsessed not with seeking answers to his questions, but with endlessly repeating the questions to which he has already decided there are no answers. Patterson holds that Satan is "driven by the need to know the truth" about Jesus's identity and mission; but as the eternal enemy of all Milton's elect heroes who seek and defend Truth, Satan is repelled by the real truth about anything.[78] He has spent the entire poem insisting to Jesus that truth is relative, that exceptional subjectivity for the godly is a delusion, that a nebulous providence cannot allow him to know anything for sure, and that the only path to power and security is through one's own secular standards and politic self-determination.

Jesus, on the other hand, appears to become increasingly vague in his responses to Satan even as he becomes increasingly sure—at least, sure enough—of his heroic identity and his quest. Whatever narrative vision his wandering trials have granted him, however, would be meaningless to Satan, who is always already convinced that providential illumination cannot be real or trustworthy. To Satan, divinely imparted self-assuredness looks indistinguishable from infuriating ambiguity, as is the case with Jesus's riddling: "Think not but that I know these things, or think / I know them not; not therefore am I short / Of knowing what I ought" (4.286–88). We, the audience, are also not fully privy to what Jesus knows about himself and his destiny; but like the poem's hero (and like Adam in *Paradise Lost* or the "serviceable" cast of the *Nativity Ode*), we know all that we need to at present. It would be a grave mistake for us to assume along with Satan that what we do not know does not exist to be known, that "there is no 'there' there."

The critical impulse to reduce *Paradise Regained* to antinarrative silence seems linked to the urge to decouple it from romance or any other genre. For instance, Patterson proposes that the answer to whether the Son's kingdom is "Real or Allegoric" is "neither," but we would do much better to accept the full weight of the romance trope and say that it is both.[79] The kingdom of God that would "to pieces dash / All monarchies besides" may have been a powerful symbol in the hearts and minds of the community that resisted the restoration of royalism, but Milton and his fellow Puritan republicans would have insisted that its status as merely symbolic was temporary, just as Jesus does. Milton's Christian narrative, as "the reality of which the dragon-killing romance is a parody," features a real hero destined to overcome a real foe in real time and finally for all time. Even though (as Michael warns Adam) the Son's battle with Satan remains deferred and never takes the form of a martial "Duel" (12.387), the fact and the providentially ordained outcome of their combat still stand as bulwarks of generic conventionality against Satan's innovative ambiguation. When Jesus stands on the pinnacle, he stands against his enemy's attempts to strip all absolute meaning from sacred identity, godly heroism, and narrative temporality and to locate the self as the only absolute power. Undaunted by all temptations to value romance's surface over its structure, to choose politic calculation over faithful submission, and to create a new story to suit his own needs in his own time, Jesus takes his place within the story that has already been written and waits for its next adventure. His heroic subjectivity possesses him so strongly that Satan flees before that profoundly interiorized conviction, "smitten with amazement," unable to withstand what he refuses to understand (4.562).

In that moment, the romance plot within *Paradise Regained* has reached its predestined climax: Jesus has "vanquish[ed] / Temptation" and "regain'd lost Paradise" (4.607–8). Yet the challenges of Milton's poem do not disappear. Jesus may have attained the knowledge he needs, but the audience has heard few revelations and seen little action. And as countless readers have noted, the larger story does not end with Jesus's descent from the pinnacle. He can only now "on [his] glorious work / ... enter, and begin to save mankind," and the horizon of the romance landscape remains wide open as he returns "Home to his Mothers house" (4.634–35, 639). As one quest episode concludes, another begins. But the divine romance of *Paradise Regained* is neither endless nor aimless. J. Martin Evans has argued that Milton regards contemplation as a predecessor to action rather than a replacement for it, and that *Paradise Regained* signals the continuation of the Christian story rather than the dissolution of narrative: "Although the final lines return Christ to his mother's house, Milton has made it clear that the 'Queller of Satan' (4.634) is only on the brink of his divine mission. The real action is just about to begin."[80] The poem *does* continually promise "real" romance heroism in an indefinite future—but given those promises, why does Milton return Jesus to Mary's house at all? Why do the last lines of the poem gesture toward further patience and quiet contemplation rather than to action?

To begin to answer this question, we must return to the visionary summit, Spenser's device in *The Faerie Queene* that so inspired Milton. The Redcrosse Knight, Adam, and Jesus are all granted visions of sacred narrative as they stand on great heights. When Redcrosse descends from his momentary prospect above his story, his vision fades as his eyes readjust to the mortal world; he must return, only imperfectly enlightened, to the Christian warrior's burden of action within time. Adam's mortal sight is also too weak for a full understanding of history, and he returns from the mountain poised to enter the active world with mixed faith and doubt. But *Paradise Regained* ends not with Jesus's spectacular battle with Satan or his commencement of active labors: it ends with his quiet return to his mother's house. Had Spenser made a similar move, the Legend of Holiness would have concluded with Redcrosse relaxing in the castle of Cœlia, his combat with the dragon still ahead. A historicist explanation is possible: while Spenser is immediately concerned with the next tasks facing his elect nation, Milton's England has been derailed from its course. But this rationale seems insufficient. Unlike Redcrosse and Adam, Jesus does not lose his grasp on the narrative vision he has received. When he comes down from his mountain or his pinnacle, his descent is only physical. In effect, Jesus dwells in his visionary moment even after it has passed: he finds it down on the ground, whether at the angels' banquet in the wilderness or in Mary's house, amid everyday life. From that time on, his universal prospect and his private home are one and the same.

Paradise Regained's concluding evocation of Jesus at home with his mother also recalls the quiet scene at the end of the *Nativity Ode*, which finds the "Courtly Stable" full of angels waiting with Mary in "order serviceable," peacefully anticipating her baby's remote heroic future (237–44). Returning from his first romance quest, Jesus reenters this domestic space as an adult who can consciously participate in the experience of standing "serviceable" to sacred narrative, simultaneously aware of its "Full and perfect" arc and of his present place within its meandering course. He sees the story at once from a divine, authorial height and through the lowly striving of a human character like Mary, uniting Spenser's two kinds of romance perspective. Stuart Curran has proposed that by the poem's end Jesus "lives without time," "liberated from the constraints of time and history."[81] In a sense, this is so, but the full extent of Jesus's heroic accomplishment (and of Milton's generic accomplishment) is only clear if we recognize that he also lives *within* time, *dedicated to* the occluded demands of historical narrative as they arise and become known. Both Jesus and Milton remain committed to providential romance as a genre ideally suited to the tempest of time, and to the post-Restoration Puritan moment in particular, in that it embodies the tension between the doubts and disappointments of the present and the triumphant promise of the future, using that tension to drive the story of the godly community onward through its political vicissitudes and toward its final vanishing point. While Satan's royalist-inflected romance attempts to shed an artificial light on the darkness of history, Milton's renewed chance at true romance depends both on the hero's providential illumination and on his willingness to wander, or to stand and wait, in the human world of darkened narrative vision.

CHAPTER 4

"My Victorious Triumphs Are All Thine"

The Politics of Love and Elect Community in
Lucy Hutchinson's Order and Disorder

Percy Herbert, Margaret Cavendish, and John Milton all determined, in their own ways, that postwar ideological romance had to confront the challenges of contingency and variable subjectivity, and that both heroism and identification with a romance community might depend less on assured narrative vision than on one's response to narrative uncertainty. Milton, in his generic conflict with royalist romance, continued to insist on the legitimacy of divinely inspired heroic subjectivity, opposing the Hobbesian proposition that since no such thing could be proven, it effectively did not exist. In her biblical epic *Order and Disorder*, Lucy Hutchinson is similarly adamant. As we will see, though, she is invested in resisting a different royalist model: one that affirms the authenticity of heroic subjectivity but rejects its exclusivity to an "elect" subset of believers. This chapter, and the final one that follows, explore a subtle shift in seventeenth-century attitudes to romance: some writers, instead of concerning themselves with the genre's subversive power (for good or ill) to identify subjects within already-demarcated ideological communities, grew more interested in its potential to envision and construct new communities, and to repair old divides in subjectivity. While Hutchinson refuses to indulge the idea that romance might mend rifts in religion or politics—a possibility that inspired her royalist contemporary, John Dryden—her tacit return to romance in *Order and Disorder* does help her renegotiate some of the ruptures in genre, narrative perspective, and gendered heroic subjectivity that troubled her *Memoirs* of her husband.

Scholarship on *Order and Disorder* is only now emerging from its infancy, but one assertion in its preface has already attracted attention. Hutchinson warns potential readers who "understand and love the elegancies of poems" that they will find "nothing of fancy" in her work, and avows that a literary imagination has no place in biblical hermeneutics: "Had I a fancy, I durst not have exercised it here; for I tremble to think of turning Scripture into a romance; and shall not be troubled at their dislike who dislike on that account, and profess they think no poem can be good that shuts out drunkenness, and lasciviousness, and libelling satire, the themes of all their celebrated songs. These . . . dislike not the poem so much as the subject of it."[1] Hutchinson seems to smear romance as an ungodly form, and (as with Milton) many scholars have taken her at her word. Long before the poem's authorship was known, C. A. Moore read it as "a veiled rebuke of Milton" for his highly inventive retelling of Genesis in *Paradise Lost*.[2] Many decades later, David Norbrook, who discovered, attributed, and edited the complete twenty-canto text of the poem, likewise acknowledges that Hutchinson "may have been hitting at Milton" for his "[addition] to the text" of Scripture.[3] Hutchinson does indeed seem to equate such "fancy" with a crass and impious treatment of God's word as "romance," a genre she associates not only (perhaps) with Milton but also with loose and disorderly Cavalier writing.

Yet Norbrook also regards Hutchinson's rebuke of "fancy" with a healthy measure of skepticism: he finds *Order and Disorder* "far from artless" and reads the poem as suggesting that "human artifice can be redeemed" by God.[4] Even in the poem's preface, Hutchinson begins to imagine precisely this sort of artistic redemption. Referring to her earlier translation of Lucretius's pagan account "of the original of things," she claims that *Order and Disorder* began as a form of personal prayer and penitence: "These meditations were not at first designed for public view, but fixed upon to reclaim a busy roving thought from wandering in the pernicious and perplexed maze of human inventions; whereinto the vain curiosity of youth had drawn me" (3). In essence, Hutchinson began to compose her poem in her hope of redemption from a "roving," "wandering" romance of the mind; her meditations on scripture have led her, by God's grace, away from the Lucretian "maze" of atomistic contingency and into a providential and teleological narrative of creation. Not at all unlike Milton in *Paradise Lost* and *Paradise Regained*, Hutchinson turns away from the ideologically corrupt romance of fortune, but rather than truly rejecting the genre, she instead embraces the romance of providence, the plot of which follows the ever-purposeful trials and triumphs of the elect. The poem that she began in search of redemption *from* romance will, by its (unfinished) end, prove to be another model for a Puritan redemption *of* romance.

As Robert Wilcher has noted, "Romance was a narrative genre that had appealed to [Hutchinson's] adolescent imagination during the 1630s":[5] in her fragmentary autobiography, Hutchinson recalls that as a girl, "I thought it no sin to learne or heare wittie songs and amorous sonnetts or poems, and twenty things of that kind, wherein I was so apt that I became the confident in all the loves that were managed among my mother's young weomen."[6] Norbrook suggests that she was probably one of the seventeenth century's many admirers of Sidney's *Arcadia*; he observes parallels between Sidney's romance imagery and Hutchinson's in her elegies and points out that elegy 11 "gives her husband the Sidneian name of 'Philocles.'"[7] But apart from Norbrook's passing note, Wilcher is the one other scholar to date who has concerned himself specifically with Hutchinson's *Order and Disorder* and a godly treatment of the romance tradition.[8] He provides a useful overview of some of the epic's romance elements, arguing that while "features of fictional romance" are "deliberately eschewed in the 1679 volume," which included only the first five cantos and their account of the Creation and the Fall, elements of the genre "became prominent in the narrative expansion of later episodes."[9] Wilcher points to sections in which Hutchinson invents psychological interiority for her biblical characters and to passages featuring love and marriage, most notably Jacob and Rachel's pastoral courtship. He claims that these "features of fictional romance" are sparse in the poem's first half and chiefly involve the emotional and erotic experiences of women. The chapters of Genesis that do not feature "the marriages and other sexual liaisons of the patriarchs" give Hutchinson scope for "moral and religious 'meditations'" and "occasional political observations" but "offer little to stimulate an imagination nourished in its early years on amorous sonnets and romances."[10] In Wilcher's reading, feminine romance occasionally emerges to enrich certain episodes of *Order and Disorder*, but romance does not underpin the poem's narrative form or purpose.

Wilcher is right to draw our attention to the elements of romance in *Order and Disorder*, and Hutchinson's engagement with the mode often does pertain to love and marriage. However, while this chapter is indebted to his work, I would like to move beyond a straightforward enumeration of some of the romance episodes in the poem, and I hope to complicate Wilcher's definition of the genre based on Pierre Huet's seventeenth-century opinion that "Romances . . . have Love for their principal Theme, and meddle not with War and Politicks but by accident"—an opinion that his contemporaries often did not share, as we have seen.[11] As Wilcher shows, Hutchinson did *not* necessarily "tremble to think of turning Scripture into a romance." It remains for us to determine how she, like Milton, understood her adult relationship to the genre and why she turned to it so often in *Order and Disorder* after repudiating it. First, I hope to show that Hutchinson does not clearly distinguish between romance that is erotic, psychological, or pastoral (i.e., feminine) and romance that is martial, heroic, or political (i.e., masculine)—indeed, her poem reconsiders some of the generic and gendered gaps that emerged in her *Memoirs*. For Hutchinson, as for Sidney and even Milton, the eroticism of romance is inextricably connected to her sense of heroism, and private emotion and action in her text have direct relationships to public politics and governance. It is thus not quite true that Hutchinson reserves romance for the poem's second half; such content runs throughout her text, connecting later episodes in Genesis and passages in the poem to earlier ones. Second, I propose that Hutchinson's self-contradictory tendency to "[turn] Scripture into a romance" is neither an accident nor merely an offshoot of her youthful enthusiasm for the genre. Rather, like Milton, Hutchinson takes royalist modes of erotic and heroic romance into account in composing *Order and Disorder* and combats them not with anti-romance but with right romance as the exclusive province of a godly republican audience—in her case, an explicitly Calvinist elect community whom God has predestined as the heroes of history. While Wilcher regards Hutchinson's reflections on "the mystery of 'election' as one of [her] moral and religious 'meditations'" rather than an example of "creative engagement," we will see that her treatment of elect exceptionalism lays fundamental groundwork for her postwar Puritan romance, and that it reappears as a major theme throughout diverse instances of her engagement with the mode.[12] Before we return to Hutchinson's Genesis epic, a consideration of romance as a strategy in John Dryden's poem "Astraea Redux" will help illuminate how *Order and Disorder* presents a godly audience with treatments of exclusive elect community, erotic love, chivalric heroism, and teleological narrative that actively resist both Cavalier literature and royalist political ideology.

PATRILINEAL ROMANCE AND EROTIC UNIVERSALISM IN DRYDEN'S "ASTRAEA REDUX"

Dryden's jubilant panegyric, written to celebrate Charles II's return to England more than a decade after his father's execution, does not approach the royalist narrative of a tyrant's usurpation of the throne and the rightful heir's recovery of it by recounting the story chronologically, as a prose romance might. Still, "Astraea Redux" undoubtedly embraces the discourse of epic romance as a mode of understanding history, celebrating Charles's restoration, and advocating for royalist policy. Dryden's young king appears not simply as another Aeneas or Augustus, the Virgilian harbinger of a new golden age, but also as the tempest-tossed hero of countless classical, medieval, and early modern romances of fortune and providence.

Having been driven "into exile from his rightful throne," the "Heir to his father's sorrows with his crown" is "Forced to suffer for himself and us," his people (75, 50–52).[13] Charles is "tossed by fate" until "His manly courage over[comes]" ill fortune and he returns to rule his kingdom at last (51, 56). As the expectations of romance dictate, the sources of the hero's strife are directed, however indirectly, to guide him to safety and triumph: "those loud storms that did against him roar / Have cast his shipwrecked vessel on the shore" of his kingdom, where Charles's romance will conclude in his reunion with his loving subjects in a symbolic marriage (123–24). Dryden's poem, conceiving romance as reparative rather than exclusive, depicts the Restoration as the harmonious telos to the turbulent national story, and even hints at theological universalism: God has blessed and redeemed all English people equally in their blissful union with the king.

"Astraea Redux" reminds us that while Herbert and Cavendish's postwar uneasiness with providential or "mystical" romance was widespread among royalist writers, that discomfort was not ubiquitous. Although Dryden's poem attributes events to various forces, including fate and astral influences, it insists on God as the final authority, wholeheartedly embracing a divine design to history and a narrative shape in which all of the hero's sorrows and wanderings are directed to restore him to his rightful place. In his epigraph, with its beautifully free translation of Virgil's fourth eclogue, Dryden conforms to the classical tendency to depict historical time as cyclical: "The last great age, foretold by sacred rhymes, / Renews its finish'd course; Saturnian times / Roll round again." In the body of the poem, however, his vision of predestined history unfolds according to the more linear modus operandi of a Christian providence.[14] Charles II's peaceful restoration illustrates Christ's mercy on sinful England:

> Heaven would no bargain for its blessings drive,
> But what we could not pay for, freely give.
> The prince of peace would, like himself, confer
> A gift unhoped, without the price of war. (137–40)

This free grace is granted to an entire nation that does not deserve it; Dryden begins to suggest that neither he nor God have marked out an exclusive subset of English men and women as special beneficiaries of the happy ending to the nation's story. Still, the "prince of peace" has his own policy for conferring such gifts: they are best given and best received when their absence has been long felt. Knowing "his blessing's worth," God in his providence "took care, / That we should know it by repeated prayer; / Which stormed the skies and ravished Charles from thence, / As heaven itself is took by violence" (141–44). In other words, he has deliberately authored and presided over a lengthy national romance. Even in rejoicing at the king's miraculous return, Dryden's language evokes the "violence" that "ravished" him away in the first place and reminds his audience how many times their pleas for deliverance had to be "repeated" before they were granted; the story of Charles's loss and recovery is linear and orderly in retrospect, but (by God's will) it did not appear that way while it was still in progress. Although Dryden's divine romance belongs to all England, not to an ideological subset of its people, his God is like Milton's or Hutchinson's in that he chastens, rewards, and teaches his people through the patterns of genre.

Indeed, once the unfolding of history has allowed him to see the full arc of the divine plot, Dryden's poetic voice resembles Milton's Adam in questioning how best to "express" his "doubtful thoughts" that must "both regret and bless" Charles's and England's "sufferings" (71–72). And like Hutchinson in her autobiographical writing, Dryden ultimately chooses to celebrate the fact that he was born in an age of historical romance—one of heroism and hardship:

> Some lazy ages lost in sleep and ease
> No action leave to busy chronicles:
> Such whose supine felicity but makes
> In story chasms, in epoches mistakes;
> O'er whom time gently shakes his wings of down
> Till with his silent sickle they are mown.
> Such is not Charles's too too active age,
> Which, governed by the wild distempered rage
> Of some black star infecting all the skies,
> Made him at his own cost like Adam wise. (105–14)

The present period may be "too too active," subject to great suffering and "cost," yet it seems that Dryden's speaker would hardly have it otherwise. A peaceful era is "lazy" and finally "lost," doomed to be "gently . . . mown" into historical oblivion; it creates a dull blank or even a nihilistic rift within the great "story" of time and offers no material to great storytellers. The age of Charles II may appear to be "governed by . . . some black star," but it is really (or also) authored by God, and it offers the kind of wisdom that can only be attained by one who—"like Adam"—lives through the tempest of the story rather than the "chasm" of peaceful ignorance.

Dryden further distinguishes himself from a Cavendishesque approach to romance by downplaying the role of personal agency in shaping history. Like Milton's characters, the historical figures in "Astraea Redux" may err when they mistake the right occasion for heroic action, such as Sir George Booth, whose 1659 military campaign on Charles's behalf ended in defeat. Dryden commends Booth's dutiful courage but rebukes his "valour" as "forward": "The attempt was fair; but heaven's prefixed hour / Not come" (145–48). Divine illumination alone can determine the right time for the right agent to act—and in this case, it is General Monck "whom Providence designed" to deliver England from the "real bonds" of "false freedom" (151–52).[15] Unlike the conclusion of *Paradise Lost*, however, which emphasizes the centuries of anticipation and struggle that both pre- and postdate the arrival of the Messiah, and which reminds us that neither Adam's firstborn son nor his grandchildren nor any of his conceivable descendants will complete the narrative that Adam's fall began, "Astraea Redux" comforts its audience with the conventional romance promise of the next generation. History enabled Dryden to rejoice in a real-world exemplar of patrilineal romance, in which a faithful son recovers what was stolen from his father; and also of intergenerational romance (like those beloved by Shakespeare), in which young people set the foolish mistakes of their parents to rights.

The poem opens by setting up tension between the younger generation (among whom Dryden counts himself) and their puritanical elders: "Youth, that with joys had unacquainted been, / Envied grey hairs, that once good days had seen: / We thought our sires, not with their own content, / Had ere we came to age our portion spent" (26–29).[16] But by the time the poem ends, this fear has been allayed by the restoration of the young king and by *his* restoration of England to an even happier state than it had enjoyed under his father. Charles may be "Heir to his father's sorrows with his crown," but he is also destined to see those sorrows end, undoing the ill suffered and the damage done by the previous generation (52).[17] His time of trial proves to be precisely that—a test rendering him worthy of his crown and ensuring that he will wear it with care: "Inured to suffer, ere he came to reign, / No rash procedure will his actions stain" (87–88). Charles II's diplomatic future reign is implicitly contrasted with his father's past, which may at times have been marred by rashness as a result of Charles I's sheltered youth. By the poem's end, the young people who lamented the wrongs of their "sires" will welcome their monarch's return and collectively perform the role of the bride in the historical romance's royal wedding, with both representatives of generational promise uniting in one flesh and one nation.

Crucially, the happy ending to the exiled king's story is represented not by a martial conquest, but by Charles's loving marriage to his subjects after long strife and separation.[18] Dryden's England, deprived of her royal bridegroom before the consummation of their union, has spent years envying her happier sisters on the continent and bemoaning the ill fortune that keeps her from her lord: "And heaven that seemed regardless of our fate, / For France and Spain did miracles create . . . / While our cross stars denied us Charles's bed, / Whom our first flames and virgin love did wed" (13–20). For Dryden, the rebellious people and their monarch are star-crossed lovers rather than enemies in war. Even the rebellion itself ought to be understood not as political hostility between irreconcilable foes, but as the folly of an amorous quarrel: instead of traitors, the people are "Like early lovers, whose unpractised hearts / Were long the May-game of malicious arts," subjecting the faithful Charles to the mistrust and fickleness of the archetypal coy or harsh mistress (211–12).[19] But Dryden assures the king that, like all romance lovers who put their love to the test, "since reformed by what we did amiss / We by our sufferings learn to prize our bliss" (209–10).[20] Regretting their vanity, his subjects "With double heat renew their fires again," and now that they have endured separation from their beloved as a fitting punishment for their foolishness, the much-anticipated wedding night is finally at hand (214).

This consummate reunion accomplishes more than ending a quarrel: it effectively wipes the quarrel from history and memory, an erotic Oblivion Act comparable to the legislation that pardoned countless republicans after monarchy was restored.[21] Dryden performs this erasure with another metaphor of marriage and sexuality in identifying the ship that carried Charles back to England: "The Naseby, now no longer England's shame, / But better to be lost in Charles's name, / (Like some unequal bride in nobler sheets) / Receives her lord" (230–33). The *Naseby*, originally named to celebrate the 1645 battle that dealt a crushing defeat to the royalists, was rechristened the *Royal Charles* when it arrived in Holland to transport the king home. By bearing the weight of Charles's body and by taking his name, Dryden suggests, the vessel's former "shame" is "lost" along with the name that commemorated that ignominy.[22] England's feminine inferiority submits to the king's masculine authority and is claimed and transfigured by it; the ugly shame of civil war morphs first into the alluring shame of the "unequal" virgin bride in her marriage bed and then into unashamed wedded union. Through the power of love and marriage, the original significance of the old name is transformed, then forgotten. A similar process occurs as Dryden imagines the ship nearing the white cliffs of Dover, whose color again initially signifies shame. The poet assures the monarch that his eager eyes do not deceive him: "As you meet it, the land approacheth you. / The land returns, and in the white it wears / The marks of penitence and sorrow bears" (253–55). Yet Charles's love and forgiveness remake England's remorse into something new: tears of regret turn into "tears of joy, for your returning spilt," which "Work out and expiate our former guilt" (274–75). Likewise, Dryden soon re-signifies whiteness—"And now time's whiter series is begun, / Which in soft centuries shall smoothly run"—and the color of England's contrition implicitly becomes the color of its purity and perfection as the king's bride (292–93). Mingling the imagery of amorous reunion and High Anglican (or Catholic) penitence, Dryden represents the mutual love between the king and his people as a force that transforms all the sufferings of the past two decades into the blessings of a completed romance narrative. The poem's earlier hints at universalism merge with its erotic romance: the entire nation is redeemed; all subjects are reinscribed as feminine in shame but then as masculine in marriage; and most important, everyone is now a royalist.[23] Dryden's royal romance has rejected exclusive ideological community in favor of all-inclusive erotic union.

Lois Potter has pointed out that the dramatic and prose Stuart romances which idealized the relationship between Charles I and Henrietta Maria, delineated a distinctively royalist stance on eroticism and marriage in which true love valorizes compromise, transcending worldly divisions of nationality and religion that might otherwise have kept apart the king and his French Catholic queen.[24] "Astraea Redux" takes a similar position in celebrating the restored relationship between Charles II and his universally beloved subjects: love overcomes all obstacles and heals all wounds, even those caused by bitter civil strife. Erotic love, in this royalist mode, is a nebulous yet tremendously potent force that sweeps away abstruse political and philosophical concerns. Of course, as Potter, Erica Veevers, and Victoria Kahn have demonstrated, it erects different ideologies in their place and is far from apolitical. The royalist politics and poetics of eroticism extol monarchy as the only form of government that can effect a perfect union between the state and its people, pointing to harmonious love as both the rationale and the result of policies such as the Indemnity and Oblivion Act of 1660 and the subsequent Test Acts and Act of Uniformity that mandated membership in the Anglican Communion. Love conquers all, joining royalists and republicans, fostering religious harmony through conformity, and reuniting spouses whom violence or misunderstanding have thrust apart. This universalizing spirit of love, which proceeds from Charles II as the messianic prince of peace, inspires Dryden's ardent patriotism in "Astraea Redux"—and Hutchinson's burning contempt in *Order and Disorder*.

"MIXED MARRIAGES" PRODUCE MONSTERS: SPIRITUAL MISCEGENATION AND TYRANNY IN *ORDER AND DISORDER*

In her epic poem, Hutchinson expresses scorn and revulsion for the royalist perspective on universalizing love that we find in "Astraea Redux" and elsewhere. But while she takes pride in the idea that her poem will repel

Cavalier readers because it abhors "lasciviousness," her biblical narrative does not distinguish itself from royalist models of romance by shunning eroticism. Instead, godly love in *Order and Disorder* plays a vital role in the divine romance by eschewing Dryden's royalist policy of prioritizing harmonious union over religious and political agreement: according to the poem's conception of right romance, unity of ideology must precede unity in marriage.[25] Hutchinson's romance community of believers, conventionally Sidneian in its erotic foundation, can essentially be defined as the class of the elect according to the Calvinist dogma of double predestination, and so is more exclusive than ever.

Hutchinson's uncompromising stance on erotic love emerges within the poem's early cantos and arises out of martial chivalric rhetoric. It is founded on her identification of the Fall, together with God's promise that Eve's "seed" will break the head of the serpent, as the "first beginning" of the "great war" between "two opposèd seeds":

> Two sovereign champions here we find,
> Satan and Christ contending for mankind.
> Two empires here, two opposite cities rise,
> Dividing all in two societies:
> The little Church and the World's larger State,
> Pursuing it with ceaseless spite and hate. (5.80–81, 85–90)

While Christ and Satan are the "champions" of this cosmic combat, humans serve as lesser warriors: "each age [is] with new combatants supplied," and the "great war" has been "Carried along more than five thousand year, / With various success on either side' (5.82–84). Yet the "little Church" finds "Hope in the promise' of God's "most certain oracle," while "Hell and the World fight upon desperate terms" (5.92–94): both sides know that the war is predestined to end with Christ's exclusive "society" victorious. This interpretation of Genesis as the beginning of the narrative of Christian salvation is a theological commonplace, which Hutchinson couches in the language of epic romance.[26] Her expanded reading of the divine "oracle," however, extends her reformation of the mode for a godly community. God's promise, she explains, contains his "Precepts and rules" for the "new obedience" of his chosen people (5.210). Chief among these is the forbidding of any association with the seed of Satan:

> Our first injunction is to hate and fly
> The flatteries of our first grand enemy;
> To have no friendship with his cursèd race,
> The interest of the opposite seed t'embrace. (5.213–16)

Much is contained within this prime directive. First, there is Hutchinson's assumption that it is "ours"—in other words, that she and her readers are among the community of the elect, the protagonists and "combatants" in the sacred heroic narrative for whom the command is intended. Next, there are several polarizing absolutes: that all who do not fall into this first person plural are the "cursèd race" of the "grand enemy," that their "interest" is diametrically opposed to that of the godly, and that the two factions must therefore have nothing to do with each other (other than battle). Last, there is a hint of sexual prohibition in particular within the broader rule of separation: "The interest of the opposite seed" suggests philosophical and political concerns, but the ban on "friendship" and "embrac[ing]" verges into the personal and the erotic. Crucially, any eroticism in Hutchinson's lines is restrictive rather than inviting; she gestures toward the possibility of sexual congress with the "opposite seed," but only to dismiss it as repugnant.[27] Her formulation renders Dryden's universalist erotics unthinkable.

Order and Disorder's postlapsarian narrative makes the theme of spiritual miscegenation, and God's hatred of it, explicit. After murdering his brother Abel, Cain, the first reprobate in the Calvinist tradition, "found a wife who left for him her God" and "Both founders of the Worldly State became" (6.350–51). An unholy marriage in which a woman subordinates her religion to her desire produces the entirety of the "cursèd race" that is destined to wage war on the elect for millennia to come. (Notably, the Geneva Bible's annotations suggest that Cain's son Lamech, by taking two wives, was the first to profane "the lawful institution of marriage, which is, that two should be one flesh"; Hutchinson, who imagines marriage already corrupted by Cain's wife's abandonment of God for her reprobate husband, sees no need to include Lamech or his bigamy in her poem.[28]) She then identifies Seth, Adam and Eve's third child, as "the founder of the Holy State," but notes that from the inception of history, God's elect community has been in danger of losing its numbers to the "Worldly State" through intermarriage: "Seth's offspring did God's ways decline, / Mixed with Cain's impious brood, yet of that line / In every age some few with pure hearts sought / The Lord of Life and to their children taught" (7.1–4). The combat between the "two opposite cities" becomes a reproductive battle as well as an ideological one, though as ever, the elect are destined to win, regardless of their army's small size. Although Cain and his wife's "family increased," Hutchinson notes, "Oft are they multiplied who are not blessed," their increase becoming rankness of nature devoid of providential purpose, while "The holy seed still with advantage dies / That it in new and glorious form might rise" (6.353–54, 429–30).

As the narrative continues, Hutchinson's emphasis on God's prohibition of love between the elect and reprobate communities leads her into vociferously Calvinist readings of scripture, such as Genesis 6:1–4, in which "the sons of God saw the daughters of men that they were fair, and they took them wives of all that they liked." In so doing, these "Sons of God"

> all the greater ends of marriage slight,
> Conducted by their sensual appetite;
> With profane wives defiling that pure bed
> Which God to holy use determined,
> To be a seminary for his plants
> And fill his city with inhabitants. (6.533–40)

The sons of God, for Calvinist adherents to the Geneva translation, are not angelic beings but "the children of the godly which began to degenerate," while the "daughters of men" are "those that came of wicked parents."[29] Hutchinson adopts this reading, adding her own observation that the defilers of marriage risk depopulating the Holy State. She emphasizes that the profane union of the reprobate with the "Sons of God" causes monstrous births to follow: "But these mixed marriages produced a brood / That stained the earth with violence and blood; / Men of prodigious valour, strength and size / Whose monstrous crimes were no less prodigies" (6.541–44). For Hutchinson, the grotesqueness of "these mixed marriages" has nothing to do with the union of humans with angels or demons, nor with intercourse between physically or nationally distinct peoples. Rather, the abomination is *spiritual* miscegenation; the erotic and social "embracing" of the "opposite seed" generates the race of monsters that God's chosen "combatants" must battle.[30]

Hutchinson proposes that early spiritual miscegenation also introduced false religion into the world, which she associates with the gaudy trappings of Catholicism or High Anglicanism: under the "Oppression" of the monstrous "brood," "sincere worship was no more allowed / But driven out by the tumultuous crowd / Who new ways of invoking God begin, / Bringing vain pomp and men's inventions in" (6.547–50). Her expanded version of Genesis 6:1–4 considers the values and aims of both Caroline erotic romance and Caroline conciliatory policy and turns them upside down.[31] In *Order and Disorder*, no love can justify the union of two peoples waging constant spiritual war with each other. By implication, fallen Protestants who commit spiritual miscegenation in the name of love and dynastic reproduction (e.g., Charles I and his son, in taking Catholic wives) or for the sake of money, status, or security (e.g., nonconformists who submit to the Test and Uniformity Acts and join the politic body of the king's church) have been seduced by seventeenth-century Duessas and threaten to reintroduce corruption into God's chosen nation, "fill[ing] his city" with the wrong "inhabitants." These sins, like the "mixed marriages" at the dawn of history, are victories for Satan in the cosmic war, and Hutchinson brands those who commit or celebrate them "proud rebels," reserving (as usual) the accusation of rebellion for royalists, collaborators, or their analogues (6.555).[32] God's love and election are reserved for true believers, for whom marriage can never be a compromise:

> Yet though more generally among mankind
> False worship was advanced and truth declined,
> There were a few that yet continued pure
> Nor these polluted mixtures would endure,
> But God in his own ordinances sought
> And men his undefilèd precepts taught. (6.557–62)

Only the "few" who keep themselves "pure" through their strict adherence to God's law, shunning spiritually unequal partners, are fit to lead the Holy State. This entity is neither strictly political nor merely spiritual; it retains autonomy despite the Worldly State's tyranny, since its "ordinances" are divine rather than human and the seat of its government is the home and family, yet it is ruled by "devout patriarchs" whose leadership of their "chaste pious wi[ves]" and "holy offspring" stretches beyond the private sphere to "[warn] and [rebuke] those reprobates of old" (6.637, 618–20).[33]

As Wilcher argues, Hutchinson embellishes scripture with her own creative content more and more frequently as the poem progresses. In cantos 17 and 18, the story of Jacob and Esau offers an opportunity to illustrate her renunciation of erotic compromise: her expansion on Esau's two marriages invokes several tropes of royalist erotic romance, then demolishes them. Esau demonstrates his reprobation in violating God's "first injunction" for the elect: despite being Isaac's favorite son, he "Undutiful in his behaviour proves . . . / Matching with the accursèd Canaanites" (17.466–68). Yet Hutchinson does not end here, as the text of Genesis does; instead, she digresses by inviting us to imagine Esau as a conventional romance hero in thrall to love—or, more specifically, as a Drydenesque star-crossed wooer who convinces himself that love conquers all. Hutchinson inverts first a story in which the "rough, yet bold" hunter is "entrapped" and "subdued" by the beauty of Aholibamah, and next Esau's interior monologue as he reasons his way through the values of royalist romance (17.505, 470–81):

> Nor did he check but flattered his desire.
> 'Can I,' said he, 'burn with a nobler fire?
> If Nature in creation have designed
> Man must be linked with womankind,
> What should I seek in her that I must wed
> But beauty wherewith pleasure may be fed?
> Is't not a princess that inflames my love?
> Can any other choice so happy prove?
> My father tells me they're a cursèd brood,
> But why should he appoint me my own food? . . .
> When I at home have made a nobler choice,
> Wherein 'tis fit my father should rejoice.' (17.483–96)

Subjectively (and faultily) assured of his own heroism within his personal romance, Esau tells himself that no sentiment can be "nobler" than the love of a beautiful woman, which accords with the primal order of "Nature," and no choice of a beloved could be more "happy" than a "princess" of royal blood. Esau's reasoning then takes an explicitly Caroline turn: the fact that his love is forbidden by the ideology of his community only intensifies its merit. Why should it matter that he is a Hebrew and his lady a Canaanite if he loves her? Why should religious and political difference dictate his private desires, particularly when the public good of marriage to a princess and harmony with her nation will result? How can the archaic rules and enmities of an older generation stand in the way of young love, especially if its practical benefits could easily reconcile all parties? Esau's passion is strong enough that it outweighs all other concerns yet (in his view) manages to satisfy them anyway—the very happy situation in which the lovers of Caroline court drama or Dryden's Restoration celebration find themselves. Charmed by Esau's courtly conduct, Aholibamah gives "free assent unto his wishes," just as the enamored people of "Astraea Redux" do.

But this sort of unprejudiced, universalist love is never a virtue for Hutchinson. Because Esau desires Aholibamah only for "base ends," his ardor quickly cools, and he reenacts the same erotic romance with a different Canaanite woman.[34] Finally, Hutchinson envisions the domestic aftermath of Esau's two marriages, in which the illusory ideal of interideological harmony evaporates. His "godly, sober" mother Rebecca attempts to make the best of her new daughters-in-law and strives "with pious kindness ... / To instruct them in God's worship, and correct / Those vanities which graceless dames affect" (17.519–24). But the Canaanites refuse to assimilate: "they, proud of their princely families, / Her and her pious counsels much despise, / Practise their idol-worship in despite" (17.525–27). Like England's two consecutive Catholic queens, Henrietta Maria and Catherine of Braganza, Esau's foreign princesses show no interest in changing their religion or their lavish habits to match the expectations of their husband's society, drawing him instead toward allegations of "sinful riot" (17.520). Similar perversions, we may imagine, will be the result of the ill-advised "marriage" Dryden celebrates between England and the hedonistic Charles II. In a final interjection of her voice into Esau's story, Hutchinson suggests that the only solution to such "mixed marriages" is a strikingly Miltonic one: the would-be hero should "those wicked women have divorced / And to his father's will his own resigned" (18.362–63). Unlike Caroline romance and policy, which celebrate the harmonious union of opposed religions and imagine the king and his people as reconciled lovers, extolling true love as a great obliterator of ideological distinctions and healer of old wounds, *Order and Disorder* upholds such barriers to politic affection with militant zeal. In the world of Hutchinson's biblical epic, romance could never build community by overriding spiritual difference; rather, spiritual difference hinders true love and stands in the way of the elect community's right romance.

"'TIS ONLY LIKE DESIRES LIKE THINGS UNITE": GODLY LOVE AND GOVERNANCE

Tarnishing royalist portrayals of tolerant love as mere "lasciviousness," however, does not mean that *Order and Disorder* disavows eroticism. On the contrary, Hutchinson's stance against spiritual miscegenation leads her to a perspective on love that combines the natural law of Lucretius (whom she had renounced in nearly the same breath as romance in her preface) with a staple formula of erotic romance:

> 'Tis only like desires like things unite:
> In union likeness only feeds delight.
> Where unlike natures in conjunction are,
> There is no product but perpetual war,
> Such as there was in Nature's troubled womb
> Until the severed births from thence did come. (3.263–68)[35]

This explanation of Adam's need for a mate like himself forms the foundation for godly love throughout the rest of the poem and introduces certain links to romance long before Hutchinson repudiates others. Hutchinson modifies the mode's medieval tradition that the elite must (and do) love only the elite, revising it into a Calvinist principle that the elect must (and do) truly love only the elect.[36] This concept permits her to adopt both subversive and conservative stances on marriage and its ramifications, public and private. The erotic atomic principle that "only like desires like things unite" points to several of her more radical positions. First, as we have seen, her postulate that the mingling of "unlike natures" precludes love grounds her suggestion that "mixed marriages," even royally sanctioned ones, are perversions void under natural and divine (if not human) law. Next, her Lucretian philosophy undergirds her belief in the essential likeness and equality of men and women in creation, a theme that plays into her reconsideration of gendered heroism throughout the poem. Hutchinson is like many biblical commentators in her emphasis on Eve's creation out of Adam's body and on the couple's becoming "one flesh" again in marriage ("We, late of one made two, again in one / Shall reunite"); however, as Shannon Miller has pointed out, she is unique in her interpretation that this reunion is achieved by reproduction ("When marriage male and female doth combine, / Children in one flesh shall two parents join"), which grants both parents equal status in relationship to their offspring—an important idea given that the visionary insights of *Order and Disorder* are frequently God's ambiguous promises of progeny (3.406–7, 415–16).[37]

Finally, the tenet that "likeness only" can produce true "union" allows for Hutchinson's implication that the "war" that inevitably results from "unlike natures in conjunction" may occur on a national level as well as a domestic or atomic one. Original human likeness, and attraction to that likeness, are the sources of both godly marriage and reproduction *and* godly governance. In a remarkably swift progression, Hutchinson proposes that man's "Need of a suitable and a kind aid" applies not only to a spouse "To whom he might his joys communicate," but to all sociopolitical relationships. The erotic desire to unite and share freely with one's equal partner as a solution to loneliness and spiritual stagnation becomes the foundation of the entire state, and even a justification for the redistribution of wealth: just as it is "not good" that Adam should be alone in Eden, "It is not good virtue should lie obscure, / That barren rocks rich treasures should immure, / Which our kind Lord to some, for all men gave, / That all might share of all his bounties have" (3.345–48). In a political community rooted in likeness and cemented by godly love, "the great" are not "permitted to retreat" from their care of "the simple and the weak," who—like Eve—risk harm from "strong and subtle foes" when left "alone" (3.355–60). Hutchinson concludes that, beginning with Adam and Eve but continuing throughout history,

> Men for each other's mutual help were made,
> The meanest may afford the highest aid,
> The highest to necessity must yield:
> Even princes are beholding to the field. (3.361–64)

She annotates the final line with a marginal reference to Ecclesiastes 5:9: "The profit of the earth is for all: the king himself is served by the field." Anyone who fails to live by this law of mutuality both "Injures himself" by cutting himself off from erotic and social conversation and "others doth betray / Whom Providence committed to his trust" (3.365–67). England's kings are the implicit objects of this criticism; rather than governing their "associates" with the humility and love of spiritual equals granted social and material power, they have assumed absolute superiority and forced their "partners" into "conjunction" with an "unlike nature," thereby ensuring "perpetual war," whether on the battlefield or in the heart. Such a parody of marriage, Hutchinson suggests, must be acknowledged as a tyrannical imposition rather than disguised as a bride's comely submission to her loving groom. She has moved with astonishing speed from a conventional literary law of erotic attraction and a basic Lucretian principle to a radical political stance. If "only like desires like things unite," then the political equivalent of spiritual miscegenation—the tyranny of a reprobate monarch over an elect community—is anathema to the laws of God's created universe (whether erotic, material, or spiritual), and the righteous response to it is the divorce that both Esau and England are too servile to choose.[38]

As we track Hutchinson's use of the romance tenet of love-in-likeness to its radical conclusion, we find conservative principles interwoven along the way. She responds to her belief that all human beings—male and female, rich and poor—are equal in creation by simultaneously deconstructing and upholding gendered and sociopolitical hierarchy. "The great," whether husbands, the wealthy, or the powerful, may be joined to "the weak" in a bond of "mutual help," but in order for each group to perform its sacred duty, their relational inequality must stand; God has given the riches of the earth "to some, for all," but the rich must first possess them in order to exercise their virtue by sharing them with their poor dependents. Hutchinson's paradoxical perspective calls for radical reform while necessarily preserving many essentials of the status quo, including restriction of leadership to an elite minority: she imagines government by an aristocracy of the elect, defined (in her case) as those "few with pure hearts" who uphold the Holy State in "every age" by keeping the law of love, reproduction, and social fellowship only with others like themselves.[39] These true "Sons of God" who shun spiritual miscegenation and the tyranny it breeds are uniquely fit for good marriage and good governance, both of which are predicated at once on "mutual help" and worldly hierarchy. Hutchinson here turns to the rules of romance to imagine an elect community that is founded not only on spiritual likeness and equality, but also on temporal difference and disparity.

Just as conservative politics enter into Hutchinson's most reformist ideology, her romance tropes are at their most earnest *and* their most traditional in Jacob's courtship of Rachel in book 19. While Hutchinson ironizes and parodies the genre in Esau's wooing of his Canaanite wives, her turn to pastoral romance at the end of the poem is startling in both its conventionality and its sincerity. Rachel's resemblance to the beautiful and universally beloved shepherdesses of Sidney's *Arcadia* and Shakespeare's *The Winter's Tale* (and even royalist pastoral drama) must be intentional: the shepherds introduce her to Jacob as "the only loadstone, the bright star / By whose light all our youth attracted are" (19.212–14). Hutchinson's blazon of the shepherdess pays further self-aware yet unironic tribute to tradition and highlights the conservative model of romance heroism in which birth, beauty, and virtue are inextricably intertwined:

> of that noble kind
> Was Rachel's beauty that it showed a mind
> Worthy of such a cabinet: Nature the mould
> Formed to those gemlike virtues it should hold.
> Vigour and courage in her bright eyes shone,
> On the large forehead wisdom had a throne.
> A blushing modesty, accompanied
> With tempting sweetness, did her motions guide.
> The opening of her lips was eloquence. . . .
> In every smile was gentleness and truth. . . .
> Her voice was harmony, her radiant hair
> Chaste Love's strong band, not lust's alluring snare. (19.287–300)

Hutchinson notes that Rachel differs from the wicked women earlier in the poem *not* in being "insensible of Love"—a cold defect of character that "would a stain to all her beauties prove"—but in that "when that fire into her bosom came / It burnt as purely as a martyr's flame" (19.305–8). Attraction and desire do, and should, affect the elect as they do the reprobate; in fact, they do so with greater legitimacy, strength, and constancy. Here again, we see the vitality of romance to Hutchinson through Helen Cooper's description of "women's sexuality" in medieval romance as "one of the key factors that enables a restoration of social and providential order. Such an emphasis functions as a strong generic marker—this is what romance is *about*."[40]

As twin brothers, Jacob and Esau share a courtship that is outwardly similar, and yet no two desires could be less alike according to the fundamentals of the poem's cosmology. Jacob, too, is instantly enamored of his cousin Rachel's beauty at their first meeting, but he is attracted at the same time by the bond of kinship between them: "Nature's force he felt / Contending with the late intruder, Love, / Which should more powerful in his bosom prove. / He tells her who he is, nor then forbears / To claim that dear relation with joy's tears" (19.254–58). Hutchinson makes no distinction between Jacob and Rachel's likeness in virtue, their likeness in blood as "noble" descendants of Abraham, and "Nature's force" attracting their "seed" to its original likeness; all are features of their elect condition, which generates their desire for each other on an atomic level, justifies it as legitimate and pure, and ensures the continuance of the Holy State. Notably, this godly attraction is "heterosexual" only in the "usual" sense of gender difference—which, as Will Fisher and Lisa Jardine have argued, may have been only one of the "conceptual rubrics" by which early modern people understood their own sexual desires and relations.[41] Although neither scholar considers religion or spiritual condition among these possible rubrics, Hutchinson treats them as the most vital considerations. And in all ways but a rather superficial one, Jacob and Rachel's desire for each other is desire for sameness. Because Jacob is drawn toward his own familial, cultural, spiritual, and material likeness, he has a sincere right to the romance rhetoric Hutchinson used to condemn Esau. The very amorousness that leads Esau further into sin makes Jacob into the unironic hero of Hutchinson's Puritan pastoral romance, the upholder of God's nation, and an embodiment of the divine and natural law that only "like desires" and like "natures in conjunction" can form the building blocks of love, a stable material universe, and a thriving political state.

We might well compare Hutchinson's privileging of Jacob and Rachel's elect romance over the reprobate Esau's to her account of her and her husband's courtship in the *Memoirs*. As we saw in chapter 2, she describes how her husband-to-be falls suddenly in love with her after refusing to "be entangled in any of [the] fine snares" of ladies adorned "with all the gayety and bravery that vain weomen put on to sett themselves off"; she notes that his "extravagant perplexity of soule concerning [Lucy] . . . had not bene admirable in another light person, but in him, who was from his childhood so serious and so rationall in all his considerations, it was the effect of a miraculous power of providence, leading him to her that was destin'd to make his future joy."[42] John Hutchinson's erotic passion would be condemnable in a lesser man, but in a person of his intelligence and virtue, it serves as evidence of God's providential work within the elect mind and heart. Hutchinson is not so bold in the *Memoirs* as to identify herself and her husband explicitly as elect lovers and the "light person" or the "vain weomen" as lustful reprobates, but the parallels with *Order and Disorder*'s Calvinist classification of love and lust are undeniable. Their attraction leads, Hutchinson coyly adds, to "a more handsome management of love than the best romances describe":[43] this true story, authored by providence, admits yet also surpasses the conventions of genre.[44] Likewise, although *Order and Disorder*'s preface expresses abhorrence for "turning Scripture into a romance," the poem as we have it concludes with a pastoral love affair and a significantly revised stance: that the heroic and erotic stories ordained by God are like, but infinitely better than, "the best romances" produced by human art or policy. As we have seen, however, John and Lucy's romance in the *Memoirs* becomes strained by the tension between his assured spiritual vision of his role in the narrative of the elect and her struggle to accept and enact what she cannot see; the characters of Genesis allow Hutchinson to reimagine a godly romance subjectivity that does not fracture so easily along gendered lines.

"WHAT WILL FULL RESTORATION BE?": RETHINKING TELEOLOGY, GENDER, AND NARRATIVE VISION

"Love is the cément of the Holy State," pronounces the narrator in comparing Cain and Seth's offspring. "Nor hath it place or fellowship with hate" (6.419–20). The elect community, uniquely capable of true love and sincere political fellowship, must resist any temptation to pollute itself with those whom "lust or interest . . . in leagues combines, / But holy love or friendship never joins" (6.415–16). And while elect sexuality is always oriented toward the future of the Holy State—springing from and flowing toward "God, the fountain of all love" (6.422)—Hutchinson represents all ungodly activity, including sex and reproduction, as purposeless and stagnant,

> as a declining stream
> That breaks off its communion with its head,
> By whom its life and sweetness late were fed,
> Turns to a noisome, dead, and poisonous lake,
> Infecting all who the foul waters take. (4.22–26)

We might be inclined to see a version of Lee Edelman's queer anti-futurism being denounced here, and yet for the most part, what Hutchinson condemns as "declining" is the *usual* sort of sexuality and childbearing, which in her formulation is just as "dead" as the sin of Sodom.[45] In fact, the Sodomites' homosexual practices are quite briefly remarked on as just one instance of the city's "lascivious love"; Hutchinson's concern with the socially normative sin of "heterosexual" spiritual miscegenation eclipses her interest in other perversions (13.12). As we see in Jacob and Rachel, the only love that has a future is the exceptional elect desire of like for like, and this futurism is consistent with the structure of right romance. Like so many of her radical Protestant fellows and predecessors, Hutchinson endows the marginalized community of the elect with a long yet productive and progressive narrative, while excommunicating their superficially dominant enemies from teleological temporality.[46] However superficially alike their respective versions of erotic romance may appear, one is destined to for propagation, continuance, and a sacred end, wheres the other is going nowhere.

Jacob and Rachel's marriage, like the Hutchinsons', marks the conclusion of a micro-romance within the ongoing transhistorical romance of the elect, authored by God himself. Like so many romances, Jacob's story in *Order and Disorder* breaks off unfinished with the rest of the poem, but its nonending implies that the divine romance is likewise unfinished only because it is ongoing.[47] In the poem's final line, Jacob is "Carried off . . . safe" from Laban's vengeful troops, "for God at first did send / An unseen guard of angels to attend / His servant home, though yet he knew it not, / And Bethel's certain vision had forgot" (20.144–49). Despite the fact that the heroes frequently "forget" the promised plot of their stories or fail to "perceive" their unfolding, providence still presides as author, whether of the epic romance of the Holy State or of the individual narratives of its elect members, whose unions sustain "the blessèd seed" destined to generate their community's "sovereign champion" (12.168, 5.85). Hutchinson reminds her readers that the original marriage of Adam and Eve prefigures the true end of the heroic and erotic romance of history, when Christ, having vanquished Satan in the universe's final battle, will be eternally united to his chosen bride, the Church:

> 'Henceforth no longer two but one we are. . . .
> As my victorious triumphs are all thine,
> So are thy injuries and sufferings mine,
> Which I for thee will vanquish as my own,
> And give thee rest in the celestial throne.'
> The bride, with these caresses entertained,

> In naked beauty doth before him stand,
> And knows no shame, purged from all foul desire
> Whose secret guilt kindles the blushing fire.
> Her glorious Lord is naked too, no more
> Concealed in types and shadows as before. (3.493–98)

These reconciled lovers recall Dryden's joyous national marriage yet leave it far behind. Their "nakedness" serves a triple purpose: it exalts simple, unadorned worship over High Church liturgy; it showcases the ultimate redemption of elect eroticism, made fully perfect at the end of time; and it signifies the telos of Christian art and hermeneutics, justifying their purpose and marking their ending. The "glorious Lord" is "no more / Concealed" in the "types and shadows" of history and text; in the very eschatological moment that it becomes possible to read time as a finished romance, it also becomes unnecessary, even meaningless. Typology, genre, and other such interpretive tools are finally stripped away to reveal the real thing.[48]

Long before the ends of the divine romance are realized, however, the wandering narrative of God's chosen community winds slowly (if progressively) on from one generation to the next. As Miller, Murphy, and others have observed, much of *Order and Disorder* is preoccupied with the business of reproduction: from Adam and Eve to Abraham and Sarah to Isaac and Rebecca to Jacob and Rachel, elect families constantly experience gratification, then disappointment, then renewed joy as they await the birth of the "blessèd seed," the child or children destined to carry on the physical and spiritual lineage of the Holy State in its eternal combat with "Hell and the World." For all four of these couples, the wait is long and the result unexpected, entirely out of step with the orderly patrilineal narrative of "Astraea Redux": the first three patriarchs beget firstborn sons who show early promise but are not chosen for heroic roles, and Jacob produces many children with Leah while he and his beloved Rachel remain childless. Further, Norbrook notes that "Calvin and other Protestant commentators saw the Jacob-Esau story as paralleling that of Isaac and Ishmael: the normal order of primogeniture is inverted for the sake of the elect, anticipating the belated triumph of the true church."[49] Hutchinson adopts this Reformation-era Calvinist theme and modifies it for the Restoration, repeatedly emphasizing that neither the firstborn son nor the next generation in general—both of them sources of imminent hope in

"Astraea Redux" and throughout romance-inflected royalist historiography—are legitimate symbols of sacred teleology.

The story of Esau provides *Order and Disorder*'s most emphatic polemic against primogeniture as well as spiritual miscegenation; at the same time, it reveals Hutchinson's interest in overcoming a gendered binary for romance subjectivity. In favoring his elder son, Isaac is "governed by a partial blind affection" and "Stuck to that choice which was not God's election" (18.77–78). Discovering that he has blessed Jacob instead and so been acted on "by a secret Providence / Whose workings were not obvious to his sense" (18.141–42), Hutchinson's uniquely introspective Isaac is overcome not with anger at his wife and younger son, whose deceit is justified by "powerful reason" (17.541), but with "trembling horror" at his own resistance to divine will in "dot[ing] on him the Lord / As a profane wild reprobate abhorred" (18.155–56). In the *Memoirs*, John Hutchinson was endowed with a vision of God's narrative for his Holy State, which Lucy's "partial blind affection" for her husband prevented her from seeing, much to her own dismay and self-recrimination. In *Order and Disorder*, Hutchinson makes Rebecca the heroic visionary—a representative of "female access to God" who requires no mediation from her spouse—and her husband the spouse who must repent of his confusion between worldly and godly concerns and accept her superior insight into the divine plot.[50] The law of primogeniture, so pivotal to divine right monarchy and to the royalist reading of Charles II as the hero of his family's dynastic romance, may easily run afoul of "God's election." If it does, a godly governor must abandon it and submit to legitimate divine right. Any assumption that the divine narrative accords with human birth order is either a grave error that the elect must learn to correct in themselves, as Isaac does, or else the fatal fallacy of the damned. Hutchinson imagines that after Adam's unworthy first son has murdered his second, Satan "exult[s]" at his apparent triumph over the "champion" destined to destroy him, believing "The holy seed extinguished by [Abel's] death / But God revived it in succeeding Seth" (6.424–26). The champion's victory was never contingent on either of Adam's eldest sons, nor does it depend on any other firstborn in time to come, least of all Charles II.

Beyond separating eldest sons from their traditional heroic roles, *Order and Disorder* rejects another common theme of romance that Dryden's postwar royalist narrative embraces: the hope that the suffering of one generation will be ameliorated by the young heroes of the next one. The promise of future redemption is paramount to Hutchinson's treatment of the history of the Holy State, but crucially, that salvific end lies in the deep future, never in the hands of the present population's immediate offspring. Eve is the first character in the poem to misunderstand the scope of the divine romance, imagining (like Milton's Adam) that its temporality is restricted to the life spans of herself and her children, and that her conception of her first son heralds the triumphant fulfillment of God's promise:

> When Cain was born, exultingly she thought
> She had into the world her champion brought;
> But from the error of that fond conceit
> She learned that such as live on faith must wait
> To have the promises whereon they stay
> Performed alone in God's own time and way. (6.33–38)

Hutchinson makes clear that Eve's error is not simply her assumption that her firstborn son must be the promised seed, nor even that the story's end is near at hand, but rather that she possesses any conventionally heroic power to bring that end about, when in truth it remains "obscured . . . Till the full time revealed the mystery" (6.47–48).[51] *Order and Disorder* revisits Spenser's paradoxical treatments of heroic agency in books 1 and 3 of *The Faerie Queene* and reaches a similar conclusion: human action is undeniably part of the divine plot, yet by comparison with God's will it is neither sufficient nor necessary in the usual sense of the word.[52] The bearing of children is one aspect of this rule: in *Order and Disorder*, as for Britomart, the heroically mundane task of producing a family is a providential commandment without a predictable triumph or a foreseeable end. Beginning with Eve, every mother is called to "maintain / Posterity, not frighted with the pain" in the hope of the "promise that thereby she shall / Recover all the hurt of her first fall / When, in mysterious manner, from her womb / Her father, brother, husband, son shall come" (5.221–28). Again, the mortal role in the divine romance is both a certainty and a mystery—and the mystery in which all elect parents still share cannot be quite the same as the mystery of Christ's incarnation that Eve fails to anticipate in canto 6. The precept given to women in canto 5 clearly refers to the incarnation of Christ thousands of years in Eve's future, and yet it also remains operative for Eve's living descendants, male and female joined in one flesh by their children, despite the historical fact of Jesus's birth seventeen centuries prior to Hutchinson's writing. The "full time" has "revealed the mystery" of Christ's identity as the "champion" of the Christian romance, but the mystery of both sexes' ongoing commandment to childbearing remains shrouded in time that is not yet full.

The disappointment of the republican cause, paired with the enduring Puritan belief in a providential structure for history, necessitates Hutchinson's return to this Spenserian or Sidneian style of unfinished, long-form romance—a mode that Charles II's return to power had obviated for post-Restoration royalist treatments of the genre, including "Astraea Redux." The king's return lent the royal romance a beautiful simplicity: as literary convention dictated, the loving and fruitful union of Charles II's parents perfectly performed its reproductive function and resulted in a heroic firstborn son who successfully reclaimed his father's usurped throne. Everything, in the end, had gone according to the generic plan.[53] In order to survive and retain positive ideological value, Puritan republican romance therefore required a different plan: a much more expansive one that refused to recognize that royalist "end." After introducing the Spenserian paradox of heroism within time early in her poem, Hutchinson continues to raise it, consistently stressing both the hope of futurity and the failure of immediate expectation, and so rejecting the primogeniture, imminent resolution, and narrative finality that Dryden embraces.[54]

The trial of submission to right romance temporality troubles the patriarchs as much as it does their wives, since the prophetic insights offered to the men of Genesis are typically the same as those offered to the women: bewildering promises of future progeny, not the assured, transcendent visions of a Redcrosse Knight or a John Hutchinson. Adam, Abraham, and Jacob are granted no special narrative knowledge that Eve, Sarah, and Rachel lack. When God tells a confused Abraham that his aging wife Sarah, rather than her young maid Hagar, will become the mother of his heir, Hutchinson adds an association between the unborn Isaac and the promise of the holy seed's birth made to Adam and Eve: "And now my promises shall take effect, / Nor shalt thou long the blessèd seed expect. / Yet not from Hagar's but from Sarah's womb / The children of the covenant shall come" (12.167–70). Again, the firstborn son is rejected and the human order of primogeniture gives way to a higher order. But, lest divine inheritance law seem a simple matter of radical inversion, Hutchinson invents God's revelation to Abraham that "the blessèd seed" refers not merely to an individual, but to a continuous community of godly lineage, long before (and, as we have seen, long after) it manifests itself as a specific person. Isaac both is and is not the expected heir to the promise of history, God explains:

> It is in Isaac that I have decreed
> A glorious name unto thy holy seed.
> From him the godly nations shall descend . . .
> And from a race of kings at last shall rise
> That glorious Monarch whose great victories
> Shall overthrow the powers of Death and Hell
> And them from their usurpèd realm expel. . . .
> But first a long and various tract of time
> Must be expired before thy nephews climb
> To these last glories; yet here steadfast rest
> Thy faith: the world shall be in Isaac blessed. (14.299–314)

As it turns out, Isaac is destined to be the heir whose line will *eventually* produce the *true* heir, the "sovereign champion" destined to reclaim his "usurpèd realm." But there is nothing immediate about the promised triumph of this family line: a nebulous span of time, made known to Abraham only as "long and various," separates Abraham and his son from the "glorious Monarch" whom Isaac's birth anticipates. God warns Abraham that the arrival of the "blèssed seed" remains a distant prospect, even as it is also imminent in Isaac's birth. Yet the message ends in renewed comfort, with God's reassertion of Isaac's crucial role in the protracted plot. Abraham will be long dead by the time of Christ's birth, to say nothing of the end of days (since, as we have seen, the holy seed endures after Christ's death and resurrection, continuing to emerge from the erotic union of elect women and men throughout history)—but he may "steadfast rest / [His] faith" in his own son, "here" and now. Like Spenser's Merlin providing limited solace to Britomart, Hutchinson's God offers Abraham no direct vision of his romance's end, instead exhorting him simultaneously to imagine the full landscape of sacred time and to content himself with his far more limited sight of the present occasion as he moves through the twists and turns of his own linear narrative. Unlike the assured triumph of the rightful heir in the royalist family romance, Isaac's arrival must never be mistaken for the telos of his story—and yet his failure to embody that end must not be regarded as a disappointment. God seems to present Abraham and his "nephews" with their "long and various" period of waiting—with the weight of romance—as a gift in itself. Like Ishmael, then, Charles II is the false heir of a false teleology, but his opponents have, as yet, no "glorious Monarch" of their own at hand to reclaim the "usurped realm." But both the king's success and the disappointment it spells for Puritan republicans are temporary. The future in which worldly monarchy will be obliterated might be near at hand or almost infinitely far off, but "the godly nations" may "steadfast rest / [Their] faith" not only in the uncertain future, but "here" in the unpromising present. By mysterious means, in their own children and in their community of faith, "the world shall be . . . blessed."[55]

The word "restoration," which appears frequently throughout *Order and Disorder*, refers always and only to the fulfillment of God's promises to the elect or to the triumphant conclusion of the providential narrative.[56] In a lengthy creative digression, Hutchinson characterizes the renewal of life after the Flood as "Earth's restoration" by God, but reminds her audience that, as always, each happy ending to the trials of the godly merely prefigures their ultimate joy at the end of time, which surpasses the imagination: "What will full Restoration be, if this / But the first daybreak of God's favour is?" (8.149, 27–28). The royalist "restoration," then, is doubly false for Hutchinson. It is a temporary triumph of the Worldly State, falsely represented as a righteous victory, and it is a vicissitude, celebrated as the end of the royal romance, which fails to recognize the entire arc of the romance of providence. The true Restoration is still at hand, and its glory is reserved for the Holy State alone.

In her lyrical meditation on the Flood's aftermath, Hutchinson continues to subvert the imagery of the Worldly State's romance about itself. The mountains rising "from th'imprisoning flood, / Their faces slimed, their standards dropping mud" appear "as a prince who, long in prison bound, / Comes squalid forth at first, untrimmed, uncrowned" (8.35–38). She appears to adopt the premise of "Astraea Redux"—that the world's rebirth arrives in the form of a restored prince who returns from exile to recover his lost throne—but as with the term "restoration," she appropriates her enemies' rhetoric for Puritan republicanism and so changes its meaning. The emergent figure is not an earthly prince who has overcome earthly opponents, but the earth itself, responding to God's enabling mercy. On one hand, this prince can triumph even "uncrowned"; on the other, his natural form is lowly, unadorned, and unclean before his transformation by divine grace. Only under the care of "Heaven's compassionate, kind, refreshing eye" do the mountains appear kingly: "Again they fair, again they stately grew, / Again looked down on the sunk realm where they / So long space late captived and vanquished lay" (8.39, 42–44). Hutchinson proceeds to challenge any remnants of royalist ideology that might still linger around the royal image after her appropriation and transformation of it. After depicting God's restoration of the humble mountains, she issues a dire warning to them, and to the rulers that they resemble, never to forget the sole source and sustainer of their majesty:

> But curb, fair hills; O curb your growing pride:
> He who above your covering clouds doth ride,
> Whose pity drew you from your low estate,
> When you insult will cast down your proud height. . . .
> Your new-restorèd glory shall expire. . . .
> And you, great Lords, who on the mountains reign,
> With them shall once more be destroyed again. (8.45–54)

The language of "restoration" here appears in a royalist context as the resurgence of monarchy, and Hutchinson again emphasizes the corruption and transience of the concept according to royalist usage: any restoration tainted by pride and impiety is ultimately doomed to "expire" to make way for the "full Restoration" of the elect. Finally, after appropriating the image of the returning prince, transfiguring it, and critiquing it, Hutchinson unceremoniously discards it, ending her admonition with a dismissal: "But let's not glance at judgements due to you / While we old miracles of grace review" (8.63–64). The heroic figure of royalist romance is initially useful as an emblem of salvation, but his monarchist overtones shadow "the first daybreak of God's favour" by coming to signify the resurgence of sin, and finally the image's efficacy withers before true "miracles of grace" and the distant prospect of "full Restoration." Hutchinson seeks a two-pronged victory over royalist language and symbolism by recuperating them for Puritan republicanism when the values of the opposing narratives intersect, and by casting them aside as soon as they do not, extracting the pith of the royal romance and throwing away the rind.

"What will full Restoration be?" is the question that *Order and Disorder* continually poses and invites its godly readership to contemplate.

Hutchinson offers rare and partial answers to it, as when she imagines "That glorious Monarch whose great victories / Shall overthrow the powers of Death and Hell / And them from their usurpèd realm expel" and the subsequent consummation of the marriage between the true "Monarch" and his bride, "no more / Concealed in types and shadows." For the most part, though, the question is for asking rather than answering; both the protagonists of Genesis and God's elect community of women and men throughout history are called occasionally to take heroic action, but more often to perform heroic patience. They can only trust that "God's repeated interventions in history always look forward to the future, insisting that however unclear it may seem, it will follow a coherent pattern"—the plot of providential romance.[57] Moreover, while the plot of sacred history is ongoing, visible to the heroes of the Holy State only in the rarest visionary moments, the individual believer can (and should) pursue his or her own miniature progressive narrative:

> So we, pursuing our attainments, should
> Press forward from what's positively good,
> Still climbing higher, until we reach the best,
> And, that acquired, forever fix our rest,
> Our souls so ravished with the joys divine
> That they no more to creatures can decline.
> As God's rest was but a more high retreat
> From the delights of this inferior seat,
> So must our souls upon our Sabbaths climb
> Above the world, sequestered for that time
> From those legitimate delights which may
> Rejoice us here upon a common day. . . .
> Yet is this rest but a far distant view
> Of that celestial life which we pursue
> By Satan oft so interrupted here
> That little of its glory doth appear. (3.574–85, 612–15)

This exhortation begins with Platonic language in urging a gradual "climbing higher, until we reach the best," and develops into a Neoplatonic Christian reminder of the ends of the divine narrative, when all earthly referents will be "no more." In quotidian life, the Sabbath's day of rest offers the godly the best opportunity to meditate on these ends, yet even the Sabbath is a type with an unfulfilled antitype. Long before the romance episodes of the poem's later cantos, Hutchinson's ruminations on the last day of creation—and on the end of days—seem (perhaps consciously) inspired by *The Faerie Queene*'s visionary moments, drawing both from Redcrosse's own "climb / Above the world" to catch a fleeting sight of the New Jerusalem in the distance, and from the final four perfectly "unperfite" lines of Spenser's epic romance:

> For, all that moueth, doth in Change delight:
> But thence-forth all shall rest eternally
> With Him that is the God of Sabbaoth hight:
> O thou great Sabbaoth God, graunt me that Sabaoths sight. (7.8.2)

Redcrosse is granted a narrative vision of the story's end, as is John Hutchinson in the *Memoirs*, while Britomart and Lucy must accept promises and grope through narrative obscurity; in *Order and Disorder*, Hutchinson upholds both of Spenser's variations on godly heroic subjectivity while rejecting her impression in the *Memoirs* of a gendered hierarchy to them. Adam and Eve, Abraham and Sarah, Jacob and Rachel must together doubt and hope in the promise of the future. At the same time, nothing precludes a female hero, past or present, from achieving "a far distant view / Of that celestial life," and Rebecca's narrative vision outstrips Isaac's, while their son Jacob receives a "certain vision" of God's plan that he has "forgot" in the poem's final lines (20.149). Both the patriarchs and matriarchs of *Order and Disorder* are sometimes accorded brief glimpses of God's full narrative about themselves and their progeny, but such vision fades quickly, and for the most part, men and women alike must pray and hope for what they cannot see. Likewise, Hutchinson's elect community of Puritan republicans find themselves somewhere in the middle of the romance of history, able in their time of disappointment to perceive "little of its glory." *Order and Disorder* strives to remind its reading community that the absence of present triumph only demonstrates the plot's unfinishedness: in the meantime, the godly are left with the struggle and the gift of "Press[ing] forward" to attain a momentary Sabbath's sight of something their adversaries can only feebly mimic: "full Restoration."

CHAPTER 5

"In the Next World"

John Bunyan, Aphra Behn, and the Imitation of Romance

Unlike John Milton and Lucy Hutchinson, who each confessed their youthful enthusiasm for reading romance but made statements repudiating it later in life—despite their tacit continued commitment to it in their biblical poetics—John Bunyan never made any effort to conceal the fact that he based the structure and style of *The Pilgrim's Progress* on the chapbook romances he read as a boy.[1] "Give me . . . George on horseback or Bevis of Southampton," he recalled of his early reading preferences, "give me some book . . . that tells of old fables; but for the holy Scriptures I cared not."[2] This final chapter considers the less-studied second part of Bunyan's *Pilgrim's Progress* (1684) alongside another work of prose fiction that appeared at a time when the civil wars were passing into more distant memory and the "Glorious Revolution" was poised to end the reign of the Stuart dynasty, Aphra Behn's *Oroonoko* (1688). Both texts, already known for their resistance to generic categorization, continue English writers' postwar considerations of how romance might redefine and reconstruct community, and whether it serves more to reiterate, or to repair, divisions in religion, politics, and other sites of identity. At the dawn of the eighteenth century, and just before their own deaths, Bunyan and Behn could look back on decades past and return to questions much like those that challenged Spenser and Sidney: Can romance function as a meaningful model for national, individual, or sacred history? What are its civic and religious applications and limitations? Is a community characterized by a shared commitment to romance strengthening its sense of identity and purpose or laboring under a dangerous delusion?

Behn's *Oroonoko* appeared in the same year as Bunyan's death; unlike Hutchinson and Milton, Bunyan could not have read or be responding to the royalist text with which I have paired him. The pairing, though, helps illustrate a kind of cessation of hostilities in the seventeenth-century ideological war over romance. We have grown used to a pattern in which royalist or republican writers condemn romance as their enemies' ridiculous fantasy and then find a way to recuperate it in semisecret; despite holding diametrically opposed political and religious beliefs, neither Behn nor Bunyan does this. Behn stands as a final challenge to the idea of romance as a royalist genre: her transatlantic tragedy enacts the recession of romance and offers a damning commentary on its real-world value for a politically viable community. Meanwhile, by the time Bunyan began to write fanciful allegory as a preacher of those scriptures he once dismissed in favor of tales of love and adventure, the Puritan minister actively defended his use of romance and made no attempt to obscure it in the first part of his *Pilgrim's Progress* (1678). Yet he, too, seems aware that there may be something outworn or limiting in the mode. Both writers stress romance's capacity to unite a diverse group of men and women—for Behn, a fellowship that mixes race, rank, and religion; for Bunyan, a nontraditional family of nonconformists—and yet both take care to expose their communities' cherished romances as an imitation rather than a reality, a deliberate effort to relive a heroic narrative of the past that may not be recapturable.

Here, though, the pair again diverge. Behn's *Oroonoko* reveals the weakness of her text's alliance of romance lovers, showing that their shared inclination to live life as romance "in the next world" of the American colonies neither imbues them with special status or providential protection nor even reliably ties them to each other. The community is no sooner made than marginalized, and Behn's prophetic perspective on history as a royalist woman near the end of her life reveals not the New Jerusalem but the New World, a setting she finds hostile to the ideas that allowed romance to flourish across ideological boundaries in seventeenth-century England. Bunyan, however, after several prior experiments mingling romance and

Puritan symbolism, draws the mode to the fore by deliberately orchestrating productive conflicts in part 2 of his *Pilgrim's Progress* between romance convention and the spiritual journey to the "next world" of the Celestial City. Bunyan concluded his career as a preacher and an allegorist by suggesting that romance's value lies in its ongoing ability to generate and empower a radically resistant community and in its capacity to imitate (rather than embody) sacred narrative form.

"INFINITELY PLEAS'D WITH THIS NOVEL": THE DEGRADATION OF ROMANCE COMMUNITY IN APHRA BEHN'S *OROONOKO*

Like Bunyan's *Pilgrim's Progress*, and unlike many of the earlier seventeenth-century works we have considered, Aphra Behn's *Oroonoko* is not a text whose relationship to romance needs to be excavated from beneath its author's protestations. One of the few elements of *Oroonoko* about which there is abundant critical consensus is its foundation in romance.[3] Readers even slightly versed in the tradition of Sidney's *Arcadia*—whether in 1688 or today—can hardly miss Behn's idealized description of Oroonoko's beauty, "the most exact that can be fansy'd," alongside "real Greatness of Soul, . . . refin'd Notions of true Honour, . . . absolute Generosity, and . . . that Softness that was capable of the highest Passions of Love and Gallantry."[4] His love story with Imoinda is equally familiar: two young people, alike in nobility, beauty, and virtue, are inevitably attracted to each other but face obstacles to their union before their separation, their travel to a distant land, and their unlikely (yet again inevitable) reunion. So far, Behn stresses, Oroonoko and Imoinda resemble conventional European romance protagonists in all but skin color.[5] Yet perhaps this superficial difference is what compels the structure of their romance to veer off into some other mode or genre once they arrive in the historical, mappable, white space of Surinam. Again like Bunyan, Behn makes her work's romance heritage obvious in order to interrogate romance's artifices and applications. Unable to bear his nominal slavery in Surinam or to be consoled by manufactured adventures around the island, Oroonoko leads a slave revolt that ends with his killing of the willing Imoinda and his own torture and death at the hands of the colonial government. This gruesome collapse of romance norms has been widely noted: Anita Pacheco identifies the force that "intrudes into the world of heroic romance" as realism.[6] Richard Kroll argues that *Oroonoko* comments on "the generic difference between true history and romance,"[7] Rachel Carnell and Albert Rivero note that the new narrative bears "the recognizable outlines" of tragedy,[8] and William Spengemann suggests that Behn's romance gives way to "a new way of writing fiction" whose narrative norms remained to be determined but which "we now associate with the novel."[9] A sense also prevails that this generic shift can be identified with the geographic shift between the "Old World" and the "New"; Kroll, for one, proposes that the events in Oroonoko's homeland of Coramantien "represent a site where romantic kingship is displayed and anatomized, while the events in Surinam represent a site where romantic kingship is tested."[10]

If critics concur that *Oroonoko* deliberately problematizes romance, nearly every other aspect of Behn's narrative is contentious. Laura Brown has pioneered many readings of *Oroonoko* that question not simply its ideology but its ideological coherence: is it possible to determine whether *Oroonoko* critiques or condones slavery, whether it advocates cultural radicalism or conservatism, or whether it outlines a consistently royalist platform?[11] I am chiefly concerned with the relationship between *Oroonoko*'s mixed genre and its politics, though the first two questions are imbricated within the last. A number of readers of *Oroonoko* have made two fundamental assessments of its political ideology: first, that the narrative (like its author) is essentially royalist in its representation of a virtuous prince who is degraded and brutalized by figures representing, and partly consisting of, republican Whigs;[12] but second, that its royalism is not entirely consistent or uncomplicated.[13] What might *Oroonoko*'s challenging politics have to do with its challenging genre? It has become commonplace to read the lovers' grim deaths as a lament for the impending fall of the Stuarts and, with them, the mystical splendor of absolute monarchism. In this light, Oroonoko's anti-romance demise "mark[s] the tragic fall of kings in an enterprise beset by self-serving privateers, interlopers and colonial miscreants."[14] A smaller number of readers have found that what *Oroonoko* grieves for is not precisely, or not only, royalism: for Spengemann, it is the collapse of the "Old-World dream" of colonial utopia; for Rivero, the passing of Behn's innocence; and for Warren Chernaik, the ineradicability of despotism and slavery.[15] I propose that one of the chief losses Behn laments in *Oroonoko* is the loss of romance itself as a viable narrative of English political history and of national and religious identity.[16] Oroonoko's story depicts something we have encountered many times before and will see again in Bunyan: a small community bound together by enthusiasm for and enactment of romance, united in resistance against an enemy that seeks to thwart its destiny. But by that story's end, romance's promise has failed: no matter how strong its members' conviction that they live within a progressive heroic narrative, that community finds itself forsaken by providence, stripped of the power to recover its losses or prevail over tyranny, its members too devoted to their subjective delusions to remain devoted to each other.

In 1688, Behn concludes that loyal subjects of the monarchy had better let go of the romance subjectivity that had contributed to royalist identity since the heyday of Charles I and Henrietta Maria's happy marriage—which ended, after all, in public ridicule and ugly death. We have seen how, throughout much of the seventeenth century, both royalists and republicans tended to adopt a posture of disdaining their enemies' flighty, arrogant obsession with romance while tacitly embracing the mode for their own purposes. With the civil war long over and further national turmoil on the horizon, Behn abandons this pose. Instead of denouncing romantic republicanism while pursuing romantic royalism, she relinquishes claim to the romance mode's power to represent English history, mournfully concluding that romance is not worth the competition since its function of identifying history's patterns and its heroes is illusory. The long struggle for control of a national romance was in vain: romance cannot advance any desired political reality and cannot represent the narrative form of English, human, or sacred history. Like her older friend and competitor Dryden in his "Astraea Redux," Behn briefly conceives of romance as a mode that can transcend cultural and ideological divides and construct a youthful new community poised to inhabit a better world—except that that better world is a fiction. Instead of ending with the irenic apocalypse of the Restoration, history grinds on, enslaving, humiliating, and dividing its would-be heroes. The tragedy of *Oroonoko* lies partly in the fact that even as romance creates and coheres a superficially idealized community, it disenfranchises it: Oroonoko and his friends, despite exhibiting the conventional characteristics of romance heroes (including a love of the mode itself), are destined for defeat as a viable society, in part because the impure world overpowers them but also for another crucial reason. The argument advanced by Victoria Kahn and Anthony Welch that affect and sympathy are major constituents in the postwar reconstruction of the royalists' sense of romance community holds true for *Oroonoko*, but only up to a point.[17] While Behn's text features its version of "a network of affective bonds among loving nobles," those bonds are disturbingly easy to untie or break once strained, since the network proves more devoted to the imitation of romance than to its own members.[18]

Other critics have remarked on Behn's division between the few characters who admire both romance and Oroonoko and the many who run roughshod over them, though most associate this separation with other binaries: the geographical separation between Africa and the New World, the distinction between upper and lower classes, or the ideological difference between Behn's loyal Tories and the hated Whigs.[19] While each of these readings approaches some truth, none of their distinctions can quite stand up to scrutiny. Oroonoko's heroism is tested by different forces of tyranny in both Coramantien and Surinam, encountering honorable allies and opportunistic enemies in both places. While Oroonoko's inborn royalty is visible in his body and countenance, virtue also appears to shine through the face of the mere gentleman Trefry, as we will see. The wicked Byam and his henchman Banister—"a Fellow of absolute Barbarity, and fit to execute any Villany, but . . . Rich"—are far from being commoners; the Irish brute Banister may epitomize wealth divorced from nobility of birth or nationality, but Byam is a member of the landed gentry and the descendant of English nobles (118).[20] More important, neither are Byam and Banister republicans or Whigs, despite the fact that many of the nameless English islanders under their control smack of Whiggish capitalism: Oroonoko's cruelest and most deceitful enemies are real historical figures who served as high-ranking royalist colonial officials. And as Chernaik has suggested, Oroonoko's rhetoric against tyranny can read as republican rather than royalist.[21] Race, rank, and political ideology all fail to provide a thorough and accurate determination of the virtue of *Oroonoko*'s protagonists and antagonists, but affinity for romance itself remains a reliable determiner—though crucially, it is not ultimately stronger than the markers that will divide them.

Throughout *Oroonoko*, and in both of the text's settings, a love of the lofty values and stimulating stories of romance—together with a predisposition for treating the romance mode as a model for imitation and interpretation—draws disparate individuals into an elite community of virtue. We must note that Behn's *elite* community is explicitly not an *elect* community in any Protestant sense we have encountered: as a royalist and perhaps a Catholic, Behn (like Cavendish and Dryden) found conflations of romance heroism and divine election neither attractive nor convincing. In fact, her black African hero undermines Protestantism's racial exegesis (widespread throughout, and well after, the early modern period) that took the African race to be the offspring of Ham, declared reprobate by God and cursed by Noah to unremitting slavery. Both their reprobation and their enslavement disqualified them from participation in the progressive narrative of the elect.[22] Behn's *Oroonoko* moves to spurn the religious and narrative implications of this convention. The degeneracy that is supposed to characterize Ham's descendants instead flourishes in the white enemies of the heroic and genteel African prince, who stands at the head of his romance community due to a secular nobility of spirit that never signifies any kind of Christian election. In fact, Oroonoko's sense of honor prompts him to disdain Christianity as a religion of liars and to reject the narrator's pious efforts to convert him. In positioning itself against this exegetical and historical narrative tradition, *Oroonoko* seems to resist a Protestant project outlined by Dennis Britton: he argues that "English Protestant theology and romance . . . sought to govern the construction of race" away from the Catholic romance trope of the converted heathen, for whom race and religion were more fluid.[23] Under the new framework, Protestantism comes to read "Christian identity as racial identity," with no flexibility possible.[24] Behn insists that physically and morally, Oroonoko models English romance heroism better than the white people of Surinam, despite his unconverted blackness—though her text will not remain so sure about its own or Oroonoko's power to combat the dominant narrative.

Whether the members of Behn's elite community are African or European, noble by birth or only in spirit, self-evidently royalist or not, they find deep gratification within their like-minded society, even as their romance subjectivity separates them from the majority of their neighbors. Oroonoko's membership in this small but diverse community predates his encounters with the narrator or Trefry, his chief allies in Surinam. He distinguishes himself from his own people by his interest in the heroes of European history (as soon as he and the narrator meet in Surinam, they are united by their shared admiration for the royal martyr Charles I) and by his idiosyncratic vow to be exclusively faithful to Imoinda despite Coramantien's custom of polygamy. Oroonoko's oath wins him the heart of Imoinda, who shares his affinity for the norms of European erotic romance, while dividing him from his grandfather the king; the sensibilities that harm his status at court make his love story especially appealing to the narrator in

Surinam and to her romance-reading English audience. However, Behn never suggests that the values of romance are unique to England or to Europeans. As with other writers, romance becomes a mode of thought and action that allows its followers to recognize one another and to identify themselves as distinct from the masses whose spirits are not sufficiently elevated to ascribe to it. We begin to see romance's power to form an improbable community while we are still in Coramantien: Oroonoko's wartime enemy Jamoan becomes his hostage but also his dearest friend once they have witnessed each other's martial prowess and manly virtue. Jamoan knows instinctively how to minister to Oroonoko's lovesickness for his lost Imoinda: "By a thousand Tales and Adventures of Love and Gallantry, [he] flatter'd his Disease of Melancholy and Languishment; which I have often heard him say, had certainly kill'd him, but for the Conversation of this Prince" (81). Notably, Oroonoko is gratified by Jamoan's romances not because they ease his sorrows but because they sharpen and intensify them. Behn's narrator identifies the paradoxical nature of Jamoan's treatment: it "flatter[s]" the illness that torments Oroonoko by reiterating his own experiences and exalting them to a literary height; yet at the same time that it nourishes and glorifies his "Disease," Oroonoko becomes convinced that it has saved his life by providing him with the vital "Conversation" of a sympathetic fellow romance subject. For now, the question of whether romance chiefly imparts solipsistic "Languishment" or communitarian salvation is left open.

The Jamoan episode, in which two adversaries are united by their mutual recognition and appreciation of romance tropes, repeats itself once Oroonoko arrives in Surinam. He is bought by Trefry, "a Man of Great Wit, and fine Learning" who overhears his disdainful farewell to the captain of the slave ship and his hope to "*meet with more Honour and Honesty in the next World*" (86–87). Trefry, instantly attuned to Oroonoko's innate nobility, seems poised to answer that hope:

> He ... no sooner came into the Boat, but he fix'd his Eyes on him; and finding something so extraordinary in his Face, his Shape and Mien, a Greatness of Look ... had a great mind to be enquiring into his Quality and Fortune; which, though Oroonoko endeavour'd to hide ... Trefry soon found he was yet something greater than he confess'd; and from that Moment began to conceive so vast an

Esteem for him, that he ever after lov'd him as his dearest Brother, and shew'd him all the Civilities due to so great a Man. (87)

Trefry discovers Oroonoko's rank and his moral quality simply by beholding that "something so extraordinary" about him, whatever it may be; this ability of a displaced or disguised aristocrat to radiate some indefinable allure that reveals his hidden status is a romance cliché. "Entertain'd" by Trefry with "Art and Discourse," Oroonoko soon perceives in turn "a kind of Sincerity, and awful Truth in the Face of *Trefry*; he saw an Honesty in his Eyes, and he found him wise and witty enough to understand Honour" (87–88). Mysterious virtue inheres in both these men of doubly disparate rank (master and slave, minor gentleman and prince), and it is communicated both through the body and through the elite "Discourse" that mutually delights them. Sensing an ally, Oroonoko tells his whole story to Trefry, "whom he found . . . charm'd with all the Greatnesses of his Actions; which . . . wholly vanquish'd him and subdu'd him to his Interest" (87). If Trefry were not endeared to Oroonoko through his heroic countenance alone, his account of the true romance of his life earns his complete devotion. He is eager to reciprocate the gift of Oroonoko's romance with a story of his own: being "naturally Amorous," Trefry "lov'd to talk of Love" and tells of his "fine she *Slave*" who has made every man in the vicinity, black or white, "undone" (90). The promise of a love story piques Oroonoko's interest, as it did back in Coramantien: "The *Prince* . . . never heard the Name of *Love* without a Sigh, nor any mention of it without the Curiosity of examining further into that tale, which of all Discourses was most agreeable to him" (90). While Trefry's account furthers his friendship with Oroonoko, the pair's interpretation of it sets them apart from all the other listeners, who laugh at the unwarranted "Civility" in Trefry's claim that the beautiful slave's virtuous countenance prevents him from exercising his sexual rights as her master (91). Either Trefry and Oroonoko are alone in recognizing the Sidneian norms inherent in the scenario—the impassioned lover, the chaste beloved, her disarming modesty, and his awakened virtue—or else they are alone in placing any value on them. In a moment that highlights their special status while anticipating their dangerous insulation, these three figures—Trefry, Oroonoko, and now the chaste enslaved woman—compose a tiny elite class distinguished from a larger aristocratic audience by their "true Notions of Honour and Vertue" (91).

The apex of the romance plot in *Oroonoko*, and the highest pleasure for the members of its romance community, occurs as a result of Trefry's amorous discourse: keen to see the beauty and nobility of "Clemene" for himself, Oroonoko (now called "Caesar") discovers that she is his own Imoinda. The miraculous event passes all description: "'Tis needless to tell with what transports, what extasies of Joy, they both a while beheld each other, without Speaking; then Snatcht each other to their Arms; then Gaze again, as if they still doubted whether they possess'd the Blessing: They Graspt; but when they recovered their Speech, 'tis not to be imagin'd, what tender things they exprest to each other; wondering what strange Fate had brought 'em again together" (91). Crucially, this triumph delights an audience beyond the lovers whom it directly concerns. Trefry, who in his purchasing power is perversely responsible for the happy reunion he has just witnessed, is "infinitely pleas'd with this Novel, and ... not a little satisfied, that Heaven was so kind to the *Prince*, as to sweeten his Misfortunes by so lucky an Accident" (92). Overcome with enthusiasm for the apparently providential true romance unfolding before his eyes, he is "impatient" to repeat the "Novel"—a strange new event, but also often a romance narrative—to another sympathetic listener: Behn's persona (92). The narrator and Trefry, being distinctively attuned to such things, had sensed previously that Clemene was a person "of Quality," but her value to them increases exponentially once they learn she is the female protagonist of Oroonoko's stirring romance: "When we knew *Clemene* was *Imoinda*, we cou'd not enough admire her" (92). As Oroonoko and Imoinda celebrate their reunion firsthand, Trefry and the narrator relish the vicarious experience of being a party to this "real" romance that so much resembles the stories they like best. At this moment, their central community of four seems to have reached a pinnacle of joy and cohesion: while Oroonoko and Imoinda renew their commitment to each other in marriage, the narrator and Trefry commit to restoring them and their newly conceived heir to their rightful home and throne in Coramantien.

Spengemann has described what the end of Oroonoko and Imoinda's romance might look like were it to conclude in the expected fashion: "For the happy conclusion of the romance, only the rupture between these lovers and the old king of Coramantien remains to be healed; and, as anyone familiar with the genre would know, such problems are easily dispatched. Whether Oroonoko and his gravid spouse return to the welcome of a once tyrannical parent now softened by remorse, or the king conveniently dies during their absence, or they decide to remain in America and establish a peaceful dynasty of commingled love and honor in that regained paradise, the romantic action has virtually arrived at its projected conclusion."[25] Trefry, Behn's persona, and Behn's readers all share Spengemann's impression of what might happen next to complete the formulaic plot. Oroonoko, too, has fantasized about a happy ending for himself and Imoinda that seems suddenly to lie wide open before them: barred from access to her in Coramantien, he imagines "fly[ing] with her to some unknown World, who never heard our Story" (68). As Rivero has noted, Surinam will shortly prove the "grim fulfillment" of his dream.[26] Romance has shown its capacity to delight its admirers, to soothe their woes while indulging their sense of a special subjectivity, and to draw them together while distinguishing them from all others—but here, its powers have reached their limit. By the end of the text, romance will have failed to deliver Oroonoko, and it will have disenfranchised and doomed the very community it created, whose radical interracial alliance is far weaker than it may seem.

At first, the weakness of romance is easily conflated with its temporary usefulness for forming community and consoling the dispossessed. Much as Jamoan comforted Oroonoko in his lovesickness—and perhaps himself in his captivity—by telling "Tales and Adventures of Love and Gallantry," the narrator attempts to "entertain" her new African friends through storytelling and adventuring until their hypothetical return to Coramantien (93). The pleasures of romance draw Oroonoko into an unorthodox society, one that breezily makes light of distinctions of race, rank, religion, and gender, as the royal slave comes to prefer the company of his "Great Mistress" and her female relations "much above the Men" (93). When the community is not absorbed in heroic discourse, it dabbles into heroic action: Behn devotes a significant portion of her text to episodes in which the group explores the island, interacts with exotic natives, and slays "monstrous" wild beasts (94). Yet, while these "novel" curiosities appear to feed their fellowship and give Oroonoko "occasion of many fine Discourses; of Accidents in War, and Strange Escapes," the narrator admits a darker truth: she has been "oblig'd, by some Persons, who fear'd a Mutiny," to amuse and divert Oroonoko and Imoinda (99, 93). While the friends' enjoyment of romance and of each other seems sincere, their superficially radical community is a contrived tool of the enslaving establishment, and it will never become an effective instrument of resistance against the power that deployed it.

For Oroonoko, the narrator's pretend-play eventually turns cloying, and he recognizes the phony adventures as sightseeing trips and distractions: "These were not Actions great enough for his large Soul, which was still panting after more renown'd Action" (94). Imoinda, too, begins to pine for the promised happy ending to her family romance as her pregnancy progresses. Realizing that their freedom is not forthcoming, Oroonoko finally takes matters into his own hands and attempts to inspire his fellow slaves with the romance subjectivity that has always guided his own conduct. He stresses the existential horror of their interminable slavery, which—as the tradition of Ham's curse emphasizes—lacks a romance trial's capacity to ennoble or redeem the sufferers: "He told 'em it was not for Days, Months, or Years, but for Eternity; there was no end to be of their Misfortunes: They suffer'd not like Men who might find a Glory, and Fortitude in Oppression; but like Dogs" (105). Oroonoko's gradual degradation has opened his eyes to the difference between his friendships in Surinam and his friendship with Jamoan in Coramantien: he and his fellow slaves have not been conquered "Nobly in Fight" or "by the chance of War," and his indignation at his unheroic servitude overcomes his love for his fancied hosts (105). Oroonoko urges his fellows to embrace real martial heroism—"the more Danger, the more Glory"—and the concomitant hope of providential protection and restoration: "He said, they wou'd Travel towards the Sea . . . and when they cou'd find a Ship . . . guided by Providence that way, they wou'd Sieze it, and make it a Prize, till it had Transported them to their own Countries" (106). Having spent months in Surinam talking of romance and playing at it with his English friends, he chafes against the aimlessness of their diversions and his slavery, and he orchestrates a return to the real thing.

For Behn, however, the tragic aftermath of Oroonoko's rebellion sharply exposes the failure of romance as a "real thing" that can control the shape of historical or personal narrative. We suddenly discover that while the narrator and her comrades' romance subjectivity has granted them an illusory impression of their cultural status, it gives them no political power at all. The narrator is inclined to conflate these two types of authority (which are indeed not normally separate in traditional romance): she remarks that "the better sort" have too much "Respect for Caesar" to fight him, and her scorn for the low character of Deputy Governor Byam initially conceals the weight of his authority in Surinam (107). Byam at first seems "the only violent Man" against large numbers of "the better sort" who despise his cruelty, yet the contempt that the people "of any fashion" feel for Byam proves to go hand in hand with the passivity of their privilege (107). Their admiration for Oroonoko's heroism as a "Novel" does not translate into any heroic exercise on their own part. Behn reveals the flimsiness of the community united by love of romance through its rapid disintegration when its white members' loyalty and trust are tested; the narrator joins the other fashionable women who "fly down the River, to be secur'd" from the threat of Oroonoko (111). Her comment on her decision to flee from her friend betrays both her remorse about what follows and her confusion about her status in Surinam as a cultured, aristocratic woman: "While we were away, [Byam] acted this Cruelty: For I suppose I had Authority and Interest enough there, had I suspected any such thing, to have prevented it" (111).

Whether we regard the narrator as deeply deluded about her power, terribly remiss in exercising it, or both, the fact remains that the radical community shaped by narrative pleasure and affective sympathy crumbles, while Byam easily assembles a mob united by economic interest that puts down the revolt. Kimberly Coles, who shares Britton's argument for an English nationalist project that brings with it a racializing discourse, notes that "the logic that governs conquest and colonization turns upon [unstable racial] divisions that must be 'calcif[ied],'" and so they are here.[27] Oroonoko, who threatens "the cultural construction of a cohesive English national ethnic identity" in his power to "convey more than one ethnic signature at the same time," is forced by Byam's mob—and worse, accepted by the frightened narrator—to signify as a black barbarian.[28] In Britton's words, "emergent concepts of race and Protestant theology" made certain romance miracles impossible for certain subjects.[29] Oroonoko's belief that his comrades might transform their suffering into heroic progress has proved illusory; in this new world dominated by white Protestants, the Curse of Ham *does* effectively exclude slaves from true romance.

Byam's demagoguery gives him far more real potency than either Oroonoko's moral outrage against tyranny or the narrator's mystical faith in royal power and virtue. Surinam's elite community of romance lovers finds itself literally outgunned by those who perceive that success "in the next World" of America depends on opportunistic policy and exploitation, not sentimental convictions of providential heroism.[30] In fact, the crafty Byam seems to sense that he can turn the weakness and naiveté of his rivals' romance subjectivity against them: he co-opts honest Trefry, whose face radiates

"Sincerity, and awful Truth," to help extract Oroonoko's fateful surrender by promising his freedom and appealing to his heroic virtue. Like the narrator who instinctively aligns herself with her white friends when her romance alliance is tested, Trefry implicitly trusts the Deputy Governor and agrees to act as his agent. His tearful honesty in pleading with Oroonoko is genuine, and Oroonoko does not err by trusting him per se. Both men's errors lie instead in their enduring faith in the reality of romance values and outcomes. As a white person who has read romance and only recently embarked on a vicarious experience of living it through his royal slave, Trefry is particularly credulous: ever since recognizing Oroonoko's royalty and bringing about his improbable reunion with Imoinda, he has been "infinitely pleas'd with this Novel" that he believes directs the plot of his friend's life, and he remains convinced that his story must end with his return to his rightful throne in Coramantien, accompanied by his bride and heir. Byam's fiction that Oroonoko and his royal family "shall depart free out of our Land" may be calculated to flatter not only Oroonoko's desire but also the expectations and honor of Trefry, whose romance subjectivity assures him that although he is not the hero, he is the friend and ally instrumental to the hero's perfection of his narrative. Trefry is manipulated by his enthusiasm for the values and ends of romance, and Oroonoko by the same trust in the chivalric purity of Trefry's honor that first facilitated their friendship.

Once he has discovered Byam's deceit, Oroonoko's slaying of the willing Imoinda and their unborn child highlights not only the community's political powerlessness, but also the emptiness of any appeal to providential protection or election. When Oroonoko kills his unborn heir—"the last of his Great Race"—he has destroyed the hope of restoration in the next generation that underpins royalist romance (93). Moreover, he has applied his variation on Noah's curse to his own son.[31] Behn posits at the beginning of her narrative that black Africans can take on heroic roles in romance—but by definition, the enslaved, whose lives and labor are not their own, cannot. The majority of Africans on Surinam, like the majority of white colonists who serve Byam, are unfit for heroism or freedom; even worse for the anti-Protestant romance vision of Behn and *Oroonoko*'s elite community, Oroonoko himself finally degenerates into the brutality that is supposed to characterize his race and his paganism, degraded by the racial and religious suppositions of his colonial masters.[32] His violence against Imoinda and their child, which remains heroic in the eyes of the lovers from Coramantien, horrifies the narrator with its foreign barbarism.

The narrator's fellowship with Oroonoko fails him for the same essential reasons that Trefry's does: not through a deficiency of noble sentiment, but through a privileging of the self-centered illusions of romance above the reality of romance-inspired friendship. When Oroonoko is informed that he will not recover from his wounds (and will therefore never take revenge on his enemies nor return to Coramantien), the narrator reports that "we were all (but Caesar) afflicted at this News": while Oroonoko, like Charles I, has accepted his narrative's modal shift and is settling into his final role as heroic martyr, the community that has cohered around him cannot bear for his "Tale of Love and Gallantry" to decline into tragedy (117). And rather than remain with him to witness his tragic end as it unfolds, the narrator flees the scene again: "The Sight [of his injuries] was ghastly," she reports, "his Discourse was sad; and the earthly Smell about him so strong, that I was perswaded to leave the Place ... (being my self but Sickly, and very apt to fall into Fits of dangerous Illness upon any extraordinary Melancholy)" (117). The narrator is literally unable to stomach the decay of Oroonoko's once-idealized heroic body and the gruesome collapse of his romance; her attachment to romance aesthetics results in her abandonment of the man she once believed to embody them as soon as his story becomes too "ghastly," "sad," and "Melancholy" to remain a real-life representation of the kind of "Novel" that pleases her.[33] This episode illustrates a theory of the construction of racial identity advanced by Patricia Akhimie, who argues that the pain of another body, instead of evoking human sympathy, "exist[s] ... inside an ideological blind spot" and is "difficult to pity or relieve"; "more often ... we perceive the 'bruise' as evidence of the insurmountable difference between our self and another."[34] Akhimie suggests that the wounds that might be taken as "evidence of a violent crime" are read as "the sign of a natural subservient" and of "a moral and a social inferiority."[35] This is precisely what happens between the narrator and Oroonoko: traumatized by real-world violence, their transracial bond splinters into a white woman repulsed by a black man. Even if the elite community's admiration for romance heroism lives on in the narrator's written witness to Oroonoko's life and death, that same text must record how the racial and ideological diversity of the fellowship crumbles in colonial Surinam, and its structure does not correspond to the fantasy that romance is a providential key to historical reality.

Spengemann has drawn our attention to a connection between the tragic end of *Oroonoko* and the melancholy verse that Behn composed shortly after her story's publication and just before her death. Responding to a request that she compose an effective endorsement of the "Glorious Revolution" that ended Stuart rule, Behn declines:

> My Muse . . . would endeavour fain to glide
> With the fair prosperous Gale, and the full driving Tide,
> But Loyalty Commands with Pious Force,
> That stops me in the thriving Course,
> The Brieze that wafts the Crowding Nations o're,
> Leaves me unpity'd far behind
> On the forsaken Barren Shore,
> To sigh with Echo, and the Murmuring Wind;
> While all the Inviting Prospect I survey,
> With Melancholy Eyes I view the Plains,
> Where all I see is Ravishing and Gay,
> And all I hear is Mirth in loudest Strains;
> Thus while the Chosen Seed possess the Promis'd Land,
> I like the Excluded Prophet stand,
> The Fruitful Happy Soil can only see,
> But am forbid by Fates Decree
> To share the Triumph of the joyful Victory.[36]

Spengemann suggests that we keep *Oroonoko* in mind when reading Behn's dying verse in order to perceive the "wonderful irony" in her lament that she will never enter the New World she surveys from her prophetic height:

> The Promised Land that calls the Crowding Nations across the Atlantic is, as Oroonoko discovered, an Old-World dream, already dispelled by the efforts to realize it; while the dishonored prophet, who seems to sit on the Forsaken Barren Shore of the Old World, consoling herself with the devalued bric-a-brac of antique legend, has in fact been there ahead of the rest and has already learned what it will take the Chosen Seed another two hundred years to realize—that the Old World is gone, and that the New one will require its makers to conceive an entirely new idea of their collective destiny.[37]

This perceptive reading allows us to hear in Behn's tone not only irony, but also a strange, half-mocking sympathy that connects the disenfranchised community of royalist romance with its estranged Puritan cousin. Her description of those who celebrate the "Triumph" of the Glorious Revolution as "the Chosen Seed" racing to "possess the Promis'd Land" is apt: such people, after all, are the republican-leaning Whigs and radical Protestants who had long identified themselves with the nation of Israel and its romance journey through the wilderness. But in comparing herself to Moses, that favorite visionary hero of religious reformists, Behn aligns herself *with* her ideological adversaries rather than against them. She and the "Chosen Seed" shared the same narrative goal of arriving at the "Fruitful Happy Soil," the same dream of "Ravishing" prosperity and "joyful Victory"—but as a defeated and dying royalist, Behn's "Excluded Prophet" finds herself awakened from that dream. The mountaintop prospect she has commandeered from Moses shows her not the Promised Land nor the New Jerusalem but an unvarnished vision of her nation's narrative. Although she is compelled by her "Loyalty" to the deposed Stuarts to abstain from rejoicing in England's future, Behn sounds more wistful than resentful, perhaps even feeling pity for those who have left her "unpity'd far behind": unlike them, she has seen enough of that "Inviting Prospect" to have concluded that the "Chosen Seed" may be unwittingly headed toward yet another "Barren Shore."

Both Behn and her characters have been forced to put aside their fictions about their community's "collective destiny"; Behn's opponents have yet to do so. Soon enough, she implies, they, too, will discover that the story about their identity and destiny that they cherished is "an Old-World dream," a cultural relic that will mark its adherents not as divinely predestined victors but as David Quint's "losers."[38] One of those ideological opponents, Bunyan, shares Behn's understanding of romance as a collective imitation of a dream and as a mode that poses problems for familial and political narratives, but holds on to that imitation as viable for his nonconformist Puritan community. In the intervening years before he produced part 2 of his wildly popular book—during which he had also published the similarly romance-inspired *Life and Death of Mr. Badman* (1680) and *The Holy War* (1682)—Bunyan had the time and opportunity to contemplate the merits and the limits of imitating romance as a spiritual strategy for him, his dissenting flock, and his expanding readership. Michael Davies argues that Bunyan fundamentally mistrusted romance throughout his career, and that both parts of the *Pilgrim's Progress* "should not be considered as romance at all (Puritan or otherwise) but, rather, a rewriting of romance, one that deconstructs the genre, its features and its forms, and reconstructs them within the frame of Bunyan's own theology"; Bunyan, Davies claims, wants his readers to read for the redeeming doctrine beneath the temptation of the adventure story.[39] In contrast, I want to show that Bunyan does direct his, and our, attention to the friction at various points of contact between romance convention and Christian narrative, but without ever turning away from it, exhibiting and encouraging critical self-consciousness about how elect community is constituted and how romance both enriches and constrains perspectives on sacred temporality. While Behn makes the painful decision to abandon romance on behalf of her fellow embattled Tory royalists, Bunyan remains committed to its imperfect utility for Christian nonconformists as the discourse of a loving community living in resistance to structures of power.

In part 1 of *The Pilgrim's Progress*, Bunyan's allegorical approach to genre, time, and space is relatively straightforward: Christian travels from the City of Destruction through the sins and dangers of life to the Celestial City. His heroic romance ends when he enters the City after crossing the River, an act that stands for the death of his mortal body. While the precise moment of the end of his quest cannot quite be defined—Christian is, "as it were in Heaven, before [he] came at it; being swallowed up" by an angelic host from the dreaming narrator's limited sight—the conclusion of his narrative aligns fairly neatly with the temporal and spatial attainment of his generic telos.[40] The less-studied part 2, in which Christian's wife, children, and disciples retrace his journey, complicates the questions of what constitutes spiritual romance and where its "end" lies. Both the rich potential and the difficulty in mapping Christian allegory onto romance structure emerge through two major avenues: first, Bunyan's transformation of his hero from an embattled individual to an imitative community; and second, his focus on female characters, none of whom appears as a pilgrim in part 1.[41] While Christian's romance was marked by isolated paths and unknown perils, part 2 is populated by protagonists who pay a different sort of tribute to romance convention in their metaconsciousness of heroic antecedents, their deliberate pursuit of chivalric combat, and their concern with love, courtship, and the promise of reproduction. These normative tropes contribute to Bunyan's construction of his markedly nonnormative pilgrim community.

However, the pilgrims' various goals, while all generic staples, are difficult to square with their claim to be "upon the same *Errand*" as Christian (191): once they, too, reach the Celestial City, the significance of their pursuits must diminish, just as Spenser's New Jerusalem demanded the Redcrosse Knight's forsaking of the "deeds of armes" and "Ladies loue" he had been seeking (1.10.62). The communal, feminine, and familial concerns that are unique to part 2, and that enrich Bunyan's construction of elect fellowship, also "have curious consequences for the allegory," in the words of Christopher Hill.[42] In adding these new elements, Bunyan forces us to consider the temporal, spatial, and narrative discontinuities between earthly and apocalyptic romance. In a sense, the romance genre itself is an allegory in *The Pilgrim's Progress*— the symbol rather than the essence of sacred narrative form.

"WARM WITH DESIRES": IMITATIVE COMMUNITY AND QUEER CHRISTIAN LOVE

It has become commonplace to remark that part 2 of *The Pilgrim's Progress* is simply less exciting than part 1, more focused on companionship and conversation than on combat. In 1928, Ronald Knox scoffed that "Christian goes on a pilgrimage, Christiana on a walking tour"; more recent scholarship, while less disparaging, often references the quip.[43] There *is* something touristy, even groupie-like, about Christiana and her companions' retracing of Christian's journey: at House Beautiful, Christiana and Mercy ask to have the same bed that Christian slept in, where they lie awake together talking of his adventures (224). Later, Great-heart takes them sightseeing on the battlefield where Christian fought Apollyon and points out its various attractions, the relics of Christian's chivalric valor:

> This is the place; on this ground Christian stood, and up there came Apollyon against him. And look ... here is some of your Husband's blood upon these stones to this day: Behold also how here and there are yet to be seen upon the place, some of the Shivers of Apollyon's Broken Darts.... Verily Christian did here play the Man, and showed himself as stout as could, had he been there, even Hercules himself. When Apollyon was beat, he made his retreat to the next Valley, that is called The Valley of the shadow of Death, unto

which we shall come anon. Lo, yonder also stands a Monument on which is Engraven this Battle, and Christian's Victory, to his Fame, throughout all Ages. (242)

Instead of reliving the experience of fighting Apollyon firsthand, Christiana and her party—together with part 2's readers—are encouraged to experience their collective memory of the battle as both terror and pleasure. This retracing of Christian's path and the shared remembrance it engenders allow romance to continue to flourish as a unifying center of community despite (or even because of) its explicit derivativeness. Moreover, we will see that the community that coheres around the memory of Christian's romance, while retaining its familiar properties of demarcating God's chosen heroes and excluding their enemies, also fosters new, nonnormative unions and modes of intimacy that strengthen the elect fellowship.

As Christiana's party gradually encounters other pilgrims, the newcomers reveal that "Christian's Name" is now "famous," with word of his heroism "spread abroad far and near" (294). Michael Austin reminds us that Christian's story has in fact "become a written text" avidly consumed by fictional fans of his sacred romance: Mr. Sagacity informs the dreaming narrator that "there are but few houses that have heard of him and his doings, but have sought after and got the *Records* of his Pilgrimage; yea, I think I may say, that that his hazardous Journey has got a many well-wishers to his ways" (178).[44] In other words, the real text of Bunyan's part 1 has apparently entered the fiction of part 2, "just as most of the characters that Quixote and Sancho encounter in *Don Quixote II* have read *Don Quixote*."[45] But Christian gains more than readers and "well-wishers." Valiant-for-truth articulates a recurring theme when he explains how he, too, came to set out on pilgrimage with his "*Jerusalem* Blade" at the ready (293): "We had one Mr. Tell-true came in to our parts, and he told it about, what Christian had done . . . how he had killed a Serpent that did come out to resist him in his Journey; and how he got through to whither he intended. . . . In a word, that man so told the Story of Christian and his Travels, that my heart fell into a burning haste to be gone after him, nor could father or mother stay me" (293–94). Christian's romance moves certain readers to run off in imitative pursuit, and so Christiana's band grows as new Pilgrims join her "walking tour" and pass much of their time simply "talking of *Christian*," taking mutual pleasure and comfort in recollections of his famous exploits (281).

The characters' mutual awareness of the genre they inhabit has led to many remarks that part 2 is about not only the imitation of individual heroism, but also Christian community.[46] Moreover, it is about community nurtured by storytelling: Bethany Bear argues that in both parts of *The Pilgrim's Progress*, godly "fancy" or imagination can serve as a sign of election and as a force that "sustain[s] love among Christians," and we can say the same for the right romance that delights both Bunyan's readers and his characters.[47] The elect may find evidence of their status in their enthusiasm for Christian and his heroic narrative, and even the stories they habitually share of one another's humbler "progresses" strengthen them with the reminder that trials and triumphs are common to all pilgrims. As Christiana puts it, "This relation of Mr. *Fearing* has done me Good. I thought nobody had been like me, but I see there was some Semblance 'twixt this good man and I" (256). While much of part 1 deals with the burdensome and frightening isolation of the nonconformist soul, part 2 (like Hutchinson's *Order and Disorder*) relishes the relief of being "like" and with others—a comfort furnished by shared narrative norms and repetitions. Much as communal story enables the pilgrims to recognize and reassure one another until they reach the safety of Beulah, which houses a composite "History of all the famous Acts" of Christians past for all to read (306), Bunyan's prologue to part 1 promises his readers that their election might be revealed to them by their regard for the book they hold and by their capacity to comprehend it: "Wouldst read thy self, and read thou knowest not what, / And yet know whether thou art blest or not[?]" (9).[48] Part 2's prologue offers a similar assurance: "Things that seem to be hid in words obscure, / Do but the Godly mind the more allure" (173).[49] The romance that Bunyan's audience and characters read and strive to imitate contains symbolic meaning not only within its pages, but in its very being as a sacred communal text. This multi-plotted narrative about the journey of the elect comes to symbolize, in itself, elect fellowship.

Some (most notably Roger Sharrock) have suggested that part 2's comforting communal focus renders it gentler, more inclusive, and less ideologically combative than part 1.[50] However, we must acknowledge that the text never relinquishes Protestant romance's long-standing vehemence about the exclusivity and elite status of God's chosen people, here of a piece with Bunyan's strong commitment to religious separatism. As we have seen before, this strategy follows Jameson's idea that romance upholds "a deep-rooted ideology which . . . draw[s] the boundaries of a given social order," but that social order conceives of itself as a small and select group called to resist dominant structures of power—in Bunyan's case, a nonconformist flock opposed to royalism and a state church. When Christiana implies that gentleness might take the place of resolute opposition, insisting that "surely, surely" her neighbors' "Hearts would be affected" if they could perceive Christ's love as she does, Great-heart cautions her that her spiritual sympathy is not a universal phenomenon: "To be affected with Christ and with what he has done is a thing special" (214). Bunyan designs part 2 such that the same can be said about being moved by Christian's narrative. Christiana's unregenerate neighbors scoff at the "fantastical . . . whimsical Fools" who would leave home on a godly romance quest, and the narrator notes that "the baser sort . . . had no reverence for these men, nor took they notice of their Valour or Adventures" (280). Godly romance subjectivity, as Great-heart explains, comes not from the mere "sight and consideration" of heroism, but from "an indeared Affection begot in us by it," a gift of interpretation and love not granted to "the baser sort" (214). As ever, according to the *New Arcadia*, "they only know it which inwardly feel it" (78). Elsewhere, Great-heart teaches that those who hold the pilgrims in contempt are excluded from narrative as a model for human life: "The fear of God is the beginning of Wisdom; and to be sure they that want the beginning, have neither middle, nor end" (256). Much as Milton's fallen angels move "in wandering mazes lost" (2.561), and as Hutchinson likens the Worldly State to stagnant water (4.22–26), Bunyan understands reprobation as incapacity for teleological plot.[51]

By now, we should find nothing surprising in Bunyan's reiteration of this norm of Protestant romance: as in Sidney, Spenser, Milton, and Hutchinson, the godly view the mode as a strategy for identifying themselves as members of a present community or a historical continuum of chosen heroes, categories from which the unregenerate or the reprobate are excluded. Yet Bunyan and his characters do more than retread familiar territory, and the impulse that part 2 is more interested in Christian unity and intimacy than in exclusion can still lead us onto solid new ground. Beyond simply using romance to place believers in the family of the godly, Bunyan relies on the genre's conventions to think quite unconventionally about how that family might be composed and how it might locate itself within narrative time. Central to this reimagining are the women of part 2, whose affective

"Hearts" grant them the "indeared Affection" that inspires elect heroism. At the same time, these heroines offer Bunyan a conduit for channeling erotic and reproductive concerns into his nonconformist romance in a way I argue we should recognize as queer. Bunyan's Christian queerness accommodates heterosexuality—as scholars including Carolyn Dinshaw, Carla Freccero, Will Fisher, and Melissa Sanchez have argued early modern queer studies should—but it chiefly models love as "made of affective relations" that are "heterogenous and indeterminate."[52] The intimate bonds generated by Bunyan's imitative romance are evocative of Sidney's empathetic fellowship and yet more expansive; the narrative and historical temporalities it envisions are "non- but not anti-normative in their impulses."[53]

In general, neither erotic love nor women have fared very well in Bunyan studies, even in recent years. Very few scholars have looked beyond Bunyan's claim in *Grace Abounding to the Chief of Sinners* that God "made [him] shie of women" and of communal displays of affection,[54] or attempted to complicate the consensus that he shunned real and fictional women for the sexual temptations they always embodied.[55] While Kathleen Swaim has famously argued that Christiana and Mercy allow Bunyan to imagine heroic femininity in part 2,[56] other feminist scholars such as Margaret Olofson Thickstun and Margaret Sönser Breen have seen the heroines' need for male protection and instruction as evidence of their heroism's subordination.[57] (Much more recently, Breen has also produced the only other queer reading of *The Pilgrim's Progress*, a powerful treatment to which I will return.[58]) Readings persist such as Thomas Luxon's, who finds that "Bunyan's most persistent refrain" is that "the carnal things of this world," which include wives, marriage, sexuality, and family, "are essentially worthless in the long run."[59] Luxon scarcely comments on *The Pilgrim's Progress*'s problematic second part, with its multiple female pilgrims and the four marriages that are celebrated within it. And yet part 2 is even more remarkable in that its godly women do not seem to have been included for the primary end of entering into marriages with its male pilgrims, even though these marriages are encouraged.[60] For one thing, Bunyan introduces marriage and reproduction into his sequel partly to interrogate erotic romance's vexed (but not void) relationship to Christian temporality, as we will see shortly. For another, part 2's women demonstrate that Bunyan's elect community is bound together most strongly not through traditional marriage, but through nonnormative and sometimes transgressive forms of eroticism, intimacy, and affective piety.

Bunyan's female characters and their offspring imbue the romance of part 2 with a low-frequency erotic resonance that is absent in part 1, in which the vocabulary of sexuality inevitably signals a falling away from the divine rather than an approach toward it, as with Faithful's temptation by Wanton.[61] Notably, Bunyan (like plenty of other male believers) embraces the hetero-eroticism of the Song of Songs and gives it homoerotic spiritual application when describing his personal salvation narrative in *Grace Abounding*.[62] In *The Pilgrim's Progress*, he relies on part 2's women and young men to reflect this particular element of his own religious experience—though *not* generally through interactions with one another that gesture toward heterosexual desire or future marriage. At the house of Gaius, the Song of Songs is the means by which love language is purified for the pilgrims' consumption. When Christiana's son Matthew asks whether they may lawfully eat the "very good tasted" dish of apples that their host has offered, since their "first Mother" succumbed to desire for the same fruit, Gaius answers:

> Apples were they with which we were beguil'd,
> Yet Sin, not Apples hath our Souls defil'd.
> Apples forbid, if eat, corrupts the Blood.
> To eat such, when commanded, does us good.
> Drink of his Flagons then, thou, Church, his Dove,
> And eat his Apples, who art sick of Love. (264)

The Song of Songs's imagery of wooing and lovesickness, taken here (as usual) to be an allegory of Christ's spiritual courtship of his Church, sanctions an erotic undercurrent to Bunyan's own allegory at the same time that it permits Matthew to satisfy his bodily appetite with what God has sanctified. While Gaius's house is also the site where part 2's marriages will be performed, the Song of Songs's eroticism here simply urges the little "Church" to enjoy the communal love feast that has been prepared for them, bypassing dyadic heterosexual desire in favor of their longing for Christ and for fellowship with one another.[63]

We might guess that Bunyan is displacing sexual pleasures onto gustatory and communal ones due to his own supposed discomfort with women and sex. Other evidence, though, suggests his investment not in *nonerotic* paths to Christian communion, but in *nonnormative* ones that allow part 2's eroticism to focus on a loving community of women and men rather than on heterosexual union between one man and one woman. And women are usually the sources of this intimacy and diffuse amorousness: most commonly, the erotic impulse felt by the male author of *Grace Abounding* is expressed by the female characters of *The Pilgrim's Progress*. The group's journey begins only because Christiana first becomes possessed with a longing to follow her husband to the Celestial City when a mysterious figure called Secret enters her house. After a godly greeting from this male "Stranger," "she blushed and trembled, also her heart began to wax warm with desires to know from whence he came" (182). Christiana's private sensual arousal in response to a man who is not and will not become her spouse (or, stepping outside the allegory, to a penetrating feeling that Bunyan genders male) prompts her to gather her children and pursue her husband, not out of specific desire for either Christian or Secret, but out of more generalized yearning to "come into [God's] presence" with Christian and "with Legions more, his Companions," who long in turn to welcome her into their fellowship (182).

In keeping with his representation of both his characters and his audience as imitative readers of Christian's romance, Bunyan's prologue positions his young female readers similarly to Christiana in her private moment with Secret. "Young Ladies, and young Gentle-women too" share Christiana's intimate, if not precisely sexual, desiring response when they are visited by Bunyan's Pilgrim (i.e., when they read and interpret part 1):

> Their Cabinets, their Bosoms, and their Hearts,
> My Pilgrim has, 'cause he to them imparts
> His pretty riddles in such wholesome strains
> As yields them profit double to the pains
> Of reading. (172)

These lines appear particularly transgressive when we consider that the reading of "pretty" romances or novels was commonly condemned for threatening the chastity of seventeenth-century women, as was evangelical Puritanism; Bunyan himself was tendentiously accused of sexually enticing female members of his flock.[64] Yet much as he did with Christiana and Secret, Bunyan here celebrates the "wholesome" merits of women's amorous receptivity, quite outside of reproductive marriage. For although the pilgrim possesses "their Bosoms, and their Hearts," their attraction to him—whether "he" stands for Christian, the book, or Bunyan as its author—paves the way to their desire for Christ and endows them with membership in the pilgrim community of characters and fellow readers. Breen's early argument for women's subordination throughout part 2 depends on her reading of Bunyan's female characters as inextricably "sexed," unlike their male counterparts.[65] While their feminine sexuality does render them, in Bunyan's eyes, unfit for martial action and in danger of sexual predation, it also makes them singular vessels—and, more importantly, channels—for open-ended godly erotic possibility. In these instances, Bunyan's fellowship of nonconformists has its seat in women's private spaces, their secret thoughts, and even their bodies.

Generally, though, part 2's unique erotic charge is more likely to be couched in terms of affect rather than embodiment.[66] Whereas Behn ultimately dismissed sympathy and affect as constitutive of a stable romance community in *Oroonoko*, Bunyan asserts their value as openly as he embraces romance itself. In part 2, this emotional force emerges most strongly out of the dual bond of Christian fellowship and female friendship between Christiana and Mercy. It is their relationship, rather than that of any of the heterosexual couples, that typifies the love that extends beyond the norms of marriage to permeate and bind Bunyan's pilgrim community.[67] Christiana follows the precedent of Secret by initially acting as a sort of matchmaker between Mercy and Mercy's own erotic desire for redemption, "glad at heart, not only that she had a Companion, but also for that she had prevailed with this poor Maid to fall in love with her own Salvation" (188). Mercy's love for Christ goes on to influence her mortal courtships: after rejecting a "sweet heart . . . that pretended to Religion; but a man that stuck very close to the World," Mercy vows that her own godliness "shall be to [her] as a Husband," but she eventually reconciles her zealous "Conditions" with worldly romance by becoming engaged to Christiana's son Matthew (209–10). Remarkably, though, this match is made just after Gaius proclaims himself "glad to see" Mercy and Christiana "together here, a lovely Couple" (262). Gaius advises Christiana to make her and Mercy's bond of love and companionship official through marriage: "Take *Mercy* into a nearer Relation to thee. If she will, let her be given to *Matthew* thy eldest son. 'Tis the way to preserve you a Posterity in the Earth" (262). While Matthew's contribution is essential for "Posterity" and for a legally recognized "nearer Relation," Christiana and Mercy themselves already make up a "lovely" and loving "Couple" whose tenderness toward each other brings comfort and delight to their fellow pilgrims.

Mercy and Christiana, having already been celebrated by the Interpreter as types of the inseparable Ruth and Naomi, complete their reflection of the biblical heroines' relationship by becoming a daughter- and mother-in-law whose emotional and companionate devotion to each other resembles a marriage in itself.[68] Their pairing bolsters Julie Crawford's proposal that early modern marriage was "not always already heterosexual" and that "women often retain their bonds with each other *through* marriage"; Crawford considers another mother- and daughter-in-law relationship (the Countess and Helena in Shakespeare's *All's Well That Ends Well*), which "cannot be deduced from any single desire and cannot be reduced to any single nomination."[69] At times, Christiana and Mercy's indeterminate bond appears as warm intimacy triangulated through Christian, as when they lie together in his former bed, talking of their dreams of the Celestial City. At others, it takes on the sublime cast of awe and dread in the face of each other's beauty of holiness: when the women are bathed, made "fair as the Moon" (in another reference to the Song of Songs), and clothed as brides of Christ in "fine Linen, white and clean," "they seemed to be a Terror one to the other; For that they could not see that glory each one had in her self, which they could see in each other. Now therefore they began to esteem each other better than themselves. For you are fairer than I am, said one; and, You are more comely than I am, said another" (209–10). Bunyan sees no disharmony between erotic love for Christ and ardent desire to stand in the beautiful presence of fellow believers. In a marginal gloss to a later moment when Christiana and Mercy are welcomed by their "Friends" as "Vessels of the Grace of God" and greeted "with a kiss," Bunyan's personal avowed discomfort with haptic fellowship does not interfere: the gloss states approvingly that "Christians' love is kindled at the sight of one another" (224). The two women's relationship—a remarkable commingling of loving companionship, wonder and desire, and procreative marriage (with Matthew's help as a biologically essential but affectively peripheral third party)—infuses the narrative of part 2 with the eroticism and reproductive continuity often promised by romance, while turning these elements both nonconformist Christian and queer.

Alongside Christian's inspirational heroism, it is Christiana and Mercy's emotional union that generates and sustains part 2's community, first by extending it beyond the confines of Christian's nuclear family and then by providing for the expanded family's biological and spiritual futurity. Heterosexual marriage, homoerotic intimacy, and communal love cooperate to help Christian's literal and figurative descendants "spread abroad . . . upon the face of the Earth" and "uphold" the romance of part 1 as a living, proliferating narrative (262). Hearing Christian's story moved Valiant-for-truth to forsake his father and mother and cleave to Mercy and Christiana's growing band; his detachment from his parents recalls Jesus's assurance in Matthew 19:29 that "every one that hath forsaken houses, or brethren, or sisters, or father, or mother, or wife, or children . . . for my name's sake, shall receive an hundredfold." Believers are promised not only countless brothers and sisters in Christ, but also a multiplicity of spiritual parents, children, and spouses.[70] Bunyan's community embraces godly intimacy, tinged with eroticism, as a divine gift that thrives outside of normative marriages and nuclear families: he represents it flourishing between unmarried men and women, between women together, and among women praying—or even reading the right sort of romance—seemingly alone in the privacy of "their Cabinets, their Bosoms, and their Hearts."

The common denominator that unites all these heterogenous sites of desire and fellowship is feminine presence. Bunyan may indeed have been personally "shie of women" and intimate contact, as he claims in *Grace Abounding*, but he declares in the same volume that his sincere conversion began when he discovered that his "heart would tarry" in the company of "three or four poor women" he encountered sitting together and "talking about the things of God . . . as if they had found a new world."[71] Bunyan identifies as his spiritual mothers a community of women whose greatest pleasure was to tell "how God had visited their souls with His love in the Lord Jesus"; the intimacy and erotic devotion that he finds unsettling come enviably easily to them.[72] In part 2 of *The Pilgrim's Progress*, the Interpreter shows Christiana and Mercy a tableau Christian did not see, of a hen sheltering her chicks: he explains, "I choose, my Darlings, to lead you into the Room where such things are, because you are women, and they are easy for you" (203). The hen signifies not simply biological maternity, as we might assume, but the "Methods" by which God gathers and sustains "his People" (203): Bunyan seems to regard not just motherhood, but also love, open-ended desire, and erotic romance, as comparatively "easy" for female believers, and as the means by which they generate and nourish the expansively nonconforming family of the elect.

ROMANCE AND/AS ALLEGORY: CHRISTIAN'S IMITATORS IN TIME AND SPACE

The bond between Christiana and Mercy, which radiates love outward from itself to permeate the nonconformist Christian community, is *not* the animating idea behind Breen's "speculative" but rich and compelling reading of part 2, which she regards somewhat intuitively as the queerer book of *The Pilgrim's Progress*.⁷³ Instead, Breen's work is based on theories of temporality, such as Freccero's idea, shared by Dinshaw, of "queer history as a touch across time . . . to feel a connection and to feel community."⁷⁴ She proposes that part 2 resembles explicitly queer texts in having "an ambivalent relation to models of progress" and departs from part 1 in acknowledging "that linearity doesn't always work for the spiritual pilgrim," asking:

> What if we as readers of Bunyan assume that it is narratively and spiritually viable for pilgrims to undertake a journey that is a walking tour—or a stroll or long detour? . . . Isn't their journey livelier than [Christian's] as well? Their travel includes frequent rest stops; the pilgrims eat and drink well, they talk a lot, and they burst into song . . . as they fumble along to the Celestial City, the "failed" pilgrims . . . get to have some fun. Theirs is a journey propelled by an expansive sense of belonging, whereby . . . no one gets left behind.⁷⁵

In this final section, I, too, want to explore how Bunyan reconsiders narrative time and progress in part 2, with less attention to queer temporality than to his deliberate interrogation of romance as a meaningful model for individual and communal history. Like Behn, Bunyan seems to have doubts on this score—but he resolves them differently than she does.

Romance conventions, including love and chivalry, are instrumental in constructing Bunyan's nonnormative affective community. However, alongside romance's power to generate an extraordinary fellowship in part 2 comes a challenging metaconsciousness of genre and unstable temporality. The concerns of both the female characters and their warfaring male companions cause narrative time to take on a different, much less straightforward cast in part 2 than in part 1, as Breen and others have observed. The women's investments in love and kinship, so central to Bunyan's reconceived community, also force discontinuities between romance and spiritual allegory. Whereas Christian's travel to the Celestial City took *spiritual days*, Christiana's journey through ostensibly equidistant allegorical space requires *real years* as her children grow up, marry, and have offspring of their own.⁷⁶ However, the rate at which time passes in part 2 is impossible to determine: for instance, the narrator tells us that after James's marriage to Gaius's daughter Phebe, "they yet stayed about ten days at Gaius's House, spending their time, and the Seasons, like as Pilgrims use to do" (271). In order for Christiana's sons to mature and reproduce, "ten days" must indeed stand for some number of "Seasons," but Bunyan offers us no formula for performing this calculation. Elsewhere, we are simply told that part 2's various marriages unfold "in process of time": Mercy and Matthew marry after the pilgrims have stayed at Gaius's house for "more than a Month" (265), James and Phebe also wed at "about this time" (271), and Christiana's two youngest sons take wives after resting at the house of Mnason for an ambiguous "great while" (278).

Bunyan's descriptions of the children and the illustrations added to the 1687 edition only further complicate matters. When Christiana and her family depart the City of Destruction, the narrator describes her sons as "little Children" or "Babes" (181–82); later, when Matthew first begins to "blush" at making Mercy smile, he is still identified as a "little boy" (219). Even in Gaius's house, where Christiana's sons become eligible for marriage, they remain "Boys" to whom Gaius serves "a Dish of Milk well crumbed ... *that they may grow thereby*" (263). Meanwhile, the illustrations depict their rapid growth. As they begin their pilgrimage in the first, Matthew's head reaches the waist of Mercy, his future wife. Next, when Great-heart is leading the band to House Beautiful some days or weeks later, the children stand about a head shorter than the women, and the illustrator may offer some clue to their sudden growth in the couplet below the image: "See here too how the Child doth play ye man / And weak grow strong, when Great heart leads the van." And in the final woodcut, in which the Pilgrims circle the head of Giant Despair, there is no discernible difference among their height or ages. The illustrator's images, while consistent with the narrator's account of the boys' maturation into husbands and fathers and with Great-heart's observation that they are learning to conduct themselves spiritually "like [men]" (245), offer a striking visual example of the strange temporality of part 2's romance.[77] Through them, we witness "real" time passing at a rapid rate that has tacitly slipped out of alignment with the temporal and spatial limits of part 1's spiritual allegory.

Breen suggests that the uneven "synchronic development of Mercy and Matthew exposes and in so doing undermines what Edelman has termed the normalizing drive toward reproductive futurism that the couple enacts"; her queer reading is compatible with Luxon's emphasis on how the conventional goals of feminine or family romance—love and marriage, procreation and inheritance—are concepts eliminated in Heaven or at the end of time.[78] But it does not work to read part 2 as strictly anti-futurist, as Breen herself is aware: Gaius, for instance, emphasizes that marriage and reproduction remain essential for the furtherance of the worldly church and thus to a larger sacred plot. Christian completes his romance when he enters the Celestial City and is "swallowed up" from the narrator's and our sight, but this sense of an ending is withheld from the generation that follows him. The narrator lets us witness Christiana and several of her companions passage over the River, but he leaves her children's narrative open: "As for *Christiana*'s children, the four Boys that *Christiana* brought with her, with their Wives and Children, I did not stay where I was, till they were gone over. Also, since I came away, I heard one say, that they were yet alive, and so would be for the Increase of the Church, in that Place where they were for a time" (313–14). Mercy's story, then, concludes not in the Celestial City of her dreams, but breaks off when she, Matthew, and their siblings begin their quest to continue Christian's elect line. As Gaius insists, her mission will ensure "that the Name of their Father, and the House of his Progenitors, may never be forgotten in the World" (262). But even as this concern with the communal memory and repetition of Christian's heroic exploits reinforces our impression that we are reading the next generation (both biological and spiritual) of his family romance, we must observe that the next generation's "bear[ing] up their Father's name" and "tread[ing] in their Father's steps" are not—indeed, must not be—coterminous with "com[ing] to their Father's end" (262). The young families' ostensible destination, deliberately unreached when the narrator leaves them in Beulah "yet alive . . . for the Increase of the Church," would signal both the desired end and the erasure of their story, since erotic love, reproduction, and intergenerational inheritance are staples of romantic temporality that are rendered meaningless in eschatological time.

Gaius's attempt to clarify the matter using Old Testament typology only draws further attention to its difficulty. Proposing "to take away [women's] Reproach" and affirm their heroic potential, he reminds the pilgrims that "this Sex, in the old Testament, coveted Children, if happily this or that Woman might be the Mother of the Saviour of the World" and that "Women therefore are highly favoured, and show . . . that they are sharers with us in the Grace of Life" (262–63). His lesson evokes the paradox of reproductive temporality that we observed in Lucy Hutchinson's *Order and Disorder*, as does Christiana's prophecy to her daughters-in-law that "they have been

Faithful, and a fulfilling of the Promise upon them, will be their end" (307–8). The maternal mission that part 2's elect women share cannot be the same as the Old Testament heroines' hope that their child might be the Messiah, yet the "Promise" of reproduction still somehow applies to Christiana's descendants and lends legitimate godly purpose to the marriages of Mercy and the other young women.

The prologue's introduction of Christian's family succinctly encapsulates, in a half rhyme, the troubled compatibility of sacred and romance time: "let them know that these related *were* / Unto him: yea, his wife and children *are*" (169; emphasis mine). That the travelers *are* Christian's family is information essential to our sense that the next generation is continuing his quest—but the sacred end of that quest relegates that once-crucial relation to a profane past. Marriage, that event that concludes so many romances while gesturing toward their potential for continuation, must play a more circumscribed role for Bunyan. This problem would seem consistent with Luxon's argument that marriage is aggressively devalued throughout his works, but the truth seems more complicated, and deliberately so on Bunyan's part. Christiana grieves that she has "lost her husband" and that "the loving bond of that Relation was utterly broken betwixt them"; still, she continues to rely on "husband" and "wife" throughout part 2 as titles that best explain their former (and future?) connection (180). Also indicative of the problem is the fact that Christiana varies in her description of Christian as "gone *over the River*" (180), "gotten above" (191), or simply "dead" (223). When we interpret *The Pilgrim's Progress* as a romance, we think of Christian as having traveled from one point in space to another; when we read it as allegory, we grasp that he has moved through time from life into death and through spiritual states from sin to salvation. Christiana expresses all of these possibilities at once, situated simultaneously within the allegory and outside of it, as both character and reader.

Although we might take her vacillation as evidence of the *disintegration* of romance as an adequate model of the Christian story, we must also recognize that Christiana finds herself strengthened by the *reintegration* of romance into her understanding of her personal narrative: "My Sons, I have, as you may perceive, been of late under much exercise in my Soul about the Death of your Father; not for that I doubt at all of his Happiness: For I am satisfied now that he is well. . . . Come, my Children, let us pack up, and be gone to the Gate that leads to the Celestial Country, that we may see your Father, and be with him" (183). Acknowledging to herself and to her children that their husband and father is dead, she adds that they may still "pack up" and journey to another "Country" to "be with him"; immediately after admitting the limited application of romance to their family's sad situation, she reaffirms its purpose. Christian's "Relation" to her has indeed been "broken" by his death and entrance into heaven, where the only marriage is that of Christ to his communal Church, and yet Christiana's new assurance that their "loving bond" may be repaired and restored inspires her to re-present her narrative through the genre that enacts the reunion of lovers and families. Bunyan's rhyme in the prologue likewise stresses the endurance of marriage rather than its decline: in reading time, Christiana and the children "are" Christian's family *after* they "were," not only before. Marriage is sharply devalued, then suddenly revalued as a symbol of spiritual fulfillment and as a representation of the multivalent love that joins worldly Christians to their heavenly counterparts and to each other—a sign that remains persistently useful even as it is not precisely correct.

Feminine concerns are not the only source of Bunyan's genre riddles. A number of readers have found that the highly imitative or derivative nature of part 2's adventures lowers the stakes or the interest of the romance.[79] Hill, following Knox, jokes that "Great-heart and his shooting parties just finish off work which Christian had so well begun."[80] The pilgrims largely avoid falling into Christian's perils, since Great-heart "did so faithfully tell them of *Dangers*" with the aid of his ever-present "Book or Map" (299). The question of whether the pilgrims' plot ever had any stakes that can be raised or lowered demands a consideration of Stanley Fish's characteristic but important argument that both parts of *The Pilgrim's Progress* lack the narrative uncertainty necessary for such stakes really to exist.[81] Since Bunyan's characters are predestined as either "blest or not," Fish argues, the saved are already saved and the damned are already damned; narrative "progress" is as much the delusion of the elect as it is of the reprobate, a bait and switch Bunyan has designed first to entrap his readers and then to remind them of their fallen minds and depraved literary sensibilities. The characters' (and our) shared familiarity with romance's structure stands in the way of a pure understanding of nonprogressive sacred time.[82] We have seen that Bunyan was, as Fish and Davies assert, aware of the disjunctions between his romance and his allegory. But as we conclude this section, a closer look at a few of part 2's most derivative or imitative moments should show that Bunyan saw worldly genre as a "Map" with important limits and important uses—not as a trap, a sin, or an error to discard.

Great-heart's "Book or Map"—which Bunyan glosses as "God's Book" but which also evokes part 1 itself, the source of the characters' and readers' communal knowledge—is judged by the narrator to be a gift of grace rather than an easy way out: "Then thought I with my self, who, that goeth on Pilgrimage, but would have one of these Maps about him, that he may look when he is at a stand, which is the way he must take?" (300). Familiarity with the form of the text is not, as Fish would have it, a stumbling block, but a trustworthy narrative guide providentially provided for the elect community. Colin Manlove has suggested that as a result of the pilgrims' textual foreknowledge, their few dangerous exploits are often "not a part of the pilgrimage at all, but are done almost as hobbies."[83] Indeed, Christian is a hero whom adventures *befall*, such as his assault by Apollyon and his captivity by Giant Despair, whereas in part 2, the community of reader-heroes, seeking to imitate the now-famous Christian, both *retell* his trials in lieu of experiencing similar ones and increasingly *go in search* of adventures of their own. Yet this self-conscious approach to chivalric adventure as digressive or diversionary is really nothing new in the romance genre: like Quixote, and in fact like Sidney's earlier heroes, the pilgrims seek out adventure in order to emulate the protagonists they already admire. At the same time (and as we saw in *Oroonoko*), this conventional practice also points conspicuously to the genre's norms and makes its seams visible. For instance, at Vanity-Fair, the site of Christian's imprisonment and his companion Faithful's martyrdom, the pilgrims re-recount this *"hard Chapter"* of part 1 to one another; where Christian and Faithful shared a bond of mutual suffering, their followers share a bond of mutual familiarity with and zeal for that suffering (273). Meanwhile, instead of being subjected to torment there, they seek out godly combat: the male Pilgrims "[enter] into a Covenant to go and engage" a deadly monster "like a Dragon" who menaces the town, and "with their Weapons go forth to meet" the Beast of Revelation (279). The Beast is easily routed, though not killed; like many of Spenser's battles, the men's chivalric conflict concludes in an immediate victory while obviously deferring an eschatological one. Here, part 2's self-awareness of genre again runs into temporal problems: while Christian's unsought duel with Apollyon stood for his psychological struggle against Satan—successful in one moment but potentially renewable in any other—the allegory of the pilgrims' combat within time with the Beast of the end times is much less tidy, simultaneously evocative of the warfaring Church's communal power and of its limited temporal agency.

This generic and temporal self-consciousness takes on further complexity at the site of Christian's abduction by Despair. His reader-followers naturally recognize the fabled place and together "[consult] what was best to be done": the men agree to slay the Giant and demolish Doubting Castle (282). Great-heart builds "A Monument of Deliverance" in a space "right over against the Pillar that *Christian* erected for a *Caution* to Pilgrims that came after, to take heed of entering into his Grounds," emphasizing the episode's parallelism with part 1 through both the monument's location and its inscription:

> This is the Head of him, Whose Name only
> In former times, did Pilgrims terrify.
> His Castle's down, and Diffidence his Wife
> Brave Master Great-heart has bereft of Life. (286)

The quatrain demands we ask whether Despair and Doubt have been put down only as generic tropes—a giant and his lair—by the next generation of a family romance, or whether 'Pilgrims that [come] after' have been delivered from the sins themselves for all time, a finality withheld from the battle with the Beast. Roger Pooley, asking whether such "permanence" can be "credible," points to this episode as an example of how the 1687 illustrations "significantly [affect] our interpretation of... the text."[84] Beneath the picture of the community of pilgrims playing music and dancing around Despair's severed head, the illustrator has added his own quatrain, a Spenserian note of caution that stands in striking juxtaposition to the verse composed by Great-heart:

> Tho doubting Castle be demolished,
> And the Gyant dispair hath lost his head
> Sin can rebuild the Castle, make't remaine;
> And make despair the Gyant live againe. (285)

As Pooley notes, "Together the incident and its illustration capture the mixture of the 'already' and the 'not yet' that is Bunyan's sense of the victory of

Christ."[85] This "already / not yet" paradox, of course, is essentially the same as the mystery of reproduction whereby the elect continue to anticipate the promise of the Messiah many centuries after Jesus's birth, and is what characterizes the temporal tension throughout Milton's poetics of Christian history.

While the illustrator's woodcut reinforces the allegorical ambiguity of the pilgrims' triumph at Doubting Castle, Bunyan himself already seems to be drawing his readers up to the very edge of his allegory, "right over against" the space where Great-heart's success overlays Christian's struggle—much as the pilgrims in the woodcut press close to the pole of the monument, their awed expressions suggesting simultaneous celebration and apprehension. As often happens, the boundary blurs between the real community of reading believers and the fictional community of questing pilgrims, who are themselves readers of Christian's story and of his cautionary note about the dangers of Despair. Each is called to experience, in one place and at one moment, both fear and deliverance, both romance and reality. It is probably no coincidence that the narrator also breaks in at just this moment to remind us that all these events are merely what he "saw in [his] Dream," an interruption he makes with greater frequency in part 2 than part 1 (284). The dream of romance may allow the godly to unite in envisioning the defeat of sin, but as a dream, it also acknowledges itself as mimetic or symbolic rather than real, a narrative form of this world rather than the next. Davies aptly calls Bunyan "an author with a highly sophisticated concept of what narrative can and should do," concerned "with aspects of narration which we might otherwise consider modern or postmodern: Bunyan seems to be interested in antinarrativity, in constructing stories which are difficult to enjoy as stories, rather than simply marrying popular fictive modes to a Puritan moralism."[86] I argue, though, that Bunyan's sophisticated manipulation of the superficially simple does not amount to his treatment of romance as a wholly self-consuming artifact. The worldly literary mode that Davies and Fish take to be a dangerous delusion, Bunyan exposes as the dreaming and desiring believer's illusion, which is also an imperfect allusion to divine truth.

Betty Schellenberg has observed that part 2's repetitive imitations and communal focus "[imply] a potentially unlimited multiplication of equally significant and narration-worthy pilgrimages."[87] Such unfettered narrative potential is endemic to romance in the anti-teleological sense that Patricia Parker has called "inescapable," endlessly dilating and indefinitely repeating.[88]

Bunyan certainly suggests that a final telos to the romance exists, both for individuals like Christian and for the apocalyptic Church, but the central concerns of part 2 partly undermine romance as an adequate model of that narrative in its fullest, most "real" form. Given Bunyan's extensive efforts to redeem romance and render it compatible with a Puritan salvation narrative, we should not conclude that he changes his mind in part 2 about the genre's usefulness as a model. Far from it: the sequel stresses romance's power to reconceive and reconstruct the community of the elect and to map out its teleological path. But at the same time, it reminds its readers of the limits of that progressive model and alerts us to the dilatory margins of the "Book or Map" of romance. The genre itself becomes an allegory *of* itself, in the way that Bunyan likes best: like the old pilgrim who protests that his name is not "Honesty" but simply "Honest," the romance of part 2 succeeds "not in the abstract" but in a form that exposes its mundane, human parameters (249). The worldly boundaries of this communal generic tradition are what allow Stand-fast, crossing the River, to separate the stories he has heard and imitated from the truth he is about to see and live fully: "I have formerly lived by Hearsay, and Faith, but now I go where I shall live by sight" (313).

Stand-fast makes an important distinction: reading the Christian life as romance has given him an impression of the Celestial City necessary to maintain his "Faith," but it has never given him "sight." He points us to a final moment that highlights the extent to which Bunyan has reimagined the model of Protestant allegorical romance that he inherited indirectly from Spenser a century before. Near the end of part 1, Christian and Hopeful, like Redcrosse, are offered a temporary vision of their heavenly goal when the Shepherds of the Delectable Mountains invite them to look through their "Perspective-Glass": "The pilgrims lovingly accepted the motion: so they had them to the top of an high Hill, called *Clear*, and gave them their glass to look. Then they tried to look; but the remembrance of that last thing that the Shepherds had shown them [the By-way to Hell] made their hands shake, by means of which impediment they could not look steadily through the glass; yet they thought they saw something like the Gate, and also some of the Glory of the place" (126–27). Like some other of Bunyan's allegorical persons and places, the hill Clear is named with apparently intentional imprecision, for Christian—unlike Redcrosse—cannot clearly see the holy city in the distance; he only thinks he might see "something like" it. To a fallen spectator, a pinnacle vision of the distant end of romance can never be permanent, but Christian's is the faintest and most fleeting of the many such visions we have encountered in this book. Bunyan's symbolic narrative might gesture toward "some of the Glory" of what it stands for, but it cannot show it, not even to its own characters. Indeed, by part 2, Christiana and Mercy do not imitate this particular experience: although they encounter the Shepherds, no mention is made of the Perspective-Glass. In its place, the Shepherds comfort Mercy—who is suffering the pains of pregnancy—with a "Looking glass" with the power to reveal the image of Christ, "the Prince of Pilgrims" (289). When we recall that Spenser's Britomart received, in place of Redcrosse's narrative prospect, only the troubled promise of future offspring and a glimpse of her beloved in a magic mirror, Bunyan may appear to be reiterating Spenser's delineation of unequally satisfying romance perspectives. Yet Christian is arguably the one shown much less than Mercy, and the pilgrims of part 2 are not offered Christian's vision because, in the strength of their numbers and their faith, they do not need it. The "Book or Map" they hold in their hands and hearts has supplanted the hazy view from the mountaintop. In *The Pilgrim's Progress*'s self-conscious second part, the women and men of the elect community have distinct attributes that advance their cause but share one common narrative vision as readers and imitators. Rather than requiring visionary proof that their romance is real, they possess a shared earthly text that stands for, and reminds them of the superior reality of, its unreadable heavenly counterpart.

Bunyan's narrative complexity has inspired Breen to call for "a capacious, layered definition of queer [temporality]," one that can accommodate both Edelman's anti-teleological, anti-reproductive futurist stance and a longing for progress into a better world to come.[89] She cites queer writer Mark Doty's vision of the future as a "temporal space" that, like the Celestial City in the distance, "constantly diminishes, but never vanishes" and is "shaped by . . . the weight of memory": "Is my future, then, remembering you? Inscribing the name, carrying the memory? Remembering is the work of the living, and the collective project of memory is enormous; it involves the weight of all our dead, the ones we have known ourselves and the ones we know only from stories."[90] Doty's conception beautifully evokes the pilgrim community's relationship to Christian and his romance, as well as other relationships between the living and the dead in melancholy narratives of memory such as Greville's *Life of Sidney*, Hutchinson's *Memoirs* of her husband, and even Behn's *Oroonoko*. But where Behn (like Greville) was impelled by the tragedy of the dead to renounce romance forever as a mode that could make history legible for the living, Bunyan joins Hutchinson, Milton, Spenser, and Sidney in choosing the right kind of romance as the symbol of his elect community and their resistance to temporal power. Among these reformist writers, Bunyan's idea of romance is most open to accepting and working within the limits of the genre's value; he regards it as the right mode for telling the story of individual and communal Christian heroism and history precisely because its imitation of godly heroic agency and narrative time is imperfect. Romance is not, in the end, the way, the truth, or the life—it is a map, a faithful fiction, a way of living.

Conclusion

If Behn's late work suggests that the end of the seventeenth century brought with it the tragic death of romance, we ought to recognize the extent to which this is true: pure romance as a form of high literature or political mythmaking had declined in England in the hundred years since Sidney and Spenser's aristocratic and nationalistic narratives, and mid-century royalist writers such as Herbert and Cavendish were among the last to publish "serious" prose tales of erotic or chivalric quests for politically engaged upper-class readers. Their work, moreover, was beginning to push against romance's conventional reliance on providential teleology and heroic idealism, a task that Behn effectively completed when her prince came to a tragic and barbaric end. As Michael McKeon and others have demonstrated, the prose romance—primarily a royalist genre throughout the Civil War and Restoration periods—declined, or grew up, into the novel, a form characterized by the gestures toward ostensible realism, contingent narrative, and the psychological "world within" that we find in *The Princess Cloria, Assaulted and Pursued Chastity,* and *Oroonoko*.[1] Under McKeon's formulation, the novel does not reject romance so much as accomplish its tacit incorporation and elision: by pretending to portray a fictional world in which all events are contingent yet "natural," both rationally and psychologically plausible, the novelist plays the empiricist while also adopting the role of an invisible providence.[2]

However, I have taken care throughout this book not to conflate royalist romance or prose romances with the complete picture of seventeenth-century English romance; accordingly, we should not mistake the decline or the transformation of the royalist prose romance for the death of the genre. First and foremost, Behn's disillusioned prophecy—that heroic or nationalistic romance was doomed in both the Old World and the New—was wrong. (We may recall that Greville, too, was mistaken when he forecasted the end of English romance after Sidney's death many decades earlier.) Sacvan Bercovitch has shown that romance constructions of selfhood and nationhood, dependent on providential quests and chosen heroes, flourished on American soil during the seventeenth and eighteenth centuries (and, indeed, far beyond) as the community of "the Chosen Seed" journeyed across dangerous seas and unknown territories to "possess the Promis'd Land" and triumph over their unregenerate enemies.[3] As accurate as it was, Behn's vision of oppression, suffering, and death in the New World nevertheless underestimated romance's enduring persistence, adaptability, and fluid subjectivity as a sociopolitical strategy. Second, the broad generalization that the realist novel outstripped the providential or supernatural romance after the seventeenth century overlooks another important fact: that Bunyan's *Pilgrim's Progress* achieved stunning popularity in the eighteenth and nineteenth centuries, becoming (as is commonly cited) a household staple rivaled only by the Bible itself. Bunyan's allegorical romance saw countless new editions, along with an unauthorized sequel by Thomas Sherman (which partly prompted the authentic part 2), and an anonymous part 3 after Bunyan's death. Christian, Christiana, and their many heroic companions became models of spiritual and psychological selfhood through which subjects could "read [them] sel[ves]," just as Bunyan had envisioned (9).

Together with Behn and her turn to tragic realism, the unapologetically romantic Bunyan concludes this project not only because he wrote at the crux of traditionally defined periods and because he was one of the last major seventeenth-century writers to have an adult memory of the Civil War, but also because he is unlike most other authors in these pages, in that he does not deny or conceal his debt to England's chivalric romance tradition. Despite the brief concerns about the worldliness of the genre that he expresses in the preface of *The Pilgrim's Progress*, his "apology" leaves him reasonably comfortable with it. While Milton and Hutchinson disclaimed romance in their biblical poetics only to reclaim it, Bunyan is open about the fact that his fictions are drawn both from the Bible and from *Bevis of Hampton*. The difference may be attributable partly to the disparate social standing of these Puritan writers and their intended audiences: sincere, generically straightforward romance had become increasingly associated with lower-class readers, and Bunyan, a craftsman's son raised on tales of adventure from cheap chapbooks, had a humble readership to appeal to and no intellectual or aristocratic face to save. However, the shift in Puritan romance's overtness from Milton to Bunyan may also signify something more interesting. We have explored in detail how the Civil War and the Restoration witnessed a protracted ideological battle over romance; by 1688, though, Behn's *Oroonoko* had effectively surrendered the field, judging that romance's promises to its chosen champions had failed and were not worth the fight. As Annabel Patterson suggested of Milton (I believe wrongly), later seventeenth-century royalists may really have had *their* "last chance at true romance," mined it for its remaining veins of political usefulness, and begun to move on to new modes of narrative.[4] Not all of their opponents, however, concurred that romance's value had expired, even if it was limited. While the battle was still at its height, Milton and Hutchinson felt compelled to associate romance with Cavalier vainglory or worldliness, just as royalist writers insisted that it was so much delusional Puritan nonsense. But as the two ideological models of heroic narrative became more distinctly separate from each other, Bunyan found himself free to turn to fantastical romance without much worry that he was doing wrong by his faith or his politics. Monsters, giants, and knights with magical weaponry—the kind of figures that Spenser had embraced but that Sidney had already found problematic, and that were decorously or anxiously shadowed in Milton and Hutchinson's work—could fight it out in broad daylight in *The Pilgrim's Progress*, and would continue to do so for the entertainment and Christian education of future generations of readers, including those who shared neither Bunyan's politics nor his theology.[5]

Royalists' and republicans' battle for romance far outlasted the armed conflicts of the Civil War, but as the seventeenth century and the reign of the Stuarts neared their ends, the generic competition also died down. To declare a victor, we would need to clarify the terms of victory, and it might be much easier to say that romance itself won on two fronts. Under seventeenth-century royalist treatments, the genre was gradually remodeled under ideological pressures until it became something new, experimental, and tentatively realist; meanwhile, driven by different and opposing ideological exigencies, Puritan writers were increasingly motivated to preserve and maintain a form of romance that had prevailed in earlier eras and in popular chapbook stories of questing and dragon slaying, a form dominated by providential design, absolute standards of good and evil, and exceptional heroic subjectivity. Bunyan and Behn's beliefs may have been passionately opposed, but their models of romance were no longer in competition. Behn's royalist narrative freely owns its romance roots but is exploring new, "modern" literary territories and has been hailed as the first "American novel."[6] Bunyan's Puritan fiction is unabashedly conspicuous as fantastical, allegorical romance; while apocalyptically proleptic, it is artistically nostalgic—in some ways, literally "medieval"—and can perhaps be regarded as the most influential ancestor of countless fantasy adventures, including religiously inflected twentieth-century classics by J. R. R. Tolkien and C. S. Lewis.

I do not mean to suggest at all that romance progressed or transfigured through royalist writing but remained static or regressed under Milton, Hutchinson, and Bunyan. The seventeenth century may have seen both the birth of the novel and the deliberate revaluation of certain elements of medieval romance, but writers of diverse ideologies together transformed the ways in which the romance mode purported to model history, prescribe norms for heroic subjectivity, and create community. From Sidney and Spenser to Bunyan and Behn, romance changed from the form in which God had written the narrative of humanity to a mode in which subjects actively interrogated the ambiguous relationship between providential authorship, human agency, and random chance. Even for Bunyan, romance was less the genre of history than a heuristic imitation; and if his monsters are medieval, something about his self-conscious and self-referential play with genre in part 2 of *The Pilgrim's Progress* may strike us as postmodern. Tragedy and the death of heroes, too, went from creating tension with romance (as they did in Sidney's *New Arcadia*, Greville's *Life of Sidney*, and Hutchinson's *Memoirs* of her late husband) to becoming incorporated with it: postwar royalist romances, *Paradise Lost*, *Order and Disorder*, and *Oroonoko* are all concerned with how to accomplish the obligatory integration of romance and tragedy, and it can be easy to forget that the allegory of *The Pilgrim's Progress* demands that it also end with the deaths of most of its protagonists. Hobbes feared that romance offered its readers a naïve sense of their own invincibility, but in the decades after *Leviathan*, the same literary strategy that empowered its subjects typically also called on them to question their heroism, the inevitability of their temporal success, and the cohesion of their communities.

The methods whereby romance draws ideological communities into coherence have been the final major subject of this project. Here, too, we find remarkable consistencies alongside remarkable transformations. "They only know it which inwardly feel it" (78)—the defense of Sidney's Pyrocles that makes romance a matter for the private psyche, a source of individual and communal power that need not look outside itself for validation, and an extraordinary affective experience that might form intimate and transgressive bonds among the few who shared it—was a formulation that continued to express the ideological power offered by the strategy of romance throughout the seventeenth century. Romance subjectivity and exclusivity allowed royalist and republican readers to interpret Sidney and Spenser as they pleased, armed William Cavendish and John Hutchinson against their cynical enemies and skeptical wives, divided Milton's Jesus from Satan and Hutchinson's Holy State from the Worldly State, and enabled Bunyan's and Behn's heroes and readers to ally with companions in their quest against the unregenerate who would hinder it. However, romance soon became more than a litmus test for locating the spiritual elect or the cultural elite and excluding their supposed adversaries. It became a field for exploring the problems inherent in its own nonrational subjectivity, where heroes could grapple not just with their enemies but also with the elusiveness of assurance about their identities, obligations, and destinies. Finally, it became an instrument not simply for identifying preexisting "elect" communities, but also for working to reimagine and rebuild them. For Dryden, struggling in his poetry to heal the wounds of the Civil War, the vision of romance community was one of universal (royalist) union rather than exclusivity and exceptionalism, and for Behn, romance nourished the abortive hope that an elite English heroic subjectivity need not remain divided by politics or religion, or even by race and nationality. Even Bunyan, for whom election and double predestination were at least as important as they were for Sidney or Spenser, strongly suggested in *The Pilgrim's Progress* that creating community through romance meant much more than separating those who were "blest" from those who were "not" (9): it also meant envisioning a Christian fellowship constituted and sustained by nonnormative bonds of love and kinship, by heroic imitation, and by the repetition of shared story. This final element, perhaps, was romance's greatest and most enduring promise, embraced by each of the writers in these pages: that when idealism seemed destined only for tragedy, and when a collective quest seemed to have gone hopelessly astray, a community of would-be heroes might survive through the story that always remained, ready to be told again.

NOTES

INTRODUCTION

1. Hobbes, *Elements*, 50–51.
2. Ibid., 63.
3. Hobbes, *Leviathan*, 9.
4. Kahn, *Wayward Contracts*, 145. Smith also discusses Hobbes's relationship to romance and its writers in *Literature and Revolution*, esp. 159–60.
5. See, for example, Fuchs on recognizing romance by sight in *Romance* (1–2).
6. Cooper, *English Romance in Time*, 10.
7. Ibid., 9. Cooper's reference to a "family resemblance" is linked to the "horizon of expectations" that Jauss has identified as constituting a literary form familiar to audiences (*Towards an Aesthetic of Reception*, 79).
8. Fuchs, *Romance*, 9.
9. Ibid.
10. Frye, *Secular Scripture*, 15, 53–54, 58–59.
11. Parker, *Inescapable Romance*.
12. Cavallaro, *Chivalric Romance*, 1–2.
13. Quint, *Epic and Empire*, 9.
14. Sidney, *Defence of Poesie*, C4r.
15. Fuchs, *Romance*, 9.
16. Without being strongly concerned with genre, Guibbory's *Map of Time* discusses the tension, and frequent interaction, between seventeenth-century visions of history as progressive, regressive, cyclical, or random.
17. Fludernik, *Towards a "Natural" Narratology*, 22. Cited in Cooper, *English Romance in Time*, 47.
18. Cooper, *English Romance in Time*, 47.
19. Frye, *Secular Scripture*, 31.
20. Welch, "Epic Romance, Royalist Retreat," 578, 572.
21. Smith, *Literature and Revolution*, 243.
22. Rose, "Gender, Genre, and History"; Hackett, *Women and Romance Fiction*; Dowd and Eckerle, *Genre and Women's Life Writing*; Eckerle, *Romancing the Self*.
23. Fuchs, *Romance*, 78; Cooper, *English Romance in Time*; Goodman, *Chivalry and Exploitation*.
24. Veevers, *Images of Love and Religion*; Coiro, "Ball of Strife"; Britland, *Drama at the Courts of Queen Henrietta Maria*.
25. Patterson, *Censorship and Interpretation*; Salzman, *English Prose Fiction*; Kahn, *Wayward Contracts*; Zurcher, *Seventeenth-Century English Romance*; Potter, *Secret Rites and Secret Writing*.
26. Newcomb, *Reading Popular Romance*; Das, *Renaissance Romance*.
27. Smith, *Literature and Revolution*, 236; see also 234–49. Zurcher, in *Seventeenth-Century English Romance*, likewise offers a reading of Harrington's *Oceana* but spends many more pages on royalist prose.
28. Jameson, "Magical Narratives," 142, 158.
29. Ibid., 160, 140.
30. Heng, *Empire of Magic*, 18.
31. Werth, *Fabulous Dark Cloister*.
32. Fuchs, *Romance*, 65.
33. McKeon, among others, notes that by the seventeenth century, romance was often invoked in a "trivializing or pejorative" sense (*Origins of the English Novel*, 27).

34. Donne, *John Donne*, 288. Fuchs has presented a reading of lyric romance in the sonnets of Petrarch (*Romance*, 64).

35. Sanchez, *Erotic Subjects*, 4–5.

36. Freccero, "Tangents (of Desire)," 91–92; Dinshaw, *Getting Medieval*, 12–13.

37. Friedlander, "Desiring History," 3, 9.

38. A major source for this debate is Traub, "New Unhistoricism in Queer Studies"; for a useful overview of it, see Friedlander, "Desiring History."

39. Lake, *Christ's Conflict*, 4. Subsequent references appear parenthetically.

40. For other arguments that one may experience daily life and history through the hermeneutic of genre, including romance, see Lamb, "Merging the Secular and the Spiritual"; Smith, *Literature and Revolution*, 243; White, *Fiction of Narrative*.

41. Helsby, *Letters*, Folger Shakespeare Library ms. X.d.493 (5).

42. Ibid.

43. Ibid.

44. Helsby, *Letters*, Folger Shakespeare Library ms. X.d.493 (3).

45. Hatton's politics are difficult to discern from her correspondence. She discusses them most directly in this letter, in a difficult passage in which she condemns the hypocrisy and "selff love" of both sides in the war (ibid.).

46. Ibid.

47. For a discussion of romance and male intimacy in royalist writing, see Kahn, *Wayward Contracts*, 223–51.

48. Bercovitch, *Puritan Origins*.

49. McKeon, *Origins of the English Novel*, 88–89.

50. Gleckman, "Malvolio and Puritan Assurance," 9.

51. Hobbes notes the revolutionary danger inherent in the fact that claims to sacred vocation could never be disproven and might seem to be confirmed by chance (*Leviathan*, 293).

52. Smith poses a claim about epic that I wish to make a version of, in more detail, about romance: "The history of the epic during the English Revolution is a process . . . in which kinds of subjectivity are 'discovered'—as epic and heroic patterns are worked upon by divided perceptions and divided ideological requirements. . . . [Epic] enabled religious difference to be voiced as a state of mind . . . an odyssey of subjectivity. Where this might involve an inward turn for the defeated and withdrawn Royalist, puritan republicanism was most heroically engaged in its inwardness" (*Literature and Revolution*, 232–33).

53. Patterson, *Censorship and Interpretation*, 167–210; Potter, *Secret Rites and Secret Writing*, 72–112. Crawford observes that the "interpretive strategies" of texts also functioned as political code for other communities (*Mediatrix*, 28).

54. Kahn, *Wayward Contracts*, 223–51; Welch, "Epic Romance, Royalist Retreat."

55. Crawford, *Mediatrix*, 6.

56. Lake, *Antichrist's Lewd Hat*.

57. Helsby, *Letters*, Folger Shakespeare Library ms. X.d.493 (3).

58. Sidney, *Arcadia*, 78.

59. Cooper, *English Romance in Time*, 251.

60. Bunyan, *Pilgrim's Progress*, 173.

CHAPTER 1

1. Werth, *Fabulous Dark Cloister*.

2. Michael Brennan traces this popular story in "Thy Necessity Is Yet Greater."

3. For discussions of the relationship between Sidney's popular image and the appropriation of his works, see Hager, "Exemplary Mirage"; and Hillyer, *Sir Philip Sidney*.

4. Weiner, *Poetics of Protestantism*, 3.

5. Worden, *Sound of Virtue*.

6. Sinfield, *Faultlines*.

7. Duncan-Jones, *Sir Philip Sidney*.

8. Even scholars who have made these attempts have acknowledged the challenge of doing so. Weiner admits that "the term 'Calvinist' is as temporally confusing as its English equivalent, 'Puritan'" (*Poetics of Protestantism*, 8), and Worden notes that Sidney's Protestantism "carries light creedal baggage" (*Sound of Virtue*, 32).

9. Stillman, *Philip Sidney*. This argument has strongly influenced recent Sidney scholarship.

10. Ibid., 113.

11. Weiner, Worden, and others oppose several earlier arguments that Sidney's

prose fictions celebrate erotic love and romance heroism, including Davis, *Map of Arcadia*; Lawry, *Sidney's Two Arcadias*; Connell, *Sir Philip Sidney*.

12. Weiner, *Poetics of Protestantism*, 100.

13. Arguments that Sidney revises the New Arcadia to portray more admirable heroes are more common. See, for example, Lindheim, *Structures of Sidney's Arcadia*; and Schneider, *Sidney's (Re)Writing of the "Arcadia."*

14. Worden, *Sound of Virtue*; Skretkowicz, *European Erotic Romance*, 169. Skretkowicz finds Sidney ambivalent about erotic love and ultimately inclined toward parodying it as politically irresponsible (169, 202–3).

15. See C. Kinney, "On the Margins of Romance" and "Chivalry Unmasked"; Lamb, "Exhibiting Class"; Davis, "Web of His Story." For readings that see Sidney supporting the potential compatibility of unironic romance and Protestantism, see Dana, "Providential Plot"; Brumbaugh, "Cecropia and the Church of Antichrist" and "*Jerusalem Delivered*"; Mentz, "Reason, Faith, and Shipwreck"; A. Kinney, "Poetics of Romance"; Skretkowicz, *European Erotic Romance*; Werth, *Fabulous Dark Cloister*; Crowley, "Sireno and Philisides"; Werlin, "Providence and Perspective."

16. For a rich study of *Arcadia*'s afterlives, see Alexander, *Writing after Sidney*.

17. The term is Stanley Fish's, in *Self-Consuming Artifacts*.

18. Sidney, *Defence of Poesie*, C4r. Skretkowicz argues that Sidney turns to romance to create "intellectual and spiritual bonds among disparate Protestant communities of quasi-republican inclination" (*European Erotic Romance*, 2). Gerard reads Sidney as a community builder in "Within the Zodiac of Wit," 91.

19. Irish details this relationship in "Friendship and Frustration."

20. Stillman, *Philip Sidney*, 59–60.

21. Sanchez, *Erotic Subjects*, 11.

22. Cooper, *English Romance in Time*, 241 (emphasis mine).

23. Das, *Renaissance Romance*.

24. Stillman, *Philip Sidney*, 39.

25. Sidney, *Arcadia*, 268. Subsequent references appear parenthetically.

26. See, for instance, Mornay's *Woorke concerning the trewnesse of the Christian religion*, of which Sidney began a translation before his death.

27. Baker emphasizes the Calvinist terminology of the repenting sinner's softened heart in "Sidney, Religious Syncretism, and Henry VIII."

28. Stillman, *Philip Sidney*, 53.

29. As the *New Arcadia* opens, Strephon and Claius make a similar appeal while discussing their transformation through love of Urania: "Who can better witness that than we, whose experience is grounded upon feeling?" (5).

30. Cooper, *English Romance in Time*, 219–20 (emphasis in the original).

31. Ibid., 258.

32. Crawford, "Sidney's Sapphics," 991.

33. Ibid., 994.

34. Sanchez, *Erotic Subjects*, 4.

35. Crawford, "Sidney's Sapphics," 998, 1005n; Lamb, *Gender and Authorship*, 75–76.

36. Stillman, *Philip Sidney*, 164.

37. Ibid., 165.

38. Wood argues that the *New Arcadia*'s moral philosophy encourages optimism about Amphialus ("'If an excellent man should err'").

39. Sidney, *Defence of Poesie*, C2r. For insightful discussions of this issue, see Lee, "Sidney's Two Roads," 103–5; Werlin, "Providence and Perspective."

40. Stillman, *Philip Sidney*, 113.

41. Crawford, "Sidney's Sapphics" and *Mediatrix*.

42. Kinney, "On the Margins of Romance."

43. Kinney, "Sidney's *Arcadia*," 398. See also Kinney's "On the Margins of Romance" and Lamb's similar argument in "Exhibiting Class" (60–62).

44. Davis, "Web of His Story," 62–63.

45. Werth, *Fabulous Dark Cloister*, 43–45.

46. Lee identifies a lack of moral exemplarity as the characteristic that separates Mopsa's "humorous commentary on episodic storytelling" from Musidorus's episodic narrative ("Sidney's Two Roads," 89). Werlin suggests that Sidney portrays Mopsa and her family as "clearly lack[ing] the

princes' moral liberty" ("Providence and Perspective," 36).

47. Parker, *Inescapable Romance*.
48. Jameson, "Magical Narratives," 161.
49. See, for example, Brumbaugh, "Cecropia and the Church of Antichrist."
50. Sanchez, *Erotic Subjects*, 91. Cooper, while not speaking directly of Sidney, also notes that although "romances are usually thought of as serving the ideology of the elite," to the extent that they encourage active, independent, transgressive love—especially from women—"they begin to look almost oppositional" (*English Romance in Time*, 226).
51. The connection between Cecropia and Lucretius was first made by Myrick (*Sir Philip Sidney*, 265).
52. Sanchez, *Erotic Subjects*, 91.
53. Sidney, *Defence of Poesie*, F4r.
54. See, for example, Davis (*Map of Arcadia*, 75), Lawry (*Sidney's Two Arcadias*, 155), Sanchez (*Erotic Subjects*, 91).
55. Crawford, *Mediatrix*, 40, 45.
56. Sanchez, "True Vowed Sacrifice," 100.
57. Ibid., 102.
58. Worden, *Sound of Virtue*, 340.
59. Lochman, "Friendship's Passion," 78.
60. Duncan-Jones, *Sir Philip Sidney*, 288. For other arguments that the *New Arcadia* reveals Sidney's loss of psychological or political faith, see McCoy (*Rebellion in Arcadia*, 26, 216) and Sedinger ("Sidney's New Arcadia").
61. Werlin, "Providence and Perspective," 33.
62. See, for example, Mallette, *Spenser and the Discourses of Reformation England*; Werth, *Fabulous Dark Cloister*; Hodges, "Reformed Dragons."
63. Berger, *Allegorical Temper*, 240.
64. King, *Spenser's Poetry and the Reformation Tradition*, 202.
65. King, "Sidney and Spenser," 149.
66. Mikics, *Limits of Moralizing*, 60.
67. Parker, *Inescapable Romance*, 64.
68. Kinney, "Romance," 122.
69. For a discussion of the complex relationship between human and providential narrative perspectives in *The Faerie Queene*, see McCabe, *Pillars of Eternity*.
70. The invisibility of God's church on earth, and the challenge Spenser faced in attempting to represent it, is the subject of Falck's "Heavenly Lineaments."
71. Hadfield argues that in light of Stillman's recent case for Sidney's Philippism, it is worth maintaining that "the principal texts that inspired Spenser's religious imagination were those of the mainstay of English Reformation thought, John Calvin" ("Spenser and Religion," 22). Broaddus likewise sees Redcrosse's adventures as a transposition of Calvinist doctrine ("Spenser's Redcrosse Knight").
72. Cooper, *English Romance in Time*, 218.
73. Spenser, *Faerie Queene*, 3.2.27, 39. Subsequent references appear parenthetically.
74. Coles, "Gender in the 1590 *Faerie Queene*," 357.
75. Ibid., 361.
76. Ibid., 353–55.
77. Britomart's nurse and squire, Glauce, quietly drops out of book 3 after the meeting with Merlin.
78. Coles, "Gender in the 1590 *Faerie Queene*," 358.
79. Ibid.
80. Hadfield reiterates the important point that "confessional labels do not always help to distinguish or classify varieties of religious belief in early modern England" ("Spenser and Religion," 22).
81. A similar moment occurs in book 2, when Arthur, reading from a book of prophecy, is forced to break off before he learns his own future (2.10.68). Likewise, Guyon stops reading the history of Fairie Land once he reaches the reign of Gloriana, but the narrator reminds us that the book "Ne yet has ended" (2.10.70).
82. Mallette, *Spenser and the Discourses of Reformation England*, 155.
83. Coles, "Gender in the 1590 *Faerie Queene*," 358; King, "Sidney and Spenser," 148.
84. King, "Sidney and Spenser," 147–48.
85. Crawford, *Mediatrix*, 40, 45.
86. Coles, "Gender in the 1590 *Faerie Queene*," 357.
87. Ibid., 353, citing Luciano, "Unrealized," 228.
88. Redcrosse's ancestry is notably not Briton like Artegall's, but Saxon; as

in Merlin's prophecy, historical enmities vanish in anticipation of Tudor peace and Protestant unity.

89. King remarks on Spenser's conflation of elitism and election by noting that "what Calvin says about salvation could just as easily be said about knightly or kingly identity through birth: it 'is freely offered to some while others are barred from access to it.' . . . Just as one must be born a knight, so one must be born as one of God's Elect to be saved; both systems emphasize an identity given or inherited from the 'father,' with God being the father in the second case" ("Sidney and Spenser," 151).

90. For Mallette, too, the major thrust of Contemplation's vision, as with Merlin's prophecy, makes Elizabeth a necessary yet insufficient component of Protestantism's providential plot (*Spenser and the Discourses of Reformation England*, 46).

91. King, "Sidney and Spenser," 149.

92. King observes that "only when the hero has withdrawn an aspiration toward romance, as traditionally conceived in terms of knightly prowess and self-sufficiency, can the hero then begin to move toward a condition of moral stability that truly is romance in its deepest, Edenic sense" (ibid., 150).

93. As Sean Kane points out, *The Faerie Queene*'s chivalric "frame of militant faith" is never "dismissed . . . the contradictions of holiness can only be resolved in a timeless vision of the New Jerusalem, and a temporal view of the work to be done" (*Spenser's Moral Allegory*, 48–49).

94. Mikics reads this moment to mean that "the poetic world cannot reconcile the earthly and the heavenly, romance and its Christian message" (*Limits of Moralizing*, 60). I propose that the paradoxical reconciliation of earthly and heavenly romance is precisely what Contemplation insists on, and what Redcrosse must see in order to grasp, however briefly, his full purpose.

95. As Watkins puts it, "Spenser both envisions and defers an imminent exaltation of time into eternity. The moment Redcrosse's victory over the Dragon seems to usher in the church's apocalyptic marriage to the Lamb, the marriage rites turn out to be just a betrothal" ("'And yet the end was not,'" 157).

96. Mikics, *Limits of Moralizing*, 62.

97. Parker, *Inescapable Romance*, 64.

98. Arthos remarks that the poet and "[his] own uncertainties" are as much the subject of *The Faerie Queene* as the trajectories of the heroes; Spenser, "in the image of . . . the questing knight," turns to romance in an effort to "lead his own thought and hope to eternity and satisfaction" (*On the Poetry of Spenser*, 65–66).

99. Cooper, *English Romance in Time*, 361–408.

CHAPTER 2

1. This short, strange pamphlet has received little commentary to date. It is mentioned in Heffner et al., "Spenser Allusions," 223–24; and in Black and Celovsky, "Lost Works." For more comprehensive treatments, see King, "'Faerie Leveller'"; Hulse, "Spenser, Bacon"; Nicosia, "Reading Spenser."

2. Anonymous, *Faerie Leveller*, 7. Subsequent references appear parenthetically.

3. Both Nicosia ("Reading Spenser") and King ("'Faerie Leveller'") propose Sheppard as the author. Sheppard would later compose a Spenserian tribute to Charles I, *The Faerie King*.

4. Nicosia, "Reading Spenser," 287.

5. King, "'Faerie Leveller,'" 298. For studies of Spenser's legacy among seventeenth-century republicans, see O'Callaghan, "*Shepheards Nation*"; Norbrook, *Poetry and Politics*.

6. Nicosia remarks that Sheppard and other mid-seventeenth-century writers "often represented the future as if it were already past to translate political aspiration into compelling historical fact" ("Reading Spenser," 288).

7. Meserole explains that the seventeenth-century spate of Puritan anagrammatics "had as its basis the Puritan belief that nothing in this world, including nomenclature, was haphazard. God had . . . intended that a person's name, if carefully examined, could reveal aspects of his character" (*American Poetry*, xxx).

8. The Jonathan cited by Sheppard is probably the Levite priest of Judges 18:30. This obscure reference may be meant both to reinforce Sheppard's credibility as a student of scripture and to suggest that the proper "priestly" authority can guide the audience through Spenser's riddling romance. I am grateful to Christopher Martin for this identification and suggestion.

9. Nicosia points out that the typology employed throughout *The Faerie Leveller* is literary and semi-secular as well as biblical: Spenser's fictional Artegall becomes a prophetic type of Charles I, who (in theory) subsequently fulfills the Legend of Justice in real historical time ("Reading Spenser").

10. This reassignment of a heroic identity for Charles is consistent with Spenser's original method, in which a number of different characters all serve as figures for Elizabeth. For a study of romance-influenced portrayals of Charles I in the visual and literary arts, see Corns, *Royal Image*, esp. Coiro, "Ball of Strife."

11. Hulse points out that "at the same time that it paints the antiroyalist forces all with one brush, the pamphlet seeks to divide them.... Sheppard has aimed his fable at the exact points most likely to provoke dissension and conflict" ("Spenser, Bacon," 340).

12. King, "'Faerie Leveller,'" 301.

13. Nicosia notes that "after all, the practice of weighing and judging is fundamentally interpretive" ("Reading Spenser," 290).

14. Milton, *Complete Prose Works*, 390. Given that mid-century allusions to book 5 of *The Faerie Queene* are rare, Milton's striking reference to Talus a year after the publication of *The Faerie Leveller* might suggest that he was aware of it.

15. For two studies of Sidneian romance's importance to the Stuarts and their followers, see Patterson, *Censorship and Interpretation*, 167–84; and Spiller, "Speaking for the Dead," 229–51.

16. Such scholars include Larson (*Fulke Greville*), Wooden ("Rhetorical Design"), Martin ("Between Duty and Selfness"), Spiller ("Counsel of Fulke Greville"), and Alexander (*Writing After Sidney*, 220–61).

17. Greville, *Life of the Renowned Sr Philip Sidney*, 134, 247. Subsequent references appear parenthetically.

18. Herman, "Bastard Children of Tyranny," 998.

19. Ibid., 998–99. It may be telling that the frontispiece of the *Life* identifies its author as "a Servant to" Elizabeth, who had retained moderate popularity across factions, without mention of Greville's official relationship to James I. While Herman proposes that nostalgia for Elizabeth could translate into nostalgia for Charles I, the publisher's description of Greville elides the Stuart dynasty after their crushing loss of power.

20. Gouws has made a preliminary argument for a republican reception of the 1652 *Life* but expresses skepticism that the text was widely purchased or read when it first appeared ("Early Readers of Fulke Greville").

21. This inclination to read Sidney into England's future—to explain him as a Puritan before Puritanism was well established, and as a republican when that movement was still inchoate—is also evident in contemporary criticism. For studies that explore the living Sidney's participation in sixteenth-century discourses of republicanism, see Raitiere, *Faire Bitts*; Worden, *Sound of Virtue*.

22. Hager has argued that the *Life of Sidney* "is a version of a genre conventionalized by Foxe's *Acts and Monuments*, the Protestant saint's life" ("Exemplary Mirage," 3.)

23. Further references to "Sidney" in this section usually refer to the idealized subject of the *Life*.

24. Alexander suggests that in Greville's high praise for Sidney in this passage, "Sidney's figures of speech inflect Greville's language," haunting his friend's writing (*Writing after Sidney*, 231).

25. In the *Defence of Poesie*, Sidney defines the poet's role as "not onely to make a *Cyrus* . . . but to bestow a *Cyrus* vpon the worlde, to make many *Cyrus*'s, if they wil learne aright, why, and how that Maker made him" (C2r).

26. Candido notes that "what is most curious about Greville's statement here is

that it does not characterize Sidney's behavior as a simple renunciation of art for life; rather it emphasizes the importance of both elements in a new and distinctly mimetic form of artistic expression" ("Fulke Greville's Biography," 5).

27. A royalist reader, of course, could attach a different significance to Sidney's innate leadership "by right."

28. While Herman argues that the *Life* idealizes Elizabeth at the expense of James ("Bastard Children of Tyranny"), Greville's Elizabeth is idealized only to the (limited) extent that her beliefs and policies accord with Sidney's.

29. Greville's imagery also invokes Jesus's mountaintop vision of earth's kingdoms and his placement by Satan on the pinnacle of the temple, subjects that Milton would later take up in *Paradise Regained*.

30. Martin argues that "conditioned by his own cautious pragmatism, Greville cannot bring himself to condone the personal drives which lay behind Sidney's fatal vulnerability" ("Between Duty and Selfness," 26). The author's struggle between desire to idealize the fallen subject and regret for the subject's self-caused fall is also a central feature of Margaret Cavendish's and Lucy Hutchinson's respective memoirs of their husbands.

31. For a more extensive discussion of this topic, see Wilkes, "Left . . . to Play the Ill Poet in My Own Part."

32. Alexander notes that "Greville is never an imitator of Sidney's style. One of the ways in which he can keep going the dialogue that began in Sidney's lifetime is to keep writing in the voice with which he started . . . argumentative, moralizing, and complicated" (*Writing after Sidney*, 225).

33. Cavendish, *Life of the Thrice Noble, High and Puissant Prince William Cavendishe*, c2r. Subsequent references appear parenthetically. I refer to Margaret Cavendish as "Cavendish" when discussing her as the author of the *Life*, but as "Margaret" when she appears as a participant within it. I refer to William Cavendish, who is very much a literary fantasy in his own biography, as "William."

34. Pepys, *Diary*, 484, 630. A. Bennett points out that Pepys's diary indicates he was at least entertained enough by her "ridiculous History" to stay up all night reading it ("Fantastic Realism," 194).

35. Kahn, *Wayward Contracts*, 180.

36. Cavendish's dismissal of exaggerated historiography may be tongue-in-cheek even in her preface: only a paragraph after her denunciation of the republicans' likening their heroes to the "most famous . . . Greeks and Romans," she compares her husband to "another Scipio" (d1v).

37. For another discussion of Cavendish's "strategic appropriation" of romance as a royalist woman, see Rees, *Margaret Cavendish*, 44.

38. While we are accustomed to thinking of Margaret Cavendish as a writer of romances, her husband also enjoyed the genre, and his relationship to it was political as well as personal. The Earl of Newcastle was once mocked by the Parliamentarian Lord Fairfax, whom he had challenged to wage a more heroic (and antiquated) form of warfare, as a man who "follow[ed] the rules of Amadis de Gaule, or the Knight of the Sun" (Firth, *Life of William Cavendish*, xii–xiii).

39. For a discussion of the romance trope of the restoration of the rightful heir, see Cooper, *English Romance in Time*, 324–60.

40. The concept of *fin amour* is broadly equivalent to that of "courtly love," although the latter term is the invention of literary critics, while the former actually appears in a number of foundational medieval texts. Sanchez identifies the erotic tradition that informs the *Life of William* as "Petrarchan" (*Erotic Subjects*, 10), though the early modern Petrarchan tradition was itself an offshoot of the medieval *fin amour*—and originally, as Cooper has argued, of medieval traditions of feminine desire (*English Romance in Time*, 230).

41. Kahn, *Wayward Contracts*, 180.

42. By the rules of *fin amour*, William is a more perfect lover than any character Spenser or Sidney produced; both writers' male lovers are particularly susceptible to self-interestedness. But in Lady Mary Wroth's 1621 *Urania*, written as a companion romance to Sidney's *New Arcadia* and featuring a female protagonist, the profoundly interiorized experience of suffering

for love takes on a higher value than any external reward for one's patience.

43. Cavendish is far from crafting a romance out of her own marriage in her short, cool account of their courtship in the *Life* (P2r). Her chronicle of the same courtship in her autobiographical *True Relation* is somewhat warmer, though even here she rejects "Amorous Love" as "a Disease, or a Passion, or both" (*Paper Bodies*, 47). For a discussion of Cavendish's engagement with romance in her autobiography, see Dodds, "Margaret Cavendish's Domestic Experiment."

44. Kahn, "Margaret Cavendish," 562, 562n; Sanchez, *Erotic Subjects*, 179.

45. Dinshaw, *Getting Medieval*, 12–13; Freccero, "Tangents," 92.

46. Sanchez, *Erotic Subjects*, 4.

47. Ibid., 4n.

48. I am grateful to Mary Baine Campbell for this observation.

49. Sanchez, *Erotic Subjects*, 4, 9, 178.

50. The *fin amour* tradition inevitably relies on some form of gender fluidity. Most often, a male lover submits to the service of a lady and abases himself before her, inverting their usual gendered hierarchy; if the lover is female, she occupies the abject position yet fills the masculine role in the strength of her devotion. This aspect of the *fin amour* tradition is particularly well treated in Barbara Newman's *From Virile Woman to WomanChrist*, 137–67.

51. See, for example, Sanchez, *Erotic Subjects*, 177–79; Mendelson, *Mental World of Stuart Women*, 41–50; Norbrook, "Margaret Cavendish and Lucy Hutchinson," 194; Fitzmaurice, "Margaret Cavendish's *Life of William*," 93–94.

52. Fitzmaurice, "Margaret Cavendish's *Life of William*," 95; Sanchez, *Erotic Subjects*, 6.

53. Fisher, "Erotics of Chin Chucking," 7–8; Sedgwick, *Epistemology of the Closet*, 12.

54. Hyde, *Selections*, 256.

55. Hutchinson, *Memoirs*, ed. Firth and Hutchinson, 117. William Cavendish's romance sensibilities evidently damaged his reputation even among other royalists, as Brownley has noted (*Clarendon*, 122).

56. Sanchez, *Erotic Subjects*, 58.

57. Battigelli, *Margaret Cavendish*, 4.

58. Sidney, *Arcadia*, 78. In following Sidney, Cavendish again positions herself in an interesting relationship to her fellow royalist Hobbes. By associating romance with republicanism in her preface, she seems to agree with Hobbes that it is a civic evil, and she also follows his premise that William's imaginative romance for one transforms his weakness into a subjective, perhaps illusory, sense of power. She finds a way around Hobbes's condemnation of the genre, though, in showing that this power does not make her husband dangerous, since he channels all his heroic energy into love for the king.

59. Sanchez, *Erotic Subjects*, 178; Crawford, *Mediatrix*, 4.

60. Norbrook has remarked that "Cavendish has no time for the providential explanations of events that preoccupied so many royalist as well as Puritan historians" ("Margaret Cavendish and Lucy Hutchinson," 194). But while Cavendish's disdain for providential history is a pillar of her corpus, she admits it into the *Life* for William's sake.

61. Sanchez, *Erotic Subjects*, 177. Sanchez continues, "Cavendish's opposition to absolutism should not be equated with a rejection of monarchy as such. Rather, she endorses a return to a Sidneian view that noble subjects have a duty to restrain both their own impulses and those of their sovereign."

62. Ibid., 178–79.

63. Fitzmaurice, "Margaret Cavendish's Life of William," 98.

64. Crawford, *Mediatrix*, 3.

65. Kahn, "Margaret Cavendish," 560.

66. Hutchinson, *Memoirs*, ed. Sutherland, 38. Subsequent references appear parenthetically.

67. Norbrook, "Margaret Cavendish and Lucy Hutchinson," 194, 185. Both women wrote their accounts of their husbands' lives at around the same time, but Hutchinson's highly charged republican text was not printed during Charles II's reign.

68. Cook, "Story I Most Particularly Intend," 273.

69. Ibid., 275.

70. Keeble, "But the Colonel's Shadow," 231. Eckerle rightly objects that "this

argument both reifies the reductive interpretation of romance as a feminine genre and ignores the romance elements that Hutchinson retains" (*Romancing the Self*, 102n44).

71. Looser argues that for Hutchinson, carefully controlled elements of romance "are not only acceptable but necessary to honest history writing" and "true romance" comes "from God rather than from fancy" (*British Women Writers*, 45). Seelig (*Autobiography and Gender*) and Eckerle (*Romancing the Self*) also affirm Hutchinson's turn to romance in the *Memoirs*.

72. Cook argues that in the *Memoirs* Hutchinson "tells her own story as much as ... that of her husband" ("Story I Most Particularly Intend," 272). Eckerle disagrees, calling the text "truly the story of the man rather than of herself or their marriage" (*Romancing the Self*, 100). I find neither argument quite right: John Hutchinson *is* the central figure of the *Memoirs* and the source of its guiding vision, but the narrative is also marked by Lucy Hutchinson's determination of her role in it relative to his.

73. A number of scholars have addressed the question of Lucy Hutchinson's agency versus her subordination to her husband. Keeble has argued that Hutchinson figures her total submission ("But the Colonel's Shadow"). On the opposite end of the spectrum, Longfellow has mined Hutchinson's *Memoirs* and her *Elegies* for evidence of proto-feminism (*Women and Religious Writing*, 180–208). Throughout his extensive body of work on Hutchinson, Norbrook has advocated for a more nuanced appreciation of her intertwined gestures toward wifely submission and female agency, and Looser argues that "to label one of the selves as more true is to miss the point of their combination" (*British Women Writers*, 40); I hope to follow their example here.

74. Lucy Hutchinson's descendant Julius, who prepared the original manuscript of the *Memoirs*, expresses skepticism at episodes of Hutchinson's life writing that "[savour] almost too much of the ridiculous for the gravity of an historian" but acknowledges that while some may be "untrue," literary exaggerations about his ancestor were not unusual: he had been told "other tales [of him], resembling the legends of romance" (*Memoirs*, ed. Firth and Hutchinson, 38n, 390n).

75. Achinstein has argued that in the erotic and devotional blazons—typically of Christ—that we encounter in seventeenth-century Protestant women's writing, "romance became deployed ... precisely because it worked to accommodate erotic desires as agency" ("Romance of the Spirit," 435). Throughout the *Memoirs*, Hutchinson grapples with the relationship between her romance agency and her husband's. For a reading of the blazon and female agency in Hutchinson's work, see Hammons, "Polluted Palaces."

76. Cook proposes that a "fitting analogy" for the structure of the *Memoirs* "would be that of concentric circles, with the life of John Hutchinson as the outer and central rings, beginning and ending the story, and the history of the period, and God's dealings with the English falling in between" ("Story I Most Particularly Intend," 272). Looser describes the text's structure as Hutchinson's use of "multiple genres to mirror each other: romance as a reflection of politics as a reflection of providence, stretching toward the absolute" (*British Women Writers*, 41).

77. Eckerle, *Romancing the Self*, 103.

78 In Eckerle's formulation, "The man who scorns love ... is not punished by Cupid's arrow but directed by" divine providence (ibid., 103).

79. For a study of the desiring woman's role in medieval romance, see Cooper, *English Romance in Time*, 218–68.

80. Looser observes that "Hutchinson describes the war as a series of conflicts among those who loved God, country, city, family, power, or themselves in the wrong order or in the wrong amounts" (*British Women Writers*, 46).

81. Eckerle has suggested that seventeenth-century women's life writing often "adopt[s]" the tone of "tragic" rather than "triumphant" romance "as they explain the problems they faced during courtship, marriage, and widowhood and often attempt to defend their behavior in response to these problems"

(*Romancing the Self*, 89). Looser, too, describes Hutchinson's historiographical style as resembling "tragic romance" (*British Women Writers*, 35).

82. Although most readers of the *Memoirs* have not questioned Lucy Hutchinson's version of events surrounding John's recantation, Hirst ("Remembering a Hero") and Lobo ("Lucy Hutchinson's Revisions of Conscience") have offered provocative arguments that her story contains dubious elements and that she may be trying to recast her husband as an unsullied republican in the wake of a recantation that was possibly his idea all along. Hirst's and Lobo's cases remind us once again that the subjects of these politically charged, generically complex memoirs may be best understood in context as literary characters rather than historical figures. Norbrook has called for our scholarly appreciation of the irresolvable ambiguities of the case ("Memoirs and Oblivion").

83. Murphy has noted that while Hutchinson's preface "promises her children that her text will preserve the memory of their father," this "transcendence of time becomes threatened" at the end of the *Memoirs* by the appearance of Lucy's ghost (*Familial Forms*, 149). Murphy returns to the challenging image in "I Remain, an Airy Phantasm." Keeble ("But the Colonel's Shadow") cites Lucy's shade as further evidence of her wifely subordination, but I believe we can also read the ghost as a sign of her generic agency and her ongoing struggle to locate a role in heroic romance for the female believer.

CHAPTER 3

1. Herbert, *Princess Cloria*, 319. Subsequent references appear parenthetically.

2. Milton, *Complete Poems and Major Prose*, 694. Unless otherwise noted, subsequent references to Milton's works are from this edition (abbreviated *CPMP* or cited parenthetically).

3. For a reading of *Comus* as a post-Shakespearean staged romance, see Mulready, *Romance on the Early Modern Stage*.

4. Milton, *CPMP*, 728–29.

5. Ibid., 697.

6. Ibid., 793.

7. Ibid., 795.

8. For Milton's privately appreciative references to *Arcadia*, see Mohl, "Milton's Commonplace Book," 463–64.

9. Lewalski, "Milton"; Frye, "Typology of *Paradise Regained*"; Quilligan, *Milton's Spenser*; Burrow, *Epic Romance*; Lahive, "Reading and Writing Romance."

10. Williamson, "Milton the Anti-Romantic"; Fish, "Things and Actions Indifferent"; Schwartz, "From Shadowy Types"; Loewenstein, *Milton and the Drama of History*; Taylor, "Milton and the Romance of History."

11. Patterson, "*Paradise Regained*," 197; Kinney, *Strategies of Poetic Narrative*; Steadman, *Moral Fiction*; Nardo, "John Phillips, John Milton."

12. A recent exception is Cooper, who argues that Milton was motivated by genre theory and ethical anxieties in "Milton's King Arthur."

13. See Smith, *Literature and Revolution*; Zurcher, *Seventeenth-Century English Romance*.

14. Lahive, "Reading and Writing Romance," 532.

15. Milton, *CPMP*, 694.

16. Chaucer's *Franklin's Tale* offers a romance about three aristocrats who try to behave virtuously while entangled in a love triangle and asks the audience to debate, at the end of the tale, "Which was the moste fre" (*Canterbury Tales*, l.1622).

17. Milton, *Complete Poetry and Essential Prose*, 907.

18. Danielson, *Milton's Good God*; Fallon, "'Elect above the Rest'"; Shuger, "Milton Über Alles."

19. Fallon, "'Elect above the Rest,'" 110.

20. Shuger, "Milton Über Alles," 403.

21. Milton, *CPMP*, 90.

22. Frye, *Secular Scripture*, 29. Lahive also invokes "Frye's emphasis on the revolutionary nature of romance" to explain its appeal to Milton and suggests that the "fit audience" is called to decode the complex romance of *Paradise Lost* ("Reading and Writing Romance," 532).

23. Salzman, *English Prose Fiction*; Kahn, *Wayward Contracts*.

24. Salzman, *English Prose Fiction*, 156.

25. For discussions of the relationship between seventeenth-century romance and Hobbes's political theory, see Kahn, *Wayward Contracts*; Smith, *Literature and Revolution*, 159–60, 233–49; Zurcher, *Seventeenth-Century English Romance*.

26. Echoing Salzman, Smith also notes that *Cloria* "provides reactions rather than answers" to the problems of history and to the decline of sincere and straightforward royalist romance (*Literature and Revolution*, 237).

27. Salzman, *English Prose Fiction*, 174.

28. Cavendish, *Description of a New World*, X4r–X4v.

29. Battigelli has also noted that Cavendish uses scientific skepticism to undermine the religious dogmatism that she blamed for the civil wars, replacing prophets with scientists ("Political Thought / Political Action").

30. Cavendish, *Philosophical Letters*, 231.

31. Cavendish, *World's Olio*, Y3v. Cavendish's sense of providence is very close to that of Hobbes, from whom it is likely derived: "Things *to come* have no being at all; the *future* being but a fiction of the mind, applying the sequels of actions past to the actions that are present; which with most certainty is done by him that has most experience, but not with certainty enough. And though it be called prudence when the event answereth our expectation; yet in its own nature it is but presumption. . . . The best prophet naturally is the best guesser; and the best guesser, he that is most versed and studied in the matters he guesses at" (*Leviathan*, 14).

32. Cavendish, *Assaulted and Pursued Chastity*, Ff2v. Subsequent references appear parenthetically.

33. Travellia also disfavors "Divine books," arguing that "they raise up such controversie, as they cannot be alayd againe, tormenting the minde about that they cannot know whil'st they live" (Gg1r).

34. Kahn argues that Cavendish "uses the concerns of romance to counter the Hobbesian response" to England's political crisis; she also points out that Cavendish's decision to employ rather than dismiss romance is sometimes "less a simple rebuttal of Hobbes . . . than an adaptation of [his] arguments concerning the power of self-interest" (*Wayward Contracts*, 172, 192).

35. Travellia recalls several heroines of Shakespearean comedy and romance, perhaps most notably the clever and pragmatic Marina of *Pericles*; this precedent may indicate Shakespeare's similar interrogations of dramatic romance. (I am grateful to an anonymous reader for this observation.)

36. Gallagher, "Embracing the Absolute."

37. Kahn, "Reinventing Romance," 630.

38. Kahn, *Wayward Contracts*, 231.

39. Williamson, "Milton the Anti-Romantic," 18.

40. Patterson, "*Paradise Regained*," 200.

41. Kinney, *Strategies of Poetic Narrative*, 129.

42. Lahive, "Reading and Writing Romance," 535.

43. Williamson, "Milton the Anti-Romantic," 19.

44. For a discussion of this problem in royalist romance, see Kahn, *Wayward Contracts*, esp. 227–33.

45. Quilligan, *Milton's Spenser*, 108.

46. See Revelation 12:7–9.

47. Schwartz, "From Shadowy Types," 134, citing Fish, "Things and Actions Indifferent."

48. Mary Beth Rose has discussed Milton's passive heroism, particularly as gendered feminine (*Gender and Heroism*, 85–99). Miltonic heroism is indeed often passive and sometimes feminized, though the potential for active heroism in the providentially correct moment always stands as a crucial aspect of the hero's calling.

49. Erin Murphy has noted that the "tangle of historical styles" in books 11 and 12, including "tragic, cyclical, millenarian, and typological," contribute to a "problem of narrative" (*Familial Forms*, 126, 117). Adam's greatest difficulty with this narrative is that it undermines his "ability to authorize": to license and control the actions of his offspring, and also to determine the narrative's shape (ibid., 124).

50. Spenser's Redcrosse makes a similar about-face, from expressing his yearning for "Ladies loue" in one stanza to

overzealously renouncing "ioyes so fruitlesse" in the next (1.10.62–63).

51. Loewenstein, *Milton and the Drama of History*, 123–24. See also Hillier, "So Shall the World Goe On."

52. Schwartz, "From Shadowy Types," 134–36.

53. Milton understood romance as a genre that mediated between deferral and fulfillment, and between enlightenment and ignorance, at least as early as *Areopagitica* (1644), which famously compares humanity's slow quest for Truth to Plutarch's ancient romance of Isis and Osiris: "the sad friends of Truth . . . imitating the carefull search that *Isis* made for the mangl'd body of *Osiris*, went up and down gathering limb by limb still as they could find them. We have not yet found them all, Lords and Commons, nor ever shall doe, till her Masters second comming; he shall bring together every joynt and member, and shall mould them into an immortall feature of loveliness and perfection" (*CPMP*, 1018).

54. Quint, "Expectation and Prematurity."

55. Ibid., 208–9.

56. It is worth noting that in 1629, well before the royalists' exilic writing, the young Milton feels free to conflate Fate and Providence unproblematically and without further explanation. We might compare his lack of concern over terminology here to God's sharp clarification in *Paradise Lost*: "Necessitie and Chance / Approach not mee, and what I will is Fate" (7.172–73).

57. Rajan, "In Order Serviceable," 13.

58. Evans, *Miltonic Moment*, 35–37. For another reading that also finds that "joylessness" prevails in the poem, see Meier, "Milton's *Nativity Ode*," 7.

59. Quint, "Expectation and Prematurity," 215.

60. With good reason, it has become commonplace to connect the conclusion of the *Nativity Ode* to the final line of Milton's sonnet on his blindness: "They also serve who only stand and wait."

61. I follow Lewalski in finding it unproblematic to categorize *Paradise Regained* as both a brief epic and a romance. See, respectively, *Milton's Brief Epic* and "Milton."

62. Lewalski, "Milton," 68–70.

63. Frye, "Agon and Logos," 136.

64. Fish, "Inaction and Silence," 44–45.

65. Fish, "Things and Actions Indifferent," 166.

66. Ibid., 181–83.

67. Patterson, "*Paradise Regained*," 201.

68. I am grateful to John Rogers for this observation.

69. Like many romances, *The Princess Cloria* also opens with an errant protagonist (Cassianus) wandering through an unfamiliar country and encountering a (legitimately) hospitable stranger.

70. Satan scoffs at the libertine Belial's suggestion that the devils entrap Jesus with "Amorous Nets," arguing that many great men "[make] small account / Of beauty and her lures . . . / on worthier things intent," but he tries the tactic anyway, just to make sure (2.162, 193–95).

71. Lewalski, "Milton," 67.

72. For an argument on patience as republican resistance in the poem, see Norbrook, "Republican Occasions."

73. Zwicky identifies the distinction between Satanic and messianic understandings of time as the difference between the Greek concepts *chronos* and *kairos* ("*Kairos* in 'Paradise Regained'").

74. While Adam, creation's first lover, is innately horrified by violence but drawn to erotic romance, Jesus sees no appeal in amorous tropes but initially finds himself attracted to a romance of valor.

75. For another argument that heroic action in the temporal world is consistently deferred in *Paradise Regained*, but never denied its ultimate importance and eventuality, see Norbrook, "Republican Occasions," 136.

76. Fish, "Things and Actions Indifferent," 166.

77. Gay also interprets Satan's reading of Jesus's horoscope in the "Starry Rubric" as his mistaken reliance on both empty symbols and irreligious fatalism ("Astrology and Iconoclasm").

78. Patterson, "*Paradise Regained*," 202.

79. Ibid.

80. Evans, *Miltonic Moment*, 121–22.

81. Curran, "Paradise Regained," 219–20.

CHAPTER 4

1. Hutchinson, *Order and Disorder*, 5. Subsequent references appear parenthetically.

2. Moore, "Miltoniana," 321. Prominent Miltonists such as Shawcross (*Milton*) and Wittreich ("Milton's Transgressive Maneuvers") have followed Moore's summary of Hutchinson's work. Mayer, too, agrees that Hutchinson meant to rebuke *Paradise Lost* for romanticizing scripture ("Lucy Hutchinson," 317). Milton's and Hutchinson's perspectives on creative biblical poetics is also the subject of Wilcher's "'Adventurous Song.'"

3. Norbrook, "Poem and Its Contexts," xxv. Norbrook also points out that we cannot be certain that the composition of *Order and Disorder* postdates that of *Paradise Lost*, finding it "not wholly implausible" that either Milton or Hutchinson might have had "access to the other's manuscript" through their "mutual friend, the Earl of Anglesey, to whom each of them entrusted sensitive manuscripts" (xiv, xvii). See also Norbrook's "Lucy Hutchinson, John Milton."

4. Norbrook, "Poem and Its Contexts," xxix, xxxi.

5. Wilcher, "Lucy Hutchinson and Genesis," 28.

6. Hutchinson, *Memoirs*, ed. Sutherland, 289.

7. Norbrook, "Lucy Hutchinson's Elegies,'" 473.

8. Lahive briefly discusses Wilcher's reading in "Reading and Writing Romance." Several additional scholars have considered Hutchinson's turn to romance in her *Memoirs* of her husband: see, for example, Looser, *British Women Writers*; Seelig, *Autobiography and Gender*; Eckerle, *Romancing the Self*.

9. Wilcher, "Lucy Hutchinson and Genesis," 25.

10. Ibid., 35.

11. Huet's definition of romance is cited by Wilcher ("Lucy Hutchinson and Genesis," 35) and Salzman (*English Prose Fiction*, 179).

12. Wilcher, "Lucy Hutchinson and Genesis," 35.

13. Dryden, *John Dryden*, 9–17. Subsequent line-number references appear parenthetically.

14. For discussions of Dryden's complex treatment of the patterns of historical time, see Barbeau, *Intellectual Design*; Guibbory, *Map of Time*, 213–53; Winn, "Past and Present."

15. Montaño also points to "Astraea Redux" in remarking on Dryden's providentialist view of history and his skepticism regarding the efficacy of military agency (*Courting the Moderates*, 98).

16. Twenty-first-century millennial readers may be unusually well equipped to understand these poignant lines.

17. "Astraea Redux" helps extend forward in English history Das's argument that romance animates clashes and mediations between younger and older generations (*Renaissance Romance*).

18. For a discussion of Dryden's devaluation of martial heroics, especially in his later poetry, see Winn, "Thy Wars Brought Nothing About."

19. Charles plays a more gender-normative role in the erotic romance of Dryden's "Astraea Redux" than in Cavendish's *Life of William*, which figured the king as the fickle mistress and William as his long-suffering lover (see chapter 2).

20. Winn suggests that these lines describe "the English as repenting their affair with Cromwell and returning to their true lover Charles" ("When Beauty Fires the Blood," 256).

21. Berensmeyer argues that "Astraea Redux" imagines a kind of "anti-republican countermemory" ("Art of Oblivion," 90).

22. Hammond notes that "such renaming reverses the revolution of the 1640s and 1650s which had involved many instances of public renaming as new leaders assumed control of the language of government, and radical groups produced new vocabularies for the description of English history and society" (*John Dryden*, 28).

23. Berensmeyer proposes that "the poem's Royalist ideological content is perfectly mirrored in its form, the 'perfect union' of subjects under a patriarchal kingship and the hierarchical order of things

poetically expressed in the well-ordered and harmonious form of the couplet. In Dryden's lines, civilization rhymes with empire and London with Rome rather than Jerusalem" ("Art of Oblivion," 90–91).

24. Potter, *Secret Rites and Secret Writing*, 77–80. Kahn likewise discusses love's conciliatory role for royalists in *Wayward Contracts*, esp. 171–95. See also Veevers, *Images of Love and Religion*.

25. Murphy has observed how Hutchinson strongly upholds marriage between people of different nationalities in her autobiographical fragment, in which she traces her own family's descent through both the Saxons and the invading Normans: "Hutchinson uses marriage as a figure of consent, which has the power to remake the relation between the conquerors and the conquered, allowing the nation to find a more peaceful future" in the intermarriage of its people, rather than in a stable line of kings (*Familial Forms*, 158). But crucially, while Hutchinson imagines that mutual love within an inter*cultural* marriage may nurture the growth of a godly state, the discordant values within an inter*faith* marriage can never do so.

26. Wilcher has noted that Hutchinson also "adopts the epic machinery of infernal councils and devilish intrigue to underpin crucial turns" elsewhere in *Order and Disorder*'s narrative, "often with the slenderest of biblical warrants" for her genre play ("Lucy Hutchinson and Genesis," 29).

27. Greville and his version of Sidney refer to this "first injunction" when Sidney in the *Life* condemns Elizabeth's proposed marriage to the Catholic Anjou as "the very first breach of Gods ordinance, in matching herself with a Prince of a diverse faith" (*Life of the Renowned Sr Philip Sidney*, 63–64). See chapter 2.

28. *Bible* (printer: Barker), 3.

29. Ibid., 4.

30. Looser, tracing the reception of Hutchinson's *Memoirs* and the fascinating history of Lucy and John Hutchinson as literary characters, describes a nineteenth-century play by John Henry Browne, *Love's Labyrinth*, featuring a soldier in the parliamentarian army in love with the daughter of a royalist soldier. Lucy "is portrayed as against the lovers because she is willing to sacrifice all forms of love for the Puritan cause," branding them "traitors"; by contrast, "King Charles vows to overcome hate and prejudice to allow [the lovers] to marry, encouraging their 'artless troth.'" Looser observes that "Brown's characterization retains and foregrounds Lucy Hutchinson's politics more than most portraits drawn of her in the nineteenth century" (*British Women Writers*, 56).

31. Wilcher suggests that "the subversively republican tenor of some of Hutchinson's reflections on such figures as Cain . . . might also be taken as a deliberate counterblast to royalist romances of the 1650s, which garnished their tales of love and war with 'divers Politicall Notions, and Singular Remarks of Moderne Transactions'" ("Lucy Hutchinson and Genesis," 35).

32. See also Norbrook, "Poem and Its Contexts," xxvii.

33. For an excellent study of the radical political dimension of the home and family in seventeenth-century England, see Gillespie, *Domesticity and Dissent*. Murphy has also discussed how the discourse of a separate domestic space in the seventeenth century "does not render the family apolitical, but rather redefines its relationship to politics for the republican cause by maintaining its separation from government" (*Familial Forms*, 136).

34. Wilcher cites Hutchinson's axiom here that "Eager desires die when fruition's past" (17.510) as "evidence of [her] familiarity with the amatory verse of Sir John Suckling, the poet of the 1630s who had the strongest influence on the . . . libertine poets of the restored Stuart court" ("Lucy Hutchinson and Genesis," 37). Given that the themes of Esau's wooing already play on those of early Caroline court drama, Hutchinson may intend for Esau's repetitive romances with his two brides to condemn the young Charles I's two controversial courtships of Catholic princesses, first the failed negotiation for the Spanish infanta and then the successful match with Henrietta Maria of France.

35. Goldberg argues that Lucretius remained a major influence on Hutchinson's writing despite her repudiation of his

atheism and of her translation of *De Rerum Natura* (*Seeds of Things*, 122–78).

36. For a compelling discussion of how the medieval and early modern romance tradition combines the theme of union between elite heirs and heiresses with the theme of mutual love as spiritual fulfillment, see Cooper, *English Romance in Time*, 218–68.

37. Miller, *Engendering the Fall*, 118–25. Longfellow (*Women and Religious Writing*, 188–90) and Mayer ("Lucy Hutchinson," 311) have also emphasized the radicalism of Hutchinson's portrayal of mutuality in marriage. Norbrook is rightly more tempered in his conclusion that Hutchinson's depiction of male and female relations in marriage incorporates both mutuality and conservative hierarchy (see "Poem and Its Contexts," xliii–lii; and "Lucy Hutchinson, John Milton," 56–61).

38. It is worth noting that if Hutchinson regards a nation's subjection to a bad king as analogous to Esau's enthrallment to his reprobate wives, she feminizes the monarch: he is the gaudy, wicked woman whom the fallen and deluded subjects uxoriously adore, and whom the godly subjects wish (and ought) to divorce. This metaphor constitutes another radical departure from Dryden's formulation and from traditional royalist political theory, which regarded the monarch as his people's husband (see Kahn, *Wayward Contracts*, 174–75); accordingly, his duty was to rule them with love, and theirs to obey him. For a reading of Milton's performance of similar manipulations of gendered conventions in his divorce tracts and political writings, see Murphy, *Familial Forms*, 84–85, 240.

39. In this, Hutchinson models Jameson's socially conservative romance for the Puritan godly—yet ironically, this act is in itself a radical protest against the entrenched, and recently reestablished, tradition of monarchy.

40. Cooper, *English Romance in Time*, 219–20 (emphasis in the original).

41. Fisher, "Erotics of Chin Chucking," 151; Jardine, "Twins and Travesties."

42. Hutchinson, *Memoirs*, ed. Sutherland, 28, 30.

43. Ibid., 52.

44. Looser, *British Women Writers*, 45.

45. Edelman, "No Future."

46. For a discussion of how republican writers constructed alternative models of kinship in resistance to normative patrilineal temporality, see Murphy, "Radical Relations."

47. Wilcher finds it "appropriate that [*Order and Disorder*] should remain unfinished, like the great English exemplars of the romance genre, Sidney's *New Arcadia* and Spenser's *Faerie Queene*. . . . In that incompleteness . . . it forces a marriage between the Puritan writer's understanding of the human story derived from her Bible-centred conception of universal history and the ongoing flow of human stories that are the life-blood of romance" ("Lucy Hutchinson and Genesis," 42).

48. Looser argues that Hutchinson uses "multiple genres to mirror each other: romance as a reflection of politics as a reflection of providence, stretching toward the absolute" (*British Women Writers*, 41). Clarke discusses the Song of Songs, the source of Hutchinson's mystical marriage trope, as "the true romance of which romantic fiction is a Satanic copy" for seventeenth-century nonconformist women (*Politics, Religion, and the Song of Songs*, 160).

49. Norbrook, *Order and Disorder*, 217n.

50. Murphy, "I Remain, an Airy Phantasm," 101. Murphy points out that Hutchinson departs from Calvinist tradition by not blaming Rebecca for her deceit (99). Bennett, who reads *Order and Disorder* as feminist liberation theology, identifies Rebecca as a particular heroine for Hutchinson for her exercise of right reason at the intersection of the domestic and the public sphere ("Mary Astell, Lucy Hutchinson," 155–56).

51. Miller has argued that Hutchinson "revise[s] aspects of Genesis . . . to suggest how maternal procreation can be used as a counter to seventeenth-century patriarchal theory" (*Engendering the Fall*, 109). Miller's case is convincing insofar as the women of *Order and Disorder* participate fully in the conflict between the Holy and Worldly States, but we must keep in mind that Hutchinson places firm limits on the power

of human parents and their equally human offspring to resist worldly order. The only decisive challenge to the hierarchy of the Worldly State belongs to the "champion" Christ, and it will be "Performed alone in God's own time and way" (6.38).

52. In contrast to the many books on Spenser and Milton, no study of Hutchinson's literary relationship to Spenser has yet been made. (Goldberg's *The Seeds of Things* discusses both Spenser and Hutchinson in relationship to Lucretius, but not to each other.) However, Hutchinson's allegory of Divine Vengeance (8.187–250) and her episode personifying Sleep and Night (14.43–147) resemble Spenserian as well as Virgilian material. Given Spenser's enduring popularity throughout the seventeenth century and Hutchinson's youthful fondness for love poetry and romances, it seems highly likely that she had at least some familiarity with *The Faerie Queene*.

53. In Potter's words, "Events had transformed the fantastic prophecies into reality, and the mock tragedy into true tragicomedy" (*Secret Rites and Secret Writing*, 112).

54. For another perspective on the "troubled promise of reproduction" in *Order and Disorder*, see Murphy, *Familial Forms*, 152–75.

55. Murphy argues that "Hutchinson highlights the threat of relying upon reproduction as the ground of stability, instead embracing the power of sacred history. The promise of the future, however, is not enough. Her commitment to the form of typology comes only after she has been able to challenge this system to respect the present, as well as provide a bridge to the future" (ibid., 174–75).

56. Norbrook reminds us that the word "restoration" had simultaneous deep significance for royalism, Puritanism, and even secular republicanism ("Poem and Its Contexts," xxxix).

57. Ibid., xxxi–xxxxii.

CHAPTER 5

1. Sharrock has objected to seeing *The Pilgrim's Progress* as "an imitation of a chivalric romance," preferring to read it as "something growing out of oral narrative like the fairy- or folk-tale" ("Life and Story," 56). However, we have Bunyan's own testimony about his reading habits to consider; and at any rate, it seems unnecessary to reject the relevance of one form in favor of its close cousin.

2. Bunyan, *Miscellaneous Works*, 333.

3. Brown discusses *Oroonoko* as a romance at length in "The Romance of Empire."

4. Behn, *Oroonoko*, 62. Subsequent references appear parenthetically.

5. For a discussion of the literary conventions that constitute Oroonoko's identity as a heroic aristocrat, see Hoegberg, "Caesar's Toils."

6. Pacheco, "Royalism and Honor," 503.

7. Kroll, "Tales of Love," 602.

8. Carnell, "Subverting Tragic Conventions"; Rivero, "Aphra Behn's 'Oroonoko.'"

9. Spengemann, "Earliest American Novel," 409.

10. Kroll, "Tales of Love," 582. Spengemann also finds something uniquely American about Behn's new discourse and its incompatibility with old-world romance ("Earliest American Novel").

11. Brown argues that "the treatment of slavery in *Oroonoko* is neither coherent nor fully critical" and suggests that the text may also reveal Behn's ambivalence toward her royalism ("Romance of Empire," 55). Many readers concur with Brown that *Oroonoko* condemns slavery insofar as it has demeaned Oroonoko's kingship and his spiritual nobility, but not as an inherent evil, and that in this respect it is socially conservative. See also Guffey, "Aphra Behn's *Oroonoko*"; Starr, "Aphra Behn and the Genealogy of the Man of Feeling"; Ferguson, "Juggling the Categories"; Iwanisziw, "Behn's Novel Investment"; Dickson, "Truth, Wonder, and Exemplarity."

12. Guffey popularized the reading of Oroonoko as an allegorical stand-in for a royal Stuart, in his case the soon-to-be-deposed James II ("Aphra Behn's *Oroonoko*"). Numerous scholars have followed him, including Duffy, who identifies Oroonoko as the Duke of York (*Oroonoko*), and Brown, who reads him as a figure for another royal martyr, Charles I

("Romance of Empire," 57–59). Many critics read Oroonoko as a composite of these and other Stuarts, and/or a representative of absolute monarchy more generally.

13. Brown has argued that *Oroonoko*'s royalism is beset by contradictions ("Romance of Empire," 55–56); both she and Mendelson (*Mental World of Stuart Women*, 120) suggest that Behn may have sympathized with antiroyalists, perhaps as a result of her relationship with the republican William Scot during her time in Surinam. Pacheco posits that the text is "distinctly royalist" but that "its effort at ideological closure is undermined .. by its reliance on the unstable discourse of [aristocratic] honor" ("Royalism and Honor," 491–92). Chernaik has chosen not to assume Behn's royalism, pointing out that Oroonoko's speeches on liberty and tyranny echo republican rhetoric ("Captains and Slaves"); and Dickson has argued that Behn's hero recalls Sidney's Elizabethan humanism in a manner not comfortably compatible with hard-line pro-Stuart absolutism, a dichotomy we also observed in Greville's *Life of Sidney* in chapter 2 ("Truth, Wonder, and Exemplarity," 588). Kroll argues that *Oroonoko* occasionally appears unsympathetic to absolutism because Behn's objective is to offer a cautionary tale to James II ("Tales of Love," 576–78).

14. Iwanisziw, "Behn's Novel Investment," 95. Visconsi similarly argues that Oroonoko's tragedy signifies, for Behn, the dominance of England's "barbarous national character which prefers violence and personal independence to the mercy and moral prudence of kingly government" ("Degenerate Race," 673).

15. Spengemann, "Earliest American Novel," 414; Rivero, "Aphra Behn's 'Oroonoko,'" 447; Chernaik, "Captains and Slaves," 104.

16. Although Rivero suggests that *Oroonoko* is based on the "lofty heroic French romances" that Behn and her royalist contemporaries enjoyed reading ("Aphra Behn's 'Oroonoko,'" 451–53), we are by now familiar enough with the prevalence of romance through a long thread of English literary and political discourse to see that Behn also had this rich native tradition to refer to, as acknowledged by Dickson in his discussion of Behn and Sidney ("Truth, Wonder, and Exemplarity").

17. Kahn, *Wayward Contracts*, esp. 223–51; Welch, "Epic Romance, Royalist Retreat."

18. Welch, "Epic Romance, Royalist Retreat," 591.

19. According to Kroll, romantic kingship flourishes in Coramantien but cannot survive in Surinam ("Tales of Love"). Pacheco remarks that the text divides "the English colonists into two distinct camps: those people 'of quality' who recognize and respect Oroonoko's royalty . . . and the rabble" ("Royalism and Honor," 502). Visconsi sees the rabble as representations of Behn's "republican and Whig opponents," who fail to recognize or respect kingship that "inheres somatically" by romance convention ("Degenerate Race," 674, 682). Rivero finds that Behn's "'romantic' colonial fiction . . . is the romance of decorous, upper-class sentiments" and argues for Behn's belief that "if properly conducted by the right aristocratic sort of people . . . the colonial enterprise can have salutary effects" ("Aphra Behn's 'Oroonoko,'" 451–52).

20. Pacheco acknowledges this obstacle to her reading ("Royalism and Honor," 496).

21. Chernaik, "Captains and Slaves."

22. Milton, possibly because of his rejection of double predestination, does not include the episode with Noah and his sons in Adam's vision of biblical history in *Paradise Lost*, but the orthodox Calvinist Hutchinson enthusiastically rehearses the curse in *Order and Disorder* (9.205–11). The reprobation of Ham's descendants, she explains, revivified the Worldly State after the Flood, and so allowed Satan to rekindle "The fatal war . . . / Against the new foundation of mankind" (9.213–14). Ham's black "children" are "Excluded from the special blessing" of their cousins; their literal and moral "slavery" binds them to fight for the wrong side of Hutchinson's spiritual war, and so they are "Cut . . . off" from the romance of the elect (9.277–78, 271, 287).

23. Britton, *Becoming Christian*, 32.

24. Ibid., 33.

25. Spengemann, "Earliest American Novel," 395.
26. Rivero, "Aphra Behn's 'Oroonoko,'" 449.
27. Coles, "West of England," 470.
28. Ibid., 467–68.
29. Britton, *Becoming Christian*, 35.
30. Pacheco summarizes the situation: "The ideology that works to affirm an endangered tradition simultaneously connives its destruction" ("Royalism and Honor," 503).
31. In Hutchinson's words, "Who sentences his sons his own sins dooms / And his own executioner becomes" (9.236–37).
32. Coles argues that an ambiguously racialized figure such as Oroonoko must be forced to bear a single racial signature because he "reminds an English audience of the barbarism upon which their civilization is founded, and that the 'degeneration' of the English" in the colonial setting (which we see in Byam and his fellows) "might well be a return to first principles" ("West of England," 468).
33. Rivero argues that "the narrator, having lovingly fashioned [Oroonoko and Imoinda's] attractive bodies, now details their defacement and dismemberment as a way . . . of expiating the guilt she feels over her inability to have done anything to have helped them avoid their fate. . . . It seems as though the author, having made their beautiful bodies, must now unmake them, must render them repulsive" ("Aphra Behn's 'Oroonoko,'" 457).
34. Akhimie, "Bruised with Adversity," 187.
35. Ibid., 191, 188.
36. Cited in Spengemann, "Earliest American Novel," 414.
37. Ibid.
38. Quint, *Epic and Empire*, 9.
39. Davies, "Stout and Valiant Champions," 110.
40. Bunyan, *Pilgrim's Progress*, 163. Subsequent references appear parenthetically.
41. The first Bunyan scholar to make the argument that the "hero" of part 2 is "the group," instead of either Christiana or Great-heart, was Schellenberg ("Sociability and the Sequel," 319).
42. Hill, *Tinker and a Poor Man*, 229.

43. Knox, *Essays in Satire*, 206.
44. Austin, "Figural Logic of the Sequel," 498.
45. Ibid.
46. Readings that focus prominently on Christian community in part 2 include Knott, "Bunyan and the Holy Community"; Batson, *John Bunyan*, 47–53; Schellenberg, "Sociability and the Sequel"; Swaim, *Pilgrim's Progress, Puritan Progress*; Steen, "'Over this Jordan.'"
47. Bear, "Fantastical Faith," 671.
48. For an argument that Bunyan intended part 1, despite its broad readership, to be directed exclusively to Calvinist dissenters like his flock, whom he regarded as the elect, see Dutton, "Interesting, but Tough."
49. Of course, both promises contain an ominous corollary: if readers do not find themselves "allure[d]" by Bunyan's allegorical romance, they evidently fall into the category of the "or not" rather than of the "blest."
50. See Sharrock, *John Bunyan*; Freeman, *English Emblem Books*, 208; Keeble, "Christiana's Key," 2; Seed, "Dialogue and Debate"; Turner, "Bunyan's Sense of Place"; Sim, "Safe for Those," 158. For arguments that part 2's tone remains exclusive and combative, see Hammond, "Pilgrim's Progress"; Steen, "'Over this Jordan.'"
51. Part 1's Ignorance offers the most discussed and most spectacular example: shunted straight to hell from a trapdoor at the gates of the Celestial City, he was never on the progressive heroic journey he believed himself to be.
52. Dinshaw, *Getting Medieval*, 12–13.
53. Freccero, "Tangents (of Desire)," 99.
54. Bunyan, *Grace Abounding*, 86.
55. Ezell is a notable exception, though her reading seeks to show not that Bunyan approved of female sexuality, but that his "acute sense of the sexual politics of his time and place . . . informs the numerous examples he offers in his writings of women characters and relations between the sexes" ("Bunyan's Women," 68).
56. Swaim, *Pilgrim's Progress, Puritan Progress*, 160–97.

57. Thickstun, "From Christiana to Stand-fast"; Breen, "Sexed Pilgrim's Progress."

58. Breen, "Pilgrim's Art."

59. Luxon, "One Soul versus One Flesh," 87.

60. Hill has remarked that part 2 "deals specifically with the salvation of women—single women or widows, not dependent on men" (*Tinker and a Poor Man*, 230).

61. S. J. Newman makes the rare claim that "sex is no longer the danger of Part I but the erotic accessibility of a more temperate zone. . . . Fertility and procreation are now signs of grace" ("Bunyan's Solidness," 239–40).

62. Bunyan, *Grace Abounding*, 27–28.

63. For a discussion of the intersection of the Song of Songs and romance, see Clarke, *Politics, Religion, and the Song of Songs*, esp. 159–61.

64. For a helpful discussion of this allegation and its repercussions for Bunyan, see Ezell, "Bunyan's Women."

65. Breen, "Sexed Pilgrim's Progress."

66. Scholars have long remarked that Bunyan's affective register becomes much more pronounced in part 2: Baird points out that "prominence is given to human emotions and sentiments" rather than to doctrine (*John Bunyan*, 92), and Batson notes that "emotions, desires, relationships, and joys receive strong emphasis" (*John Bunyan*, 53).

67. Sharrock notes somewhat vaguely that the "touching and interesting" relationship between Christiana and Mercy contributes to the "considerable softening of the atmosphere" in part 2 ("Life and Story," 63).

68. Ruth's vows to her mother-in-law Naomi are often read at weddings: "Whither thou goest, I will go: and where thou dwellest, I will dwell: thy people shall be my people, and thy God my God Where thou diest, will I die, and there will I be buried. The Lord do so to me and more also, if ought but death depart thee and me" (Ruth 1:16–17).

69. Crawford, "All's Well," 40, 39, 43.

70. Luxon discusses Bunyan's use of this text in his sermons, but seems to take a literal or biological view of these familial goods, which Christ technically can restore even though they mean nothing "in the long run" ("One Soul versus One Flesh," 87). In part 2, however, Bunyan is deeply invested in the spiritual family that emerges when biological relation is acknowledged to be not meaningless, but markedly secondary.

71. Bunyan, *Grace Abounding*, 14–15.

72. Ibid., 14.

73. Breen, "Pilgrim's Art," 71.

74. Freccero, "Tangents (of Desire)," 92.

75. Breen, "Pilgrim's Art," 72, 74–75.

76. Batson, among others, represents the temporality of part 2 as "relaxed," "without haste," and lacking in "urgency," but does not note its allegorical inconsistency with part 1 (*John Bunyan*, 48–49). Hill notices that time in part 2 seems "elusive" since "Christiana's children grow up from infancy to marriageable age" (*Tinker and a Poor Man*, 223).

77. The boys' amorphous, rapidly shifting age may speak to Bunyan's concept of Christian wisdom; he noted that his *Book for Boys and Girls* was designed not only with real children in mind, but also "spiritual children" in need of childlike theological tools. Breen makes a similar point in "Sexed Pilgrim's Progress" (450).

78. Breen, "Pilgrim's Art," 73; Luxon, "One Soul versus One Flesh."

79. Batson's note that "Part Two lacks the dangers, and perhaps the adventures of Part One" is typical (*John Bunyan*, 48).

80. Hill, *Tinker and a Poor Man*, 229.

81. Fish, *Self-Consuming Artifacts*, 229–38. Dutton, too, discusses the problem of progress in the context of double predestination ("Interesting, but Tough").

82. For a reading that discusses the concept of nonlinear "progress" in the early modern period to challenge Fish's "modern sense" of the word, see Hill, *Tinker and a Poor Man*, 221–23. Edwards has also argued against Fish's reduction of the word's meaning ("Journey in *The Pilgrim's Progress*").

83. Manlove, "Image of the Journey," 24.

84. Bunyan, *Pilgrim's Progress*, ed. Pooley, xlvi.

85. Ibid.

86. Davies, "Stout and Valiant Champions," 130.

87. Schellenberg, "Sociability and the Sequel," 319.
88. Parker, *Inescapable Romance*.
89. Breen, "Pilgrim's Art," 66.
90. Ibid., 68, citing Doty, *Heaven's Coast*, 2–6.

CONCLUSION

1. McKeon, *Origins of the English Novel*.
2. Ibid., 105–9.
3. Bercovitch, *Puritan Origins*; Spengemann, "Earliest American Novel," 414.
4. Patterson, "*Paradise Regained*."
5. Dutton discusses Bunyan's legacy in works such as Mark Twain's *Adventures of Huckleberry Finn* and Louisa May Alcott's *Little Women*, noting the challenge of interpreting *The Pilgrim's Progress* without a predestinarian framework to Christianity and the fact that this did not deter most readers ("Interesting, but Tough").
6. Spengemann, "Earliest American Novel."

BIBLIOGRAPHY

Achinstein, Sharon. "Romance of the Spirit: Female Sexuality and Religious Desire in Early Modern England." *English Literary History* 69 (2002): 413–38.

Akhimie, Patricia. "Bruised with Adversity: Reading Race in *The Comedy of Errors*." In *The Oxford Handbook of Shakespeare and Embodiment*, edited by Valerie Traub, 186–96. Oxford: Oxford University Press, 2016.

Alexander, Gavin. *Writing after Sidney: The Literary Response to Sir Philip Sidney, 1586–1640*. Oxford: Oxford University Press, 2007.

Anonymous. *The Faerie Leveller: or, King Charles his Leveller descried and deciphered in Queene Elizabeths dayes. By her Poet Laureat Edmond Spenser, in his unparaleld Poeme, entituled, The Faerie Queene. A lively representation of our times*. London, 1648.

Arthos, John. *On the Poetry of Spenser and the Form of Romances*. Freeport, N.Y.: Books for Libraries Press, 1970.

Austin, Michael. "The Figural Logic of the Sequel and the Unity of 'The Pilgrim's Progress.'" *Studies in Philology* 102, no. 4 (2005): 484–509.

Baird, Charles W. *John Bunyan: A Study in Narrative Technique*. Port Washington, N.Y.: Kennikat Press, 1977.

Baker, Christopher. "Sidney, Religious Syncretism, and Henry VII." *Studia Neophilologica* 86, no. 1 (2014): 17–36.

Barbeau, Anne. *The Intellectual Design of John Dryden's Heroic Plays*. New Haven, Conn.: Yale University Press, 1970.

Batson, E. Beatrice. *John Bunyan: Allegory and Imagination*. London: Croom Helm, 1984.

Battigelli, Anna. *Margaret Cavendish and the Exiles of the Mind*. Lexington: University Press of Kentucky, 1998.

———. "Political Thought / Political Action: Margaret Cavendish's Hobbesian Dilemma." In *Women Writers and the Early Modern British Political Tradition*, edited by Hilda Smith, 40–55. Cambridge: Cambridge University Press, 1998.

Bear, Bethany Joy. "Fantastical Faith: John Bunyan and the Sanctification of Fancy." *Studies in Philology* 109, no. 5 (2012): 671–701.

Behn, Aphra. *Oroonoko*. Edited by Joanna Lipking. New York: Norton, 1997.

Bennett, Alexandra. "Fantastic Realism: Margaret Cavendish and the Possibilities of Drama." In *Authorial Conquests: Essays on Genre in the Writings of Margaret Cavendish*, edited by Line Cottegnies and Nancy Weitz, 179–94. London: Associated University Presses, 2003.

Bennett, Joan. "Mary Astell, Lucy Hutchinson, John Milton, and Feminist Liberation Theology." In *Milton in the Age of Fish: Essays on Authorship, Text, and Terrorism*, edited by Michael Lieb and Albert C. Labriola, 139–66. Pittsburgh: Duquesne University Press, 2006.

Bercovitch, Sacvan. *The Puritan Origins of the American Self*. New Haven, Conn.: Yale University Press, 1975.

Berensmeyer, Ingo. "The Art of Oblivion: Politics of Remembering and Forgetting in Restoration England." *European Journal of English Studies* 10, no. 1 (2006): 81–96.

Berger, Harry. *The Allegorical Temper: Vision and Reality in Book II of Spenser's Faerie Queene*. New Haven, Conn.: Yale University Press, 1957.

The Bible. Translated according to the Ebrew and Greeke, and conferred with the best translations in diuers languages. With most profitable Annotations vpon all the hard places, and other things of great importance, as may appear in the Epistle to the Reader. London: Christopher Barker, 1583.

Black, Joseph L., and Lisa Celovsky. "'Lost Works,' Suppositious Pieces, and Continuations." In *The Oxford Handbook of Edmund Spenser*, edited by Richard A. McCabe, 349–64. Oxford: Oxford University Press, 2010.

Breen, Margaret Sönser. "The Pilgrim's Art of Failure and Belonging: Dialogues Between Bunyan and Queer Studies." *Bunyan Studies* 18 (2014): 61–77.

———. "The Sexed Pilgrim's Progress." *Studies in English Literature* 32, no. 3 (1992): 443–60.

Brennan, Michael G. "'Thy Necessity Is Yet Greater Than Mine': The Re-Mythologizing in the Literary and Visual Arts of Fulke Greville's Water-Bottle Anecdote (1750–1930)." *Sidney Journal* 28, no. 2 (2010): 1–40.

Britland, Karen. *Drama at the Courts of Queen Henrietta Maria*. Cambridge: Cambridge University Press, 2009.

Britton, Dennis. *Becoming Christian: Race, Reformation, and Early Modern Romance*. New York: Fordham University Press, 2014.

Broaddus, James. "Spenser's Redcrosse Knight and the Order of Salvation." *Studies in Philology* 108, no. 4 (2011): 572–604.

Brown, Laura. "The Romance of Empire: *Oroonoko* and the Trade in Slaves." In *The New Eighteenth Century*, edited by Laura Brown and Felicity Nussbaum, 41–61. London: Methuen, 1987.

Brownley, Martine Watson. *Clarendon and the Rhetoric of Historical Form*. Philadelphia: University of Philadelphia Press, 1985.

Brumbaugh, Barbara. "Cecropia and the Church of Antichrist in Sir Philip Sidney's *New Arcadia*." *Studies in English Literature* 38, no. 1 (1998): 19–43.

———. "*Jerusalem Delivered* and the Allegory of Sidney's Revised *Arcadia*." *Modern Philology* 101, no. 3 (2004): 337–70.

Bunyan, John. *Grace Abounding, with Other Spiritual Autobiographies*. Edited by John Stachniewski and Anita Pacheco. Oxford: Oxford University Press, 1998.

———. *The Miscellaneous Works of John Bunyan*, vol. 1: "Some Gospel-Truths Opened," "A Vindication of Some Gospel-Truths Opened," and "A Few Sighs from Hell," edited by T. L. Underwood, with Roger Sharrock. Oxford: Clarendon Press, 1980.

———. *The Pilgrim's Progress*. Edited by Roger Pooley. London: Penguin, 2008.

Burrow, Colin. *Epic Romance: Homer to Milton*. Oxford: Clarendon Press, 1993.

Candido, Joseph. "Fulke Greville's Biography of Sir Philip Sidney and the 'Architectonic' Tudor Life." *South Central Review* 2, no. 1 (1985): 3–12.

Carnell, Rachel. "Subverting Tragic Conventions: Aphra Behn's Turn to the Novel." *Studies in the Novel* 31, no. 2 (1999): 133–51.

Cavallaro, Dani. *The Chivalric Romance and the Essence of Fiction*. Jefferson, N.C.: McFarland, 2016.

Cavendish, Margaret. *Assaulted and Pursued Chastity*. In *Natures Pictures Drawn by Fancies Pencil to the Life*, Ff2v–Mm4v. London, 1656. Women Writers Online, Women Writers Project, Northeastern University.

———. *The Description of a New World, Called "The Blazing-World."* London, 1668. Women Writers Online, Women Writers Project, Northeastern University.

———. *The Life of the Thrice Noble, High and Puissant Prince William Cavendishe.* London, 1667. Women Writers Online, Women Writers Project, Northeastern University.

———. *Paper Bodies.* Edited by Sylvia Bowerbank and Sara Mendelson. Peterborough, Ont.: Broadview Press, 2000.

———. *Philosophical Letters.* London, 1664. Women Writers Online, Women Writers Project, Northeastern University.

———. *The World's Olio.* London, 1655. Women Writers Online, Women Writers Project, Northeastern University.

Chaucer, Geoffrey. *The Canterbury Tales.* Edited by A. C. Cawley. London: Everyman, 2003.

Chernaik, Warren. "Captains and Slaves: Aphra Behn and the Rhetoric of Republicanism." *Seventeenth Century* 17, no. 1 (2002): 97–107.

Clarke, Elizabeth. *Politics, Religion, and the Song of Songs in Seventeenth-Century England.* Basingstoke, U.K.: Palgrave Macmillan, 2011.

Coiro, Ann Baynes. "'A Ball of Strife': Caroline Poetry and Royal Marriage." In *The Royal Image: Representations of Charles I*, edited by Thomas Corns, 26–46. Cambridge: Cambridge University Press, 1999.

Coles, Kimberly Anne. "Gender in the 1590 *Faerie Queene*." In *Edmund Spenser in Context*, edited by Andrew Escobedo, 352–62. Cambridge: Cambridge University Press, 2017.

———. "West of England: The Irish Specter in *Tamburlaine*." In *The Blackwell Companion to Tudor Literature*, edited by Kent Cartwright, 459–74. Oxford: Wiley-Blackwell, 2010.

Connell, Dorothy. *Sir Philip Sidney The Maker's Mind.* Oxford: Clarendon Press, 1977.

Cook, Susan. "'The Story I Most Particularly Intend': The Narrative Style of Lucy Hutchinson." *Critical Survey* 5, no. 3 (1993): 271–77.

Cooper, Helen. *The English Romance in Time: Transforming Motifs from Geoffrey of Monmouth to the Death of Shakespeare.* Oxford: Oxford University Press, 2004.

———. "Milton's King Arthur." *Review of English Studies* 65 (2013): 252–65.

Corns, Thomas, ed. *The Royal Image: Representations of Charles I.* Cambridge: Cambridge University Press, 1999.

Crawford, Julie. "*All's Well That Ends Well*; or, Is Marriage Always Already Heterosexual?" In *Shakesqueer. A Queer Companion to the Complete Works of Shakespeare*, edited by Madhavi Menon, 39–47. Durham, N.C.: Duke University Press, 2011.

———. *Mediatrix: Women, Politics and Literary Production in Early Modern England.* Oxford: Oxford University Press, 2014.

———. "Sidney's Sapphics and the Role of Interpretive Communities." *English Literary History* 69, no. 4 (2002): 979–1007.

Crowley, Timothy D. "Sireno and Philisides: The Politics of Piety in Spanish Pastoral Romance and Sidney's *Old Arcadia*." *Studies in Philology* 110, no. 1 (2013): 43–84.

Curran, Stuart. "*Paradise Regained*: Implications of Epic." *Milton Studies* 17 (1983): 209–24.

Dana, Margaret. "The Providential Plot of the *Old Arcadia*." *Studies in English Literature* 17, no. 1 (1977): 39–57.

Danielson, Dennis. *Milton's Good God: A Study in Literary Theodicy.* Cambridge: Cambridge University Press, 1982.

Das, Nandini. *Renaissance Romance: The Transformation of English Prose Fiction, 1570–1620.* Farnham, U.K.: Ashgate, 2011.

Davies, Michael. "'Stout and Valiant Champions for God': The Radical Reformation of Romance in *The Pilgrim's Progress*." In *John Bunyan: Reading Dissenting Writing*, edited

by N. H. Keeble, 103–32. Bern: Peter Lang, 2002.
Davis, Alex. "'The Web of His Story': Narrating Miso's Poem and Mopsa's Tale in Book 2 of the *New Arcadia*." *Sidney Journal* 26, no. 2 (2008): 49–64.
Davis, Walter R. *A Map of Arcadia: Sidney's Romance in Its Tradition*. New Haven, Conn.: Yale University Press, 1965.
Dickson, Vernon Guy. "Truth, Wonder, and Exemplarity in Aphra Behn's 'Oroonoko.'" *Studies in English Literature* 47, no. 3 (2007): 573–94.
Dinshaw, Carolyn. *Getting Medieval: Sexualities and Communities, Pre- and Postmodern*. Durham, N.C.: Duke University Press, 1999.
Dodds, Lara. "Margaret Cavendish's Domestic Experiment." In *Genre and Women's Life Writing in Early Modern England*, edited by Michelle M. Dowd and Julie A. Eckerle, 151–68. Aldershot, U.K.: Ashgate, 2007.
Donne, John. *John Donne: The Major Works*. Edited by John Carey. Oxford: Oxford University Press, 1990.
Doty, Mark. *Heaven's Coast*. New York: HarperCollins, 1996.
Dowd, Michelle M., and Julie A. Eckerle, eds. *Genre and Women's Life Writing in Early Modern England*. Aldershot, U.K.: Ashgate, 2007.
Dryden, John. *John Dryden: The Major Works*. Edited by Keith Walker. Oxford: Oxford University Press, 1987.
Duffy, Maureen, ed. *Oroonoko and Other Stories*. London: Methuen, 1986.
Duncan-Jones, Katherine. *Sir Philip Sidney: Courtier Poet*. New Haven, Conn.: Yale University Press, 1991.
Dutton, Richard. "'Interesting, but Tough': Reading *The Pilgrim's Progress*." *Studies in English Literature* 18 (1978): 439–56.
Eckerle, Julie. *Romancing the Self in Early Modern Englishwomen's Life Writing*. Farnham, U.K.: Ashgate, 2015.
Edelman, Lee. *No Future: Queer Theory and the Death Drive*. Durham, N.C.: Duke University Press, 2004.
Edwards, Philip. "The Journey in *The Pilgrim's Progress*." In *The Pilgrim's Progress: Critical and Historical Views*, edited by Vincent Newey, 111–17. Liverpool, U.K.: Liverpool University Press, 1980.
Evans, J. Martin. *The Miltonic Moment*. Lexington: University Press of Kentucky, 1998.
Ezell, Margaret J. M. "Bunyan's Women, Women's Bunyan." In *Trauma and Transformation: The Political Progress of John Bunyan*, edited by Vera J. Camden, 63–80. Stanford, Calif.: Stanford University Press, 2008.
Falck, Claire. "'Heavenly Lineaments' and the Invisible Church in Foxe and Spenser." *Studies in English Literature* 53, no. 1 (2013): 1–28.
Fallon, Stephen. "'Elect above the Rest': Theology as Self-Representation in Milton." In *Milton and Heresy*, edited by Stephen Dobranski and John Rumrich, 93–116. Cambridge: Cambridge University Press, 1998.
Ferguson, Margaret. "Juggling the Categories of Race, Class, and Gender: Aphra Behn's *Oroonoko*." In *Women, "Race," and Writing in the Early Modern Period*, edited by Margo Hendricks and Patricia Parker, 209–24. London: Routledge, 1994.
Firth, Charles Harding, ed. *The Life of William Cavendish, Duke of Newcastle*. London: Routledge, 1886.
Fish, Stanley. "Inaction and Silence: The Reader in *Paradise Regained*." In *Calm of Mind*, edited by Joseph A. Wittreich, 38–42. Cleveland: Press of Case Western Reserve University, 1971.
———. *Self-Consuming Artifacts*. Berkeley: University of California Press, 1972.
———. "Things and Actions Indifferent: The Temptation of Plot in *Paradise Regained*." *Milton Studies* 17 (1983): 163–85.
Fisher, Will. "The Erotics of Chin Chucking in Seventeenth-Century England." In *Sex before Sex: Figuring the Act*

in Early Modern England, edited by James M. Bromley and Will Stockton, 141–70. Minneapolis: University of Minnesota Press, 2013.

Fitzmaurice, James. "Margaret Cavendish's Life of William, Plutarch, and Mixed Genre." In Authorial Conquests: Essays on Genre in the Writings of Margaret Cavendish, edited by Line Cottegnies and Nancy Weitz, 80–102. London: Associated University Presses, 2003.

Fludernik, Monika. Towards a "Natural" Narratology. London: Routledge, 1996.

Freccero, Carla. "Tangents (of Desire)." Journal for Early Modern Cultural Studies 16, no. 2 (2016): 91–105.

Freeman, Rosemary. English Emblem Books. London: Chatto and Windus, 1948.

Friedlander, Ari. "Desiring History and Historicizing Desire." Journal for Early Modern Cultural Studies 16, no. 2 (2016): 1–20.

Frye, Northrop. "Agon and Logos." In The Prison and the Pinnacle, edited by Balachandra Rajan, 135–63. Toronto: University of Toronto Press, 1973.

———. The Secular Scripture: A Study of the Structure of Romance. Cambridge: Harvard University Press, 1976.

———. "The Typology of Paradise Regained." In Milton: Modern Essays in Criticism, edited by Arthur E. Barker, 429–46. Oxford: Oxford University Press, 1965.

Fuchs, Barbara. Romance. New York: Routledge, 2004.

Gallagher, Catherine. "Embracing the Absolute: The Politics of the Female Subject in Seventeenth-Century England." Genders 1 (1988): 24–39.

Gay, David. "Astrology and Iconoclasm in Milton's 'Paradise Regained.'" Studies in English Literature 41, no. 1 (2001): 175–90.

Gerard, Christian Anton. "Within the Zodiac of Wit: Philip Sidney, William Scott, and the Right Reader Turned Right Poet." Sidney Journal 33, no. 1 (2015): 91–107.

Gillespie, Katharine. Domesticity and Dissent in the Seventeenth Century: English Women's Writing and the Public Sphere. Cambridge: Cambridge University Press, 2004.

Gleckman, Jason. "Malvolio and Puritan Assurance." Appositions 10 (2017). http://appositions.blogspot.com/2017/08/jasongleckmanpuritanassurance.html.

Goldberg, Jonathan. The Seeds of Things: Theorizing Sexuality and Materiality in Renaissance Representations. New York: Fordham University Press, 2009.

Goodman, Jennifer. Chivalry and Exploitation, 1298–1630. Woodbridge, U.K.: Boydell Press, 1998.

Gouws, John. "Early Readers of Fulke Greville, The Life of the Renowned Sir Philip Sidney (1652)." Notes and Queries 62, no. 4 (2015): 595–97.

Greville, Fulke. The Life of the Renowned Sr Philip Sidney. With the true Interest of England as it then stood in relation to all Forrain Princes: And particularly for suppressing the power of Spain Stated by Him. His principall Actions, Counsels, Designes, and Death. Together with a short Account of the Maximes and Policies used by Queen Elizabeth in her Government. London, 1652

Guffey, George. "Aphra Behn's Oroonoko: Occasion and Accomplishment." In Two English Novelists: Aphra Behn and Anthony Trollope, edited by George Guffey and Andrew Wright, 1–41. Los Angeles: University of California. William Andrews Clark Memorial Library, 1975.

Guibbory, Achsah. The Map of Time: Seventeenth-Century English Literature and Ideas of Pattern in History. Urbana: University of Illinois Press, 1986.

Hackett, Helen. Women and Romance Fiction in the English Renaissance. Cambridge: Cambridge University Press, 2000.

Hadfield, Andrew. "Spenser and Religion—Yet Again." Studies in English Literature 51, no. 1 (2011): 21–46.

Hager, Alan. "The Exemplary Mirage: Fabrication of Sir Philip Sidney's

Biographical Image and the Sidney Reader." *English Literary History* 48, no. 1 (1981): 1–16.

Hammond, Brean. "*The Pilgrim's Progress*: Satire and Social Comment." In *The Pilgrim's Progress: Critical and Historical Views*, edited by Vincent Newey, 118–31. Liverpool, U.K.: Liverpool University Press, 1980.

Hammond, Paul. *John Dryden: A Literary Life*. London: Macmillan, 1991.

Hammons, Pamela. "Polluted Palaces: Gender, Sexuality and Property in Lucy Hutchinson's 'Elegies.'" *Women's Writing* 13, no. 3 (2006): 392–415.

Heffner, Ray, Dorothy E. Mason, Frederick M. Padelford, and William Wells. "Spenser Allusions in the Sixteenth and Seventeenth Centuries: Part II (1626–1700)." *Studies in Philology* 69, no. 5 (1972): 173–351.

Helsby, Mary Hatton. *Letters*. Folger Shakespeare Library ms. X.d.493 (3, 5, 6).

Heng, Geraldine. *Empire of Magic: Medieval Romance and the Politics of Cultural Fantasy*. New York: Columbia University Press, 2003.

Herbert, Percy. *The Princess Cloria; or, The Royal Romance*. London, 1661.

Herman, Peter C. "'Bastard Children of Tyranny': The Ancient Constitution and Fulke Greville's *A Dedication to Sir Philip Sidney*." *Renaissance Quarterly* 55 (2002): 969–1004.

Hill, Christopher. *A Tinker and a Poor Man: John Bunyan and His Church, 1628–1688*. New York: Knopf, 1989.

Hillier, Russell M. "'So Shall the World Goe On': A Providentialist Reading of Books Eleven and Twelve of *Paradise Lost*." *English Studies* 92, no. 6 (2011): 607–33.

Hillyer, Richard. *Sir Philip Sidney, Cultural Icon*. New York: Palgrave Macmillan, 2010.

Hirst, Derek. "Remembering a Hero: Lucy Hutchinson's *Memoirs* of Her Husband." In *Ashgate Critical Essays on Women Writers in England, 1550–1700*, vol. 5: *Anne Clifford and Lucy Hutchinson*, edited by Mihoko Suzuki, 263–72. Aldershot, U.K.: Ashgate, 2009.

Hobbes, Thomas. *Elements of Philosophy*. London, 1656.

———. *Leviathan*. Edited by Edwin Curley. Indianapolis: Hackett, 1994.

Hodges, Kenneth. "Reformed Dragons: *Bevis of Hampton*, Sir Thomas Malory's *Le Morte Darthur*, and Spenser's *Faerie Queene*." *Texas Studies in Language and Literature* 54, no. 1 (2012): 110–31.

Hoegberg, David. "Caesar's Toils: Allusion and Rebellion in *Oroonoko*." *Eighteenth-Century Fiction* 7, no. 3 (1995): 239–58.

Hulse, Clark. "Spenser, Bacon, and the Myth of Power." In *The Historical Renaissance: New Essays on Tudor and Stuart Literature and Culture*, edited by Heather Dubrow and Richard Strier, 315–46. Chicago: University of Chicago Press, 1988.

Hutchinson, Lucy. *Memoirs of the Life of Colonel Hutchinson*. Edited by Charles Harding Firth and Julius Hutchinson. London: George Bell and Sons, 1908.

———. *Memoirs of the Life of Colonel Hutchinson*. Edited by James Sutherland. London: Oxford University Press, 1973.

———. *Order and Disorder*. Edited by David Norbrook. Oxford: Blackwell, 2001.

Hyde, Edward, Earl of Clarendon. *Selections from "The History of the Rebellion."* Edited by Gertrude Huehns. Oxford: Oxford University Press, 1978.

Irish, Bradley J. "Friendship and Frustration: Counter-affect in the Letters of Philip Sidney and Hubert Languet." *Texas Studies in Literature and Language* 57, no. 4 (2015): 412–32.

Iwanisziw, Susan. "Behn's Novel Investment in 'Oroonoko': Kingship, Slavery and Tobacco in English Colonialism." *South Atlantic Review* 63, no. 2 (1998): 75–98.

Jameson, Fredric. "Magical Narratives: Romance as Genre." *New Literary History* 7, no. 1 (1975): 135–63.

Jardine, Lisa. "Twins and Travesties: Gender, Dependency, and Sexual Availability in *Twelfth Night*." In

Erotic Politics: Desire on the Renaissance Stage, edited by Susan Zimmerman, 65–77. New York: Routledge, 1992.

Jauss, Hans Robert. *Towards an Aesthetic of Reception*. Translated by Timothy Bahti. Minneapolis: University of Minnesota Press, 1982.

Kahn, Victoria. "Margaret Cavendish and the Romance of Contract." *Renaissance Quarterly* 50, no. 2 (1997): 526–66.

———. "Reinventing Romance; or, The Surprising Effects of Sympathy." *Renaissance Quarterly* 55, no. 2 (2002): 625–61.

———. *Wayward Contracts: The Crisis of Political Obligation in England, 1640–1674*. Princeton, N.J.: Princeton University Press, 2004.

Kane, Sean. *Spenser's Moral Allegory*. Toronto: University of Toronto Press, 1989.

Keeble, N. H. "'But the Colonel's Shadow': Lucy Hutchinson, Women's Writing, and the Civil War." In *Literature and the English Civil War*, edited by Thomas Healy and Jonathan Sawday, 227–47. Cambridge: Cambridge University Press, 1990.

———. "Christiana's Key: The Unity of *The Pilgrim's Progress*." In *The Pilgrim's Progress: Critical and Historical Views*, edited by Vincent Newey, 1–20. Liverpool, U.K.: Liverpool University Press, 1980.

King, Andrew. "Sidney and Spenser." In *A Companion to Romance. From Classical to Contemporary*, edited by Corinne Saunders, 140–59. Malden, Mass.: Blackwell, 2004.

King, John. "'The Faerie Leveller': A 1648 Royalist Reading of 'The Faerie Queene,' V.ii.29–54." *Huntington Library Quarterly* 48, no. 3 (1985): 297–308.

———. *Spenser's Poetry and the Reformation Tradition*. Princeton, N.J.: Princeton University Press, 1990.

Kinney, Arthur. "A Poetics of Romance." *Sidney Journal* 26, no. 2 (2008): 1–16.

Kinney, Clare. "Chivalry Unmasked: Courtly Spectacle and the Abuses of Romance in Sidney's 'New Arcadia.'" *Studies in English Literature* 35, no. 1 (1995): 35–52.

———. "On the Margins of Romance, at the Heart of the Matter: Revisionary Fabulation in Sidney's 'New Arcadia.'" *Journal of Narrative Technique* 21, no. 2 (1991): 143–52.

———. "Romance." In *Edmund Spenser in Context*, edited by Andrew Escobedo, 120–29. Cambridge: Cambridge University Press, 2016.

———. "Sidney's *Arcadia*, Romance, and the Responsive Woman Reader." In *A Companion to Tudor Literature*, edited by Kent Cartwright, 395–411. Chichester, U.K.: Wiley-Blackwell, 2010.

———. *Strategies of Poetic Narrative*. Cambridge: Cambridge University Press, 1992.

Knott, John R. "Bunyan and the Holy Community." *Studies in Philology* 80, no. 2 (1983): 200–225.

Knox, Ronald. *Essays in Satire*. London: Dutton, 1928.

Kroll, Richard. "'Tales of Love and Gallantry': The Politics of *Oroonoko*." *Huntington Library Quarterly* 67, no. 4 (2004): 573–605.

Lahive, Colin. "Reading and Writing Romance in *Paradise Lost* and *Paradise Regained*." *Literature Compass* 12, no. 10 (2015): 527–37.

Lake, Arthur. *Christ's Conflict with and Conquest of the Tempter*. Folger Shakespeare Library ms. V.a.394.

Lake, Peter, with Michael Questier. *The Antichrist's Lewd Hat: Protestants, Papists and Players in Post-Reformation England*. New Haven, Conn.: Yale University Press, 2002.

Lamb, Mary Ellen. "Exhibiting Class and Displaying the Body in Sidney's *Countess of Pembroke's Arcadia*." *Studies in English Literature* 37, no. 1 (1997): 55–72.

———. *Gender and Authorship in the Sidney Circle*. Madison: University of Wisconsin Press, 1990.

———. "Merging the Secular and the Spiritual in Lady Anne Halkett's

Memoirs." In *Genre and Women's Life Writing*, edited by Michelle M. Dowd and Julie A. Eckerle, 81–96. Aldershot, U.K.: Ashgate, 2007.

Larson, Charles. *Fulke Greville*. Boston: Twayne, 1980.

Lawry, Jon S. *Sidney's Two Arcadias: Pattern and Proceeding*. Ithaca, N.Y.: Cornell University Press, 1972.

Lee, Christine. "Sidney's Two Roads to Arcadia: Romance and the Narrative of Experience." *Sidney Journal* 31, no. 2 (2013): 77–105.

Lewalski, Barbara. "Milton: Revaluations of Romance." In *Four Essays on Romance*, edited by Herschel Baker, 55–70. Cambridge: Harvard University Press, 1971.

———. *Milton's Brief Epic*. Providence: Brown University Press, 1966.

Lindheim, Nancy. *The Structures of Sidney's Arcadia*. Toronto: University of Toronto Press, 1982.

Lobo, Giuseppina Iacono. "Lucy Hutchinson's Revisions of Conscience." *English Literary Renaissance* 42, no. 2 (2012): 317–41.

Lochman, Daniel T. "Friendship's Passion: Love-Fellowship in Sidney's *New Arcadia*." In *Discourses and Representations of Friendship in Early Modern Europe, 1500–1700*, edited by Daniel T. Lochman, Maritere López, and Lorna Hutson, 65–79. Surrey, U.K.: Ashgate, 2010.

Loewenstein, David. *Milton and the Drama of History*. Cambridge: Cambridge University Press, 1990.

Longfellow, Erica. *Women and Religious Writing in Early Modern England*. Cambridge: Cambridge University Press, 2004.

Looser, Devoney. *British Women Writers and the Writing of History, 1670–1820*. Baltimore: Johns Hopkins University Press, 2000.

Luciano, Dana. "Unrealized: The Queer Time of *The Hermaphrodite*." In *Philosophies of Sex: Critical Essays on The Hermaphrodite*, edited by Renée Bergland and Gary Williams, 215–41. Columbus: Ohio State University Press, 2012.

Luxon, Thomas. "One Soul versus One Flesh: Friendship, Marriage, and the Puritan Self." In *Trauma and Transformation: The Political Progress of John Bunyan*, edited by Vera J. Camden, 81–99. Stanford, Calif.: Stanford University Press, 2008.

Mallette, Richard. *Spenser and the Discourses of Reformation England*. Lincoln: University of Nebraska Press, 1997.

Manlove, C. N. "The Image of the Journey in 'Pilgrim's Progress': Narrative versus Allegory." *Journal of Narrative Technique* 10, no. 1 (1980): 16–38.

Martin, Christopher. "Between Duty and Selfness: Greville's *Life of Sidney*." *Mid-Hudson Language Studies* 9 (1986): 19–28.

Mayer, Robert. "Lucy Hutchinson: A Life of Writing." *Seventeenth Century* 22 (2007): 305–35.

McCabe, Richard. *The Pillars of Eternity: Time and Providence in "The Faerie Queene."* Dublin: Irish Academic Press, 1989.

McCoy, Richard. *Sir Philip Sidney: Rebellion in Arcadia*. New Brunswick, N.J.: Rutgers University Press, 1979.

McKeon, Michael. *The Origins of the English Novel, 1600–1740*. Baltimore: Johns Hopkins University Press, 1987.

Meier, T. K. "Milton's *Nativity Ode*: Sectarian Discord." *Modern Language Review* 65 (1970): 7–10.

Mendelson, Sara Heller. *The Mental World of Stuart Women: Three Studies*. Brighton, U.K.: Harvester Press, 1987.

Mentz, Steven. "Reason, Faith, and Shipwreck in Sidney's 'New Arcadia.'" *Studies in English Literature* 44, no. 1 (2004): 1–18.

Meserole, Harrison. *American Poetry of the Seventeenth Century*. University Park: Pennsylvania State University Press, 1985.

Mikics, David. *The Limits of Moralizing: Pathos and Subjectivity in Spenser and Milton*. Lewisburg, Pa.: Bucknell University Press, 1994.

Miller, Shannon. *Engendering the Fall: John Milton and Seventeenth-Century*

Women Writers. Philadelphia: University of Pennsylvania Press, 2008.

Milton, John. *Complete Poems and Major Prose*. Edited by Merritt Y. Hughes. Indianapolis: Hackett, 2003.

———. *The Complete Poetry and Essential Prose of John Milton*. Edited by William Kerrigan, John Rumrich, and Stephen M. Fallon. New York: Random House, 2007.

———. *Complete Prose Works of John Milton*. New Haven, Conn.: Yale University Press, 1953.

Mohl, Ruth. "Milton's Commonplace Book." In *Complete Prose Works of John Milton*, vol. 1: *1624–1642*, edited by Don M. Wolfe, 344–513. New Haven, Conn.: Yale University Press, 1953.

Montaño, John Patrick. *Courting the Moderates: Ideology, Propaganda, and the Emergence of Party, 1660–1678*. Newark: University of Delaware Press, 2002.

Moore, C. A. "Miltoniana (1679–1741)." *Modern Philology* 24 (1927): 321–39.

Mornay, Philippe Duplessis. *A Woorke concerning the trewnesse of the Christian religion, written in French: Against atheists, Epicures, Paynims, Iewes, Mahumetists, and other infidels. By Philip of Mornay Lord of Plessie Marlie. Begunne to be translated into English by Sir Philip Sidney Knight, and at his request finished by Arthur Golding*. London, 1587.

Mulready, Cyrus. *Romance on the Early Modern Stage*. Basingstoke, U.K.: Palgrave Macmillan, 2013.

Murphy, Erin. *Familial Forms: Politics and Genealogy in Seventeenth-Century English Literature*. Lanham: University of Delaware Press, 2011.

———. "'I Remain, an Airy Phantasm': Lucy Hutchinson's Civil War Ghost Writing." *English Literary History* 82, no. 1 (2015): 87–113.

———. "Radical Relations: The Genealogical Imaginary and Queer Kinship in Milton's *Paradise Regained*." In *One First Matter All: New Essays on Milton, Materialism, and Embodiment*, edited by Kevin Donovan and Thomas Festa, 81–107. Pittsburgh: Duquesne University Press, 2017.

Myrick, Kenneth. *Sir Philip Sidney as a Literary Craftsman*. Lincoln: University of Nebraska Press, 1965.

Nardo, Anna. "John Phillips, John Milton, *Don Quixote*, and the Disenchantment of Romance." *Mosaic* 47, no. 2 (2014): 169–86.

Newcomb, Lori Humphrey. *Reading Popular Romance in Early Modern England*. New York: Columbia University Press, 2002.

Newman, Barbara. *From Virile Woman to WomanChrist*. Philadelphia: University of Pennsylvania Press, 1995.

Newman, S. J., "Bunyan's Solidness." In *The Pilgrim's Progress: Critical and Historical Views*, edited by Vincent Newey, 225–50. Liverpool, U.K.: Liverpool University Press, 1980.

Nicosia, Marissa. "Reading Spenser in 1648: Prophecy and History in Samuel Sheppard's *Faerie Leveller*." *Modern Philology* 114, no. 2 (2016): 286–309.

Norbrook, David. "Lucy Hutchinson, John Milton, and the Republican Biblical Epic." In *Milton and the Grounds of Contention*, edited by Mark R. Kelley, Michael Lieb, and John T. Shawcross, 37–63. Pittsburgh: Duquesne University Press 2003.

———. "Lucy Hutchinson's 'Elegies' and the Situation of the Republican Woman Writer (with Text)." *English Literary Renaissance* 27, no. 3 (1997) 468–521.

———. "Margaret Cavendish and Lucy Hutchinson: Identity, Ideology and Politics." *In-Between* 9, no. 1 (2000): 179–203.

———. "Memoirs and Oblivion: Lucy Hutchinson and the Restoration." *Huntington Library Quarterly* 75, no. 2 (2012): 233–82.

———, ed. *Order and Disorder*. Oxford: Blackwell, 2001.

———. "The Poem and Its Contexts." Introduction to *Order and Disorder*, by Lucy Hutchinson, xii–lviii. Oxford: Blackwell, 2001.

———. *Poetry and Politics in the English Renaissance*. Oxford: Oxford University Press, 1984.

———. "Republican Occasions in *Paradise Regained* and *Samson Agonistes*." *Milton Studies* 42 (2002): 122–48.

———. *Writing the English Republic: Poetry, Rhetoric and Politics, 1627–1660*. Cambridge: Cambridge University Press, 1999.

O'Callaghan, Michelle. *The "Shepheards Nation": Jacobean Spenserians and Early Stuart Political Culture, 1612–1625*. Oxford: Clarendon, 2000.

Pacheco, Anita. "Royalism and Honor in Aphra Behn's *Oroonoko*." *Studies in English Literature* 34, no. 3 (1994): 491–506.

Parker, Patricia. *Inescapable Romance: Studies in the Poetics of a Mode*. Princeton, N.J.: Princeton University Press, 1979.

Patterson, Annabel. *Censorship and Interpretation: The Conditions of Writing and Reading in Early Modern England*. Madison: University of Wisconsin Press, 1984.

———. "*Paradise Regained*: A Last Chance at True Romance." *Milton Studies* 17 (1983): 187–208.

Pepys, Samuel. *Diary of Samuel Pepys*. Edited by John A. Smith. London: Macmillan, 1905.

Potter, Lois. *Secret Rites and Secret Writing: Royalist Literature, 1641–1660*. Cambridge: Cambridge University Press, 2009.

Quilligan, Maureen. *Milton's Spenser: The Politics of Reading*. Ithaca, N.Y.: Cornell University Press, 1983.

Quint, David. *Epic and Empire: Politics and Generic Form from Virgil to Milton*. Princeton, N.J.: Princeton University Press, 1993.

———. "Expectation and Prematurity in Milton's 'Nativity Ode.'" *Modern Philology* 97, no. 2 (1999): 195–219.

Raitiere, Martin N. *Faire Bitts: Sir Philip Sidney and Renaissance Political Theory*. Pittsburgh: Duquesne University Press, 1984.

Rajan, Balachandra. "In Order Serviceable." *Modern Language Review* 3 (1968): 13–22.

Rees, Emma. *Margaret Cavendish: Gender, Genre, Exile*. Manchester, U.K.: Manchester University Press, 2003.

Rivero, Albert. "Aphra Behn's 'Oroonoko' and the 'Blank Spaces' of Colonial Fictions." *Studies in English Literature* 39, no. 3 (1999): 443–62.

Rose, Mary Beth. *Gender and Heroism in Early Modern English Literature*. Chicago: University of Chicago Press, 2002.

———. "Gender, Genre, and History: Seventeenth-Century English Women and the Art of Autobiography." In *Women in the Middle Ages and the Renaissance: Literary and Historical Perspectives*, edited by Mary Beth Rose, 245–78. Syracuse, N.Y.: Syracuse University Press, 1986.

Salzman, Paul. *English Prose Fiction, 1558–1700: A Critical History*. Oxford: Clarendon Press, 1985.

Sanchez, Melissa. *Erotic Subjects: The Sexuality of Politics in Early Modern England*. Oxford: Oxford University Press, 2011.

———. "'The True Vowed Sacrifice of Unfeigned Love': Eros and Authority in *The Countess of Pembroke's Arcadia*." *Sidney Circle Journal* 22, nos. 1–2 (2004): 89–104.

Schellenberg, Betty. "Sociability and the Sequel: Rewriting Hero and Journey in *The Pilgrim's Progress*, Part II." *Studies in the Novel* 23, no. 3 (1991): 312–24.

Schneider, Regina. *Sidney's (Re)Writing of the "Arcadia."* New York: AMS Press, 2008.

Schwartz, Regina. "From Shadowy Types to Shadowy Types: The Unendings of Paradise Lost." *Milton Studies* 24 (1988): 123–39.

Sedgwick, Eve Kosofsky. *Epistemology of the Closet*. Berkeley: University of California Press, 2008.

Sedinger, Tracey. "Sidney's *New Arcadia* and the Decay of Protestant Republicanism." *Studies in English Literature* 47, no. 1 (2007): 57–77.

Seed, David. "Dialogue and Debate in *The Pilgrim's Progress*." In *The Pilgrim's*

Progress: Critical and Historical Views, edited by Vincent Newey, 69–90. Liverpool, U.K.: Liverpool University Press, 1980.

Seelig, Sharon Cadman. *Autobiography and Gender in Early Modern Literature*. Cambridge: Cambridge University Press, 2006.

Sharrock, Roger. *John Bunyan: The Pilgrim's Progress*. London: Edwin Arnold, 1966.

———. "Life and Story in *The Pilgrim's Progress*." In *The Pilgrim's Progress: Critical and Historical Views*, edited by Vincent Newey, 49–68. Liverpool, U.K.: Liverpool University Press, 1980.

Shawcross, John. *Milton: A Bibliography for the Years 1624–1700*. Binghamton, N.Y.: Medieval and Renaissance Texts and Studies, 1984.

Shuger, Debora. "Milton Über Alles: The School Divinity of *Paradise Lost* 3.183–202." *Studies in Philology* 107, no. 3 (2010): 401–15.

Sidney, Philip. *The Countess of Pembroke's Arcadia (The New Arcadia)*. Edited by Victor Skretkowicz. Oxford: Clarendon Press, 1987.

———. *The Defence of Poesie*. London: William Ponsonby, 1595.

Sim, Stuart. "'Safe for Those for Whom it is to be Safe': Salvation and Damnation in Bunyan's Fiction." In *Johr. Bunyan and His England, 1628–1688*, edited by Anne Laurence, W. R. Owens, and Stuart Sim, 149–60. London: Hambledon, 1990.

Sinfield, Alan. *Faultlines: Cultural Materialism and the Politics of Dissident Reading*. Oxford: Clarendon Press, 1992.

Skretkowicz, Victor. *European Erotic Romance: Philhellene Protestantism, Renaissance Translation and English Literary Politics*. Manchester, U.K.: Manchester University Press, 2009.

Smith, Nigel. *Literature and Revolution in England, 1640–1660*. New Haven, Conn.: Yale University Press, 1994.

Spengemann, William. "The Earliest American Novel: Aphra Behn's *Oroonoko*." *Nineteenth-Century Fiction* 38, no. 4 (1984): 384–414.

Spenser, Edmund. *The Faerie Queene*. Edited by A. C. Hamilton, Hiroshi Yamashita, and Toshiyuki Suzuki. Harlow, U.K.: Pearson Longman, 2007.

Spiller, Elizabeth. "The Counsel of Fulke Greville: Transforming the Jacobean 'Nourish Father' Through Sidney's 'Nursing Father.'" *Studies in Philology* 97, no. 4 (2000): 433–53.

———. "Speaking for the Dead: King Charles, Anna Weamys, and the Commemorations of Sir Philip Sidney's *Arcadia*.' *Criticism* 42, no. 2 (2000): 229–51.

Starr, G. A. "Aphra Behn and the Genealogy of the Man of Feeling." *Modern Philology* 87, no. 4 (1990): 362–72.

Steadman, John. *Moral Fiction in Milton and Spenser*. Columbia: University of Missouri Press, 1995.

Steen, Abram. "'Over this Jordan': Dying and the Nonconformist Community in Bunyan's *Pilgrim's Progress*." *Modern Philology* 110, no. 1 (2012): 47–73.

Stillman, Robert E. *Philip Sidney and the Poetics of Renaissance Cosmopolitanism*. London: Routledge, 2008.

Swaim, Kathleen. *Pilgrim's Progress, Puritan Progress: Discourses and Contexts*. Urbana: University of Illinois Press, 1993.

Taylor, Luke. "Milton and the Romance of History." *Milton Studies* 56 (2015): 301–29.

Thickstun, Margaret Olofson. "From Christiana to Stand-fast: Subsuming the Feminine in *The Pilgrim's Progress*." *Studies in English Literature* 26, no. 3 (1986): 439–53.

Traub, Valerie. "The New Unhistoricism in Queer Studies." *Publications of the Modern Language Association* 128, no. 1 (2013): 21–39.

Turner, James Grantham. "Bunyan's Sense of Place." In *The Pilgrim's Progress: Critical and Historical Views*, edited by Vincent Newey, 91–110. Liverpool, U.K.: Liverpool University Press, 1980.

Veevers, Erica. *Images of Love and Religion: Queen Henrietta Maria and Court Entertainments.* Cambridge: Cambridge University Press, 1989.

Visconsi, Elliott. "A Degenerate Race: English Barbarism in Aphra Behn's 'Oroonoko' and 'The Widow Ranter.'" *English Literary History* 69, no. 3 (2002): 673–701.

Watkins, John. "'And Yet the End Was Not': Apocalyptic Deferral and Spenser's Literary Afterlife." In *Worldmaking Spenser: Explorations in the Early Modern Age,* edited by Patrick Cheney and Lauren Silberman, 156–74. Louisville: University Press of Kentucky, 2000.

Weiner, Andrew D. *Sir Philip Sidney and the Poetics of Protestantism: A Study of Contexts.* Minneapolis: University of Minnesota Press, 1978.

Welch, Anthony. "Epic Romance, Royalist Retreat, and the English Civil War." *Modern Philology* 105, no. 3 (2008): 570–602.

Werlin, Julianne. "Providence and Perspective in Philip Sidney's *Old Arcadia.*" *Studies in English Literature* 54, no. 1 (2014): 25–40.

Werth, Tiffany Jo. *The Fabulous Dark Cloister: Romance in England after the Reformation.* Baltimore: Johns Hopkins University Press, 2011.

White, Hayden. *The Fiction of Narrative: Essays on History, Literature, and Theory, 1957–2007.* Edited by Robert Doran. Baltimore: Johns Hopkins University Press, 2010.

Wilcher, Robert. "'Adventurous Song' or 'Presumptuous Folly': The Problem of 'Utterance' in John Milton's *Paradise Lost* and Lucy Hutchinson's *Order and Disorder.*" *Seventeenth Century* 21, no. 2 (2006): 304–14.

———. "Lucy Hutchinson and Genesis: Paraphrase, Epic, Romance." *Oxford Journals: English* 59 (2010): 25–42.

Wilkes, G. A. "'Left . . . to Play the Ill Poet in My Own Part': The Literary Relationship of Sidney and Fulke Greville." *Review of English Studies* 57 (2006): 291–309.

Williamson, George. "Milton the Anti-Romantic." *Modern Philology* 60, no. 1 (1962): 13–21.

Winn, James. "Past and Present in Dryden's 'Fables.'" *Huntington Library Quarterly* 63, nos. 1/2 (2000): 157–74.

———. "'Thy Wars Brought Nothing About': Dryden's Critique of Military Heroism." *Seventeenth Century* 21, no. 2 (2006): 364–82.

———. *"When Beauty Fires the Blood": Love and the Arts in the Age of Dryden.* Ann Arbor: University of Michigan Press, 1992.

Wittreich, Joseph. "Milton's Transgressive Maneuvers: Receptions (Then and Now) and the Sexual Politics of *Paradise Lost.*" In *Milton and Heresy,* edited by Stephen Dobranski and John Rumrich, 244–66. Cambridge: Cambridge University Press, 1998.

Wood, Richard. "'If an Excellent Man Should Err': Philip Sidney and Stoical Virtue." *Sidney Journal* 26, no. 2 (2008): 33–47.

Wooden, Warren. "The Rhetorical Design of Fulke Greville's *Life of Sidney.*" *Proceedings of the PMR Conference* 8 (1983): 109–18.

Worden, Blair. *The Sound of Virtue: Philip Sidney's Arcadia and Elizabethan Politics.* New Haven, Conn.: Yale University Press, 1996.

Zurcher, Amelia. *Seventeenth-Century English Romance: Allegory, Ethics, and Politics.* New York: Palgrave Macmillan, 2007.

Zwicky, Laurie. "*Kairos* in 'Paradise Regained': The Divine Plan." *English Literary History* 31, no. 3 (1964): 271–77.

INDEX

Abraham, 133–34, 175, 181–83
Adam
    in Lake's sermons, 14
    in Milton, 124–25, 128–39, 143–44, 152–54, 160, 180
    in Dryden, 161
    in Hutchinson, 171–72, 177
Aeneas, 41, 84, 159
affect
    queer, 12, 37–40, 50–51, 56, 91–94, 175, 209–14
    and Sidneian romance subjectivity, 24, 35, 37–40, 50–51, 231
    in royalist romance, 22, 91–94, 191–92, 199
    in anti-royalist romance, 22, 174–75, 208–14, 215, 251n56
Akhimie, Patricia, 201
Alexander the Great, 2, 14
American literature and culture, 20, 228, 230
Anglicanism, 12, 21, 163–64, 167, 178
apocalypse
    in Bunyan, 205, 221, 223, 230
    in Milton, 131, 135, 137, 140
    Restoration as, 163–4, 191
    in Spenser, 58, 61, 71, 237n95
Arthurian romance, 91, 124, 143
    See also medieval romance
assurance, theology of. *See* election, theology of
atheism, 48–49, 118, 132, 247n35
Augustus, Emperor, 159
Austin, Michael, 206

Battigelli, Anna, 96
Bear, Bethany, 207
Behn, Aphra
    attitudes to romance, 26, 187–91, 198, 203–4, 215, 227

Oroonoko, 26, 187–91, 198, 203–4, 215; genre of, 189–90
    political beliefs, 190, 202–3, 249n13
    religious beliefs, 21, 192–93, 200
Bercovitch, Sacvan, 20, 228
Berger, Harry, 52
Bevis of Hampton, 187, 229
    See also medieval romance
blazon, 103, 174, 241n74
Booth, George, 161
Breen, Margaret Sönser, 209, 212, 215–17, 224
Britland, Karen, 8
Britton, Dennis, 193, 199
Brown, Laura, 190
Buchanan, George, 43
Bunyan, John
    attitudes to romance, 26–27, 187–89, 203–5, 215
    Grace Abounding to the Chief of Sinners, 38, 209–11
    Life and Death of Mr. Badman, 203
    political beliefs, 138, 208
    religious beliefs, 21, 231, 250n48 (*see also* nonconformists)
    The Holy War, 203
    The Pilgrim's Progress, 26, 187–89, 204–25, 228–31; part 1 vs. part 2, 204–7, 209–10, 214–16, 219–24
    and temporality, 12, 215–22
    and women, 208–14, 250n55

Calvin, John, 20, 38, 178
    See also Calvinism
Calvinism
    theology of, 20, 32, 35–36, 49 (*see also* election, theology of; predestination, theology of)
    and early modern identity, 20–21, 31, 55 (*see also* Protestantism, diversity of)

Calvinism (*continued*)
  in Spenser, 65–66
  in Hutchinson, 158, 165–67, 171, 176, 178
Carnell, Rachel, 190
Castiglione, Baldessare, *The Courtier*, 35
Catherine of Braganza, Queen, 170
Catholicism
  and cultural heritage, 29, 38, 46, 71, 163, 193
  and early modern identity, 21, 22, 31–32, 35, 164, 192
  as represented by English Protestants, 33, 46, 54, 62, 86, 167–68, 170
Cavallaro, Dani, 6
Cavendish, Margaret
  Assaulted and Pursued Chastity, 4, 25, 99, 116, 120–25, 127, 143, 146
  attitudes to romance, 10, 24–25, 90–92, 96–97, 99, 100, 119–21, 155, 240n57
  Life of William Cavendish, 24, 74, 90–102, 105–8, 111–12, 119–20, 136
  Philosophical Letters, 119–20
  political beliefs, 91–92, 97–99
  religious beliefs, 21, 119–20, 122–23, 148, 192
  The Blazing World, 119
  The World's Olio, 120, 128
Cavendish, William, 74, 90–100, 105–7, 231, 239n38
Charles I, King, 2–3, 82–83, 94, 117, 123, 146, 162
  anti-royalist critiques of, 113, 168, 246n34
  as heroic martyr, 125, 193, 201, 248n12
  marriage to Henrietta Maria, 8, 164, 181, 191
  portrayed as romance hero, 8, 10–11
  in Sheppard's *Faerie Leveller*, 24, 74–81
Charles II, King
  anti-royalist critiques of, 168, 170, 179, 183
  in Cavendish's *Life of William*, 91–100
  portrayed as romance hero, 116–18, 145; in Dryden's "Astraea Redux," 25, 159–64
  as Arethusius in Herbert's *The Princess Cloria*, 118
Chaucer, Geoffrey, *Canterbury Tales*, 45, 114, 242n16
Chernaik, Warren, 190, 192
Clarendon, Earl of, 94

Class, social, 9, 46, 48, 75, 79–81, 84, 114, 173, 192–99, 227, 229, 237n89, 249n19
  See also conservatism vs. radicalism in romance
classical romance, 32, 33, 41, 84, 120, 159, 244n53
Coiro, Ann, 8
Coles, Kimberly, 56, 62, 64, 199
conservatism vs. radicalism in romance, 2, 9, 26–27, 46–47, 79–81, 114, 173, 190, 207–8, 236n50, 242n22, 247n39
conscience, 22, 50, 76, 81, 106, 115
  See also subjectivity of romance
conversion narratives, 22, 35–38, 193, 210, 214
Cook, Susan, 101
Cooper, Helen, 3–4, 7–8, 26, 33, 38–39, 55, 71, 174
Crawford, Julie, 22, 39, 42, 50, 64, 98, 213
Cromwell, Oliver, 2, 3, 7, 17–18, 24, 74–79, 245n20
Curran, Stuart, 154
Cyrus the Great, 14, 238n25

Danielson, Dennis, 115
Das, Nandini, 8, 34
David, King, 14, 140, 145–47
Davies, Michael, 203–4, 219, 222
Davis, Alex, 32, 45
Dinshaw, Carolyn, 12, 91, 209, 215
divorce, 114 170, 173, 247n38
Don Quixote, 1, 5, 206, 220
Donne, John, 11–13, 19
Doty, Mark, 224
Dowd, Michelle, 8
drama, relationship to romance, 8, 33–34, 50, 87, 133, 164, 170, 174
dreams
  prophetic, 102, 130, 135 (*see also* prophecy)
  and romance in Bunyan, 203–4, 222
Dryden, John
  "Astraea Redux," 25, 158–64, 170, 178–79, 183, 191
  attitudes to romance, 25, 155–56
  relationship to Milton, 160
  religious beliefs, 21, 160, 163, 192
Duncan-Jones, Katherine, 31, 51
Duplessis-Mornay, Philippe. *See* Mornay, Philippe Duplessis

Eckerle, Julie, 8, 104
Edelman, Lee, 176, 216, 224

Eikon Basilike, 10–11, 113
election, theology of, 20–21, 35, 178, 192–93
  in Bunyan, 207–8, 231–32
  and community, 21–22, 55, 135
  in Hutchinson, 26, 103, 107, 155, 158, 166, 171, 174–75
  in Milton, 25, 115–16, 125
  in Spenser, 55, 65–66, 237n89
  relationship to romance, 20–21
Elizabeth I, Queen
  relationship to Sidney, 31, 43, 82, 85–86
  seventeenth-century legacy, 75, 82–93, 100, 238n19, 239n28
  in Spenser's *Faerie Queene*, 56–57, 59, 61–62, 64, 66, 71
epic, relationship to romance, 4–6, 8–9, 34, 57, 71, 124, 140, 157, 159, 234n52, 244n61
Evans, J. Martin, 139, 153
Eve
  in Bunyan, 210
  in Hutchinson, 165, 171–72, 177, 180
  in Milton, 124–25, 128–31, 135, 139, 144

Fallon, Stephen, 115
fin amour, 91–99, 239n40, 240n50
  See also medieval romance
Fish, Stanley, 113, 131, 141–42, 148–50, 219–20, 222
Fisher, Will, 93, 175, 209
Fitmaurice, James, 93, 98
Fludernik, Monika, 7
Freccero, Carla, 12, 91, 209, 215
free will, in theology and narrative, 31, 41, 49, 58–59, 62–63, 66, 128, 180
friendship
  female, 37–39, 212–14
  male, 43, 82, 92–94, 194–95
  in the *New Arcadia*, 37–39, 43, 51–52
  in *Order and Disorder*, 166, 176
  in *Oroonoko*, 194–95, 198, 200–201
Frye, Northrop, 5–7, 9, 116, 141–42
Fuchs, Barbara, 4, 6, 8

Gallagher, Catherine, 123
Geneva Bible, 166–67
Gleckman, Jason, 21
Glorious Revolution, 23, 187, 202–3
God, as author of romance, 2, 7, 11, 14, 21, 230
  in Dryden, 160–61
  in Hutchinson, 105, 176–77

  in Milton, 120, 129, 131, 150, 154
  in Spenser, 68
Golden Age, 137, 159–60
Goodman, Jennifer, 8
Greek romance. *See* classical romance
Greville, Fulke
  attitudes to romance, 32, 74, 83, 87–89
  author of tragedies, 49, 82, 87–89
  Life of the Renowned Sir Philip Sidney, 24, 74, 82–89, 92, 105–6, 224
  religious beliefs, 21, 82

Hackett, Helen, 8
Ham, curse of, 193, 198–200, 249n22
  See also election, theology of; race and romance
Harrington, James, 9
Hatton, Mary, 13, 16–19, 23, 234n45
Helsby, Randolph, 13, 16–19, 23
Heng, Geraldine, 9
Henrietta Maria, Queen, 8, 77, 164, 170, 191, 247n34
Herbert, Percy
  attitudes to romance, 25, 116, 123–25, 155, 159
  The Princess Cloria, 25, 111, 116–19, 126–27, 131, 143–46, 149
Hercules, 2, 84
Herman, Peter, 83
Hill, Christopher, 205, 219
historiography, relationship to romance, 4, 10, 24, 73–110, 120, 179, 190
history
  cyclical vs. linear, 160, 233n16, 243n49
  experienced as genre, 5–7, 9–12, 23, 33–34, 74, 109, 133, 230, 234n40
Hobbes, Thomas
  attitudes to providentialist and spiritual claims, 20–21, 112, 122, 127, 155, 234n51, 243n31
  attitudes to romance and imagination, 1–2, 5–6, 10, 12, 19–20, 30, 48, 111, 118, 231; alternatives to Hobbesian view, 14, 25, 94, 112, 117, 121, 240n57, 243n34
  Elements of Law, 1–2
  Leviathan, 2, 231, 243n31
  political philosophy, 5, 9, 118–19
Huet, Pierre, 158
Hulse, Clark, 75
humanism, 31, 39, 42, 249n13

Hutchinson, John, 74, 100–109, 175, 179, 181, 186, 231, 242n81
Hutchinson, Lucy
  attitudes to romance, 10, 25–26, 100–102, 156–59, 169–70, 176, 187
  autobiographical fragment, 100, 102, 157, 169
  elegies, 157
  Memoirs of the Life of Col. Hutchinson, 25, 74, 94, 100–12, 156, 158, 175–76, 179
  Order and Disorder, 25, 110, 155–59, 164–86, 207–8, 217
  relationship to Lucretius, 156–57, 171–73
  relationship to Milton, 156–58, 170, 245n3
  relationship to Sidney, 157–58, 165, 174
  relationship to Spenser, 180–83, 186, 248n53
  religious beliefs, 20, 103, 158, 160, 165–67
  views on marriage, 165–72, 175–77, 241n72, 246n25

Indemnity and Oblivion Act of 1660, 163–64
Israel, nation of, 60–61, 147, 202–3
  See also typology

James I, 82, 85, 100
James II, 126, 248n12
Jameson, Fredric, 9, 46, 81, 114, 207–8
  See also romance, conservative vs. radical
Jardine, Lisa, 175
Jesus, as knight or hero of romance
  in Hutchinson, 100, 165, 177, 181–82, 185
  in Lake's sermons, 13–16
  in Milton, 131, 134–35, 138, 140–54

Kahn, Victoria, 2, 8, 22, 25, 91, 99, 116–17, 123, 164, 191
Keeble, N. H., 101
Kempe, Margery, 38
King, Andrew, 53, 62–63
King, John, 52, 75, 81
Kinney, Clare, 32, 45, 53, 124
Knox, Ronald, 205, 219
Kroll, Richard, 189–90

Lahive, Colin, 113, 125
Lake, Arthur, 13–19
Lake, Peter, 22

Lamb, Mary Ellen, 32, 39
Langland, William, *Piers Plowman*, 65
Languet, Hubert, 31, 33–34, 42–43, 52
Levellers, 75–76, 78–79
Lewalski, Barbara, 141–42, 144
Lewis, C. S., 230
Lochman, Daniel, 51
Loewenstein, David, 113, 133
Lok, Anne, 38
Looser, Devoney, 101
Lucretius, *De Rerum Natura*, 48, 156, 171
Luther, Martin, 31, 38
Luxon, Thomas, 209, 216, 218

magic, 3–4, 9, 45–46, 55, 57, 104, 120, 224, 229
Malory, Thomas, *Mort d'Arthur*, 91
Manlove, Colin, 220
marriage
  of Christ and Church, 11–12, 52, 177–78, 185, 210, 219 (*see also* Song of Songs)
  experienced as romance, 17, 91, 99, 101, 103–6, 109, 157–58, 169–70, 175–77, 191
  of monarch to subjects, 25, 159, 162–64, 170, 173
Mary, mother of Jesus, 139–40, 146, 153–54
Mary, Queen of Scots, 100
McKeon, Michael, 20, 227
medieval romance, 3–4, 8, 19, 27, 114, 120, 138, 159, 230
  as Catholic, 29, 71
  and chivalric combat, 13, 146, 228
  and eroticism, 33, 38–39, 55, 91, 105, 143, 171, 174, 239n40
  See also memes in romance
Melanchthon, Philip, 31, 34–36, 43
  See also Philippism
memes in romance, 3–4, 11, 17, 45, 57, 64
  dragon-slaying, 8, 13, 68–69, 77, 130, 134, 138, 141–42, 152–53, 206, 220, 230
  intergenerational family, 162, 170, 178–82, 196–98, 216–18, 200, 221
  lady adrift at sea, 3, 18, 63, 71, 110, 120
  restoration of ruler, 61, 68, 90, 116, 118, 140, 145–48, 152, 159, 162, 181–85, 196–97, 200
  shipwreck, 3–4, 18, 106, 121, 159
  tempest, 18, 41–42, 63, 71, 102, 159
  unknown or disguised noble hero, 3, 44–45, 65, 140, 143, 194–95

Mikics, David, 53, 70
Miller, Shannon, 171, 178
Milton, John
    Apology for Smectymnuus, 112, 114–16, 146
    Areopagitica, 11, 112, 244n53
    attitudes to romance, 10, 25, 112–16, 123–25, 129, 136, 140–42, 155–187
    Comus, 112, 116, 140, 148
    Doctrine and Discipline of Divorce, 112, 114–15
    Eikonoklastes, 82, 112–13, 129
    and heroic patience, 118–19, 123, 125, 144, 243n48
    Nativity Ode, 117, 136–40, 152, 154
    Of Education, 112
    Paradise Lost, 5, 13, 113, 115–17, 119, 124–39, 143–44, 148, 152, 157, 161–62, 208
    Paradise Regained, 13, 113, 116–17, 130–31, 140–54, 157
    relationship to Spenser, 76, 82, 112, 114, 124, 130–31, 138, 143, 153–54 (*see also* Spenser, Edmund, appropriations of)
    religious beliefs, 20–21, 115–16, 136, 160
monarchy, theories of, 85, 91–92, 97–98, 117, 119, 144, 164, 170, 173, 179, 240n60, 247n38
Monck, George, 161
Moore, C. A., 156
Mornay, Philippe Duplessis, 35, 42, 235n26
Moses, 13, 90, 100, 105, 134, 202–3
Murphy, Erin, 178

Naseby, battle of, 163
Neoplatonism, 35–6, 43, 185
Newcomb, Lori Humphrey, 8
Nicosia, Marissa, 75
Noah, 133, 193, 200, 249n22
    See also Ham, curse of
nonconformists, 20–21, 168, 188, 203–4, 207–8, 212–14, 247n48
    See also Protestantism, diversity of
Norbrook, David, 100–101, 156–57, 178
Nottingham, battle of, 101
novel, 4, 190, 196, 199–201, 211, 227–28, 230

Pacheco, Anita, 189
Parker, Patricia, 5–6, 8, 45, 53, 70, 222
pastoral, 4, 157–58, 173–76
Patterson, Annabel, 8, 22, 113, 116, 124, 142, 150–52, 229

Pepys, Samuel, 10, 90, 91, 239n34
Petrarchan tradition, 93, 234n34
Philippism, 31–38, 41, 42, 46, 48–49, 51–52, 83
Plato. *See* Neoplatonism
Pooley, Roger, 221–22
Potter, Lois, 8, 22, 162
predestination, theology of, 20–21, 31, 35, 49, 103, 107, 165, 219, 231
    See also Calvinism; election, theology of; Protestantism, diversity of
prophecy
    ambivalence of, 145–46, 151
    as insight into narrative structure, 23–24, 26, 30, 40, 68–69
    archetype of mountaintop vision, 54, 64–69, 86, 130–35, 153, 202, 223–24
    archetype of vision of offspring, 54–55, 57–64, 102, 130, 181–82, 217–18
    Sidney as prophet, 83, 86, 89
    Spenser as prophet, 24, 74–81
Protestantism
    diversity of, 20–21, 31, 35–36, 73, 234n8, 236n80
    relationship to romance, 20–21, 26–27, 29–30, 193, 199
    in Bunyan, 207–8, 223
    in Hutchinson, 177
    in Sidney, 29–30, 39–40, 45, 50, 73
    in Spenser, 29–30, 52–54, 63
providence, definitions of, 119–20, 122, 228, 243n31, 244n56
    See also God, as author of romance; Puritanism
Puritanism
    and anti-Puritan critique, 75–76, 79, 90, 100, 117–20, 136, 162, 203, 211, 229
    and early modern identity, 21–22, 83 (*see also* Protestantism, diversity of)
    for Bunyan, 188–39, 203
    for Hutchinson, 157–58, 167–68, 175, 181, 183–84
    for Milton, 116, 125, 131, 136, 152, 154
    and romance subjectivity, 20–22, 229–30, 234n52 (*see also* Protestantism, relationship to romance)

queer affect in romance. *See* affect, queer
queer temporality, 12–13, 56, 64, 176, 215–17, 224
Questier, Michael, 22
Quilligan, Maureen, 128
Quint, David, 6, 8, 127, 203

race and romance, 188–89, 192–93, 197–201
Rajan, Balachandra, 139
Raleigh, Walter, 53
realism, 87, 189, 227–28, 230
Reformation, 9, 11, 48, 178
reproductive futurism, 12
　in Behn, 200
　in Bunyan, 204, 212–13, 216–18, 222, 224
　in Hutchinson, 167, 171–72, 176–78, 180–82
　in Milton, 130, 133, 135
　in Spenser, 54–64
republicanism, relationship to romance, 9–10, 22, 25, 73–74, 125, 203, 229, 231, 235n18
　in Greville's *Life of Sidney*, 82–90
　in Hutchinson's *Memoirs*, 100–111
　in Hutchinson's *Order and Disorder*, 158, 172–73, 181, 183–84, 186
　in Milton's *Paradise Regained*, 147–48, 152
Rivero, Albert, 190, 197
Roland cycle, 146
roman à clef, 116–17, 126
romance
　critical definitions of, 3–9, 233n7
　early modern critiques or parodies of, 10, 16–17, 22, 44–46, 73, 87–88, 90, 100–101, 103, 111, 129, 156, 229
　as gendered feminine, 19, 47–48, 101, 130, 132, 156–58, 186, 205, 212, 216–17, 241n69 (*see also* women as writers and readers of romance)
　as gendered masculine, 19, 25, 74, 101, 132, 176
Rose, Mary Beth, 8
royalism, relationship to romance
　critical views of, 7–9, 22, 227
　and historiography, 89–100
　post-Restoration optimism, 159–65, 181
　post-war pessimism and skepticism, 111–12, 116–32, 135–36, 142–46, 151, 155, 159, 181, 187–92, 230–31 (*see also* Hobbes, Thomas, attitudes to romance and imagination, alternatives to Hobbesian view)
　in pre-war Stuart court, 8, 116, 164, 170, 191
　as wartime prophecy, 73–82
Rubens, Peter Paul, 8, 77

Saint George, 8, 65, 68, 77, 130

Saint Paul, 14–15
Salzman, Paul, 8, 116–18, 143
Sanchez, Melissa, 12, 33, 39, 49–51, 91–94, 96–98, 209
Satan, as romance figure
　in Bunyan, 205–6, 220
　in Hutchinson, 100, 165, 177, 179
　in Lake's sermons, 13–16
　in Milton, 124–31, 133–35, 138, 141–53
　in Spenser, 68–69, 138
Schellenberg, Betty, 222
Schwartz, Regina, 113, 130–31, 135, 141, 150
Sedgwick, Eve, 94
Shakespeare, William, 162, 174, 213, 243n35
Sharrock, Roger, 207
Sheppard, Samuel, *The Faerie Leveller*, 24, 74–82
Sherman, Thomas, 228
Shuger, Debora, 115
Sidney, Mary, 39
Sidney, Philip
　appropriations and receptions of, 11, 24, 41, 74, 82–89, 94, 111, 113, 157, 195
　Astrophil and Stella, 39
　attitudes to romance, 6, 24, 32–34, 39–40, 45, 47–48, 52 (*see also* Sidney, Philip, *Defence of Poesie*)
　death of, 30–31, 82, 86–89
　Defence of Poesie, 30–31, 82, 86–89
　New Arcadia, 24, 29–52, 73, 87–88, 98, 100–101, 113
　Old Arcadia vs. *New Arcadia*, 32, 34, 51
　religious beliefs, 20, 31–32 (*see also* Philippism)
Sinfield, Alan, 31–32
Skretkowicz, Victor, 32
Smith, Nigel, 8–9, 113, 117
Song of Songs, 35, 210, 213, 247n48
　See also marriage, of Christ and Church
Spengemann, William, 190, 196–97, 202
Spenser, Edmund
　appropriations and receptions of, 16, 24, 74–82, 112, 114, 124, 130, 138, 143, 186, 221
　attitudes to romance, 24, 29–30, 52–53, 63–64, 67–68, 70–71, 74, 237n94
　The Faerie Queene, 4, 24, 29–30, 52–71, 74, 77–80, 110, 138, 186
　religious beliefs, 20, 54–55, 59, 236n71
Stewart, Potter, 3
Stillman, Robert, 31–33, 39, 42
stoicism, 32, 47, 49–51, 89, 93, 119

storytelling and community, 43–45, 126, 195–97, 207, 220, 224–25, 232
Stuart dynasty, 3, 8, 23, 164, 187, 190, 202–3, 229, 248n12
  See also James I; Charles I; Charles II; James II
subjectivity of romance, 2, 20, 22–24, 30, 34–42, 54, 231
Swaim, Kathleen, 209

Taylor, Luke, 113
Test Acts, 164, 168
Thickstun, Margaret Olofson, 209
Tiberius, Emperor, 145, 147
Tolkien, J. R. R., 230
Tories, 192, 204
tragedy, relationship to romance, 23, 74, 224–25, 230–32
  in Behn, 88, 190–91, 198, 201, 227–28
  in Cavendish, 90
  in Greville, 83, 87–89
  in Hutchinson, 106–10
  in Milton, 128, 132–33
  in postwar royalist romance, 123, 125, 230–31
  in Sidney, 33–34, 40–41, 49–52
  in Spenser, 60–61, 68–71
trauma, romance as response to, 9–12, 109–10, 123, 181, 186
typology, 24, 60, 67–69, 74–77, 130, 133–35, 141, 178, 185–86, 212, 217, 238n9

unfinished romance, 31, 41, 51–52, 56, 62–64, 67–71, 177, 181, 186, 247n47
Uniformity Act, 164, 168
universalism, theology of, 25, 137–38, 159–60, 164, 166, 231

Veevers, Erica, 8, 164
Virgil, 159–60, 248n53

Weamys, Anna, 41
  See also Sidney, Philip, appropriations and receptions of
Weiner, Andrew, 31–32
Welch, Anthony, 7–8, 22, 191
Werlin, Julianne, 52
Werth, Tiffany, 9, 29, 45–46
Whigs, 190, 192, 203, 249n19
Wilcher, Robert, 157–58, 168
Williamson, George, 113, 124–25
women, as readers and writers of romance, 8, 16–19, 39, 96, 211–12, 214
Worden, Blair, 31–32, 51
Wroth, Mary, 239n42

Zurcher, Amelia, 8, 113
Zutphen, battle of. *See* Sidney, Philip, death of

www.ingramcontent.com/pod-product-compliance
Lightning Source LLC
Chambersburg PA
CBHW021938290426
44108CB00012B/887